Part I: THE SMALL FINDS

Part II: GLASS

Part III: FAUNAL AND HUMAN
        SKELETAL REMAINS

Frontispiece. Silver mask (Warden, **36**).

University Museum Monograph 67

THE EXTRAMURAL SANCTUARY OF DEMETER AND PERSEPHONE AT CYRENE, LIBYA
FINAL REPORTS
Donald White, Series Editor
VOLUME IV

Part I: THE SMALL FINDS
P. Gregory Warden

Part II: GLASS
Andrew Oliver

Part III: FAUNAL AND HUMAN SKELETAL REMAINS
Pam J. Crabtree and Janet Monge

Published by
THE UNIVERSITY MUSEUM
University of Pennsylvania
Philadelphia
1990

for
THE LIBYAN DEPARTMENT OF ANTIQUITIES
As-Saray Al-Hamra
Tripoli
People's Socialist Libyan Arab Jamahiriya

Design, editing, production
 Publications Department
 The University Museum

Printing
 Science Press
 Ephrata, Pennsylvania

Endpapers taken from F.W. and H.W. Beechey, *Proceedings of the Expedition to Explore the Northern Coast of Africa from Tripoly Eastward* (London 1828)

Library of Congress Cataloging-in-Publication Data
(Revised for vol. 4)

The Extramural Sanctuary of Demeter and Persephone at
 Cyrene. Libya.

 (University Museum monograph : 52. 56. 67)
 Arabic and English
 Spine title: Cyrene final reports
 Excavations conducted by the University of
Pennsylvania, Philadelphia and the Department of
Antiquities of the People's Socialist Libyan Arab
Jamahiriya.
 Two folded plans in pocket, v. 1.
 Includes bibliographical references and indexes.
 Contents: v. 1. Background and introduction to the
excavations / Donald White -- v. 2. The East Greek,
island, and Laconian pottery / Gerald P. Schaus --
v. 4. Excavations in the Extramural Sanctuary of Demeter
and Persephone at Cyrene, Libya.
 1. Demeter (Greek deity)--Cult. 2. Persephone (Greek
deity)--Cult. 3. Excavations (Archaeology)--Libya.
4. Sanctuary of Demeter and Persephone (Cyrene)
5. Cyrene (Ancient city) 6. Libya--Antiquities.
I. White, Donald, 1935-   II. University of
Pennsylvania. University Museum. III. Libya.
Maslahat al-Athar. IV. Title. V. Title: Cyrene final
reports. VI. Series. VII. Series: University Museum
monograph ; 52, etc.
DT239.C9E98   1984   939'.75   83-19866
ISBN 0-934718-50-4 (set)

Copyright © 1990
The University Museum
University of Pennsylvania
Philadelphia
All rights reserved
Printed in the United States of America

In memory

Kyle M. Phillips, Jr.

P. Gregory Warden is chairman of the Department of Art History at Southern Methodist University in Dallas, Texas; he also serves as the editor of *Perspective*, a journal of the architectural history of Texas and the Southwest. He received his Ph.D. from Bryn Mawr College in 1978; the subject of his dissertation was the metal artifacts from Poggio Civitate (Murlo, Siena).

His research interests include the Etruscans, metalworking, ancient bronzes, and architecture. He has excavated at the sites of Poggio Civitate in Italy and at Cyrene in Libya. Presently, he is at work on several projects—a study of the bronzes from the Mediterranean Section of The University Museum; a monograph on the architecture and patronage of Neronian Rome; a study of the iron objects excavated at Castelnuovo Berardegna (Siena, Italy); and an article on Founders' Hall, a Neoclassical building at Girard College, Philadelphia.

Andrew Oliver, Jr., has been director of the Museum Program at the National Endowment for the Arts since 1982. Formerly Associate Curator of Greek and Roman Art at the Metropolitan Museum and director of the Textile Museum in Washington, D.C., he has specialized in the decorative and industrial arts of the classical world, in particular jewelry, silverware, bronzes, ivory, glass and ceramics. His publications include *Greek and Roman Jewelry in the Brooklyn Museum* (with Patricia F. Davidson), *Silver for the Gods, 800 Years of Greek and Roman Silver*—an exhibition catalogue for the Toledo Museum of Art—and several articles on Hellenistic and Roman glass in the *Journal of Classical Studies*. Forthcoming is a study of the Hellenistic pottery from Sardis in Turkey. For many years he has been associated with the excavations at the Sanctuary of Apollo at Kourion in Cyprus, conducted by his wife, Diana Buitron.

Pam J. Crabtree is an Assistant Professor of Anthropology at Princeton University. She received her Ph.D. in Anthropology from the University of Pennsylvania in 1982. The results of her dissertation research will be published by East Anglian Archaeology as *West Stow, Suffolk: The Anglo Saxon Animal Husbandry*.

Her area of specialization is zooarchaeology. In addition to the animal bones from Cyrene, Crabtree has studied the faunal collections from a wide range of archaeological sites in Europe and the Near East. She is currently co-editing a volume of essays on early animal domestication in Europe and the Near East which will be titled, *Early Animal Domestication and Its Cultural Context*. The book will be a memorial volume dedicated to Dexter Perkins, Jr., and Patricia Daly and will be published by the Museum Applied Science Center for Archaeology of The University Museum.

She is currently excavating the Late Natufian site of Salibiya I in the Jordan Valley in collaboration with Douglas V. Campana and Anna Belfer-Cohen of the Hebrew University of Jerusalem.

Janet Monge is Keeper of Physical Anthropology Collections at The University Museum. As a graduate student in physical anthropology at the University of Pennsylvania, she is currently working on her dissertation in molding and casting in a paleontological context. She has been involved with The University Museum Casting Program since 1977 and has served as Assistant Director since 1978.

Table of Contents

TEXT ILLUSTRATIONS xv

FIGURES xvi

PLATES xvii

MINOR ABBREVIATIONS xix

BIBLIOGRAPHICAL ABBREVIATIONS xx

ACKNOWLEDGMENTS xxiv

EDITOR'S PREFACE xxvi

PART I. THE SMALL FINDS 1

    INTRODUCTION 3
        The Catalogue 4

  I. FIGURINES 6
        Bronze Figurines (**1-25**) 6
            Birds (**1-15**) 6
            Frogs (**16** and **17**) 8
            Fragmentary Figurines (**18-21**) 9
            Bronze Lions (**22-24**) 9
            Bronze Ape (**25**) 10
        Ivory Figurines (**26-28**) 10
        Faience Figurines (**29-35**) 11
        Summary 12

  II. JEWELRY AND ORNAMENTS 14
        Attachments and Metal Reliefs (**36-46**) 14
            Rosettes (**40-43**) 16
            Fragments of Gold and Silver Foil (**44-46**) 16
        Beads and Pendants (**47-165**) 17
            Bronze and Biconical Tube Beads (**47-49**) 17
            Coiled Beads (**50-52**) 17
            Collar Beads (**53-58**) 18
            Disk Beads (**59-62**) 18
            Melon Beads (**63-68**) 19
            Striated Bead (**69**) 20
            Spherical Beads (**70-77**) 20
            Tubular Beads (**78-83**) 20
            Silver Beads (**84** and **85**) 21
            Axe Pendants (**86-89**) 21

	Bovine Pendants (**90** and **91**)	22
	Conical Pendants (**92-97**)	22
	Crescent Pendants (**98** and **99**)	22
	Drop-Shaped Pendants (**100-105**)	23
	Janiform Pendants (**106** and **107**)	24
	Leaf-Shaped Pendant (**108**)	24
	Lion Pendants (**109** and **110**)	24
	Pomegranate Pendants (**111** and **112**)	24
	Poppy-Head Pendants (**113-118**)	24
	Scarab Pendant (**119**)	25
	Bronze Shell Pendants (**120-136**)	25
	Shell Pendants (**137-142**)	26
	Tooth Pendants (**143** and **144**)	27
	Triangular Pendants (**145-148**)	27
	Vase Pendants (**149-153**)	27
	Heart Pendants (**154-158**)	28
	Miscellaneous Pendants (**159-165**)	28
Decorated Bead (**166**)		29
Bracelets (**167-169**)		29
Toggles (**170** and **171**)		30
Buttons (**172-174**)		30
Hair Coils (**175-187**)		30
Earrings (**188-191**)		31
Fibulae (**192-203**)		32
	Spectacle Fibulae (**192-198**)	32
	Bow Fibulae (**199-203**)	33
Pins (**204-243**)		33
	Straight Pins with Rolled Heads (**204-206**)	33
	Disk- and Knob-Headed Pins (**207-229**)	34
	Wheel-Shaped Pinhead? (**230**)	35
	Pin Caps (**231** and **232**)	35
	Pin Fitting (**233**)	36
	Silver Pin (**234**)	36
	Bone and Ivory Pins (**235-237**)	36
	Bone and Ivory Pin Terminals (**238** and **239**)	36
	Bone Disk Pinheads (**240-243**)	37
Rings (**244-264**)		37
	Finger Rings (**244-259**)	37
	Miscellaneous Rings (**260-264**)	39
Summary		40
III. HARDWARE AND TOOLS		42
Hardware (**265-314**)		42
	Attachments (**265-276**)	42
	Base and Stand (**277** and **278**)	43
	Chains (**279-281**)	43
	Clamps, Fasteners, and Dowels (**282-291**)	43
	Cotter Pins (**292** and **293**)	44
	Disk (**294**)	44
	Furniture Hinges, Bolts, and Fittings (**295-302**)	44
	Nails and Spikes (**303-308**)	45

Rivets (**309** and **310**)	45
Rods and Bars (**311**)	45
Wire (**312-314**)	46
Implements and Tools (**315-366**)	46
Bronze Implements (**315-318**)	46
Blades (**319-326**)	46
Chisels (**327-331**)	47
Hooks (**332** and **333**)	47
Implements of Bone and Ivory (**334-344**)	47
Metal Implements (**345-351**)	48
Needles (**352-356**)	49
Adze, Hammer, and Pick-Axe (**357-359**)	49
Sickle (**360**)	49
Spindle Whorls (**361-364**)	49
Strainers (**365** and **366**)	50
Summary	50
IV. WEAPONS	51
Arrowheads (**367-372**)	51
Sling Pellets (**373-375**)	52
Spearhead Points (**376-381**)	52
Summary	52
V. VESSELS	53
Faience Vessels (**382-389**)	53
Metal Vases (**390-402**)	54
Vessels (**390-393**)	54
Handles (**394-402**)	54
Stone Vessels (**403-463**)	55
Alabastra (**403-413**)	55
Lekythos (**414**)	56
Leutrophoros (**415**)	56
Vase (**416**)	56
Cups, Bowls, or Pyxides (**417-429**)	57
Lids (**430-432**)	57
Basins (**433-446**)	57
Grinding Instruments (**447-450**)	58
Pestles (**451** and **452**)	59
Offering Tables or Trays (**453-456**)	59
Measuring Stone (**457**)	59
Feet (**458-460**)	59
Palettes (**461** and **462**)	60
Mortar? (**463**)	60
Ostrich Eggshells (**464**)	60
Tridacna Shells (**465-473**)	60
Undecorated *Tridacna* (**465** and **466**)	61
Engraved *Tridacna* (**467-473**)	61
Summary	62

VI.	MISCELLANEOUS FINDS	64
	Loom Weights (**474-491**)	64
	Pyramidal Loom Weights (**481-486**)	64
	Shell-Shaped Loom Weights (**464-486**)	64
	Disk-Shaped Loom Weights (**487-489**)	65
	Conical/Biconical Loom Weights (**490-491**)	65
	Astragals (**492-501**)	65
	Bronze Astragals (**492-499**)	65
	Bone Astragals (**500** and **501**)	66
	Fish Vertebrae (**502-504**)	66
	Gaming Die (**505**)	66
	Stone Tool (**506**)	67
	Shells (**507-510**)	67
	APPENDIX I	68
	Find Spot Index	68
	APPENDIX II	79
	Concordance of Catalogue Numbers with Excavation Inventory Numbers	79
	APPENDIX III	83
	Bronze Rings	83
PART II.	GLASS	87
I.	GLASS	89
	Core-formed Glass (**1-71**)	89
	Alabastra (**1-7**)	89
	Amphoriskoi (**8-16**)	90
	Aryballoi (**17-19**)	90
	Oinochoai (**20-22**)	90
	Shape Uncertain (**23-38**)	91
	Pendant (**39**)	91
	Eye Beads (**40-56**)	91
	Bead with Threads (**57**)	93
	Plain Beads (**58-63**)	93
	Melon or Lobed Beads (**64-68**)	93
	Rods (**69-71**)	93
	Cast Glass (**72-98**)	94
	Opaque (**72-81**)	94
	Translucent, Monochrome (**82-96**)	95
	Blown Glass (**97-173**)	96
	Mold-Blown (**97**)	96
	Open Shapes (**98-160**)	96
	Ribbed Bowls (**98** and **99**)	96
	Bowls and Cups with Wheel-Cut Linear and Faceted Decoration (**100-109**)	96
	Undecorated Cups or Bowls: Rounded, Fire-Polished Rims (**110** and **111**)	97
	Cups and Bowls: Rims with Threads on Exterior (**112-118**)	97

	Bowls with Folded Rims (**119-123**)	98
	Bowls with Folded Rim and Corrugated Trimming (**124-134**)	98
	Dish and Cup with Other Types of Folded Rims (**135** and **136**)	98
	Rims Formed by a Double Fold (**137-140**)	99
	Cup Handles (**141-144**)	99
	Bases (**145-160**)	99
	Closed Shapes: Bottles, Flasks, and Unguentaria (**161-173**)	100
	Square Bottle (**161**)	101
	Bottle Handles (**162** and **163**)	101
	Flasks with Funnel Necks (**164** and **165**)	101
	Unguentaria (**166-171**)	101
	Glass with Applied Decoration (**172** and **173**)	101
	APPENDIX I	102
	The Glass Head from the Sanctuary of Demeter and Persephone at Cyrene (**174**)	102
	APPENDIX II	104
	Find Spot Index	104
	APPENDIX III	108
	Concordance of Catalogue Numbers with Excavation Inventory Numbers	108
PART III.	FAUNAL AND HUMAN REMAINS FROM CYRENE	111
I.	FAUNAL SKELETAL REMAINS FROM CYRENE	113
	Introduction	113
	The Faunal Remains From the Sanctuary of Demeter and Persephone	113
	Introduction	113
	Composition of the Faunal Assemblage	113
	Aging Evidence	115
	Butchery	117
	Measurements	118
	Conclusion	118
II.	HUMAN SKELETAL REMAINS FROM CYRENE	124
	Introduction	124
	Individual I	124
	Aging	124
	Pathology	125
	Individual II	125
	Conclusion	126
	APPENDIX I	127
	ARABIC SUMMARY	157
	FIGURES	
	PLATES	

Text Illustrations

Frontispiece	Silver mask (Warden **36**)	iv
Figure 1.	Trench Plan of the Site	xxxi

Part I

Warden Illustration 1.	Frog Hinge (**17**)	8
Warden Illustration 2.	Rosette	16
Warden Illustration 3.	Bronze Biconical Tube Bead, Type A	17
Warden Illustration 4.	Coiled Bead, Type B	17
Warden Illustration 5.	Collar Bead, Type C	18
Warden Illustration 6.	Disk Bead, Type D	19
Warden Illustration 7.	Melon Bead, Type E	19
Warden Illustration 8.	Spherical Bead, Type F	20
Warden Illustration 9.	Tubular Bead, Type G	21
Warden Illustration 10.	Silver Bead, Type H	21
Warden Illustration 11.	Arrowhead, Type A	51
Warden Illustration 12.	Arrowhead, Type B	51
Warden Illustration 13.	Arrowhead, Type C	51
Warden Illustration 14.	Arrowhead, Type D	51
Warden Illustration 15.	Pyramidal Loom Weight, Type A	64
Warden Illustration 16.	Shell-Shaped Loom Weight, Type B	64
Warden Illustration 17.	Disk-Shaped Loom Weight, Type C	65

Part III

Crabtree Figure 1.	Relative Importance of Animal Species Identified at Cyrene	115
Crabtree Figure 2.	Ages at Death for Cyrene Pigs	116
Crabtree Figure 3.	Mandible Wear Stages for Pigs at Cyrene	117

Figures

Part I

Warden Figure 1.   Pendants
Warden Figure 2.   Shell Pendants
Warden Figure 3.   Jewelry
Warden Figure 4.   Pins
Warden Figure 5.   Chain
Warden Figure 6.   Miscellaneous Iron Implements
Warden Figure 7.   Miscellaneous Implements
Warden Figure 8.   Stone Alabastra
Warden Figure 9.   Stone
Warden Figure 10. Marble
Warden Figure 11. Stone

Part II

Oliver Figure 1.   Glass
Oliver Figure 2.   Glass
Oliver Figure 3.   Glass
Oliver Figure 4.   Glass

Plates

Part I

Warden Plate 1.	Figurines
Warden Plate 2.	Figurines
Warden Plate 3.	Figurines
Warden Plate 4.	Figurines
Warden Plate 5.	Figurines
Warden Plate 6.	Figurines
Warden Plate 7.	Figurines
Warden Plate 8.	Figurines
Warden Plate 9.	Figurines
Warden Plate 10.	Figurines
Warden Plate 11.	Figurines
Warden Plate 12.	Jewelry and Ornaments
Warden Plate 13.	Jewelry and Ornaments
Warden Plate 14.	Jewelry and Ornaments
Warden Plate 15.	Jewelry and Ornaments
Warden Plate 16.	Jewelry and Ornaments
Warden Plate 17.	Jewelry and Ornaments
Warden Plate 18.	Jewelry and Ornaments
Warden Plate 19.	Jewelry and Ornaments
Warden Plate 20.	Jewelry and Ornaments
Warden Plate 21.	Jewelry and Ornaments
Warden Plate 22.	Jewelry and Ornaments
Warden Plate 23.	Jewelry and Ornaments
Warden Plate 24.	Jewelry and Ornaments
Warden Plate 25.	Jewelry and Ornaments
Warden Plate 26.	Jewelry and Ornaments
Warden Plate 27.	Jewelry and Ornaments
Warden Plate 28.	Hardware and Tools
Warden Plate 29.	Hardware and Tools
Warden Plate 30.	Hardware and Tools
Warden Plate 31.	Hardware and Tools
Warden Plate 32.	Hardware and Tools
Warden Plate 33.	Hardware and Tools
Warden Plate 34.	Hardware and Tools
Warden Plate 35.	Hardware and Tools
Warden Plate 36.	Hardware and Tools

Warden Plate 37.   Hardware and Tools
Warden Plate 38.   Hardware and Tools
Warden Plate 39.   Hardware and Tools
Warden Plate 40.   Vessels
Warden Plate 41.   Vessels
Warden Plate 42.   Vessels
Warden Plate 43.   Vessels
Warden Plate 44.   Vessels
Warden Plate 45.   Vessels
Warden Plate 46.   Vessels
Warden Plate 47.   Vessels
Warden Plate 48.   Vessels
Warden Plate 49.   Vessels
Warden Plate 50.   Miscellaneous Finds
Warden Plate 51.   Miscellaneous Finds
Warden Plate 52.   Miscellaneous Finds

Part II

Oliver Plate 1.   Core-Formed Glass: Alabastra
Oliver Plate 2.   Core-Formed Glass: Amphoriskoi
Oliver Plate 3.   Core-Formed Glass: Aryballoi and Oinochoai
Oliver Plate 4.   Core-Formed Glass: Shape Uncertain
Oliver Plate 5.   Core-Formed Glass: Pendant and Beads
Oliver Plate 6.   Core-Formed Glass: Beads and Rods;
                   Cast Glass: Opaque
Oliver Plate 7.   Cast Glass: Translucent and Monochrome
Oliver Plate 8.   Cast Glass and Blown Glass
Oliver Plate 9.   Blown Glass: Open Shapes
Oliver Plate 10.   Blown Glass: Open Shapes
Oliver Plate 11.   Blown Glass: Open Shapes
Oliver Plate 12.   Blown Glass: Open Shapes
Oliver Plate 13.   Blown Glass: Open Shapes
Oliver Plate 14.   Blown Glass: Open Shapes
Oliver Plate 15.   Blown Glass: Open Shapes
Oliver Plate 16.   Blown Glass: Open Shapes and Closed Shapes
Oliver Plate 17.   Blown Glass: Closed Shapes
Price Plate 1.   The Glass Head

Part III

Crabtree Plate 1.   Faunal Remains from Cyrene

Minor Abbreviations

D.	diameter	not inv.	not inventoried
est.	estimated	P.H.	preserved height
ext.	extension	P.W.	preserved width
H.	height	St.	stratum
L.	length	Th.	thickness
Max.	maximum	W.	width

Bibliographical Abbreviations

This series of reports adopts the standard abbreviations used by the *American Journal of Archaeology*. The works listed below are supplementary and include references cited throughout the volume.

Aegina	A. Furtwängler, *Aegina* (Munich 1906).
Alarcão 1965	J. and A. Alarcão, *Vidros Romanos de Conimbriga* (Coimbra 1965).
Argive Heraeum	C. Waldstein, *The Argive Heraeum*, 2 vols. (Oxford 1905).
Artemis Orthia	R. M. Dawkins, ed., *The Sanctuary of Artemis Orthia at Sparta*, JHS supp. vol. 5 (London 1929).
Barag 1985	D. Barag, *Catalogue of Western Asiatic Glass in the British Museum*, vol. 1 (London 1985).
Beck	H. C. Beck, *Classification and Nomenclature of Beads and Pendants* (York, Pennsylvania 1973).
Boardman, *GGFR*	J. Boardman, *Greek Gems and Finger Rings* (London 1970).
Calvi 1968	M. C. Calvi, *I vetri romani del Museo di Aquileia* (Aquileia 1968).
Charleston 1964	R.J. Charleston, "Wheel-Engraving and -Cutting: Some Early Equipment, I; Engraving." *JGS* 6 (1964) 83-100.
Clairmont 1963	C. W. Clairmont, *The Excavations at Dura-Europos, Final Report* IV, Part V, *The Glass Vessels* (New Haven 1963).
ClRh 3	G. Jacopi, *Scavi nella necropolis di Jalisso, 1924-1928, ClRh*, vol. 3 (Rhodes 1929).
ClRh 4	G. Jacopi, *Esplorazione archeologica di Camiro, ClRh*, vol. 4 (Rhodes 1931).
ClRh 6-7	G. Jacopi, *Esplorazione archeologica di Camiro 2, ClRh*, vol. 6-7, Pt. 1 (Rhodes 1933).
Conimbriga 7	J. Alarcão, R. Etienne, A. Moutinho Alarcão, and S. da Ponte, *Fouilles de Conimbriga*, vol. VII: *Trouvailles diverses—conclusions genérales* (Paris 1979).
Cooney 1960	J.D. Cooney, "Glass Sculpture in Ancient Egypt," *JGS* 2 (1960) 11-43.
Corinth 12	G. R. Davison, *Corinth*, vol. 12: *The Minor Objects* (Princeton 1952).
Corinth 13	C.W. Blegen, H. Palmer, R.S. Young, *Corinth*, vol. 13: *The North Cemetery* (Princeton 1964).
Cummings 1980	K. Cummings, *The Technique of Glass Forming* (London 1980).
Czurda-Ruth 1979	B. Czurda-Ruth, *Die römischen Gläser von Magdalensberg* (Klagenfurt 1979).
Délos 18	W. Deonna, *Délos*, vol. XVIII: *Le Mobilier délien* (Paris 1938).
Delphi 5	P. Perdrizet, *Fouilles de Delphes V: Monuments figurés, petits bronzes, terre cuites, antiquités diverses* (Paris 1908).
Doppelfeld 1965-6	O. Doppelfeld, "Das neue Augustus-Porträt aus Glas im Kölner Museum," *KölnJb* 8 (1965/66) 7-11.
Emporio	J. Boardman, *Excavations in Chios 1952-1955, Greek Emporio*, BSA supp. vol. 6 (Oxford 1967).

Fabbricotti 1985	E. Fabbricotti, "Influenze Attica a Tolemaide nel 2 sec. d.C." In G. Barker *et al.* eds., *Cyrenaica in Antiquity, Society for Libyan Studies Occasional Papers* I, *BAR International Series* 236 (Oxford 1985) 219-30.
Final Reports 1	D. White, *The Extramural Sanctuary of Demeter and Persephone at Cyrene, Libya* I: *Background and Introduction to the Excavations* (Philadelphia 1984).
Final Reports 2	G. Schaus, *The Extramural Sanctuary of Demeter and Persephone at Cyrene, Libya* II: *The East Greek, Island, and Laconian Pottery* (Philadelphia 1985).
Final Reports 3	S. Lowenstam, M. Moore, P. Kenrick, and T. Fuller, *The Extramural Sanctuary of Demeter and Persephone at Cyrene, Libya* III, Pt. I: *Scarabs, Inscribed Gems, and Engraved Finger Rings;* Pt. II: *Attic Black Figure and Black Glazed Pottery;* Pt. III: *Hellenistic and Roman Fine Wares;* Pt. IV: *Conservation of Objects* (Philadelphia 1987).
Fossing 1940	P. Fossing, *Glass Vessels before Glass Blowing* (Copenhagen 1940).
Goldstein 1979A	S. M. Goldstein, *Pre-Roman and Early Roman Glass in The Corning Museum of Glass* (Corning 1979).
Goldstein 1979B	S.M. Goldstein, "A Unique Royal Head," *JGS* 21 (1979) 8-16.
GRJ	R. A. Higgins, *Greek and Roman Jewellery* (London 1961).
Grose 1981	D.F. Grose, "The Hellenistic Glass Industry Reconsidered," *Annales du 8e Congrès de l'Association Internationale pour l'Histoire du Verre* (Liège 1981).
Grose 1982	D.F. Grose, "The Hellenistic and Early Roman Glass from Morgantina (Serra Orlando) Sicily," *JGS* 24 (1982) 20-9.
Guido 1978	M. Guido, *The Glass Beads of the Prehistoric and Roman Periods in Britain and Ireland* (London 1978).
Harden 1936	D. B. Harden, *Roman Glass from Karanis* (Ann Arbor 1936).
Harden 1968A	D.B. Harden, "The Canosa Group of Hellenistic Glasses in the British Museum," *JGS* 10 (1968) 21-47.
Harden 1968B	D.B. Harden, "Ancient Glass, I: Pre-Roman," *ArchJ* 125 (1968) 46-72.
Harden 1981	D. B. Harden, *Catalogue of Greek and Roman Glass in the British Museum, Vol. 1: Core- and Rod-formed Vessels and Pendants and Mycenaean Cast Objects* (London 1981).
Harden and Price 1971	D. B. Harden and J. Price, "The Glass," *Excavations at Fishbourne 1961-1969,* Vol. 2: The Finds (Reports of the Research Committee of the Society of Antiquaries of London, XXVII, London 1971), 317-368.
Hayes 1975	J. W. Hayes, *Roman and Pre-Roman Glass in the Royal Ontario Museum* (Toronto 1975).
Hogarth, *Ephesus*	D. G. Hogarth, *et al.*, *Excavations at Ephesus* (London 1908).
Isings 1957	C. Isings, *Roman Glass from Dated Finds* (Groningen 1957).
Jacobsthal	P. Jacobsthal, *Greek Pins* (Oxford 1956).
Knossos	J. N. Coldstream, ed., *Knossos. The Sanctuary of Demeter, BSA* supp. vol. 8 (Oxford 1973).
Lancel 1967	S. Lancel, *Verrerie antique de Tipasa* (Paris 1967).
Lindos 1	C. Blinkenberg, *Lindos,* vol. 1 (Berlin 1931).
Marshall	F. H. Marshall, *Catalogue of the Jewellery, Greek, Etruscan, and Roman in the Department of Antiquities, British Museum* (London 1907).
Matheson 1980	S. B. Matheson, *Ancient Glass in the Yale University Art Gallery* (New Haven 1980).

Mildenberg	A. P. Kozloff, ed., *Animals in Ancient Art from the Leo Mildenberg Collection* (Cleveland 1981).
Naucratis 1	W. M. F. Petrie, *Naucratis Part I: 1884-5* (London 1886).
Naucratis 2	E. A. Gardner, *Naucratis Part II: 1885-6* (London 1888).
Niessen	S. Loeschke and H. Willers, *Beschreibung römischer Altertümer gesammelt von Carl Anton Niessen* (Cologne 1911).
Notarianni 1979	G. M. Notarianni, *Vetri antichi nelle collezioni del Museo Civico Archeologico di Bologna* (Istituto per la Storia di Bologna, Bologna 1979).
Oliver 1968	A. Oliver, "Millefiori Glass in Classical Antiquity," *JGS* 10 (1968) 48-70.
Olympia 4	A. Furtwängler, *Die Bronzen und die übrigen kleineren Funde von Olympia, Olympia, die Ergebnisse der von dem Deutschen Reich veranstalteten Ausgrabungen*, vol. IV, E. Curtius and F. Adler, eds. (Berlin 1890).
Olynthos 10	D. M. Robinson, *Excavations at Olynthos X: Metal and Minor Miscellaneous Finds* (Baltimore 1941).
Perachora 1	H. Payne, *Perachora* (Oxford 1940).
Perachora 2	T. J. Dunbabin, *Perachora II* (Oxford 1962).
Petrie, *Amulets*	W. M. F. Petrie, *Amulets* (London 1941).
Petrie, *Objects*	W. M. F. Petrie, *Objects of Daily Use* (London 1927).
Petrie, *Weights*	W. M. F. Petrie, *Ancient Weights and Measures* (London 1926).
Platz-Horster 1976	G. Platz-Horster, *Antike Gläser* (Antikenmuseum, Berlin Staatliche Museen Preussischer Kulturbesitz, Berlin 1976).
Price 1985	J. Price, "Late Hellenistic and Early Imperial Vessel Glass at Berenice," in G. Barker *et al.* eds. *Cyrenaica in Antiquity, Society for Libyan Studies Occasional Papers* I, *BAR International Series* 236 (Oxford 1985) 287-296.
Reinach	S. Reinach, *Répertoire de la statuaire grecque et romaine*, 6 vols. (Paris 1897-1930).
Richter, *Bronzes*	G. M. A. Richter, *Greek, Etruscan and Roman Bronzes* (New York 1915).
von Saldern 1970	A. von Saldern, "Other Mesopotamian Glass Vessels (1500-600 B.C.)." In A.L. Oppenheim *et al.*, *Glass and Glassmaking in Ancient Mesopotamia* (Corning 1970) 203-208.
von Saldern *et al.* 1974	A. von Saldern *et al.*, *Gläser der Antike, Sammlung Erwin Oppenländer* (Hamburg 1974).
von Saldern 1975	A. von Saldern, "Two Achaemenid Glass Bowls and a Hoard of Hellenistic Glass Vessels," *JGS* 17 (1975) 37-46.
Schuler 1959	F. Schuler, "Ancient Glassmaking Techniques. The Molding Process," *Archaeology* 12 (1959) 47-52.
Smith 1957	R. W. Smith, *Glass from the Ancient World* (Corning 1957).
Snodgrass, *Armour*	A.M. Snodgrass, *Arms and Armour of the Greeks* (London 1967).
Spartz 1967	E. Spartz, *Antike Gläser* (Kassel 1967).
Tocra 1	J. Boardman and J. Hayes, *Excavations at Tocra 1963-1965, The Archaic Deposits I*, *BSA* supp. vol. 4 (Oxford 1966).
Tocra 2	J. Boardman and J. Hayes, *Excavations at Tocra 1963-1965, The Archaic Deposits II and Later Deposits*, *BSA* supp. vol. 10 (Oxford 1973).

Voscinina 1967	A. I. Voscinina, "Frühantike Glassgefässe in der Ermitage," *Die griechische Vase*, Wissenschaftliche Zeitschrift der Universität Rostock, Jahrgang 16 (1967). Gesellschafts- und- Sprachwissenschafliche Reihe, Heft 7/8, 555-560.
Walters	H. B. Walters, *Catalogue of the Bronzes, Greek, Roman, and Etruscan in the Department of Greek and Roman Antiquities, British Museum* (London 1899).
Webb	V. Webb, *Archaic Greek Faience* (Warminster, England 1978).
Welker 1974	E. Welker, *Die römischen Gläser von Nida-Heddernheim* (Frankfurt 1974).
White, *First Report*	D. White, "Excavations (1972-1973) 171-195.
Second Report	D. White, "Excavations in the Demeter Sanctuary at Cyrene 1971. Second Preliminary Report," *LA* 9-10 (1972-1973) 171-195.
Third Report	D. White, "Excavations in the Sanctuary of Demeter and Persephone at Cyrene 1973: Third Preliminary Report," *AJA* 79 (1975) 33-48.
Fourth Report	D. White, "Excavations in the Sanctuary of Demeter and Persephone at Cyrene. Fourth Preliminary Report," *AJA* 80 (1976) 165-181.
Sixth Report	D. White, "Excavations in the Sanctuary of Demeter and Persephone at Cyrene, Sixth Preliminary Report, *LA* 15-16 (1978-1979) 181-183.

Acknowledgments

I am grateful to Professor Donald White of the University of Pennsylvania for asking me to work on the "small finds" from his excavations at the Sanctuary of Demeter and Persephone, Cyrene. His constant encouragement and enthusiasm for Cyrenaican studies, and all his help while I was at The University Museum from 1980 to 1982, the period in which much of this manuscript came to fruition, greatly facilitated my work. The opportunity to visit Cyrene to study the small finds in the summer of 1981 was also essential to this project, and I am grateful to Professor White for the hospitality and cordiality that made that season a memorable experience.

To Professor Susan Kane, Oberlin College, I owe a debt of gratitude for suggesting to me the possibility of moving away from my Italo-centric interests to the wider concerns of the classical Mediterranean. Her passion for Cyrenaican research also served to encourage my own work, and I look forward to her volume on Cyrenaican sculpture in this series of excavation reports.

I should also acknowledge my debt to Kyle Meredith Phillips, Jr. I am first of all indebted to him for reading this manuscript. As always, his insight and clarity of vision were instrumental. This entire volume has been dedicated to Professor Phillips, but I wish to take this opportunity to acknowledge my own larger and more personal debt to him. From my first season in 1970 at his excavations at Poggio Civitate, while I was still an undergraduate at the University of Pennsylvania, Kyle encouraged me to pursue a career in classical archaeology. Later on at Bryn Mawr he continued to provide the inspiration that allowed me to finish a thesis and a dissertation on topics of Etruscan archaeology. Kyle was an exemplary teacher and scholar. As an advisor and friend he never said the expected or the mundane, his approach was always fresh and insightful, and he had a truly original mind. He was the premier Etruscologist in America, one of the great American archaeologists of his generation, as well as an authority on Roman art and Greek vase painting. His death in August of 1988 has left a gap that can never be filled.

I wish to thank Dr. David Reese for providing me with information about shells and other faunal remains. Some of his comments on specific finds from Cyrene are mentioned in the text, but I am also grateful for the great amount of information that he forwarded to me, and for his unselfish and unstinting assistance in making his extraordinary knowledge of faunal remains available to me. I am also grateful to Professor David Mitten, Harvard University, for his advice about some of the more enigmatic bronzes.

I am especially grateful to Southern Methodist University for the institutional support I have received since coming here in 1982. A Provostial research grant allowed me to work on the final aspects of this study. A semester sabbatical gave me the time to finalize some aspects of my research. I wish to thank Dr. Eugene Bonelli, Dean of the Meadows School of the Arts, for his support in these matters. I should also mention Eileen Coffman, graduate assistant in the Department of Art History, for her help in organizing the morass of material that evolved into this publication.

My final acknowledgment is to the editorial staff of the Publications Department of The University Museum. Karen Vellucci and Ann Bonn, colleagues as well as editors, made this publication possible. Karen Vellucci steered this manuscript through the labyrinthine halls of The University Museum and overcame all obstacles. Ann Bonn's ruthless editorial pencil greatly improved my own work. Cathy Ambrose, Georgianna Grentzenberg, Anita Liebman, Patti Maddaloni, Antonia Montague, and Adam Watson also contributed to the final product.

P. Gregory Warden
Department of Art History
Southern Methodist University

Editor's Preface

Once again as series editor I have the happy task of thanking, on behalf of myself and my four co-authors, the University of Pennsylvania, The University Museum, and the Museum's director, Dr. Robert H. Dyson, Jr., for their most generous financial support of this book, whose entire production has been realized from A to Z without any external subvention. But it is Karen Vellucci, the Managing Editor of the Museum's Publications Department, who deserves our most particular thanks for translating what started out as abstract institutional support into literary reality. Its appearance is entirely due to her energetic and wise management of the legion of financial, editorial, artistic and personal responsibilities which inevitably beset a cooperative project of this sort. Anne Bonn, Georgianna Grentzenberg, and once again Anita Liebman have contributed their own individual skills and greatly deserve our thanks. Dr. Jamal El Harami, Department of Archaeology of the University of Riyadh and an old friend of The University Museum, has generously contributed his time to the translations of the Arabic summaries of this and volume three. Finally, Professor Alan Mann of the University of Pennsylvania's Department of Anthropology requires special thanks for initially analysing the site's human skeletal remains and then arranging for the final work to be carried out on the complete faunal sample by his former students, P. Crabtree and J. Monge, who are of course the authors of the present study.

The Cyrene project is further indebted to the individual colleagues who have undertaken to study the material embodied in this volume. P.G. Warden, who writes about the sanctuary's small finds, was able to spend the 1981 final work season at Cyrene in studying the site's voluminous miscellaneous artifacts, whereas A. Oliver had something less than ten days in 1977 to work up the glass. By way of further contrast, Crabtree and Monge had to make do with samples of faunal material brought to The University Museum for study from Libya. None consequently took part in the actual archaeological retrieval of the material that lies at the core of their respective studies and should not be held responsible for the variable nature of the samples with which they have agreed to deal. Had, for example, the faunal specialists been present when the site was being dug, the collection of skeletal remains would have been done on a more thorough and systematically controlled basis, and this in turn would have left them with a larger selection. As matters stand, although the present faunal sampling falls short of the ideal, it represents what is perhaps the best that one could expect under circumstances that placed major restraints on the exportation of physical remains. Oliver's research into the site's glass was limited more by time than the size of his final sample. Fortunately it was possible to supplement his 1977 observations with notes taken by M. McClellan, who excavated at Cyrene during 1978 and 1979. A specialist himself in ancient glass, McClellan has contributed a number of entries to the present glass catalogue as well as undertaking much of its editing. We are further grateful to J. Price, a member of the Society for Libyan Studies' research team at Sidi Khrebish, who has agreed to publish the important glass head that forms the subject of Appendix I to the glass chapter. Finally, given the sheer magnitude of the miscellaneous small finds, the project is particularly fortunate that Warden was able to devote a full season to their study in Cyrene and that this took place at the conclusion of the field work rather than earlier.

Much of the glass and miscellaneous small find studies are based on artifacts that were individually catalogued as "finds" following their initial recovery, which means in practical effect that a record has been preserved of their three-dimensional location within each separate archaeological context, defined throughout by "area," "trench," and "stratum"[1] (see Fig. 1). Certain specimens were selected as representative of larger samples of similar artifacts that were stored by area, trench, and stratum but not individually catalogued.[2] This is typically the case with repetitive examples of iron, shell, certain classes of terracotta,

---

1. "Area" refers to location by gridsquare, "trench" the individual test opening within each gridsquare context, and "stratum" the specific layer within each trench. See White, *Final Reports* 1, 56.

2. Ibid., 76 n. 29.

and, to a lesser degree, glass. On the other hand, with virtually no exception, none of the faunal remains were catalogued but instead were sequestered following their excavation by area, trench, and stratum into bags for eventual shipment to Philadelphia.

As in the case of the second and third volumes in this series, the authors of the current volume have provided indices of their catalogued entries organized by area, trench, stratum, catalogue number, and date.[3] The main purpose of these find-spot indices is to illustrate the chronological limits of each context according to each class of object; eventually these data will be synthesized into a single master-index in order to date the site's various architectural and occupational phases.[4] Their inclusion here should serve to remind the reader that all of the material selected for study have a contextual significance that transcends their interest as individual objects.

The faunal remains and animal models provide a case in point. Beginning with the former, Crabtree's study confirms the observations already made in the series' opening volume about the heavy preponderance of swine bones, which is reckoned to constitute 77.6% of the identifiable faunal remains.[5] In addition the author has observe traces of butchery, which she believes provides a strong argument for the practice of ritual feasting.[6] In most instances the butchery marks appear on the forelimbs, while the hindlimbs rarely display traces of cutting or chopping. The hindparts, primarily femora and pelves, were discarded in an earth fill mixed with charcoal and ash in the F14/G14 backfill behind the Middle Sanctuary's early Imperial T10 retaining wall (Fig. 1).[7] This bears out the conclusion that the sanctuary's principal sacrificial animal was routinely separated into parts that were reserved either for eating or for burnt sacrifice if not for ritual burial ('the rite of casting down'),[8] and that in addition the differentiated parts ended up in separate dumps inside the sanctuary. We are perhaps seeing the same process at work in the recently discovered Hellenistic Sanctuary of Demeter on the acropolis of Mytilene where Reese has been able to identify a predominance of pig hind parts among the faunal remains thus far excavated.[9] In any case, no permanent, masonry-built ash-altars were installed within the excavated part of the sanctuary. On the other hand, a variety of portable stone altars that range in size from ca. 0.90 m. in height down to miniature-scale thymiateria were recovered and await future publication. The larger portable altars, of which less than half a dozen exist, might have been used for burnt offering of animal flesh, but as a class could not have accomodated continuous animal sacrifice on a large scale. We do not know where the fill behind the Middle Sanctuary retaining wall originated, but it clearly was introduced from some other sector of the sanctuary, perhaps the level of the still largely unexcavated Upper Sanctuary where the missing ash altar(s) may have been located, if they existed at all.

As for model representations of animals, votive stone and terracotta pigs have been recovered in respectable numbers[10] but, somewhat surprisingly, not in the metal and other materials studied by Warden. The small bronze animal offering of preference depicts instead domestic fowl in the form of rooster, hen, duck/goose, and pigeon; wild birds are represented by a single bronze falcon. Yet the sole avian remain to be identified out of the total sample of 2494 bones studied by Crabtree and Monge is *one* chicken bone. Unless the bird remains were completely consumed by fire, buried in some still unexcavated portion of the sanctuary, or carried home for consumption,[11] the site's entire range

---

3. Schaus, *Final Reports* 2, 108-20. Lowenstam, *et al.*, *Final Reports* 3, in which see Lowenstam, 19, 20; Moore, 44-52; Kenrick, 12-18. In the case of the present volume see below Warden, 68-78 and Oliver, 104-107.

4. The first installment will appear as part of *Final Reports* 5: D. White, *The Site's Architecture, Its First Six Hundred Years* (forthcoming).

5. *Final Reports* 1, 20-21.

6. See my remarks in *Final Reports* 3, xi. See also P. Crabtree and J. Monge, "The Faunal Remains from the Sanctuary of Demeter and Persephone at Cyrene, Libya," *Masca Journal* 4, No. 3 (October 1987) 142.

7. *Final Reports* 1, 83-88, figs. 83-88. *Final Reports* 2, xxii. *Final Reports* 3, xii.

8. The eating and burial of pigs are discussed by W. Burkert, *Homo Necans, the Anthropology of Ancient Greek Sacrificial Ritual and Myth* (Berkeley 1983) 256-58. Also *Final Reports* 1, 20-21. For burnt sacrifice see W. Burkert, *Greek Religion* (Cambridge, Mass. 1985) 60-64. The ritual slaughter of animals is discussed *ibid*. 55-59. It will be interesting to learn if the burnt pig bones found in the Demeter Sanctuary at Acrocorinth bore traces of butchery, i.e. were prepared for eating, in light of that important site's dining facilities. See R. Stroud, *Hesperia* 34 (1965) 10.

9. C. Williams and H. Williams, "Excavations at Mytilene, 1987," *Canadian Mediterranean Institute Bulletin* (1987) 10. The familiar Demeter sanctuary at Priene included an ashlar masonry pit that held pig bones at the time of its excavation. See T. Wiegand and H. Schrader *Priene*, (Berlin 1904) 154-155; M. Schede, *Die Ruinen von Priene* (1964) 93-94, fig. 107. Burkert, *Homo Necans* (above n. 8) 257 n. 5, makes the plausible assumption that the pigs were buried and not eaten, but one may suspect that the Priene remains were never eon of offerings see C. Greenewalt, *Ritual Dinners in Early Historic Sardis* for traces of butchery. For more on the underground deposits (Berkeley 1978) 33 n. 3; *Final Reports* 1, 21-22. The existence of underground "megara" in Demeter sanctuaries will be discussed in the forthcoming volume on the Cyrene sanctuary's initial six hundred years of architectural development.

10. See Crabtree and Monge below, pl. 1. The terracottas await publication by J. Uhlenbrock, the stone sculptures by S. Kane.

11. These are the necessary preconditions to Warden's remarks on the appropriateness of bird offerings to Demeter, see below Warden, 7-8, Citing cock offerings to the Kore, Burkert, *Greek Religion* (above n. 8) 55, 268 nn. 2 and 3, says that poultry sacrifices were common in antiquity, but that the offering of other types of birds was comparatively rare.

of gold, bronze, ivory, and faience animal models (which, in addition to birds, include a monkey, lions, rams, and frogs) bore no direct relationship to the living animal routinely sacrificed to the resident deities, with the one, possibly coincidental exception of sheep.[12]

Place of origin may have played a part in the process. If the votives were produced locally, as was certainly the case with many of the sanctuary's still unpublished terracotta animal votives, and perhaps sold in the vicinity of the sanctuary, their presence may be explained as much on the grounds of availability as any focused religious meaning. This may well be the only explanation that is needed for the relative plentifulness of the bronze poultry models, which seem to be local productions, as well as the scarcity of the site's imported bronze monkey, frog, lion, and falcon; faience lion, ram and falcon; and ivory ram.

Again in regard to place of origin, the excavation failed to produce any external evidence to help determine where its glass might have been made, and Oliver does not suggest local manufacture for any of the wares under study. A single cullet was discovered at Apollonia by the University of Michigan team during the 1960s, but by itself this argues nothing. Glass-making installations, however, are notoriously elusive to find but can in theory be set up almost anywhere. Given the amount of glass retrieved from the sanctuary, one may at least wonder, apparently against prevailing wisdom,[13] if at least some of the later cast and blown pieces did not have a Pentapolis origin. Obviously a sanctuary is an unlikely place in which to set up a glass factory, but the terraced land[14] east of the Upper Sanctuary Propylaeum (S20) would have made a convenient place for selling temple goods such as cooking, eating and drinking vessels, terracotta and bronze figurines, and glassware to visiting worshippers. One wonders then if some limited manufacturing could not have taken place here as well.

A further gap in our understanding of the glass has to do with its original disposition within the sanctuary. The presence, for example, of cored sherds in the F13/G13, 1 and 2 backfill behind the early Imperial T10 retaining wall tells us nothing because, as we have already seen, the source(s) of that fill cannot be determined. If glass artifacts were exhibited as votive dedications inside any of the independent shrine houses, there is no evidence from sherd concentrations to indicate which of the sanctuary's six of so house structures[15] were used, with the possible exception of the S11 chamber discussed below. It is perhaps noteworthy that no glass vessels were excavated either on or near the stone benches that ran across the backs of the S5 and S7 independent shrine houses.

The site's two largest glass concentrations were found in the D16/17 trenches (Fig. 1) from the vicinity of the S11 storage chamber and the C15/16 trench associated with the F2 fountain house. In other words, both accumulations were excavated in the general area of the sanctuary's upper southwest corner and, as such, border the extramural early Imperial lamp and pottery dump (S18) which contained large quantities of Hellenistic ceramic eating and drinking wares.[16] The dump itself, however, produced relatively little glass of importance, apart from the glass head discussed in Appendix I of Part II. This fact makes it unlikely that the glass from D16/17 and C15/16 had anything to do with the ritual dining activities otherwise attested by the dump's ceramics. The Hellenistic period S11 storage chamber, awaiting publication in the next volume of this series, was not fully excavated but appears, as the name implies, to have served a more utilitarian than ceremonial purpose. In any case, the glass finds indexed as coming from the second stratum of the three D16/17 trenches were all part of the earthquake debris and have no direct relevance for the chamber's function. On the other hand, the St. 3 glass finds were probably part of a larger cache of artifacts including terracotta figurines that were warehoused in the S11 chamber. The final answer to where and how the glass was used will only be reached if more excavation is carried out in the extramural southwest quadrant surrounding the S18 dump.

The largest accumulations of miscellaneous sixth- and fifth-century B.C. pendants and miniature bronze animals come from D12/13, B and D12/13, F (Fig. 1), trenches that lie between the later Archaic pseudo-isodomic peribolos wall (T1) and the later Archaic, early Classical period S2 and S4 structures.[17] The same grounds produced exceptional quantities of early inscribed gems and scarabs[18] as well as East Greek and Island imported Archaic sherds.[19] Large numbers of

---

12. Sheep and goat make up about 15% of the sanctuary's identifiable faunal material. For more on ovicaprid remains from the Demeter sanctuaries at Cnidus, Knossos, and Acrocorinth, see *Final Reports* 1, 20 n. 6.

13. According to J. Price, all of the late Hellenistic to early Imperial glass wares found at Berenice were imported. See "Late Hellenistic and Early Imperial Vessel Glass at Berenice: a Survey of Imported Tableware Found during Excavations at Sidi Khrebish, Benghazi," in G. Barker *et al.*, *Cyrenaica in Antiquity*, Society for Libyan Studies Occasional Papers I, BAR International Series 236 (Oxford 1985) 287-96.

14. *Final Reports* 1, 44-46, figs. 3, 40-42.

15. Ibid., 118, fig. 119.

16. Ibid., 92-93, fig., 119. *Final Reports* 3, xi. The dump site corresponds to the C17 trenches recorded on Fig. 1 of the present volume.

17. *Final Reports* 1, 118, fig. 117.

18. *Final Reports* 3, xi.

19. *Final Reports* 2, xxii. Surprisingly, the amount of Attic black figure recovered from the same contexts is contrastingly exiguous, see *Final Reports* 3, Moore, 45.

early miscellaneous small artifacts were also excavated from the open space (C13, 1) west of the S4 structure, which again proved to be a rich source for East Greek and Island Archaic pottery.[20] A large percentage of the apparently early 458 bronze rings tabulated by Warden came from D12/13, F, as well as D15/16, 1, south of the Archaic S6 Shrine House, and the adjacent ground (D16/17, 1) later associated with the Hellenistic S11 storage chamber previously discussed. Despite the fact that a proper understanding of the early buildings in this sector is inhibited by the effects of intensive later building as well as incomplete excavation, the grounds were clearly used to house at least three, possibly four independent structures[21] that belong to the Archaic-early Classical phases of the sanctuary's development. Why this zone produced numerous Archaic Island and East Greek sherds but relatively few traces of Laconian and Attic Black Figure pottery presumably has something to do with the still undisclosed function of these structures. Area C10/11, A (Fig. 1) that lies directly south of the Imperial Propylaeum (S20) and thus a short distance to the west of the S2 structure produced a fairly large number of glass fragments. These, however, occur only in upper, later Roman period strata that have no direct connection with any of the adjacent buildings, including the gateway, and fail to tell us anything about the use to which the glass was put. Finally, the fill dumped behind the T10 retaining wall separating the Middle from the Lower Sanctuary (Fig. 1, F13/G13, 1 and 2, F14/G14, 1) contained large numbers of the miscellaneous small artifacts studied by Warden as well as a dense accumulation of all types of Archaic pottery including Laconian and Attic Black Figure. On the other hand, its glass finds were relatively sparse. As so often stated, this fill is contextually useless for interpreting the original uses to which its various objects were put in the sanctuary.

More attention has been place in the above discussion on the implications of the earlier finds that the later. This fact notwithstanding, readers of this series may be already familiar with the view of D. Roques that the A.D. 262 earthquake to which the initial destruction of the sanctuary has been attributed in fact never took place in Cyrene and that the destruction was caused exclusively by the earthquake of A.D. 365.[22] More will be said about this interesting point of view when the site's later coins, sculptures, lamps, and architecture are published. In the meantime nothing emerges from the present studies by Warden and Oliver to offset our belief that sanctuary activity was largely over by the middle of the third century A.D. and that this state of affairs had been caused by an earthquake. We further believe that some limited attempt was made to clean up the Middle Sanctuary after 262 and that the site's final obliteration was caused by the A.D. 365 disaster. Hence, the two latest pieces of glass (Oliver Cat. **167** and **173**) are attributed merely to the first to fourth centuries A.D., while the late Roman gold sheets (Warden Cat. **37** and **39**) are placed no later than the early third century A.D.

There are, finally, the human skeletons published by Monge. One was a three to three-and-a-half-year-old child while the other has been described as either a well-developed fetus of full-term infant. Contrary to earlier published remarks which spoke of the fragmentary remains of three individuals,[23] Monge demonstrates that only two children are involved. The 1978 seasonal report includes a fairly detailed description of the circumstances of their discovery that can be summarized as follows.[24] The two skeletons were found ca. 1.30 m. north of the intersection of gridlines F and 12 (Fig. 1). The body of the older infant lay in a shallow crevice formed by the splitting apart under earthquake pressure of the heavy ashlar capping of the later Imperial T20 retaining wall (Fig. 1). At the time of its discovery its remains were buried in a thin layer of St. 1 A.D. 365 earthquake debris. The body had fallen on its back with its head pointing west. Wedged into the narrow gap, the head was pressed forward so that the chin rested against its chest. The right arm lay parallel to is side, the left was extended over the pelvis. No traces of clothing or any other form of costuming were recovered. The excavators found no evidence for a pit around the body to suggest that it had been hurriedly buried in scooped-out earthquake debris. Instead, to judge from the unceremonious way in which the remains were positioned between the masonry blocks, the body appears to have been accidentally buried. Our guess is that the unfortunate child was knocked over backwards into the gap in the wall where, either stunned or unconscious, it was suffocated by sliding debris. The skull and much of the rest of the body were well preserved, and the fact that no parts display traces of gnawing by rodents or other types of scavengers provides a further reason for believing that the body did not remain exposed to the air after death. What bone breakage there was took place when the bones had dried out and is better explained as the result of prolonged

---

20. *Final Reports* 2, xxii.
21. These are the S2 and S4 structures, the S6 Sacred House, and the P2-P6 rubble wall units that may have been originally part of a three-room naiskos. They await publication in volume five, but see *Final Reports* 1, 117-118, figs. 115, 117.
22. D. Roques, *Synésios de Cyrène et la Cyrénaïque du Bas-Empire* (Paris 1987) 43-44, 96, 97, 209, 319. For the effects of both earthquakes on the sanctuary see *Final Reports* 1, 123, "earthquakes." Also see "Cyrene's Sanctuary of Demeter and Persephone, a Summary of a Decade of Excavation," *AJA* 85 (1981) 27-28.
23. *Final Reports* 1, 62, fig. 56.
24. White, *Sixth Report, LA* 15-16 (1978-1979) 181-183. fig. 11, pl. LVI, d.

earth pressure than by trauma at the actual moment of death.

The newborn's sparse remains, belonging mainly to its right side, were discovered near the skull of the three-year-old child. Why only these parts of its skeleton survive and how someone so young found its way into the sanctuary represent something of an archaeological conundrum, since no trace of an accompanying adult came to light. The soil, however, immediately south of the two children lies under the expedition's Decauville railway line and was never tested. The missing parent either must still lie under the track or somehow survived the earthquake. It would be difficult to explain how a fetus' bones could escape being mixed with those of its mother, which is why I believe the remains belong instead to a newborn child. The loss of the left side of the body may simply be the result of a very shallow interment on sloping ground; the remainder was washed or carried away. In any case, the two represent the sole vestige of the human population that once thronged this sanctuary; their extreme youth gives a double poignancy to their association with its final anguish.[25]

---

25. For more on the place of children in the sanctuary see D. White, "Two Girls from Cyrene, Recent Discoveries from the Sanctuary of Demeter at Cyrene," *OpRom* 9:24 (1973) 207-215.

Fig. 1. Trench Plan of the Site (by Carl Beetz).

Part I

The Small Finds

Introduction

The 510 objects catalogued here are representative of more than 4,000 objects and fragments grouped under the general rubric of small finds. The assemblage is heterogeneous and includes many objects related to groups of similar objects being published elsewhere in this series devoted to the extramural Sanctuary of Demeter and Persephone at Cyrene. Generalizations and conclusions about any single object type are thus limited until the data from the other studies become available. For example, vessels can be discussed only when the evidence for the coarse ware, painted wares, lamps, and glass has been taken into account. Some classes of objects have been excluded from this study because they merited individual attention, for example the coins and the engraved gems, although they, too, are "small finds." The arbitrary nature of the assemblage presented in this study is important to keep in mind, for the conclusions reached here will have to be tempered and refined by the additional evidence presented in the other publications of the sanctuary.

The most important point that can be made about the nature of the assemblage as a whole is the overwhelming preponderance of objects that were apparently personal possessions, objects that are of a seemingly luxurious nature. Small figurines, jewelry, personal ornaments and other such objets de luxe as *Tridacna*-shell palettes were the most popular dedications, particularly in the early periods. For this reason, the objects in the assemblage are often made of those materials normally associated with luxury items: ivory, bone, bronze, silver, gold, ostrich eggshell, and seashell, as opposed to iron, lead, terracotta, or wood. Admittedly, this picture is partly the result of the vicissitudes of preservation; however, even when the poor preservation of, say, the iron objects is taken into account, the functional objects form only a small percentage of the whole. Also, these functional objects, for instance tools or hardware which seem not to be dedicatory in nature, tend to date to the end of the sanctuary's history.

The largest and most clearly definable group of objects dates to the Archaic period. This is partially due to the nature of Archaic small finds, which are easily identifiable and datable, but also results from the incontrovertible fact that the Archaic finds by far outnumber all the other objects combined. The sanctuary was either appreciably wealthier or more popular in the Archaic period, or else the fashion of dedication changed over time. This last possibility, that offerings of jewelry or figurines were later replaced by offerings of other kinds, can only be considered in light of the entire corpus of finds from the sanctuary.

The earliest objects may well antedate the traditional date for the establishment of the Greek settlement at Cyrene. This is the case with the engraved *Tridacna* shells (**467-473**), which seem to have been decorated in the first half of the seventh century B.C. The ivory ram (**26**), although not as precisely datable, is also quite early; it is certainly seventh century, but might date to the end of the century. The carnelian "poppy-head" pendants (**113-118**), the ivory spectacle fibulae, (**192-198**), and some of the metal pins, for instance the silver pin (**234**) which dates to the end of the seventh century B.C., are also early.

Of certain Archaic date, although probably sixth rather than seventh century B.C., are the faience figurines (**29-35**), the ivory axe pendants (**86-89**), the crescent pendants (**98 and 99**), the leaf pendant (**108**), the heart pendants (**155-158**), the hair coils (**175-186**), the earrings (**188-191**), the metal fibulae (**199-203**), many of the bronze pins, the faience vessels (**382-389**), and many of the stone vases. Ascribable to the Archaic period on the basis of style or context are an even greater variety of objects: many of the bronze figurines (**1-25**), the silver mask (**36**), a silver disk-rosette (**43**), the melon beads (**63-68**), the spherical beads (**70-77**), tubular beads (**78-83**), bovine pendants (**90 and 91**), the conical pendants (**92-97**), the ivory drop-shaped pendants (**100-105**), the janiform pendants (**106 and 107**), the gold lion pendants (**109** and **110**), the shell pendants (**120-136**), and many of the other ornament types, including some of the bronze rings.

More generally datable to either the late Archaic or Classical period are the collar beads (**53-58**) the vase pendant (**152**) and the alabaster alabastra (**403-413**).

Classical finds are much rarer. They include the biconical beads (**47-49**), the bronze frog-hinge (**17**), some of the silver and bronze rings (for example **255** and **256**), the bronze ladle handle (**402**), and the stone pyxides (**424**, **425**, and **429**).

The finds attributable to the Hellenistic and Roman periods are relatively fewer given the greater length of this last chronological division. They include the gold diadem (**38** and **39**), the silver rosettes (**40-42**), the ivory bracelets (**167** and **168**), bone buttons (**172-174**), a bronze ring (**257**), the ivory and bone rings (**258** and **254**), an iron base (**277**), bronze plaques, dowels, bronze and bone hinges (**295-297**), many of the nails, the stone finger pestles (**451** and **452**), and at least some of the stone vases. Many of the more functional pieces of hardware, tools, implements, and so on, although not precisely datable, also belong to this last group.

In terms of chronology the picture is clear: very rich dedications during the Archaic period, and dedications of decreased wealth, in decreased quantities, from the beginning of the Classical period onward.

The imported objects can be divided into three main groups: mainland Greek, East Greek, and Egyptian or Egyptianizing. These three groups seem to be fairly evenly divided.

The imports from the Greek mainland are mainly Peloponnesian. They include the ivory ram (**26**), indisputably the product of a Peloponnesian workshop. Possibly from the same source, on the basis of its style, is the unusual bronze janiform figurine (**21**). The same holds true for the janiform pendants (**106** and **107**). The ivory double-axe pendants (**86-88**), along with similar examples found at Tocra, are also mainland imports, closely paralleled throughout the Peloponnesos. They enjoyed a wider distribution than the ivory rams. The ivory spectacle fibulae (**192-198**) may be imports too, however, both the Cyrene fibulae and the examples found at Tocra are dissimilar enough from the mainland types to suggest the possibility of local production. A good number of the bronze pins may also have been produced in the Peloponnesos, where they are paralleled at several sites. All the mainland imports seem to be very early; they date to the end of the seventh or to the sixth century B.C.

The East Greek imports include the faience figurines (**29-35**) and vessels (**382-389**). The bronze monkey (**25**), two of the bronze lions (**22** and **24**), several of the stone pyxides, and a bronze fibula (**202**) may be of Ionian origin. All these objects are Archaic in date, with the exception of the pyxides, which can be assigned to the Classical period.

The Egyptian objects include the bronze frog (**16**) and falcon (**13**) figurines; the carnelian poppy-head pendants (**113-118**); the heart and face pendants (**154-158**, and **159** and **160**), the faience lentoid jar (**387**), the alabastra (**403-413**), some of the stone vases, and, perhaps, the ostrich eggshell fragments (**464**). Although they are no greater in total number, the Egyptian objects form the most varied group in terms of types of objects and materials. Here again, most of the objects are of an early date.

A few of the finds, for instance the engraved *Tridacna* shells (**467-473**), are of clear eastern Mediterranean origin, but might have reached Cyrene either by direct importation or via East Greek traders.

Much more unusual are two imports from Italy: the bronze frog-hinge from an Etruscan *infundibulum* (**17**), and a bronze duck-handle from a strainer (**402**) that was probably manufactured in Magna Graecia. Both are of Classical date, and along with a bronze ladle from the second Artemisium at Cyrene, are testament to rare trade connections with the West in the fifth century B.C.

The Catalogue

The amount of material is large, and some object types were found in great quantity. The catalogue is representative rather than comprehensive. There is neither the space nor the need to catalogue every example of every type. Therefore, it includes examples of each type of (identifiable) object that was found and attempts to give a total impression of the entire assemblage, keeping in mind the usual and necessary caveat for studies of this type: any selective process is naturally arbitrary, and the natural biases of preservation, excavation, and scholarship will necessarily affect the outcome. Certain media will be slighted—iron, for instance, because iron objects are often so badly preserved as to be unrecognizable. There is also the tendency to emphasize the spectacular and idiosyncratic at the expense of the mundane.

It has been a primary tenet in trying to organize such a myriad assortment of objects that function is the most important determinant. In studying material from a cultic context, it is the function of the object, its function as perceived by the dedicant, that determines its meaning as an offering. More arbitrary divisions by medium or technique would merely obscure this most basic aspect. For this reason the small finds have been organized in this catalogue according to their function. They are organized in chapters, each containing a broad category of objects—figurines, jewelry and ornament, hardware and tools, weapons, vessels, and miscellaneous objects. Within each chapter they are arranged by artifact type and under each typological subheading, in the case of larger classes of objects, they have been further divided into more manageable groups. Pendants, for instance, are one of the largest groups in terms of variety of types, and they have been divided into a number of typological groups, arranged alphabetically. Vases, instead, are first subdivided according to medium and then further divided according to shape. The only major exception to this functional arrangement is the first chapter, on the figurines, which groups together all the representations of full-bodied animals and humans. This is done for the sake of convenience, since it is often difficult to determine the original function of a figurine. Some may have been pendants, others attachments or decorative revetments, still others just dedicatory figures. It also follows the strictures of common sense that figurative art should be treated separately, both for stylistic reasons and because figurines might have an important symbolic or representative meaning.

Integrated into the catalogue are discussions of function, chronology, source of manufacture, and context of the finds. Discussion of this sort normally follows each major group of entries. For information regarding the general history of the site, its excavation, and summaries of the stratigraphy the reader is referred to the first volume in the series of publications on the Demeter Sanctuary.

The catalogue entries attempt to follow the format used in previous studies in this series. They include the catalogue number assigned to them in this study, the excavation inventory number, the type of object, the grid designation of the find, and a plate or figure reference. The second line gives the dimensions, and a brief description follows. If the object has been published, bibliographic references are given at the beginning of the catalogue description. Comparanda are presented following entries of similar object types. Conclusions of an immediate nature, the number of such objects found, evidence for dating, and possible place of manufacture are provided at the end of each chapter.

I

Figurines

Bronze Figurines
1-25

Among the most pleasing finds from the Demeter Sanctuary at Cyrene is a group of small bronze figurines, almost all of them animals. The figurines were found singly and come from all areas of the site.

Of the Cyrene menagerie of figurines, the majority are birds, but among themselves these birds differ widely as to type and rendering. They include doves or pigeons, water birds, hens, roosters, and a bird of prey.

BIRDS
1-15

1 ROOSTER
Pl. 1   71-285   E11   3   3
L. 0.042; H. 0.048; Th. 0.013
White, *Second Report*, pl. 94e.
Bronze. Missing beak and comb. Straight legs and neck, long curving tail. Feathering of wings indicated by shallow incision. Small protuberance on chest, perhaps remains of suspension ring. A pendant?
6th century B.C.

2 ROOSTER
Pl. 1   73-330   D12   A scarp   3
L. 0.045; H. 0.048
Bronze. Fighting cock, striding forward vigorously, on oval plinth with tenon on underside. Large feet, small body, and long neck. Head has prominent comb, long beak, and bulging eyes. Legs bent. Long sickle-shaped tail with short underfeathers.
6th to 5th century B.C.

3 ROOSTER
Pl. 1   73-331   D12   A scarp   3
H. 0.043
Bronze. Worn and corroded, almost no surface detail preserved. Missing part of tail. Short feet but no base or plinth. Long, curving tail pierced for suspension. A pendant?
6th century B.C.

4 ROOSTER
Pl. 2   73-1131   D12/E12   D   3
L. 0.051; H. 0.060; Th. 0.018
Bronze. Corroded. Legs bent at sharp angle. Long, curving tail, pierced. Small wings close to body, decorated with longitudinal hatching and light cross-hatching.
6th century B.C.

5 ROOSTER
Pl. 2   74-857   C10/11   A (beta)   3
L. 0.029; H. 0.053; Th. 0.009
Bronze. Long straight legs, separated from each other only by shallow groove. Long, curving tail. Small wings close to body. Long, straight neck. Plume and comb well delineated. No sign of suspension hole or base.
6th century B.C.

6 HEN
Pl. 2   71-459   E11   3   3
L. 0.014; H. 0.039; W. 0.014
White, *Second Report*, pl. 94f.
Bronze. Probably a hen. Head worn, little detail preserved. Head turned back. High, short tail. Wings set off slightly from body, scored to indicate feathering. Legs set on small oval plinth.
6th century B.C.

7 HEN
Pl. 2   76-1220   C12/13   1   4
L. 0.024; H. 0.043; Th. 0.013
Bronze. Stylized bird, possibly a hen. Short legs, wide tail feathers, long neck, and oval head with detailing of beak or eyes. Holes through neck and between feet.
6th century B.C.

8 PIGEON
Pl. 3   77-1084   C12   1   4a
L. 0.030; H. 0.030; Th. 0.015
Bronze. Possibly a pigeon. Broken at feet. Small beak, large circular eyes, and long, slightly upturned tail. Each wing articulated by two deep grooves.
Archaic.

9 PIGEON
Pl. 3   74-1134   D12/13   F   3
L. 0.031; H. 0.033; Th. 0.016
Bronze. Heavily corroded; broken at legs. Plump body and short tail feathers. Incised to indicate feathering of wings and tail. Hole through neck.
Archaic.

10 PIGEON
Pl. 3   74-1138   D12/13   F   3
L. 0.030; H. 0.028; Th. 0.013
Bronze. Possibly a pigeon. Heavily corroded. Head turned back. Small head with long curving beak. Short neck. Long tail feathers. Smooth underside, no indication of legs. Hole through tail.
Archaic.

11 PIGEON
Pl. 3   77-1083   C13 1 4a
L. 0.029; H. 0.023; Th. 0.014
Bronze. Perhaps a pigeon. Head turned back. Wings articulated by several straight grooves. Hole through tail.
Archaic.

12 WATER BIRD
Pl. 4   77-1124   C13 1 4b
L. 0.028; H. 0.033; Th. 0.016
Archaeology (March 1979) 59.
Bronze. Striding bird on small rectangular plinth. Long beak, large circular eyes and long curving neck. Wings articulated by deep grooves. Plinth has tenon on underside.
6th century B.C.

13 FALCON
Pl. 4   74-1124   D12/13 F 3
L. 0.054; H. 0.051; Th. 0.014
White, *Fourth Report*, pl. 29, fig. 42.
Bronze. Bird of prey, probably a falcon or hawk, standing on plinth. Hooked beak, long neck, oval body, and long legs, not separated. Wings held close to body.
7th to 6th century B.C.

14 BIRD
Pl. 4   77-1114   C13 1 4a
L. 0.048; H. 0.024; Th. 0.017
Bronze. Bird in flight with loop attached to back. Small head with little detailing of beak. Long outstretched neck and stylized wings. Fan-shaped tail feathers. Similar to **11**.
Archaic.

15 BIRD
Pl. 4   77-1249   C13 1 4
L. 0.012; H. 0.018; Th. 0.010
Bronze. Fragment of bird preserving plinth, feet, and part of legs. One leg placed in front of other.

The favorite type of bird seems to be the cock (**1-5**) with prominent comb and sickle-shaped tail. Fighting cocks are commonly represented in Greek and Roman art. In the Geometric period, bird pendants, often roosters, were dedicated at Greek sanctuaries, particularly in northern Greece, Thessaly, and the Peloponnesos.[1] The Cyrene roosters may belong to this tradition. Examples of Archaic and Classical date are less common,[2] and are more often used as pendants than as freestanding figurines. Rooster figurines were quite common during the Roman period, probably because they were associated with the cult of Mercury,[3] but the Roman examples are clearly different in style from the Cyrene roosters.[4]

These roosters are difficult to date precisely. A cock from Cyprus, now in the Metropolitan Museum in New York and dated to the early sixth century by Richter,[5] has similar treatment of the tail feathers but is otherwise not close to the Cyrene examples. A bronze cock from Corinth, not unlike the Cyrene birds in some details, is dated to the fifth century B.C.;[6] and a plastic vase from Athens, of fifth century date,[7] has similar articulation of the wings and tail feathers and would support a slightly later date. Fourth-century birds, as well as later examples, are usually more stylized and have less detailed rendering of the feathers and crest, although the poses are often more three-dimensional.[8] Thus, because of their stiffer poses, compact bodies, and careful articulation of details, I would not want to date most of our bird figurines later than the middle of the fifth century B.C. The rooster with long stylized tail, plump body, and bent legs (**4**) seems quite the earliest, perhaps dating to the sixth century B.C. It is pierced through the tail and seems to have been used as a pendant. The other cocks all stood on small plinths. With their static poses and carefully articulated tail feathers they could date to anywhere in the late sixth or early fifth century B.C.

The hens, pigeons, and ducks are all probably of similar date, namely, sixth or fifth century B.C. Particularly fine is the small duck or goose (**12**), that is shown striding forward in a vigorous and characteristic manner. Its strong modeling and three-dimensional pose suggest a date in the sixth century B.C., and in fact it was found in an undisturbed Archaic level. Almost all the other birds are also from Archaic contexts. More unusual is the hawk or falcon (**13**) with its strongly linear pose and smooth profile. This type of figurine was common in Egypt,[9] and our example may be Egyptian or at least heavily Egyptianizing. It is probably of sixth century date.

At the Demeter Sanctuary there definitely seems to have been a fondness for small bronze bird dedications during the Archaic period. While the other animal types are too few in number to suggest any specific relevance to the cult, the preponderance of fowl is certainly suggestive. This predilection for gallinaceous birds is reminiscent of the fondness for small bronze bird dedications at northern Greek sanctuaries during the Geometric period. Mitten has suggested that real birds might have been popular dedications at these same sanctuaries.[10] On the evidence of the small finds,

---

1. J. Bouzek, *Graeco-Macedonian Bronzes* (Prague 1973), 13-18. *Mildenberg*, 95-98, with bibliography. *Olynthos* 10, 117 n. 187 for an extensive list of Peloponnesian types.
2. E.g., Reinach 5, 464, nos. 5 and 6, from Locri and Cyprus.
3. C.A. DeStefano, *Bronzetti figurati del Museo di Palermo* (Rome 1975), 81. J.M.C. Toynbee, *Animals in Roman Life and Art* (Ithaca 1973), 257.
4. E.g., Reinach 5.2, 77, 1-6; 4, 536, 1-6, and 538, 1-7. Niessen, pl. 127, no. 4247. The Roman examples tend to be larger, less stylized, and more varied in their poses.
5. Richter, *Bronzes*, 47, no. 73. Reinach 5, 464, no. 6.
6. *Corinth* 12, pl. 48, no. 502.
7. *BCH* 100 (1978) 648, fig. 24.
8. E.g., a fourth century B.C. bronze cock on the New York art market, called Etruscan but probably Greek; Sale Catalogue, Sotheby's New York Galleries, June 10-11, 1983: *Egyptian, Classical, and Near Eastern Antiquities* (New York 1983), 77, no. 76 (illustrated).
9. As was pointed out by White, *Fourth Report*, 177 n. 39 citing Davidson, *Corinth* 12, 67.
10. *Mildenberg*, 95.

the same may hold true at the Demeter Sanctuary at Cyrene. Birds were normally associated with Aphrodite, and, in the Roman period, with Mercury; but here at Cyrene, at least, birds might have been considered apt for Demeter as well. Certainly birds, usually doves held by female dedicants,[11] are commonly shown in Greek sculpture.

FROGS
16 and 17

16 FROG
Pl. 5   71-799   E11   2   3
L. 0.027; H. 0.017
 Bronze. Small, crouching on flat base. Large bulging eyes. Thick ridge running vertically down back.

17 FROG HINGE
Pl. 5; Ill. 1   76-1226   C12/13   1   3
L. 0.046; H. 0.014; W. 0.028
 Bronze highly stylized frog. Long head, pointed snout, bulging eyes, and streamlined body. Front legs extended far forward. Front feet pierced by rivets; loop at rear.
 Etruscan.
 6th century B.C.

These two small bronze frogs are quite different in style and function. **16** does not seem to have been pierced, and, therefore, is not a pendant, nor, seemingly, an attachment. Egyptian frogs in a similar pose, sometimes with a flat plinth, are published as weights by Petrie. Egyptian examples were popular from the New Kingdom to at least the end of the first millennium B.C.[12] They are found in a variety of media. Greek bronze frogs are not uncommon, but usually are part of

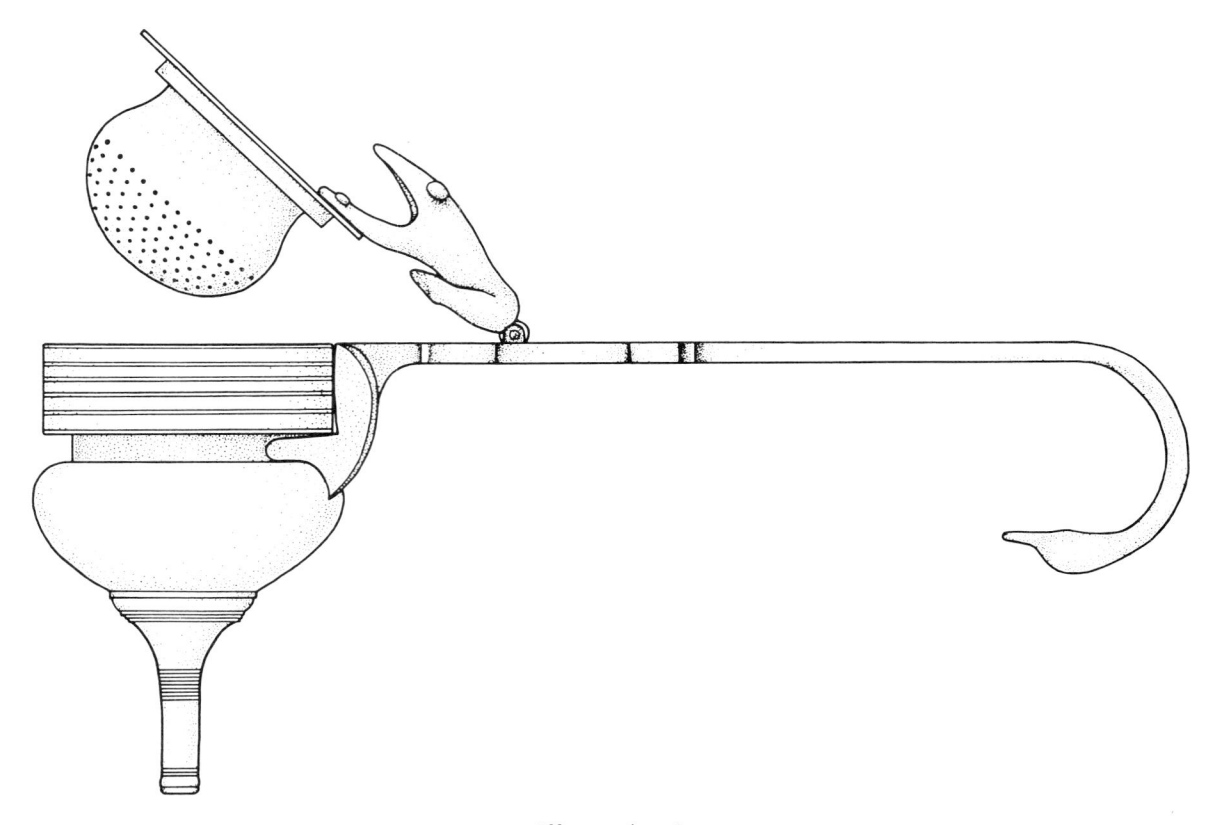

Illustration 1

---

11. Exhibition catalogue: *Greek Art of the Aegean Islands* (The Metropolitan Museum of Art, New York 1979), 162-163, nos. 119 and 120, East Greek alabastra in the shape of women holding doves.
12. Frog weights: Petrie, *Weights*, pl. 9, nos. 5083, 5146, 4775, and

4913A. Egyptian frogs: e.g., Mildenberg, 60-61, no. 47, carnelian, Dynasty 18, with bibliography. G.A. Reisner, *Catalogue général des antiquités égyptiennes du Musée du Caire: Amulets* (Cairo 1907), 188-192.

other objects—caryatid mirrors, vase spouts, etc.[13] Free-standing bronze examples are rarer[14] and do not provide any close parallels. The squatting frog **16** may have served as a weight and may be an Egyptian import.

An almost exact parallel for frog **17** is provided by a small frog from the Argive Heraeum.[15] It too has a suspension loop and two pierced front feet, and was surely made by the same workshop as the Cyrene frog. Both must have served as hinges on bronze strainer—funnels, *infundibula*. A strainer funnel from Belmonte Piceno, in the Ancona Museum,[16] has an almost identical frog on its handle. It serves as a hinge; the loop was attached to the handle and the front feet were riveted to a separate strainer which could thus be flipped out of the funnel for easy cleaning. The exact arrangement, as reconstructed for our frog (Ill. 1) is also known on an *infundibulum* in the Metropolitan Museum[17] which uses a pair of lions as a hinge. Three other strainer funnels with the same type of frog handle are known; they are of uncertain provenance but are all now in Italian museums.[18] Zuffa has shown conclusively that this type of vessel is Etruscan,[19] although it was eventually imitated in South Italy and Greece. The frog is found only on Etruscan examples,[20] and it seems reasonably certain that **17** (as well as the example from the Argive Heraeum) should be considered an Etruscan import, perhaps coming to Cyrene via South Italy, as did a South Italian strainer, with a duck handle (**402**).

FRAGMENTARY FIGURINES
18-21

18 HOOF
Pl. 6   73-890   C15/16   1   3
L. (base) 0.021; H. 0.026; W. (base) 0.022
Bronze. Fragment of animal figurine preserving a hoof resting on square plinth. Part of a horse?

19 ARM
Pl. 6   73-802   D16/17   7   1
L. 0.035
Bronze. Fragment of human figurine preserving hand and part of forearm. Bunch of grapes in palm of hand, which judging by position of thumb must be right hand.

20 FOOT
Pl. 6   76-1214   C11   1   2
L. 0.016; H. 0.005; W. 0.012
Bronze. Fragment of hollow foot resting on small plinth. Broken at instep, toes indicated by incision.

21 JANIFORM FIGURE
Pl. 7   73-1191   C15/16   1   5
H. 0.058
Bronze. Nude male with janiform head. Clear differentiation between back and front of body, although little detailing of individual features. Figure stands stiffly with both arms at sides and hands joined to hips. Faces characterized by almond-shaped eyes and small mouth. Head covered by close-fitting cap or helmet.
Peloponnesian?
Probably late 7th-early 6th century B.C.

Judging by the size of the preserved hoof and plinth, the horse (**18**) must have been a sizable piece. The other two fragments are from human figurines—**19** holds a bunch of grapes in the right hand and therefore may have represented a dedicant proffering an offering. Complete, but just as perplexing, is the janiform male figurine (**21**); it seems quite early, probably late seventh or early sixth century B.C., and perhaps of Peloponnesian manufacture.

BRONZE LIONS
22-24

22 LION
Pl. 7   71-753   D12/13   B   4
L. 0.032; H. 0.020; Th. 0.013
Bronze. Small, crouching on flat rectangular plinth. Open mouth, pronounced bulbous nose, and bulging eyes. Front legs set off from plinth and musculature articulated by

---

13. As discussed by D.G. Mitten in *Mildenberg*, 99-100, with bibliography. For a water spout with crouching frog: exhibition catalogue, *Greek Art from the Aegean Islands* (The Metropolitan Museum of Art, New York 1979), 179, no. 142.
14. Reinach 2, 778, no. 9, in the Louvre. Niessen, pl. 123, no. 4098. E. Babelon and A. Blanchet, *Catalogue des bronzes antiques de la Bibliothèque Nationale* (Paris 1895), 421, nos. 1232-1234. R.V. Nicholls, *Archaeological Reports for 1965-1966* (London 1966) 49, fig. 10.
15. *Argive Heraeum* 2, no. 31, pl. 76.
16. Ancona, Museo Nazionale inv. no. 12563/12581, from Belmonte Piceno Tomb 163. M. Zuffa, *StEtr* 28 (1960) 187-189, no. 15.
17. New York, Metropolitan Museum of Art inv. no. 11.212.2. Richter, *Bronzes*, 230, 638. A good photograph showing the hinge arrangement is provided by D.K. Hill, *JWalt* 5 (1942) 47, fig. 8.
18. M. Zuffa, *StEtr* 28 (1960) 203-204, no. 30, Rome, Villa Giulia Inv. no. 24689; p. 189-190, no. 17, Firenze, Museo Archeologico Inv. no. 1437; p. 189, no. 16, Torino, Museo Archeologico Nazionale Inv. no. 933.
19. Ibid., *StEtr* 28 (1960) 165-207. Zuffa opts for an Etruscan workshop on the basis of distribution, the early date of the Etruscan examples, and on parallel production of strainer-funnels in bucchero. His findings thus supersede E. Kunze and H. Schleif, *JdI* 53 (1939) 123-125 who argued for a Greek origin. D.K. Hill, *JWalt* 5 (1942) 46, also suggested an Etruscan origin.
20. Several *infundibula* may have been made in Campania: Zuffa, *StEtr* 28 (1960) nos. 25, 29. P.J. Riis, *From the Collection of the Ny Carlsberg Glyptothek* 2 (1938), 156, argued for a Campanian origin for the entire group. One example, found at Trebenischte, was probably a Greek imitation: Zuffa, *StEtr* 28 (1960) 174, no. 32. It differs substantially in style and form. No frogs are found on either the Campanian or Greek examples.

incision. Notch in lion's left side; hole in left side of plinth, perhaps for vertical dowel. Probably a vessel attachment.
East Greek?
Archaic.

23 LION
Pl. 8   74-272   D12/13   D   surface
L. 0.038; H. 0.018; Th. 0.014

Bronze. Small, crouching. Little articulation of head or body except for rear haunches and tail, which curves over haunch and is tucked under rear right leg. Mane modeled plastically but not articulated by incision.
Laconian?
Archaic.

24 LION
Pl. 8   76-1231   C13/D13   1   6
L. 0.034; H. 0.023; Th. 0.016

Bronze. Crouching on rectangular plinth, underside of which was a seal, now illegible. Open mouth. Tail curves over right haunch and is tucked under right leg. Rectangular cutting through side of lion, probably for a handle. Two holes through underside of lion may have held dowels.
Archaic

Lions **22** and **23** were probably attachments for bronze vessels, a common use for bronze lions during the Archaic period.[21] Lion **24** was undoubtedly a seal and has a tenon to receive a handle on one side of the body. Lions **22** and **24**, by the careful detailing of the mane, the posture of the body, the open mouth, and the articulation of the haunches and tail, resemble lions of East Greek type that were still closely related to Oriental prototypes.[22] Because of its smoothly rounded forms and lack of articulation of mane, head, and musculature, **23** seems much closer to Greek lions from mainland workshops.[23] Bronze lions were popular dedications at sanctuaries during the Archaic period.[24]

BRONZE APE
25

25 APE
Pl. 8   69-1   2   1   2
H. 0.040; W. 0.038

Bronze. Squatting, with knees tucked up close to chest. Left hand on left knee; right hand raised to side of head. Highly stylized. Not personally examined.
Archaic.

Apes are frequently represented in Greek art from the Archaic period onward,[25] squatting apes are the most common type. Corinthian plastic vases and Etrusco-Corinthian imitations thereof often take the form of squatting apes who hold one hand to the head and the other on a knee or between the legs.[26] Apes are also popular as terracotta figurines.[27] Bronze apes are found on everything from fibulae and jewelry to bronze vases, especially in Etruria where apes seem to have been extremely popular;[28] bronze figurines are less common. A bronze figurine from Rhodes, now in the British Museum, is shown in a similar squatting pose but plays the flute.[29] The Cyrene ape is datable to the first half of the sixth century B.C. because of its similarity to Corinthian and Corinthianizing ape vases.

Ivory Figurines
26-28

26 RAM
Pl. 9   73-286   E12/13   C   3
L. 0.036; H. 0.018

Ivory. Couchant ram on thin plinth. Large, thick body with prominent well-rounded haunches. Pierced horizontally through body. Head and muzzle chipped.
7th century B.C.

27 ARM
Pl. 9   74-401   Stray
L. 0.055; D. (shaft) 0.005

Ivory. Arm and hand. Cylindrical arm with no detail or modeling. Long, delicately carved fingers. Three fingers hold a sphere; other two fingers tucked under palm.
Probably Roman.

---

21. For example, on a lamp in the Louvre: A. de Ridder, *Les bronzes antiques du Louvre*, vol. 2: *Les instruments* (Paris 1915), 150, pl. 111, no. 3142.
22. For example a lion from Kameiros Tomb 6 (excavated 1864) now in the British Museum: Walters, 11, no. 139. For a similar treatment of tail and haunch: Petrie, *Weights*, pl. 9, no. 4939. For the oriental prototypes for East Greek lions: Berlin Museum, Vorderasien, *Freiplastiken und Reliefs Katalog der Originalabgüsse*, vol. 3 (Berlin 1964), pl. 21, no. 76 and from Dur-Sarrukin (Khorsabad), dated 722-705 B.C., Assyrian. Also an Assyrian lion weight in the Louvre: L. Brown, *The Etruscan Lion* (Oxford 1960), pl. 61f.
23. H. Gabelmann, *Studien zum frühgriechischen Löwenbild* (Berlin 1965), 66-74, the closest parallel to our lion may be an example from Samos, pl. 11, 1-2, considered Laconian (pp. 69-70).

24. For example the bronze lion with dedicatory inscription to Hera, from the Heraeum at Samos: exhibition catalogue, *Greek Art of the Aegean Islands* (The Metropolitan Museum of Art, New York 1979) 186, no. 150.
25. W.C. McDermott, *The Ape in Antiquity* (Baltimore 1938).
26. E.g., the Italo-Corinthian plastic vase in the Mildenberg collection: *Mildenberg*, 114-115, no. 95, with full bibliography.
27. B. Bonacelli, *StEtr* 6 (1932) 343-382.
28. R.A. Higgins, *Catalogue of the Terracottas in the Department of Greek and Roman Antiquities, British Museum*, vol. 2 (London 1959) 50-52.
29. Walters, 11, no. 144, from Kameiros, 1864.

28 LEG
Pl. 9   76-740   F13/G13   1   2
L. 0.035; Max. D. (leg) 0.008
 Ivory. Small leg. Part of figurine or doll. Very well modeled calf and ankles; delicate incision for toes. Remains of tenon at top of leg.
 Probably Roman.

The ram (**26**) is very close to a group of ivory animals from the Limenia deposit at Perachora, particularly to one specific ivory ram, Perachora A16.[30] It has the same large body and prominent haunches, as well as almost identical handling of the tucked front and back legs, and similar carving of the head and horns. Both **26** and the Perachora piece were made in the same workshop. Ivory animals similar to the Perachora examples, most of them pierced horizontally and some with seals carved on the underside of the plinth, are also known in great numbers from the Artemis Orthia sanctuary,[31] and in smaller numbers from the Argive Heraeum, Ithaca, Siphnos, and a number of other Greek sites both on the mainland and the islands.[32] The workshop has been identified as Laconian by Stubbings.[33] Our ram (**26**) is thus both early (surely at least late seventh century B.C.) and made on the Greek mainland—an heirloom perhaps dedicated by one of the early settlers at Cyrene. An ivory ram from Tocra,[34] originally a pendant but later attached to an iron fibula, belongs to the same workshop, although in details of body and head it differs somewhat from our example.

The ivory leg (**28**) was probably part of a complete human figurine, perhaps a doll. It is probably Roman. The arm (**27**) is more unusual and need not have been part of a complete figurine. The arm itself is not modeled nor is it in any way realistic, making it unlikely that it was meant to be set into, or attached onto a torso. In itself it makes perfect sense as a dedication, the offered hand which holds an offering. It, too, is probably Roman in date.

Faience Figurines
29-35

29 FEMALE FIGURINE
Pl. 9   74-977   D12/13   F   3
H. 0.059
 White, *Fourth Report*, pl. 31, fig. 44.
 Faience. Nude in rigid frontal stance with arms held straight at sides. Wide hips, large protruding stomach and breasts. Hole between left arm and waist. Dark glaze for hair, nipples, and pubic hair. Strut running vertically up back and pierced at waist level.
 Archaic.

30 INCOMPLETE FIGURINE
Pl. 10   76-979   D12/13   F   3
H. 0.042
 Faience. Figure base preserving feet and skirt. Figure shown striding. Traces of blue and green glaze.
 Archaic.

31 MALE FLAUTIST
Pl. 10   77-646   F13/G13   2   2
H. 0.046
 Faience. Frontal, preserving torso, missing legs and head. Figure holds double flute.
 Archaic.

32 GROUP
Pl. 10   77-381   F13/G13   2   2
H. 0.076; W. 0.052
 Faience. Two figurines, flautist and partially clothed male figure, standing side-by-side. Flautist wears long tunic, straight vertical pleats of which are shown from knees down, and also mantle which falls diagonally in back. Double flute is very long and extends to waist. Hair pulled back from forehead, falling to either side of head down to shoulders. Second figure (an acrobat?) wears kilt and has large rounded body with protruding stomach and buttocks. Armlet may be indicated on upper right arm. Both figures striding forward.
 Archaic.

33 LION
Pl. 11   71-146   E11   1   2
L. 0.038; H. 0.025
 Faience. Couchant, on thin rectangular plinth. Worn, little detail preserved. Eyes indicated by pin holes. Traces of green glaze on paws and mane.
 Archaic.

34 RAM(?)
Pl. 11   71-549   E15   3   3
L. 0.061; H. 0.030
 Faience. Couchant animal on thin rectangular plinth, missing much of head but possibly a ram. Worn, little detail preserved.
 Archaic.

35 FALCON
Pl. 11   76-749   F13/G13   1   2
H. 0.046; W. 0.020
 Faience. Missing lower legs and tail. Large bulging eyes. Suspension loop in back.
 Archaic.

These seven faience figurines form a small fraction of a much larger corpus of faience objects from the Demeter Sanctuary; the majority of the faience is in the form of vessels and containers (see chapter 5).

---

30. Stubbings in *Perachora* 2, 407-410, A11-A22, pl. 174. Compare pl. 174, A16,a to our Pl. 9.
31. *Artemis Orthia*, 230, pls. 148-154.
32. Stubbings in *Perachora* 2, 408 n. 5.
33. Ibid., 408. E.L.I. Marangou, *Lakonische Elfenbein-und Beinschnitzereien* (Berlin 1969), 112f. See also J. Boardman, *GGFR*, 114-117.
34. *Tocra* 2, F150, pp. 80, 83, pl. 39.

All of the figurines are of a type usually considered East Greek, most likely of Rhodian manufacture. The standing female (**29**) belongs to a group of figurines, both male and female, of similar style and attitude: a nude standing figure with arms held at the side, protruding stomach, and "Hathor" hair style. On all these figures dark glaze is used to indicate hair, nipples, and pubic hair. Figurines of this type are known from a number of Greek sites, and, because they probably represent "the gift of the worshiper,"[35] they were popular dedications at sanctuaries during the sixth century B.C. Our figurine (**29**) belongs to Webb's "Black and White Blob Group," A.b.i, which includes twenty-six examples.[36] All are from East Greek sites except for those from Sparta, Naukratis, and Tocra.[37]

More unusual is the group of flautist and kilted male, perhaps an acrobat (**32**). Single musicians, usually flautists like **31**, are known from a number of sites.[38] These musicians are sometimes shown with animals, but our example with both flautist and "acrobat" is to my knowledge unique. Although it is probably East Greek with close connections to Cypriote stone sculpture,[39] musicians of this type do have Egyptian antecedents, and faience musicians, usually larger, were manufactured in Egypt.[40]

Three faience animals were found. The lion (**33**) is paralleled in sixth century contexts at East Greek sites.[41] Rams are much rarer, and our example (**34**) is unusual, although the preservation is such that its identification will have to remain open. The falcon with suspension loop in back (**35**) is a popular type;[42] an almost exact parallel is known from Samos.[43] Datable examples have been found in the Protocorinthian deposit at Perachora,[44] in seventh-century context on Chios,[45] and in late seventh or early sixth century contexts at Tocra.[46] All these examples are East Greek, although once again such falcons are also known from Egypt. The Egyptian examples, surely the prototypes for the East Greek birds, are similar but have more carefully articulated details.[47]

Summary

Of the thirty-five figurines discussed in this chapter twenty-five are of bronze, three of ivory, and seven of faience. Most are animals: birds, lions, frogs, rams, and apes. Human figurines are rarer except among the faience examples, of which four out of seven represent humans either singly or in groups.

Birds are the most common animal represented. The popularity of roosters and hens in particular may be related to the cult of Demeter; bronze birds may have been favorite offerings because real birds were considered appropriate as dedications. The other types of animals probably had no specific cultic association, but were most likely dedicated as luxury objects. Some in fact were merely parts of larger objects: pendants, pinheads, handle revetments, and even a hinge from an elaborate bronze strainer funnel. The faience figurines were certainly mass produced; they are found at numerous Archaic sanctuaries and have no specific relevance, in terms of type represented, to the cult of Demeter.

Most of the figurines date to the Archaic period. The exceptions are four fragments, two of bronze (**19** and **20**), and two of ivory (**27** and **28**), which may be Hellenistic or Roman in date. A number of the earlier pieces are more precisely datable. The ivory ram (**26**) is probably the earliest piece; of seventh century in date and possibly an heirloom brought to Cyrene by the early colonists. The faience figurines (**29-35**) are all from the late seventh or early sixth century B.C. The bronze animals (**1-17**) are harder to date but can all be ascribed to the Archaic period on the basis of style. The bronze janiform figure (**21**) certainly has an Archaic appearance. An Archaic date is consistent with the find contexts of all these pieces, in either exclusively Archaic strata or strata with a heavy concentration of Archaic finds (see Appendix I). The popularity of figurines as dedications in the Archaic period, and their relative lack of popularity in later periods, is difficult to explain, and the phenomenon is paralleled in the case of personal ornament and jewelry (chapter 2), which

---

35. Webb, 82.
36. Webb, 84-85.
37. Webb, nos. 38, 329, 339, 317.
38. Flautists: Webb, nos. 288-306, 355-364, 392-397. Flautists are also shown sitting, crouching, or squatting. Lyre-players and drummers are rarer.
39. As was pointed out by Webb, 87.
40. Webb, nos. 580-603.
41. Webb, nos. 457-466, from Naucratis, Kameiros, Lindos, Chios, and Sounion. Examples without suspension loops: Webb, nos. 654-656.
42. Webb, nos. 482-550.
43. E. Diehl, *AA* 80 (1965) 838, fig. 12, no. 96.
44. *Perachora* 2, 513, D778, pl. 19; D787; D789.
45. *Emporio*, 241, nos. 582-6.
46. *Tocra* 2, 85, F164, pl. 40, called "probably Rhodian."
47. Petrie, *Amulets*, pl. 41. A superb Ptolemaic example in the Mildenberg collection: *Mildenberg*, 76, no. 65, with bibliography.

decrease in quantity after the Classical period. This decline may have resulted from changes in fashion rather than from any shift in economic circumstances.

The figurines seem to have been imported from a variety of areas, and no one source seems to predominate. The seven faience examples (**29-35**) are all East Greek according to the most recent studies. The bronze ape (**25**) may also be East Greek. The bronze falcon (**13**) and frog (**16**), however, are very close to Egyptian prototypes and may in fact be Egyptian. On the other hand, several pieces definitely come from Peloponnesian workshops: certainly the ivory ram (**26**), possibly the bronze janiform figure (**21**), and perhaps even the bronze lion (**23**); the other lions (**22** and **24**), however, seem closer to East Greek types. Most unusual in both the use of the figurine and in its provenience is the bronze frog (**17**) which served as a hinge for a splendid bronze funnel-strainer (Ill. 1). This *infundibulum* is of certain Etruscan manufacture and may have ended up at Cyrene via trade connections with South Italy (in fact, another bronze strainer [**402**] is probably a South Italian import). The source of the bronze birds is uncertain, although they sometimes have a general resemblance to birds portrayed on Corinthian and Attic pottery. Yet they need not be imports; they might easily have been manufactured at Cyrene. To my knowledge they form the largest group of such figurines from stratified contexts.

The overall picture provided by the figurines parallels the other groups of small finds from the Sanctuary of Demeter. The figurines are evidence of a fashion for costly and personal dedications in the Archaic period, dedications that come from a variety of sources—East Greek, Peloponnesian, Egyptian, and even Italic, with no specific dominant source area.

II

Jewelry and Ornaments

Objects of ornamental nature form the largest group of small finds from the Demeter Sanctuary. It is difficult to be precise about the exact percentage of ornamental objects because many of them, for instance the beds and pendants, are now found singly but were originally part of more complex pieces such as necklaces. Even allowing for the disproportion caused by the vagaries of preservation, it is clear that ornaments of a decorative nature, personal possessions, were favorite dedications at the Demeter Sanctuary, particularly during the Archaic and early Classical periods.

The objects are catalogued alphabetically by type. Included are attachments for jewelry, beads and pendants (for the sake of clarity the beads and pendants are grouped together: the beads alphabetized by type and then the pendants alphabetized by type with miscellaneous pendants at the end), bands, bracelets, tassels, buckles, buttons, coils and earrings, fibulae, straight pins, and rings. The quantities of each type are tabulated and discussed at the end of the chapter.

Attachments and Metal Reliefs
36-46

This small group of objects includes some of the most spectacular finds from the Demeter Sanctuary.

36 MASK
Pl. 12   74-122   D16/17   2   2
H. 0.039; W. 0.026
White, *Fourth Report*, 175, pl. 29, fig. 35.
Silver with traces of gilding. Repoussé, now flattened but originally convex, missing about one quarter of face on lower left. Frontal human face with features of black African. Tightly curled hair with deep widow's peaks, large oval eyes, wide nose and mouth.
Archaic.

37 PLAQUE
Not ill.   76-1048   C12/D12   G   3
L. 0.015; W. 0.005; Th. 0.001
Silver. Small rectangular plaque with four finished edges. Traces of incision?

38 FOIL SHEET
Pl. 12   74-170   E12/13   E   2
L. 0.042
White, *Fourth Report*, 172 n. 22.
Gold. Thin crumpled, and badly damaged. Joins **39**.

39 DIADEM
Pl. 12   74-450   E12/13   E   2
L. 0.043
White, *Fourth Report*, 172-173, n. 22; pl. 27, figs. 23-4.
Gold. Thin, broken at both ends. Stamped decoration in form of seven frontal figures who raise right arm or hold an attribute in right hand. Part of Late Roman diadem.
Severan.

The silver mask (**36**) is made from extremely thin and fragile foil and was used as an attachment on jewelry rather than as a vessel or implement attachment, perhaps forming part of a wreath, necklace, or diadem. It can be dated to the Archaic period on the basis of style. Masks with features of gorgons, satyrs, or *silenoi* are not uncommon and were often used as centerpieces for elaborate necklaces.[1] I know of no exact parallel for our mask with its African features, although it is not unusual in Archaic Greek art for satyrs to be shown with such features. Our mask may in fact be intended as a satyr mask, a type of representation common in both Greek and Punic art.[2]

---

1. E.g., Marshall, 2271, pl. 45 (satyr). Fourth century B.C.
2. For satyr masks used as Punic pendants: A. Vivesy Escudero, *La*

Necropoli di Ibiza (Madrid 1956), pl. 65, fig. 1,2; P. Cintas, *Amulettes puniques* (Institut des hautes études de Tunis, I, 1946), 54, fig. 86.

The gold foil sheets (**38** and **39**) are less enigmatic. They join to form a single strip, broken at both ends, which would have been sewn a cloth or leather backing—attachment holes are still visible along one edge of **38**. The decoration is not well preserved. All seven preserved figures are frontal and seem to hold attributes in their right hands. The figures have been described and discussed by White;[3] they all seem to be divinities. The following discussion, except where otherwise noted, follows the descriptions set forth by White.

The first figure, moving from left to right, is badly preserved; all that can be said is that the hair style is similar to that of the better preserved female figures. The second figure is definitely a woman, but it is impossible to say whether she is clothed or nude. An attribute held in the right hand has been described as possibly a torch or bunch of flowers; it seems to me definitely to be a bird, either a real bird or a statue. The third figure may again be a woman although the badly preserved details preclude certainty. The fourth figure is certainly a woman; her right hand holds a staff the top of which ends in a globe. Her hair style resembles those of the Severan period, parted in the center and falling in two masses on either side of the head. It has been suggested that she is nude to the waist; however, she might just as easily be clothed in a form-fitting garment. The scale is so small and the details so sketchy that even in this well-preserved instance it is difficult to be certain about clothing details. The fifth figure is the best preserved, the only one in which details of dress and hair style can be consistently identified. This figure is male, bearded, and has a large mass of curly(?) hair. In his right hand he holds a staff or scepter. He seems to be wearing a muscle cuirass, and even details of a leather(?) skirt can be discerned. His left shoulder may be draped with a cloak or mantle. The sixth figure has long hair arranged in a halo-like mass. The right arm is raised and holds an unidentifiable object. The seventh figure is quite badly preserved, but the head has traces of either horns or a horned headdress. This last figure may be female.

The Cyrene gold strip was part of a diadem of Late Roman date. A very close parallel is afforded by a diadem from Aleppo in the Cologne Römische-Germanische Landsmuseum; it is decorated in a similar technique and style, with a central representation of Helios flanked by rows of syncretic divinities.[4] All are frontal and hold attributes in their right hands, which are often raised. Our gold strip is thus a fragment of a similar diadem.

This type of metal strip, with frontal representation of divinities (sometimes full figures or sometimes busts set in a tondo), seems to have been popular in the eastern Mediterranean during the third and fourth centuries A.D. In addition to the example in Cologne a good parallel is provided by a gold diadem from Naukratis,[5] now in the British Museum, which is also decorated with frontal figures of divinities, both Greek and Egyptian, and possibly even a Roman emperor as Horus. Also worthy of note is a diadem, said to be from the eastern Mediterranean, decorated with busts of the seven planetary divinities, including Jupiter, and a goddess who might alternately be identified as either Demeter or Fortuna.[6] A silver diadem in the Hamburg Museum fur Kunst und Gewerbe[7] is decorated with both busts of divinities and a central horse and rider (a reference to Epona?); it may be of Thracian origin. One of the busts can be identified as Sol by its radiate crown, another as Jupiter or perhaps Serapis. These diadems are all similar in their general form, their scheme of decoration, in being decorated with divinities associated with syncretic cults, in provenance (from the eastern Mediterranean), and in their Late Roman date; the Cyrene gold strip surely forms part of this group.

Due to the poor preservation of the piece, identification of specific divinities on the Cyrene diadem is unfortunately more difficult than in the above-mentioned examples. The second figure might be identified as Demeter, in view of the fact that Demeter is sometimes portrayed on this type of diadem and because she holds a bird, an object which seems to be specifically associated with her cult at Cyrene. The loricated, bearded fifth figure is probably Jupiter and the fourth figure Juno, as suggested by White. The suggestion that Jupiter Dolichenus is specifically intended is certainly plausible, though perhaps not provable. The sixth figure has been identified as Sol Invictus, a deity portrayed on other diadems of this type, although in this case I cannot discern any specific iconographic details to substantiate the attribution. The seventh figure could be either Isis, the most likely possibility, or Hathor. All of these attributions must of course remain tentative. What seems most important is that the gold strip formed part of a Late Roman diadem that was decorated with representations of deities popular in the eastern Mediterranean syncretic cults. This type of ornament is sometimes seen on Late Roman portrait

---

3. White, *Fourth Report*, 172-173 n. 22.
4. Römische-Germanische Museum, Cologne, inv. 74.383. F. Altheim, *Die Soldatenkaiser* (1939), 281, fig. 67. *Kölner Römer-Industrierte* 17 (1970), 132, figs. 210-212.
5. Marshall, 364, no. 3045, pl. 70.

6. Hamburg, Private Collection. W. Hornbostel, *Kunst der Antike* (Mainz 1977), 484-485, no. 432.
7. Hamburg, Museum für Kunst und Gewerbe, inv. 1969.152. J. Bracker, *AA* (1974) 79-80, fig. 37. Cited by Marshall (p. 364) for this type of diadem: *OJ* 2: 245.

busts, and our piece can be dated securely to the late second or early third century A.D. by the Severan hair styles of the female figures.

It might be noted that a gold sheet with figured decoration was also found in the First Artemisium at Cyrene.[8] It is larger than our diadem and of much earlier (Orientalizing) date.

The Cyrene diadem seems to have been cut lengthwise deliberately, perhaps as part of a dedicatory ritual. Diadems similar to ours are sometimes found in tombs, and have been interpreted as part of the funerary regalia of the deceased. If this is so, our gold diadem would be a rare instance, at the Sanctuary of Demeter, of a dedication primarily funerary in nature.

ROSETTES
40-43

40 ROSETTE
Pl. 13   73-233   E10   balk   2
L. 0.016; W. 0.015
Silver. Cylindrical center filled with glass paste or enamel, two or three badly bent petals.
Roman.

41 ROSETTE
Pl. 13   73-237   E12/11   slope   1
L. 0.036; W. 0.021
Silver. Similar to 40. Central tube filled with glass paste or enamel, one and a half petals preserved. Complete petal has incised line along its length.
Roman.

42 ROSETTE
Not ill.   74-79   E12/13   E   1
L. 0.022; W. 0.020
Silver. Crumpled fragment similar to 40 and 41, preserving parts of several petals and central cylinder.
Roman.

43 DISK-ROSETTE
Pl. 13   74-1096   D12/13   F   3
D. 0.012
Gilded silver. Decorated in repoussé with rosette of eight petals. Rows of dots delineate edges of petals.
Archaic.

These four rosettes (40-43) probably served as attachments. Three of them (40-42) are of similar type: silver, with a central cylindrical tube which was filled with glass paste. Although all three examples are badly crumpled, the general form can be reconstructed (Ill. 2). The rosettes might have decorated a vessel of some kind, but might just as easily have been used for jewelry. They are unparalleled and therefore not easy to date. Because of their form and technique, I would tend to assign these pieces to the Roman period. Rosettes can also be used as pendants; a gold example was found in the First Artemisium at Cyrene. This same deposit also yielded a gold rosette used as an attachment.[9]

Illustration 2

The silver disk-rosette (43) is of a different type, flat and decorated in repoussé. It might have adorned the head of an elaborate pin, and may be compared to a silver cap from Lindos, decorated with a filigree rosette, that probably served as a terminal for a pin or small implement.[10] The disk-rosette (43) is probably of Archaic date.

FRAGMENTS OF GOLD AND SILVER FOIL
44-46

44 DECORATED CYLINDER
Pl. 13   73-1140   E10   balk   3
L. 0.018; W. 0.010
Gold foil. Decorated with raised parallel ridges to create a bark-like effect. Badly crushed.

45 STAMPED FRAGMENT
Pl. 13   77-530   D15/16   1   3
L. 0.014; W. 0.009
Gold foil. Trapezoidal in shape, with hole near one edge. Stamped decoration.

46 STAMPED FRAGMENT
Pl. 13   77-1189   C13   1   4b
L. 0.010; W. 0.008; Th. 0.001
Gold foil attached to silver foil. Decorated with groove and parallel row of raised dots.
From undisturbed Archaic context.

These three decorated fragments of gold and silver foil were probably used as attachments or revetments, or formed part of large pieces of jewelry. At least ten fragments of undecorated gold and silver foil were also found.[11]

---

8. *AfrIt* 4 (1931) fig. 17. For representations of these diadems on Roman portraits in the eastern Mediterranean: J. Inan and E. Rosenbaum, *Roman and Early Byzantine Portrait Sculpture in Asia Minor* (1966), no. 282, pl. 257.
9. *AfrIt* 4 (1931) fig. 18 (attachment) and fig. 17 (pendant plaque).

10. *Lindos* 1, 119, no. 277, pl. 12.
11. Gold foil inv. nos. 71-345 (E11,3,3), 74-450 (E12/13,E,2), 74-755 (D12.13,F,3), 74-1097 (E12/13,E,3), 76-950 (D13/E13,1,3), 77-403 (F13/G13,2,2), 77-529 (D15/16,1,3). Silver foil inv. nos. 73-1229 (C15/16,1,4), 76-1093 (D12,Balk,3s), 76-1098 (D13/E13,1,3/4).

Beads and Pendants
47-165

Beads (**47-85**) and pendants (**86-165**) are the most common small find type at the sanctuary. They are discussed together here, since differentiation between them is often arbitrary. The terminology follows Beck's classification[12] except where standard usage differs from his nomenclature. Generally, beads are defined as ornaments designed to be strung in combination, and pendants as ornaments designed to hang singly. In addition pendants generally have separately articulated suspension loop.

BRONZE BICONICAL TUBE BEADS
47-49

TYPE A (Ill. 3)

47 BICONICAL BEAD
Not ill.   74-1050   D12/13   F   3
L. 0.027
Bronze. Large, both ends flanged.
Classical.

48 BICONICAL BEAD
Pl. 14   74-1130   D12/13   F   3
L. 0.018
Bronze. Both ends flanged. Robinson, type IIIA.[13]
Classical.

49 BICONICAL BEAD
Not ill.   74-271   D16/17   2   2
L. 0.019
Bronze. Plain ends. Beck type D.1.f; Robinson, type IIIA.
Classical.

Illustration 3

In all, five bronze biconical beads were found at the Demeter Sanctuary.[14] A stone example, probably carnelian, was also found.[15] In the Cyrenaica, biconical beads have also been found at Tocra.[16] They occur sporadically throughout Greece and are common in Macedonia; examples are also known from the Balkans and Italy.[17] Robinson considers beads of this type Macedonian, but they are common enough to have been manufactured locally at most sites.

COILED BEADS
50-52

TYPE B (Ill. 4)

50 TUBULAR COILED BEAD
Not ill.   774-971   D12/13   F   3
L. 0.012; D. 0.004
Silver. Strip of foil rolled diagonally to form six-coil tube. Beck, Group XVIII.

51 TUBULAR COILED BEAD
Not ill.   76-993   C13/D13   1   7
L. 0.010
Silver. Similar to **50**. Four coils. Broken.

52 TUBULAR COILED BEAD
Pl. 14   74-1153   D12/13   F   3
L. 0.010; D. 0.006
Bronze. Similar to **50** and **51**. Three coils.

Five tubular coiled beads were excavated in the Demeter Sanctuary, four silver[18] and one bronze. Coiled beads, or spiral beads as they are sometimes called, are common throughout the Mediterranean during both the Bronze and Iron Ages. Bronze examples are normally made from wire rather than sheet metal. During the Iron Age, coiled beads were also made of glass, amber, and faience.[19] The effect of the Cyrene silver examples is strikingly similar to Late Bronze Age faience beads.[20]

Illustration 4

---

12. Beck, 1973.
13. *Olynthos* 10, 56-58, nos. 68-93.
14. Inventoried but not catalogued: 74-853, 76-1143.
15. Inv. no. 78-340.
16. *Tocra* 2, 77.

17. N. K. Sandars in *Tocra* 2, 79-80, for detailed discussion of distribution and bibliography.
18. Two more silver coiled beads were found in the same context as **51** and may have been strung on the same necklace.
19. Beck, 15.
20. M. Popham, *BSA* 75 (1980) 171, pl. 17b.

COLLAR BEADS
53-58

TYPE C (Ill. 5)

53 COLLAR BEAD
Not ill.   71-738   D12/13   B   4
D. 0.012
  Bronze. Spherical. Collar pierced twice horizontally.
  Archaic/Classical.

54 FIVE COLLAR BEADS
Not ill.   76-1151   D12/13   F   4/5
D. (individual beads) 0.006
  Bronze. Similar to **53**. Fused into two groups by corrosion.
  Archaic/Classical.

55 COLLAR BEAD
Pl. 14   74-967   D12/13   F   3
D. 0.009
  Gold. Spherical. Pierced twice horizontally. Juncture between sphere and collar decorated with two bands of small gold granules.
  Archaic.

56 COLLAR BEAD
Pl. 14   74-903   D12/13   F   3
D. 0.008
  Silver. Spherical. Pierced collar. Broken approximately in half. Juncture of sphere and collar articulated by silver band. Body decorated in filigree with rosette pattern.
  Archaic.

57 COLLAR BEAD
Pl. 14   77-1240   C13   1   4a
D. 0.009
  Ivory. Spherical. Pierced twice horizontally.
  Archaic.

58 COLLAR BEAD
Pl. 14   73-722   D12/E12   D   3
H. 0.028; D. 0.022
  Rock-crystal. Spherical. Pierced for suspension. Cracked and chipped.
  Archaic.

The most common type of metal bead found in the Demeter Sanctuary is the bronze "collar" bead, Type C (Ill. 5). Almost a hundred examples have been found,[21] sometimes in groups corroded together as they were strung. The majority are less than a centimeter in diameter. They are pierced through the collar and are clearly beads, not fibula or pin heads. Rarely, they are made of ivory, silver, or gold. The silver and gold collar beads tend to be more ornate than the bronze examples, and are often embossed or decorated with filigree.

Bronze collar beads are virtually ubiquitous during the Iron Age.[22] Small beads, similar to **53** and **54** and strung in the same manner, have been found at Tocra.

All of the gold and silver collar beads from the Demeter Sanctuary are small, of similar size, and from the same context (D12/13 F 3), and may have come from a single necklace or bangle. Several fragmentary examples of beads similar to **55** have been found in the Demeter Sanctuary,[23] and a gold collar bead with granulated collar juncture, similar to **55**, is known from Tocra.[24]

Ivory collar beads like **57**, sometimes referred to as globular pendants, were found in the Limenia deposit at Perachora;[25] Perachora also produced bronze collar beads, a mold for producing them,[26] and similar pendants of amber and gold.[27] Bone or ivory knobs of similar shape are also used as pin heads. They can be distinguished from the beads by their larger size and by the neck hole which is much larger than the horizontal hole.[28] Judging by the parallels from Perachora, ivory and bone collar beads are of Archaic date.

Illustration 5

DISK BEADS
59-62

TYPE D (Ill. 6)

59 DISK BEAD
Pl. 14   77-454   D15/16   1   3
D. 0.012; Th. 0.002
  Bone. Hole through center.

60 DISK BEAD
Pl. 14   77-495   C14/D14   2   2
D. 0.018; Th. 0.006
  Bone. Thick disk. Hole through center.

61 DISK BEAD
Not ill.   77-795   D15/E15   1   2
D. 0.020
  Bone. Irregular. Pierced

62 DISK BEAD
Pl. 14   77-746   C14/D14   2   2
D. 0.005; Th. 0.004
  Silver. Hexagonal profile.

The thin disks are one of the simplest bead types. Seventeen ivory or bone disks from the Demeter Sanc-

---

21. Inventoried but not catalogued: 71-286, 71-487, 71-488, 71-608, 71-736(4), 71-741, 74-381, 74-574, 74-821, 74-1023(2), 74-1066(2), 74-1067, 74-1068, 74-1069, 74-1070(5), 74-1071(3), 74-1072(2), 74-1073(3), 74-1074, 74-1075, 74-1076, 74-1077, 74-1082, 74-1133(2), 74-1142, 74-1154, 76-1134, 76-1137, 76-1145, 76-1148, 76-1149, 76-1150(4), 77-179, 77-431, 77-449, 77-579, 77-1086, 77-1087, 77-1243, 77-1244(2), 77-1245(3), 77-1246(5), 77-1247(2), 78-576, 78-577.
22. E.g., *Aegina*, pl. 119, fig. 34. *Tocra* 2, 157, no. 13, fig. 71. Ibid., 83, F157, fig. 40 (bone).
23. Two silver beads (74-1109, 77-308) and a gold bead (74-859) are similar to **56**. One undecorated example in silver is also known (74-901).
24. *Tocra* 1, 156, fig. 71, no. 2.
25. *Perachora* 2, A288-294, pl. 441f.
26. Ibid., pl. 79.16,18; pl. 79.12 (mold).
27. Ibid., H32, 195 (amber); 195, Ll (gold).
28. Stubbings in ibid., 441-442.

tuary were undoubtedly strung as beads; three examples (**59-61**) are representative of the type.[29] The silver bead (**62**) is disk-shaped but differs in having a hexagonal profile. All of these disks are pierced in the center, but the holes are too small for them to have served as finger rings. Faience and carnelian disks were also found.[30]

Illustration 6

MELON BEADS
63-68

TYPE E (Ill. 7)

63 MELON BEAD
Pl. 14   74-1160   D12/13   F   3
L. 0.014
Bronze. Striated and pierced longitudinally.
Archaic.

64 MELON BEAD
Pl. 14   77-1234   C13   1   4a
L. 0.011
Bronze. Similar to **63**. Prominent casting seam.
Archaic.

65 MELON BEAD
Pl. 14   77-1053   C13   1   4b
L. 0.013
Carnelian. Similar to **63** and **64**.
Archaic.

66 MELON BEAD
Not ill.   74-403   E12/13   E   2
L. 0.032
Faience. Large. Striated and pierced longitudinally.
Archaic.

67 MELON BEAD
Not ill.   76-732   F13/G13   1   2
L. 0.017
Ivory. Pierced longitudinally.
Archaic.

68 MELON BEAD
Not ill.   77-469   C14/D14   2   2
L. 0.017
Terracotta. Similar to **63-67**. Orange fabric with traces of cream paint. Cracked and chipped.
Archaic.

Melon beads are found in a variety of sizes and are made of almost every material. Twenty-seven bronze examples, similar to **63** and **64**, were found at Cyrene.[31] They sometimes occur in groups and were undoubtedly strung on necklaces. Melon beads made of faience,[32] carnelian,[33] ivory,[34] and terracotta[35] were also found in the Demeter Sanctuary. Judging by their context, the terracotta examples, about fifty in all, were strung on necklaces with other terracotta ornaments, probably spherical beads and striated tubes. Many of the terracotta melon beads retain traces of a white or cream paint; perhaps they were meant to resemble ivory beads. The ivory examples were sometimes gilded.

Melon beads are common at most Classical sites. Their origins may be traced to Egyptian prototypes— faience melon beads which date to the New Kingdom.[36] Faience melon beads have been found in Orientalizing contexts at many Greek sites,[37] and glass melon beads are also common.[38] Bronze, carnelian, and faience melon beads have been found at the First Artemisium at Cyrene and date to the Archaic period.[39] Although it is usually safer not to date this type of ubiquitous material too precisely it seems likely that our melon beads are Archaic, both in light of the comparanda and because of the contexts in which they were found. The carnelian bead (**65**) was found in an undisturbed Archaic context, and the other melon beads are all from almost exclusively Archaic strata.

Illustration 7

---

29. Inventoried but not catalogued: 71-271, 73-85, 73-118, 73-133, 73-139, 73-149, 73-703, 73-1223, 77-405, 77-532, 77-1123, 78-39, 78-296, 78-785.
30. Faience: 74-871; carnelian: 73-993.
31. Bronze melon-shaped beads: 71-451, 71-453, 71-623, 71-745, 74-572, 74-821, 74-1025, 74-1154, 74-1155, 74-1156, 74-1157, 74-1158, 74-1159, 76-1136, 76-1139, 76-1140(2), 76-1141, 76-1144(2), 77-451, 77-1059, 77-1107, 77-1127, 77-1131.
32. Another five faience examples: 73-617, 73-891, 74-748, 76-735, 78-517.
33. Eleven additional carnelian melon beads: 71-655, 73-518, 73-1103, 76-380, 76-382, 76-467, 76-728, 76-729, 77-111, 77-456, 77-1169.
34. Another six examples: 74-440, 74-745, 77-228, 77-454, 77-581, 77-1057.

35. Not included here: 76-184, 76-185, 76-250, 76-251, 76-351, 76-356, 76-362, 76-500, 76-503, 76-506, 76-507, 76-509, 76-510, 76-511, 76-531, 76-537, 76-538, 76-769, 76-774, 76-778, 76-779, 76-783, 76-962, 76-966, 76-967, 76-998, 77-48, 77-42, 77-95, 77-97, 77-99, 77-241, 77-322, 77-346, 77-418, 77-419, 77-420, 77-572, 77-901.
36. Beck 10, fig. 11, 26a and b.
37. Faience melon-shaped beads were found with Proto-Corinthian pottery at Perachora: *Perachora* 2, D832-7.
38. For glass melon beads, e.g., Hogarth, *Ephesus*, 204, pl. 45.3; *Knossos*, 116, nos. 2 and 11, fig. 25, pl. 79b; *Lindos* 1, 93, no. 148; *Clara Rhodos* 4, 337, fig. 71, no. 16.
39. *AfrIt* 4 (1931) fig. 21 (bronze), 202, fig. 26 (carnelian), 204, fig. 28.

STRIATED BEAD
69

69 STRIATED BEAD
Pl. 15   77-96   F13/G13   2   2
L. 0.023
  Terracotta. Striated longitudinally. Brown fabric.
  Archaic.

Tubular clay beads like **69**, striated longitudinally, are also common at Cyrene; 184 examples have been found. Like the terracotta melon beads which they closely resemble, they were probably cheap imitations of ivory or stone examples.

SPHERICAL BEADS
70-77

TYPE F (Ill. 8)

70 SPHERICAL BEAD
Pl. 15   71-272   D12/13   B   4
D. 0.013
  Bronze. Solid metal. Pierced.
  Archaic.

71 SPHERICAL BEAD
Pl. 15   76-1138   D12/13   F   4
D. 0.014
  Bronze. Pierced, with ring inserted in large string hole.
  Archaic.

72 SPHERICAL BEAD
Not ill.   71-821   E11   3   3
D. 0.060
  Silver. Hollow. Long suspension ring. Broken.
  Archaic.

73 SPHERICAL BEAD
Not ill.   74-1159   D12/13   F   3
H. 0.016; W. 0.014; D. 0.012
  Bronze. Solid. Found with bronze melon bead.
  Archaic.

74 SPHERICAL BEAD
Not ill.   71-822   E11   3   3
D. 0.007
  Electrum. Hollow. Flat attachments at either end.
  Archaic.

75 SPHERICAL BEAD
Not ill.   76-1046   C14/D14   1   2
D. 0.009
  Faience.
  Archaic.

76 SPHERICAL BEAD
Pl. 15   74-794   D12/13   F   e
D. 0.016
  Terracotta. Brown fabric with traces of white slip.
  Archaic.

77 SPHERICAL BEAD
Pl. 15   77-689   F13/G13   2   2
D. 0.021
  Rock-crystal. Pierced through center. Only half preserved.
  Archaic.

Spherical beads, Type F (Ill. 8), are also quite common. Most popular were the terracotta examples; they are smooth and undecorated but sometimes preserve traces of a white or cream slip. Like the terracotta melon beads, the painted spherical beads would have resembled, and probably purposely imitated, ivory or bone beads. Metal spherical beads are rarer, and normally made of bronze,[40] but silver and gold examples were also found.[41] These more valuable types are generally hollow and have a separate suspension loop. Faience spherical beads, much smaller than the metal examples, are less common.[42] One rock-crystal bead (**77**) also belongs with this group. The spherical beads are almost exclusively from levels with heavy concentrations of Archaic finds and can therefore safely be dated to the Archaic period. They may have been strung on the same necklaces as the melon beads.

Illustration 8

TUBULAR BEADS
78-83

TYPE G (Ill. 9)

78 TUBULAR BEAD
Pl. 16   71-465   E11   3   3
L. 0.009
  Bronze. Long.[43]
  Archaic.

79 TUBULAR BEAD
Not ill.   71-561   D12/13   A   3
L. 0.041; D. 0.029
  Silver. Made from hammered foil strip.[44]
  Archaic.

80 FOUR TUBULAR BEADS
Pl. 16   74-858   D12/13   F   3
L. 0.004; D. 0.004
  Gold. Made from foil strips.
  Archaic.

81 TUBULAR BEAD
Pl. 16   73-892   D12/E12   D   3
L. 0.025; D. 0.018
  Ivory. Undecorated.
  Archaic.

---

40. Additional bronze spherical beads: 71-273, 71-486, 71-652, 71-654, 71-737, 71-739, 74-573, 74-822, 74-823, 74-845, 74-1159, 76-1133, 76-1135, 76-1139, 76-1142, 76-1143, 76-1146, 77-501.
41. Gold: 77-455; silver: 77-1238, 76-1094.
42. Additional faience examples: 74-884, 76-910, 77-1122(2).
43. Two similar bronze beads were found: 74-853, 76-1143.
44. Another silver example: 74-822.

82 TUBULAR BEAD
Pl. 16   74-762   D12/13   F   3
L. 0.014
  Faience.
  Archaic.

83 TUBULAR BEAD
Not ill.   77-715   D15/16   1   3
L. 0.019; D. 0.014
  Terracotta. Undecorated.
  Archaic.

Tubular beads, Type G (Ill. 9), are also very common. They were made of bronze, silver, gold, ivory, faience, carnelian, and, most common of all, terracotta.

Tubular beads of the above type are known from most Classical sites. Metal examples, similar to our **79**, have been found at Knossos, Sparta, Aegina, and Chios.[45] The Cyrene tubular beads, like the spherical and melon beads, are mostly of Archaic date.

Illustration 9

SILVER BEADS
84 and 85

TYPE H (Ill. 10)

84 BEAD
Pl. 16   74-833   D12/13   F   3
L. 0.010; D. (each cylinder) 0.002
  Silver. Three cylinders joined together longitudinally.
  Archaic.

85 TWO BEADS
Pl. 16   77-730   D15/16   1   3
L. 0.020; W. 0.005
  Silver. Each made of three cylinders joined together longitudinally.
  Archaic?

More unusual than the preceding types, these three silver beads are made of a number of cylinders, or tubes, that are joined together longitudinally. These beads conform to Beck's Group XVII.a.2, and also may be of Archaic date.

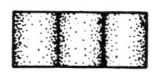

Illustration 10

AXE PENDANTS
86-89

86 DOUBLE-AXE PENDANT
Fig. 1   71-763   D12/13   A   3
L. 0.024
  Ivory. Blade edges and shaft hole articulated by incision. Traces of ivory shaft hole.
  7th or early 6th century B.C.

87 DOUBLE-AXE PENDANT
Fig. 1   74-764   D12/13   F   3
L. 0.022
  Ivory. Similar to **86**.
  7th or early 6th century B.C.

88 DOUBLE-AXE PENDANT
Fig. 1   76-1047   D12/13   A   9
L. 0.025
  Ivory. Similar to **86** and **87**.
  7th or early 6th century B.C.

89 DOUBLE-AXE PENDANT
Pl. 17   76-1221   D12/13   F   3
L. 0.021
  Bronze.
  7th or early 6th century B.C.

The four double-axe pendants form a homogeneous group. Three (**86-88**) are ivory and one (**89**) is bronze. Four similar bone or ivory pendants are known from Tocra.[46] All of these Libyan examples belong to a class of pendants popular on the Greek mainland during the Archaic period. Double-axe pendants of this type are abundant in the eighth to sixth-century levels of the sanctuary of Artemis Orthia at Sparta,[47] and also occur in the Limenia deposit at Perachora.[48] They have been found at Olynthos, Aegina, Ithaca, Siphnos, Ephesus, Megara Hybleia, Syracuse,[49] and Chios.[50] Double axes were also used as pin heads in the Archaic period,[51] but were more commonly used as pendants; they are even shown worn on necklaces in Archaic Greek art.[52] Given

---

45. Knossos: *Knossos*, 118, no. 27, fig. 25. Sparta: *Artemis Orthia* 199, pl. 85 k-n, s,t. Aegina: *Aegina*, pl. 119, fig. 65. Chios, Geometric-Archaic period: *BSA* 35 (1934-1935) 150, pl. 32,3.
46. *Tocra* 1, 165, nos. 79-82, fig. 77, and pl. 104.
47. *Artemis Orthia*, 238, pl. 163.6. Ninety-three examples.
48. *Perachora* 2, 443, A316-318, pl. 188. The Perachora examples are not incised in the same manner as the Cyrene pendants.

49. For full bibliography see Stubbings in *Perachora* 2, 443 n. 5. Ithaca: *BSA* 43 (1948) pl. 47.C32 (seventh century B.C.).
50. Chios: *Emporio* 227, no. 407. Another Chiot example from Phanai: *BSA* 35 (1934-1935).
51. *Artemis Orthia*, pl. 85, right. Hogarth, *Ephesus*, pl. 5.34.
52. As shown on a Caeretan hydria cited by Stubbings in *Perachora* 2, 443 n. 6.

this wealth of comparative material, it seems likely that the double-axe pendants (**86-89**) are of late seventh or early sixth century B.C. date and are either mainland imports or close local imitations of mainland types.

BOVINE PENDANTS
90 and 91

90 PENDANT OR PROTOME
Pl. 17   74-848   C14   1   4
L. 0.033; W. 0.033; Th. 0.0015
Bronze. Ox or cow head. Large, bulging eyes, short nose, protruding ears; mouth indicated by a double groove, nostrils by two small holes. Pierced horizontally through horns only, and vertically through length of head. Flat underside.
Probably Archaic.

91 BOVINE PENDANT
Pl. 17   74-1125   D12/13   F   3
L. 0.02; Th. 0.020
Bronze. Bull or ox head. Short horizontal horns, protruding ears, small mouth, dot nostrils. Eyes inlaid with faience or glass paste. Thick neck with skin folds indicated by shallow grooves. Pierced through upper neck.
Probably Archaic.

The ox or bull head pendant (**91**) is most closely paralleled by a bronze weight in the form of a cow or calf's head from Knossos, possibly of Egyptian origin.[53] Metal ox head weights seem to have been popular in Egypt from at least the New Kingdom onwards.[54] This type of pendant is also found in the Mediterranean during the Archaic period. Several highly stylized examples are known from Sparta,[55] as well as from Rhodes.[56] A number of other such pendants in private and public collections,[57] their provenance unknown, attest to the popularity of this form through Roman times.[58] Highly stylized bull pendants, quite different from **90** and **91**, are also known from Etruria.[59]

The bull or cow protome (**90**) may not have been a pendant at all. It is pierced both horizontally and vertically and may have been an attachment for a vessel or implement. Its smooth features and bulging eyes are not paralleled by any of the aforementioned comparanda.

CONICAL PENDANTS
92-97

92 CONICAL PENDANT
Not ill.   71-562   D12/13   B   2
H. 0.008
Silver. Thin, narrow cone. Most of suspension ring missing.
Probably Archaic.

93 CONICAL PENDANT
Pl. 17   71-767   D12/13   A   3
H. 0.007; D. 0.016
Silver. Incised chevron pattern near top of cone. Traces of gilding.
Probably Archaic.

94 CONICAL PENDANT
Not ill.   71-788   E12   1   5
H. 0.011
Silver. Solid body with small suspension loop.

95 CONICAL PENDANT
Pl. 17   74-840   D11/12   1   3
H. 0.012
Silver. Two fragments mended. Similar to **92**.
Probably Archaic.

96 CONICAL PENDANT
Not ill.   76-989   C12/13   1   3
L. 0.010; D. 0.003
Silver. Similar to **92**.
Probably Archaic.

97 CONICAL PENDANT
Not ill.   76-994   C13/D13   1   7
H. 0.013
Silver. Similar to **92**, but grooved at base of cone.

These six silver pendants are all similarly bell-shaped with a small suspension loop at the narrow end. All are small and easily could have come from a single necklace or bracelet.

CRESCENT PENDANTS
98 and 99

98 CRESCENT PENDANT
Pl. 17   77-453   C14/D14   2   2
L. 0.012
Gold. Flat with reel-shaped suspension loop. Small gold globule one end, another at center. Other end of crescent probably decorated with globule now missing.
Archaic (6th century B.C.).

---

53. J. Boardman, *The Cretan Collection at Oxford* (Oxford 1961), 52, no. 228, pl. 16.
54. Petrie, 6, pl. 9, fourth row. G. Roeder, *Ägypt. Bronzefiguren* (Berlin Mitteil. VI) 324, 479.
55. W. Lamb, *Greek and Roman Bronzes* (New York 1929), 77, pl. 23a.
56. Walters, no. 148, from Cameiros, 1864. Also, a double-bull pendant from Lindos: *Lindos* 1, pl. 643, no. 1571.
57. Galerie am Neumarkt, *Auction 22* (Zurich 1971) no. 10. M. Maass, *Antikensammlungen München, griechische und römische Bronzewerke* (Munich 1979), 47, no. 27, said to be Boeotian, seventh century B.C. Petrie, pl. 9, no. 4925. British Museum: Marshall, 1198, pl. 12 (from Rhodes, seventh century B.C.).
58. Ibid., no. 2971. Gold, from Olbia.
59. Richter, *Bronzes*, 466, nos. 1865-1866.

99 CRESCENT PENDANT
Pl. 17   77-1242   C13   1   4a
L. 0.023

Ivory, with silver suspension loop. Loop decorated with silver rosette only three petals of which are preserved.
From Archaic context. Archaic (6th century B.C.).

These small but elegant pendants (**98** and **99**) are both of Archaic date. Lunate or crescent pendants were common in the Roman period[60] and slightly less so during Hellenistic times.[61] Archaic examples such as ours are much rarer.[62] **98** is almost exactly paralleled in an early context (sixth century B.C.) at Tocra,[63] where a gold pendant dedicated at the Sanctuary of Demeter has exactly the same shape, suspension loop, and globules.[64] Crescent-shaped pendants have also been found in the Sanctuary of Demeter at Knossos.[65] The Knossos examples are silver and probably date to the Hellenistic period; a few examples, however, may be Classical.

It is significant that the crescent pendants from Tocra, Cyrene, and Knossos are all from Demeter sanctuaries. The dedication of this type of pendant to Demeter during the fourth century and the Hellenistic period has been attributed to the association of Demeter with Isis, an association which, at Cyrene at least, can be carried back to the fifth century B.C.[66] The appearance of these pendants at Tocra and Cyrene in the sixth century, and at Knossos in a Classical context, is harder to explain. At Knossos, Coldstream suggests a connection between Demeter and the native moon goddess Britomartis,[67] an explanation which does not apply to the Cyrenaica. In any case, the appearance of crescent pendants at Demeter shrines is no mere archaeological coincidence, and the evidence of crescent pendants in early contexts at Cyrene strengthens the association of lunar symbolism with the early cult of Demeter.

DROP-SHAPED PENDANTS
100-105

100 DROP-SHAPED PENDANT
Fig. 1   71-329   E11   3   3
H. 0.012

Ivory. Ovoid body, small collar. Body decorated with seven horizontal grooves. Pierced through collar. Bottom drilled.
Probably Archaic.

101 DROP-SHAPED PENDANT
Fig. 1   71-548   D12/13   B   4
H. 0.016; D. 0.008

Ivory. Elongated ovoid body, high collar. Pierced through collar.

102 DROP-SHAPED PENDANT
Pl. 17   71-563   D12/13   B   4
H. 0.011; W. 0.007

Ivory. Rectangular body, high collar. Body has three horizontal grooves. Pierced through collar.
Probably Archaic.

103 DROP-SHAPED PENDANT
Pl. 17   76-301   C13/D13   1   3
H. 0.014; D. 0.005

Ivory. Elongated oval body. Pierced at one end.
Probably Archaic.

104 DROP-SHAPED PENDANT
Fig. 1   77-229   D15/16   1   2
H. 0.026; D. 0.015

Ivory. Large ovoid body, pierced at one end. Pierced vertically through length of pendant.
Probably Archaic.

105 DROP-SHAPED PENDANT
Fig. 1   78-173   F14/G14   1   2
H. 0.013; W. 0.008

Ivory. Grooved rectangular body, similar to **102**.
Probably Archaic.

The drop-shape is one of the most common pendant types. The most popular variety is bronze with a long shaft and spherical or tear-shaped base. Surprisingly, there are no bronze examples from the Demeter Sanctuary, but six ivory examples (**100-105**) were found. The variations are virtually limitless. Drop-shaped pendants are known from as early as the Bronze Age and remain popular into the Roman period. They are found at almost every Greek site as well as in the Balkans and in Etruria.[68] The closest parallel to our examples is a stone pendant from Lindos with an ovoid body and horizontally pierced suspension loop similar to **101**.[69] Clay drop-shaped pendants from Knossos and Delos may also be cited.[70] The drop-shaped pendant is too common and widespread a type to provide useful evidence for dating.

---

60. *GRJ*, 179.
61. *Knossos*, 135-136, Coldstream cites an example from a Hellenistic context on Delos: *BCH* 89 (1965) 555-556, pls. 17 and 22e.
62. For a discussion of Archaic examples from Sparta and Ephesus, and for a representation on a Cretan flask: Boardman in *Tocra* 1, 156 n. 9. More recently: *Knossos*, 135 n. 6.
63. Boardman in *Tocra* 1, 156, no. 3, pl. 104.
64. A pierced bronze crescent from Tocra, without suspension loop, also could have been a pendant. *Tocra* 1, 159, no. 49, fig. 74.
65. *Knossos*, 135-138, nos. 38-56, fig. 30, pl. 86.
66. For the Isis-Demeter association and lunate pendants: *Knossos*, 185. The cult of Isis at Cyrene: Herodotus IV, 186.
67. *Knossos*, 185.
68. For the origins and spread of this pendant type to the west, see P. G. Warden, *OpRom* 14 (1982).
69. *Lindos* 1, pl. 10, no. 195.
70. *Knossos*, 118, no. 25, pl. 80. *Délos* 18, 303, fig. 370.

JANIFORM PENDANTS
106 and 107

106 JANIFORM PENDANT
Pl. 18   74-760   D12/13   F   3
H. 0.022; D. 0.010
   White, *Fourth Report*, 177 n. 36, pl. 28, fig. 39.
   Ivory. Back-to-back female heads. Flat, oval faces with eyes, noses, and mouths roughly indicated by incision. Long hair stacked in neat horizontal layers on either side of head. Small suspension loop on top of heads.
   Archaic.

107 JANIFORM PENDANT
Pl. 18   74-1123   D12/13   F   3
H. 0.034; W. 0.014; Th. 0.017
   Bronze. Back-to-back male heads. Large almond-shaped eyes, short noses, slightly upturned mouths, and prominent chins. Short, straight, cylindrical neck. No indication of hair. Suspension loop on top of heads.

106 and **107** are rather unusual, but relatively easy to date. The ivory example (**106**) with its Daedalic hair style and facial features is clearly Archaic in date.[71] The bronze example (**107**) is probably also early.

LEAF-SHAPED PENDANT
108

108 LEAF-SHAPED PENDANT
Pl. 18   76-951   D12/13   1   4
H. 0.014; W. 0.005
   Gold. Leaf-shaped. Leaf midrib articulated by vertical groove. Stem coiled for suspension.
   Probably Archaic.

This pendant is unique at the Demeter Sanctuary, but gold leaf-shaped pendants with midribs and suspended from chains were found in the First Artemisium at Cyrene, along with a variety of other gold leaves.[72] Bronze leaf-shaped pendants suspended from a plaque are known from Tocra,[73] and a bronze leaf from Delos with a midrib and curved back at the broad end has been identified as part of a crown.[74] Judging by the parallels from the First Artemisium, our leaf pendant is probably Archaic in date.

LION PENDANTS
109 and 110

109 LION PENDANT
Pl. 18   74-615   E12/13   E   3
L. 0.010; H. 0.009; Th. 0.006
   White, *Fourth Report*, 171 n. 15, pl. 26, fig. 16.
   Gold. Small couchant lion on oval base. Open mouth with two granules in place of canine teeth. Hollow body made from two sections of foil, seam disguised by tail. Tail formed of beaded wire, curves over rump. Base articulated by beaded wire. Reel-shaped suspension loop soldered on back. V-shaped cutting on underside of base, as if flap cut out, lifted up, and pressed down again.
   Probably Archaic.

110 LION PENDANT
Pl. 18   71-825   E11   1   3
L. 0.009; H. 0.008; Th. 0.005
   White, *Fourth Report*, 171 n. 15, pl. 26, fig. 16.
   Gold. Small couchant lion on oval base. Similar to **109**, but smaller and of cruder workmanship. Mouth closed. Seam between sections of hollow body masked by two beaded wire filigrees. Small base with identical V-shaped flap.
   Probably Archaic.

These two small gold pendants, although different in size, are of similar shape and identical manufacturing technique—foil modeled gold sections soldered together with the seams disguised by filigree and granulation. They may have been used as pendants for a pair of earrings; from the sixth century onward, earrings with pendant animals were fairly common.[75]

POMEGRANATE PENDANTS
111 and 112

111 POMEGRANATE PENDANT
Pl. 18   74-968   D12/13   F   3
H. 0.017; D. 0.009
   Silver. Pomegranate with suspension loop.

112 POMEGRANATE PENDANT?
Pl. 18   74-1087   D12/13   F   3
H. 0.028; D. 0.017
   Bronze pomegranate. Heavy and solid. Pierced rectangular flange at top, a suspension ring.

The silver pomegranate (**111**) was definitely used as a pendant. The bronze example may have been used as either a pendant or a pinhead (see **214**).

POPPY-HEAD PENDANTS
113-118

113 POPPY-HEAD PENDANT
Pl. 18   71-90   D12   2   2
L. 0.015; W. 0.007
   Carnelian. Thin shaft, pierced at top, swelling to broad pear-shaped appendage.
   Archaic.

---

71. Dated to the end of the sixth century B.C. based on its comparison to an ivory head from Perachora. White, *Fourth Report*, 177 n. 36.
72. *AfrIt* 4 (1931) 192, fig. 17.
73. *Tocra* 2, 77, F117, fig. 33.
74. *Délos* 18, 312-313, A500, fig. 379.
75. For discussion and comparanda: White, *Fourth Report*, 171 n. 15.

114 POPPY-HEAD PENDANT
Pl. 18   74-743   D12/13 F 3
L. 0.014; W. 0.007
   Carnelian. Similar to **113**.
   Archaic.

115 POPPY-HEAD PENDANT
Pl. 18   77-1055   C13 1 4b
L. 0.016; W. 0.009
   Carnelian. Similar to **113**.
   Archaic.

116 POPPY-HEAD PENDANT
Pl. 18   77-1108   C13 1 4b
L. 0.016; W. 0.009
   Carnelian. Similar to **113**.
   Archaic.

117 POPPY-HEAD PENDANT
Pl. 18   77-1235   C13 1 4b
L. 0.014; W. 0.008
   Carnelian. Similar to **113**.
   Archaic.

118 POPPY-HEAD PENDANT
Pl. 18   71-772   D12/13 A 4
L. 0.025; W. 0.010
   Carnelian. Similar to **113** but slightly larger. Narrow end pierced by silver ring. Groove at the broad end is articulated by silver band.
   Archaic.

The six carnelian poppy-head pendants (**113-118**) are all similar in size and manufacture and originally may have come from a single necklace or bangle. Poppy-head pendants are probably descendants of Late Bronze Age carnelian bottle pendants, a type found in Cyprus in thirteenth century contexts,[76] and known from Crete and mainland Greece in the LM III period.[77] Faience bottle pendants have also been found on Crete in LM IIIB context.[78] The carnelian examples are probably of Egyptian origin, but are rare in Egypt before the reign of Amenophis III (1405-1367 B.C.).[79] Merrillees has argued that the bottle pendant has its origins in Cypriot Base Ring I juglets used as containers for exporting opium.[80]

Pendant **118** is closely paralleled at Tocra, where a carnelian pendant from Deposit II, level 8, is of the same shape and also has a similar groove near the base, probably intended to receive a silver wire band. The Tocra example is from a late seventh or early sixth century context.[81] Another pendant of this type was found at Knossos,[82] and both the Tocra and Knossos examples have been termed "possibly Egyptian." Our six carnelian poppy-head pendants are thus late examples of a pendant type popular in the eastern Mediterranean from the Late Bronze Age to the Archaic period, and they may have been imported from Egypt. The Cyrene pendants should probably be dated to the late seventh or early sixth century B.C.

SCARAB PENDANT
119

119 SCARAB BEETLE PENDANT
Pl. 18   77-1120   D15/E15 1 3
L. 0.021; W. 0.014; Th. 0.009
   Silver. Hollow, with string hole through head. No articulation or modeling of body.

A single silver scarab (**119**) without detailed rendering of features was found in the excavations. It was used as a pendant, possibly suspended from a necklace which would have been strung with other types of beads or pendants.

BRONZE SHELL PENDANTS
120-136

120 SHELL PENDANT
Pl. 19; Fig. 2   71-287   D12/13 A 3
H. 0.023; W. 0.027; Th. 0.010
   White, *Second Report*, pl. 94c.
   Bronze. Radially scalloped, pierced through umbo.
   Probably Archaic.

121 SHELL PENDANT
Pl. 19   71-454   D12/13 B 4
H. 0.039; W. 0.028; Th. 0.014
   White, *Second Report*, pl. 94a.
   Bronze. Bivalve. Vertically scalloped, protruding lateral ribs. Suspension ring.
   Probably Archaic.

122 SHELL PENDANT
Not ill.   71-750   D12/13 B 4
H. 0.034; W. 0.026; Th. 0.010
   White, *Second Report*, pl. 93f.
   Bronze. Bivalve. Worn and heavily corroded. Broken at suspension loop.
   Probably Archaic.

123 SHELL PENDANT
Pl. 19; Fig. 2   73-1192   C15/16 1 4
H. 0.048; W. 0.049; Th. 0.017
   Bronze. Bivalve. Large, radially scalloped, pierced through umbo. Lateral ribs extend to form two hooks.
   Probably Archaic.

---

76. V. Karageorghis, *Excavations at Kition I. The Tombs* (Nicosia 1974), pl. 23, Kition Tomb 9; also: p. 72, no. 166, pl. 138; pp. 79-80, no. 306, pl. 138.
77. *Knossos*, 163.
78. Ibid.
79. R. Merrillees, *Antiquity* 36 (1962) 291. Idem, *SIMA* 18 (1968) 161, pl. 36,6.
80. R. Merrillees, *Antiquity* 36 (1962) 291.
81. *Tocra* 1, 166, no. 100, fig. 78.
82. *Knossos*, 163, no. 259, pl. 95.

124 SHELL PENDANT
Pl. 19   73-1225   D17/16
H. 0.037; W. 0.026; Th. 0.010
Bronze. Bivalve. Extreme lateral ribs set off from mantle, protruding slightly to either side. Suspension ring.
Probably Archaic.

125 SHELL PENDANT
Pl. 19; Fig. 2   73-1264   D12/E13   D   3
H. 0.046; W. 0.026; Th. 0.010
Bronze. Bivalve. Highly stylized, pierced through umbo. Lateral ribs protrude just above suspension hole.
Probably Archaic.

126 SHELL PENDANT
Fig. 2   74-561   E12/13   E   3
H. 0.035; W. 0.031; Th. 0.008
White, *Fourth Report*, pl. 26, fig. 17.
Bronze. Bivalve. Radially scalloped. Lateral ribs set off from mantle, protruding slightly either side. Suspension ring.
Probably Archaic.

127 SHELL PENDANT
Fig. 2   74-1122   D12/13   F   3
H. 0.045; W. 0.033; Th. 0.014
Bronze. Bivalve. Radially scalloped. Suspension ring. Corroded, restored from three pieces.

128 SHELL PENDANT
Pl. 19   74-1135   D12/13   F   3
H. 0.036; W. 0.026; Th. 0.013
Bronze. Bivalve. Suspension loop, now broken.
Probably Archaic.

129 SHELL PENDANT
Fig. 2   74-1146   D12/13   F   3
H. 0.028; W. 0.022; Th. 0.012
Bronze. Bivalve. Radially scalloped, hole through umbo. Lateral ribs project upward and slightly outward.
Probably Archaic.

130 SHELL PENDANT
Pl. 19; Fig. 2   76-1129   D11/12   1   stray
H. 0.028; W. 0.027; Th. 0.007
Bronze. Bivalve. Hole through umbo. Ribs delineated by shallow grooves.
Probably Archaic.

131 SHELL PENDANT
Pl. 19   76-1130   C12/13   1   4
H. 0.030; W. 0.020; Th. 0.007
Bronze. Bivalve. Vertically scalloped, ribs delineated by shallow grooves. Suspension ring.
Probably Archaic.

132 SHELL PENDANT
Pl. 19   76-1131   C12/13   1   3
H. 0.034; W. 0.029; Th. 0.010
Bronze. Bivalve. Hole through umbo.
Probably Archaic.

133 SHELL PENDANT
Pl. 20   76-1132   C12/D12   G   3
H. 0.035; W. 0.031; Th. 0.012
Bronze. Bivalve. Scalloped vertically, hole through umbo. Similar to **129.**
Probably Archaic.

134 SHELL PENDANT
Pl. 20   76-1227   D12/13   F   4
H. 0.040; W. 0.031; Th. 0.012
Bronze. Bivalve. Suspension ring. Ends of lateral ribs pointed and project upward slightly.
Probably Archaic

135 SHELL PENDANT
Pl. 20; Fig. 2   77-745   D15/16   1   3
H. 0.028; W. 0.023; Th. 0.007
Bronze. Bivalve. Scalloped vertically, pierced through umbo.
Probably Archaic.

136 SHELL PENDANT
Pl. 20   77-1237   C13   1   4a
H. 0.028; W. 0.026; Th. 0.009
Bronze. Bivalve. Scalloped vertically, pierced through umbo. Fragment of bronze wire embedded in suspension hole.
Probably Archaic.

Seventeen bronze shell pendants of varying form and size have been found. All are bivalve shells, probably Archaic in date.

There are two types of bronze shell pendants: those pierced through the umbo and those in which the umbo is elongated and forms a separate suspension loop. On some pendants, the extreme lateral ribs of the mantle are articulated and protrude laterally. In the most elaborate example (**123**) the ribs curve upward to form hooks.

Although real shells were often strung on necklaces, bronze imitations are surprisingly uncommon.[83] The appearance of such a large group of bronze shell pendants in the Demeter Sanctuary suggests the existence of a local workshop and perhaps some specific symbolism or significance of the shell in the worship of Demeter in this sanctuary.

SHELL PENDANTS
137-142

137 FOSSILIZED SHELL PENDANT
Not ill.   76-528   C13/D13   1   3
H. 0.034; W. 0.027
Fossil internal cast of *Chlamys* (scallop) or *Lima* (File shell). Hole drilled through center of mantle.

138 FOSSILIZED SHELL PENDANT
Pl. 20   76-968   C12/13   1   2
H. 0.038; W. 0.032; Th. 0.014
Bivalve. Hole drilled through umbo. Chipped along one edge.

139 SHELL PENDANT
Not ill.   76-971   D12/13   F   1
H. 0.023; W. 0.020; Th. 0.009
Shell. Probably recent water-worn cockle, *Cerastoderma (Cardium) edule glaucum*. Pierced below umbo.

---

83. For bronze shells: *Tocra* 1, 158, no. 11; *ClRh* 3, 72, fig. 62 (Ialysos cemetery). For a shell mold(?): *Dèlos* 18, pl. 1, no. 4.

140 FOSSILIZED SHELL
Pl. 20   77-1172   C13   1   4a
H. 0.035; W. 0.032
   Fossil *Chlamys* (scallop). Pierced just below umbo.

141 SHELL PENDANT
Pl. 20   77-112   F13/G13   2   2
H. 0.044; W. 0.025
   Shell. Cowrie *Erosaria* (*Cypraea*) *spurca*. Pierced at one end.

142 SHELL PENDANT
Pl. 20   77-645   F13/G13   2   2
H. 0.017; D. 0.052
   Shell. Limpet *Patella caerulea*. Pierced for suspension.

Actual shells and fossilized shells are much more commonly used as pendants than bronze imitations such as **120-136**.[84] Shells were often used as ornaments at Classical sites. The tradition is an old one. Necklaces of gold imitation cowries are known from Egypt as early as the Middle Kingdom,[85] and real cowries were used as ornaments in the Aegean during the Bronze Age.[86] Pierced shells, most often cowries, have been found at Knossos,[87] Thera,[88] Ephesos,[89] Perachora,[90] Delos,[91] Cyprus,[92] and in great number on Rhodes.[93] Our pierced limpet shell (**142**) is paralleled on Chios, where a cache of 270 examples was found in a context dating to ca. 600 B.C.[94] Hogarth has suggested that pierced cowries were suspended from fibulae;[95] they were more likely strung on necklaces. Cowrie pendants serving as amulets are also known from Punic sites, where they are normally found in tombs.[96] Particularly intriguing is the occurrence of pierced shells, together with bronze coins bearing the image of Demeter, in second-century B.C. tombs at Mahdia.[97] The Mahdia finds suggest a definite connection, at least in North Africa, between the shell amulet, whether real or metal imitation, and the cult of Demeter.

TOOTH PENDANTS
143 and 144

143 TOOTH PENDANT
Pl. 21   76-739   F13/G13   1   2
L. 0.040; W. 0.010
   Tooth. Crescent-shaped. Pierced through center.

144 TOOTH PENDANT
Pl. 21   77-582   F13/G13   2   2
L. 0.037; W. 0.010
   Tooth. Pierced through center.

A pierced animal tooth, similar to **143** and also probably a pendant or amulet, was found in the Limenia deposit at Perachora.[98] Another pierced tooth is known from an Archaic context on Chios.[99]

TRIANGULAR PENDANTS
145-148

145 TRIANGULAR PENDANT
Not ill.   74-831   D12/13   F   3
H. 0.028; W. 0.014; D. (ring) 0.021
   Bronze. Flat undecorated, suspended from bronze ring.

146 TRIANGULAR PENDANT
Not ill.   74-1128   D12/13   F   3
L. 0.026; W. 0.014
   Bronze. Slightly convex, suspension loop missing.

147 TRIANGULAR PENDANT
Pl. 21   77-266   D15/16   1   2
H. 0.023; D. (ring) 0.034
   Bronze foil. Suspended from thick bronze ring.

148 TRIANGULAR PENDANT
Pl. 21   73-889   C15/16   1   4
L. 0.012
   Bronze wire. Flattened at one end to form triangle, coiled at other end to form suspension loop.

These four bronze pendants of simple triangular form were made by hammering foil or wire. This type of pendant is paralleled by a bronze example from Aegina.[100] **148** has been included because it is well finished and not just a partially worked fragment of wire or foil.

VASE PENDANTS
149-153

149 VASE PENDANT
Pl. 21   73-1262   C15/D15   1B   4
H. 0.030; D. 0.024
   Solid bronze. Amphora with two large, unequal handles.

---

84. For actual and fossilized shells not used as pendants, see **508-510**, p. 67.

85. E. Vernier, *Bijoux et Orfevreries*, Catalogue général des antiquités Égyptiennes du Musée du Caire, vol. 80 (1925) 351-352, no. 53074, pl. 77.

86. E. Bielefeld, *Archaeologica Homerica C: Schmuck* (Göttingen 1967) 26, no. 179.

87. *Knossos*, 118-119, no. 30 (not illustrated), also "curled worm shell," 119, no. 31.

88. *AM* 28 (1903) 239.

89. Hogarth, *Ephesus*, 217, fig. 44.

90. *Perachora* 2, 527, K2, pl. 194.

91. *Délos* 18, 303, pierced shells on a necklace from House IV A. For another necklace from Delos: *BCH* 100 (1976) 815, fig. 23.

92. V. Karageorghis, *Excavations at Kition I. The Tombs* (Nicosia 1974), pl. 20; from the Astarte Temple, period III.

93. K.F. Kinch, *Vroulia* (Berlin 1914), 160-161, pl. 24,1-3. *Lindos* 1, 177-178, nos. 546 and 547. *ClRh* 5-6, 365, no. 8, fig. 108, pierced cowrie from the "stipe votica"; and p. 364, no. 7, fig. 109, pierced conch.

94. *Emporio*, 243, no. 606, period IV, ca. 600 B.C.

95. Hogarth, *Ephesus*, 217.

96. P. Cintas, *Amulettes puniques*, Institut des hautes études de Tunis, I, (1946), 5.

97. Ibid., 142.

98. *Perachora* 2, 527, M1, pl. 195.

99. *Emporio*, 243, no. 610.

100. *Aegina*, pl. 116, fig. 61.

150 VASE PENDANT
Pl. 21   73-1263   D12/E12   D   3
H. 0.027; W. 0.018; Th. 0.012
Solid bronze. Amphora with long body, short foot.

151 VASE PENDANT
Pl. 21   74-849   D12/13   F   3
H. 0.029; W. 0.021
Solid bronze. Trefoil oinochoe with large handle.

152 VASE PENDANT
Pl. 21   74-902   D12/13   F   3
H. 0.011; D. 0.008
Silver. Phiale, with boss in center, large strap handle. Chipped and cracked. Mended from two pieces.
Probably Archaic.

153 VASE? PENDANT
Not ill.   71-792   D11/12   A   3
D. 0.017; D. of hole 0.003
Silver. Phiale? disk with hole in center. Undoubtedly a pendant, since traces of loop or suspension strap remain along edge of disk.

The bronze vase pendants (**149-151**) may be Roman in date. A green stone miniature amphora from the House of the Masks at Delos hangs from a disk.[101] A miniature lead amphora is also known from Delos, but it need not have been a pendant.[102] Amphorae are sometimes suspended from earrings or necklaces,[103] and may have been worn as a kind of talisman.[104] Oinochoai are rarer, but like amphorae, are known from both Italic[105] and Greek contexts.[106] Even rarer are phiale pendants; **152** is probably Archaic in date and is paralleled by an example from the Demeter Sanctuary at Knossos.[107] The silver pendant (**153**) is included here because of its resemblance in form to the phiale type; however, it may be an elaborate disk pendant.

HEART PENDANTS
154-158

154 HEART PENDANT
Pl. 21   71-455   D12/13   B   4
H. 0.035
White, *Second Report*, pl. 94b.
Bronze. Heart-shaped with ribbed neck. Pierced through neck.

155 HEART PENDANT
Not ill.   77-1064   C13   1   3b
H. 0.049
Terracotta. "Wings" striated. Beck, Group XXI. B.2.a.
Archaic.

156 HEART PENDANT
Not ill.   74-915   D12/13   F   3
H. 0.023
Terracotta. Similar to **155**. Vertical striations on one side only. Broken at top.
Archaic.

157 HEART PENDANT
Not ill.   77-1046   C13   1   4b
H. 0.038
Terracotta. Similar to **155**.
Archaic.

158 HEART PENDANT
Pl. 21   N.I.   Surface
H. 0.038
Terracotta. Similar to **155**. Broken at top.
Archaic.

The bronze pendant (**154**) is clearly a variant of the Egyptian heart amulet; it even has the small lateral projections, or "wings," found on the Egyptian examples. Egyptian heart amulets are generally Ptolemaic in date, but the type may go back to as early as the third millennium B.C.[108] **154** seems to be from an Archaic context. Terracotta pendants of this type (**155-158**) are more prevalent and much closer in form to the Egyptian prototypes; all are similar to Petrie's type 7p.[109]

MISCELLANEOUS PENDANTS
159-165

159 FACE PENDANT
Pl. 21   74-846   D12/13   F   3
H. 0.026
Bronze. Elongated body with four bosses. Suspension loop.
Archaic.

160 FACE PENDANT
Pl. 21   77-1210   C13   1   4a
H. 0.033; W. 0.026
Terracotta. Roughly cross-shaped, upper projection pierced.
Archaic.

161 KEYHOLE PENDANT
Pl. 21   74-1149   D12/13   F   3
H. 0.048; W. 0.035; Th. 0.007
Bronze. Keyhole-shaped. Complete.

162 PENDANT
Pl. 21   76-1209   C12/13   1   3
H. 0.046; D. 0.027; Th. 0.009
Bronze. Ring with two arms or wings. Longer arm grooved at top, perhaps for suspension collar. Complete.

---

101. *Délos* 18, 300, fig. 368.
102. Ibid., 300, B1334, fig. 369.
103. Used as earring: Pottier-Reinach, *Nécropole de Myrina*, 215 n. 1. For the necklaces: *Lindos* 1, 98, 106 n. 240, pl. 11.
104. *BCH* 29 (1905) 402 n. 2.
105. O. Montelius, *La civilisation primitive en Italie dupuis l'introduction des métaux* (Stockholm 1895-1910), pl. 109, no. 10. Also: *NSc* (1916) 16, fig. 17; 17, fig. 21; *NSc* (1977) 226, no. 9; 227, 298.

106. Niessen, no. 3729, pl. 118; *Lindos* 1, 106, pl. 11, no. 240.
107. *Knossos*, 98-114, 143.
108. Petrie, *Amulets*, 10, pl. 1, 7a-p. G.A. Reisner, *Amulets*, Catalogue général des antiquités égyptiennes du Musée du Caire, v. 35 (Cairo 1907), 1-7, nos. 5218-5260; 105-110, nos. 12051-69; pls. 1 and 7.
109. Petrie, *Amulets*, pl. 1, 7p. Beck, 35, fig. 28, B.2.a.

163 PENDANT?
Pl. 21   73-746   D16/17   1   2
H. 0.032
Terracotta. Lump, pierced. Complete. Perhaps a pendant.

164 SEA STONE PENDANT
Not ill.   73-779   C15/16   1   4
Max. D. 0.045
Limestone. Rounded, pierced by large oval hole near one edge.

165 SEA STONE PENDANT
Not ill.   78-301   F14/G14   1   2
L. 0.033
Stone. Irregularly shaped, pierced at one end.

In its general effect, **159** resembles some of Petrie's more stylized Egyptian face pendants.[110] Also related are a number of terracotta pendants of similar shape, such as **160**.[111]

164 and **165** are sea stones that have been worn smooth, worked and pierced. They are too small to have been loom weights and are more likely amulets or charms.

Decorated Band
166

166 DECORATED BAND
Pl. 22; Fig. 3   77-1180   C13   1   4a
L. 0.040; W. 0.016; Th. 0.001
Bronze foil. Central row of bosses in repoussé, vertical row of three small bosses between each large boss. Row of small dots along upper and lower edges. Band now folded over on itself several times. Original length at least 14 centimeters.
Archaic.

This bronze band decorated with repoussé geometric patterns may have been used as a belt or as a clothing ornament. **166** seems to have been folded up originally and may have been attached to a leather backing.

Bracelets
167-169

167 BRACELET
Pl. 22   74-613   C10/11   A   1
L. 0.078; Th. 0.009; D. (est.) 0.082
Ivory. Fragment preserving more than one-third of circumference. Oval cross section.
Roman?

168 BRACELET
Not ill.   74-844   C10/11   A (beta)   2
L. 0.060; Th. 0.009; D. (est.) 0.082
Ivory. Fragment. Similar to **167**.
Roman.

169 TWO BRACELETS
Not ill.   77-1154   D12/13   F   3
D. 0.044; Th. 0.005
Bronze. Thick wire. Cylindrical grooved terminals.
Archaic or Classical.

---

110. Petrie, *Amulets*, pl. 1, 2f.

111. Six similar examples: 71-683, 71-684, 77-136, 73-1011, 77-1045, 77-1206.

Toggles
170 and 171

170 TOGGLE
Pl. 22   73-1261   C15/D15   1B   5
L. 0.040; D. (shaft) 0.006
Bronze. Cylindrical shaft with conical terminals.

171 TOGGLE
Pl. 22   78-74   F14/G14   Test   2
L. 0.023; D. 0.006
Bone. Cylindrical, grooved in center.

Two bronze examples were found; only one (**170**) has been included here.[112] Similar bronze objects from the Argive Heraeum, cylindrical shafts with conical terminals, were pinheads rather than toggles.[113] They differ from **170** in having a pierced shaft for threading onto a pin.

A very close parallel to **171** is the bone toggle A319 from the Limenia deposit at Perachora.[114] An example from Delos and a silver toggle from Kourion (Cyprus) are also close.[115] Toggles of this type are known from a number of sites.[116]

Buttons
172-174

172 BUTTON
Not ill.   78-40   C17   1   2
D. 0.019; D. (hole) 0.004
Bone. Circular. Convex on one side, slightly concave on the other. Pierced through center.
Roman.

173 BUTTON
Pl. 22   78-807   F11/G11   -   1
D. 0.017
Bone. Circular. Offset edge, slightly convex on one side. Pierced twice.
Roman.

174 BUTTON
Pl. 22   78-808   F11/G11   -   2
D. 0.015
Bone. Circular. Pierced twice. Similar to **173** but slightly smaller.
Roman.

Such buttons are extremely common in the Roman period, for example at Corinth.[117] Closer to home, earlier examples are known from Tocra [118] and from the First Artemisium at Cyrene.[119] **172-174** are probably Roman.

Hair Coils
175-187

175 HAIR COIL
Pl. 22   73-1090   D12/E12   D   3
L. 0.021; Th. 0.004
Silver. Thick wire, with grape-cluster terminals.
Probably 6th century B.C.

176 HAIR COIL
Pl. 22; Fig. 3   71-421   E12   1   5
L. 0.018
White, *Second Report*, pl. XCX,e.
Silver. Fragment. Similar to **175**, preserving terminal and small section of wire. Terminal is filigreed flower bud with granulated clusters.
Probably 6th century B.C.

177 HAIR COIL
Not ill.   74-969   D12/13   F   3
L. 0.024
Silver. Similar to **175** with grape-cluster terminals.
Probably 6th century B.C.

178 HAIR COIL
Not ill.   74-970   D11/12   1   3
D. (coil) 0.018
Silver. Similar to **175** with grape-cluster terminals, one of which is now missing.
Probably 6th century B.C.

---

112. One other example: 71-463 (E11,3,3).
113. *Argive Heraeum* 2, pl. 80, nos. 367-381.
114. *Perachora* 2, pl. 188 and A320, pl. 188.
115. *Délos* 18, pl. 77, 642, 5 and 6. Kourion: *Cesnola Atlas* iii, pl. 39, 20, as cited by Stubbings in *Perachora* 2, 443.
116. Delphi, Dodona, Sparta, Lindos, and the Argive Heraeum, as cited by Stubbings in *Perachora* 2, 443 n. 9 with bibliography.
117. *Corinth* 12, nos. 298 and 299, pl. 123.
118. *Tocra* 1, no. 84, fig. 77.
119. *AfrIt* 4 (1931) 201, fig. 25.

179 HAIR COIL
Not ill.   74-1063   D12/13   F   3   D. 0.020
White, *Fourth Report*, pl. 28, fig. 40.
Silver. Similar to **175**.
Probably 6th century B.C.

180 HAIR COIL
Not ill.   76-990   D12/13   F   3
D. (coil) 0.021
Silver. Similar to **175**. Broken into two pieces.
Probably 6th century B.C.

181 HAIR COIL
Not ill.   76-1095   C13/D13   1   6
D. (coil) 0.019
Silver. Grape-cluster terminals. Found with grape-cluster terminal of another coil.
Probably 6th century B.C.

182 HAIR COIL
Not ill.   76-1097   C13/D13   1   6
L. 0.012
Silver. Fragment preserving section of wire and spherical terminal. Traces of granulation on terminal. Burnt.
Probably 6th century B.C.

183 HAIR COIL
Pl. 22   71-751   D12/13   A   3
D. (coil) 0.024
Bronze. Ribbed terminals.
Probably 6th century B.C.

184 TWO HAIR COILS
Pl. 22   74-1081   C12/D12   G   3
D. (coil) 0.020
Bronze. Each has oval terminals.
Probably 6th century B.C.

185 HAIR COIL
Not ill.   77-268   D14/E14   1   2
L. 0.021
Bronze. Pomegranate-shaped terminals.
Probably 6th century B.C.

186 TWO HAIR COILS
Pl. 22   77-1085   C13   1   4b
D. (coil) 0.024
Bronze. Pomegranate-shaped terminals.

187 COIL
Not ill.   76-438   C13/D13   1   7
D. 0.004
Silver wire. Small wire flattened in cross section.

Hair coils of this type from Olynthos are published by Robinson as earrings or hair slides.[120] Robinson suggests that they were placed above the ears, as on an ivory statuette from Ephesus and a female head on a Cypriot vase.[121] Higgins calls this type of ornament an earring, although Hogarth identified it as a *tettix*.[122] Further evidence for use comes from funerary contexts; coils of this type are often found in tombs around the ears and head of the corpse.[123] They may have served the same purpose as Iron Age Italian fibula which were often used as hair pins and hair fasteners.

Bronze examples of these coils are often plated with gold.[124] This may explain the similarity between our bronze and silver examples, for the bronze coils, when plated with silver, would have been less expensive but virtually indistinguishable from the silver examples. Higgins considers hair coils, or slides, to be a common island type, known from Camirus and Lindos, with a splayed variant also known from Rhodes and East Greece.[125] A number of hair coils have also been found on Chios. Only one is silver; the rest are bronze, including an example with ribbed terminals like our **103**.[126] Silver coils, identified as earrings, have also been found at Knossos; these are probably fourth century B.C. or later in date, and differ from the Cyrene examples in having serpent terminals.[127] Coils similar to ours, with ribbed or conical terminals, have been unearthed at Tocra.[128] The Cyrene examples probably date to the sixth century B.C.

There are also several plain wire coils without terminals, like **187**.[129]

Earrings
188-191

188 EARRING
Pl. 22   76-991   C12/D12   G   3
L. 0.019
Silver. Hoop, with tapered ends. Outside of hoop decorated with cluster of five granules.
Probably late 7th or 6th century B.C.

189 EARRING
Not ill.   76-995   C13/D13   1   7
L. 0.016
Silver. Hoop, with tapered ends. Outside of hoop decorated with cluster of four granules.
Probably late 7th or 6th century B.C.

---

120. *Olynthos* 10, 315, pl. 18, no. 307.
121. Hogarth, *Ephesus*, 156, pl. 22. Murray Smith-Walters, *Excavation in Cyprus*, pl. 3.
122. Hogarth, *Ephesus*, 156.
123. *AthMitt* 51 (1926) 137; L. Marangou, *BCH* 99 (1975) 372 n. 19.
124. *Olynthos* 10, 90 n. 88.
125. *GRJ*, 113. *Lindos* 1, 118-119, 271-275, pl. 12. Also: Marshall, xxxiii.

126. *Emporio*, 222, nos. 35-74. Examples with ribbed terminals: nos. 373 and 374.
127. *Knossos*, 138, nos. 57-60, fig. 31, pl. 87.
128. *Tocra* 2, F116, fig. 33. Examples with ribbed terminals: *Tocra* 1, 156, pl. 104, no. 4.
129. Other spirals of this type: 74-975, 77-729 (silver), and 77-1135 (bronze).

190 EARRING
Not ill.   76-1045   C12/13   1   4
L. 0.011
   Silver. Hoop, similar to **189.** Fragmentary.
   Probably late 7th or 6th century B.C.

191 EARRING
Pl. 22   77-1173   C13   1   4a
L. 0.014
   Silver. Hoop, undecorated.
   Probably late 7th or 6th century B.C.

Of the ten silver earrings found at the Demeter Sanctuary, nine are a simple hoop with tapered ends.[130]

Tapered hoops of this type, both with and without granulated clusters, seem to have been popular on Crete and Cyprus during the Late Bronze Age;[131] they are also known from early contexts at Lefkandi[132] and from Archaic tombs in Sicily.[133] Higgins considers them a western type of earring that reached Sicily from Cyprus;[134] however, their occurrence at Cyrene and at Greek Emporio,[135] suggests a greater popularity and distribution. The Cyrene examples probably date to the late seventh or sixth century B.C., since this type of earring seems to have gone out of fashion by the fifth century. It is intriguing that bronze hoop earrings were popular at Corinth during the Byzantine period,[136] and a gold earring similar to our examples is known from a much later context at Conimbriga.[137]

Fibulae
192-203

Both bone and ivory spectacle fibulae (**192-198**) and metal bow fibulae (**199-203**) were found in approximately equal number. Seven examples of spectacle fibulae and five examples of bow fibulae have been included in this catalogue.

SPECTACLE FIBULAE
192-198

192 SPECTACLE FIBULA
Pl. 23   73-686   D16/17   1   2
L. 0.035; W. 0.029; Th. 0.003
   Ivory. Fragment, preserving part of disks. Decorated with dotted guilloche around perimeter of disks. Traces of iron on undecorated reverse.
   Archaic.

193 SPECTACLE FIBULA
Pl. 23   73-915   D12/E12   D   2
L. 0.037; Th. 0.004
   Ivory. Fragment, decorated with concentric scale pattern. Remains of iron boss in center of disk. Traces of iron on reverse.
   Archaic.

194 SPECTACLE FIBULA
Pl. 23   74-763   C13/D13   1   7
L. 0.023
   Ivory. Fragment, perimeter decorated with band of bull's-eyes.
   Possibly 6th century B.C.
   Traces of iron on reverse.

195 SPECTACLE FIBULA
Pl. 23   76-348   C13/D13   1   7
L. 0.023
   Ivory. Fragment, decorated with bull's-eyes and hound's tooth bands.
   Possibly 6th century B.C.

196 SPECTACLE FIBULA
Pl. 23   76-349   F13/G13   1   2
L. 0.037
   Ivory. Fragment perimeter decorated with guilloche band.
   Archaic.

197 SPECTACLE FIBULA
Not ill.   76-399   C12/13   1   2
D. 0.015; Th. 0.004
   Ivory. Fragment, decorated with dotted guilloche band, similar to **192.**
   Archaic.

198 SPECTACLE FIBULA
Pl. 23   77-77   F13/G13   2   2
L. 0.032; W. 0.014; Th. 0.003
   Ivory. Fragment preserving part of larger disk and entire small disk. Perimeter of large disk decorated with band of bull's-eyes.
   Possibly 6th century B.C.

Only one spectacle fibula (**198**) preserves enough of the bridge section to classify according to Stubbings' typology;[138] it belongs to his Type A with fully articulated bridge disks.

All of the spectacle fibulae are ivory. No traces of gilding, painting, or inlay are preserved, with the exception of **193**, which has traces of a central iron boss on the decorated side of the disk. Six of the fibulae are

---

130. Other earrings of this type: 71-769, 71-827, 73-721, 74-972, 76-1092.
131. *GRJ* 62, 86.
132. Ibid., 106.
133. Ibid., 120: Syracuse tomb 404, Megara Hyblaea tomb 240.
134. Ibid., 120, 127.

135. *Emporio*, 222, 350.
136. *Corinth* 12, 249, no. 2012.
137. *Conimbriga* 7, pl. 34; no. 212; p. 142: "abandon des l'habitat indigènes," hence early Imperial?
138. *Perachora* 2, 435, pl. 184, A146.

decorated simply, either with a guilloche band or a row of bull's-eyes near the disk's perimeter. Unusual is **193** with its scale pattern in the center of the disk. A similar pattern, termed "isodomic," is found on a fibula from Perachora.[139]

Ivory spectacle fibulae seem to have functioned as expensive and later variants of the ubiquitous bronze wire spectacle fibulae of the Geometric period.[140] Ivory examples are discussed in detail by Blinkenberg, and an extensive addendum of findspots has been provided by Stubbings.[141] Spectacle fibulae were common on the mainland, particularly at Sparta and Perachora, where there is good evidence for local production,[142] on the islands, in East Greece, and in South Italy and Sicily—in fact, throughout the Archaic Greek world. Most examples are seventh century in date, but sixth century examples are known from Olynthos, Corinth, Rhodes, and Halae.[143]

At Cyrene, two other spectacle fibulae were found in the early levels of the First Artemisium;[144] both are similar to our fibulae with a single band of bull's-eyes near the perimeter of the disk. Other examples were found in the Cyrenaica; ten fibulae from Tocra[145] show the same predilection for simple decoration and the use of bull's-eyes. This kind of simplified decoration may support an argument for a sixth century date and perhaps even for a local workshop.[146]

BOW FIBULAE
199-203

199 FIBULA
Pl. 23   73-1183   D17/16   1   3
L. 0.050

Bronze. Bow fibula, undecorated.
Archaic.

200 FIBULA
Fig. 3   73-1231   C15/16   1   4
L. 0.023
Iron. Bow fibula with hinged pin, missing part of pin. Undecorated.
Archaic.

201 FIBULA
Pl. 23; Fig. 3   74-1022   D11/12   1   3
L. 0.057
Bronze. Bow fibula, complete but badly bent. Transversely ribbed bow.
Probably Archaic.

202 FIBULA
Pl. 23; Fig. 3   74-1144   D12/13   F   3
L. 0.051
Bronze. Bow fibula, preserving most of bow, missing pin and hinge. Bow decorated with three heavy bead reels, one in center, one at either end.
Probably Archaic.

203 FIBULA
Pl. 23; Fig. 3   76-1248   F13   1   3
L. 0.054
Bronze. Fragment of bow fibula, preserving almost two-thirds of arc. Central portion of bow undecorated but bent sharply at right angle. Ends of bow decorated with multiple biconical reels.
Archaic.

Well-preserved examples of metal fibulae are rare at Cyrene.[147] The bronze fibula with corrugated bow (**201**) is paralleled by an example from the Argive Heraeum with the same bow shape and corrugation.[148] **202**, with elegant bead and reel moldings, is also paralleled at the Argive Heraeum and by an example from Lindos.[149] Both of our examples probably date to the Archaic period.

Pins
204-243

STRAIGHT PINS WITH
ROLLED HEADS
204-206

204 PIN
Not ill.   73-353   SW sondage   1A   3
L. 0.071

Bronze. Straight with rolled head. Shaft bends at nearly right angle before curving to form head.

205 PIN
Not ill.   73-1293   C15/D15   1B   4
L. 0.0581

Bronze. Straight with rolled head and right-angle bend, similar to **204**.

---

139. Stubbings in *Perachora* 2, 433-435.
140. For the European examples, J. Alexander, *AJA* 69 (1965) 7-23.
141. *Perachora* 2, 433-435.
142. Ibid., pl. 185, A194, an unfinished ivory spectacle fibula. Ivory wasters were also found at the site (A381, A385, p. 447).
143. *Olynthos* 10, 99, pl. 20, 344-9. *Corinth* 13, pl. 79, 159-63. Kameiros (Rhodes): *ClRh* 4, 102, fig. 89. Halae: *Hesperia* 9 (1940) 426, fig. 79. For a fourth to third century B.C. context: *AAA* (1972) 238, fig. 10, as cited by Boardman in *Tocra* 2, 80 n. 15.
144. *AfrIt* 4 (1931) 201, fig. 25.
145. *Tocra* 1, 165, nos. 72-77, pl. 104. *Tocra* 2, F151-5, pl. 40.
146. Many of the Tocra examples are of bone; five examples are from stratified context which could be as late as the sixth century B.C.
147. Other metal fibula fragments: 71-515 (pin), 73-1244 (pin), 77-457 (small bow fragment), and 76-1258 (pin).
148. *Argive Heraeum* 2, no. 882, pl. 87.
149. Ibid., no. 905, pl. 87. *Lindos* 1, no. 112, pl. 8.

206 PIN
Pl. 24   74-1152   D12/13   F   3
L. 0.021
Bronze. Straight pin with rolled head, similar to **204**. Missing part of shaft.

More than fifty pins have been found;[150] pins, in fact, seem to outnumber fibulae. Straight pins with rolled heads were among the most common types. Eight identifiable examples were found in the Demeter Sanctuary; three are included here.

Pins with rolled heads are found at most mainland Greek sanctuaries during the Archaic period.[151] They are also common in continental Europe and Italy during the Iron Age.[152] In most cases, their popularity is probably due to the ease with which they could be manufactured. Rolled pins from the Archaic period are descendants of the most popular pin type of the Bronze Age.[153] Additional rolled pins were found in the First Artemisium at Cyrene.[154]

DISK- AND KNOB-HEADED PINS
207-229

207 PIN
Pl. 24; Fig. 4   71-275   F16   1   3A
L. 0.068; D. (disk) 0.017
Bronze. Almost complete. Head formed by two knobs and large disk.

208 PIN
Pl. 24; Fig. 4   71-755   D12/13   A   4
L. 0.019
Bronze. Several knobs and large disk, largest knob decorated with vertical grooves.

209 PINHEAD
Pl. 24   71-740   D12/13   B   4
L. 0.026; Max. D. 0.024
Bronze. Knob and two collars, one collar plugged with bronze.

210 PIN
Fig. 4   71-804   E12   1   3
L. 0.068
Bronze. Long, thin shaft, now bent. Head formed by small collar and biconical knob.
Archaic.

211 PIN
Not ill.   71-798   E11   3   3
L. 0.055
Bronze. Thin, bent. Solid spherical head.

212 PINHEAD
Pl. 24   73-332   E11/D11   Balk   2
L. 0.128
Bronze. Large, broad flat disk with six transverse lines.

213 PIN
Pl. 24; Fig. 4   73-1224   D17/16   1   3
L. 0.070
Bronze. Missing only shaft point. Head formed by three spheres and disk capped by small knob.

214 PINHEAD
Pl. 24; Fig. 4   74-380   D16/17   2   4
L. 0.019; D. 0.012
Bronze. Three disks, large knob, and small pomegranate terminal. Terminal has traces of glass inlay. Head screwed onto shaft, part of which can still be seen in socket.

215 PIN
Pl. 24; Fig. 4   74-1126   D12/13   F   3
L. 0.105
Bronze. Entirely preserved but broken in two. Head formed by two spheres and disk.

216 PINHEAD
Pl. 25; Fig. 4   74-1136   D12/13   F   4
L. 0.010; D. (disk) 0.020
Bronze. Ribbed disk surmounted by small knob or finial.

217 PIN?
Not ill.   74-1145   D12/13   F   2a
L. 0.018; D. 0.006
Bronze. Shaft of either pin or small implement. Decorated with bead and reel moldings.

218 PIN
Not ill.   76-911   C12/13   1   2
L. 0.062
Iron. Pin with round head, pierced.

219 PIN?
Pl. 25   76-1228   C13/D13   1   7
D. 0.015
Bronze. Disk with central hole. Decorated on one side with impressed circles. Perhaps part of pin head. Repaired.

220 PIN
Pl. 25; Fig. 4   76-1229   D16/E16   1   1
D. 0.024
Bronze. Missing most of shaft. Hollow, conical head.

221 PINHEAD
Pl. 25; Fig. 4   77-252   D15/16   1   2
L. 0.029
Bronze. Fragment, preserving two knobs and several reel moldings. Knobs decorated with vertical grooves in groups of three.

222 PIN
Not ill.   77-449   D15/16   1   2
L. 0.011
Bronze. Small section of shaft, collar, and biconical head. Similar to **210**.

---

150. In addition to the three catalogued examples: 73-1244, 74-855, 74-1150, 74-1151, 77-961, 76-1258.
151. For an up-to-date summary of rolled pins from Greek sanctuaries: H. Phillip, *Bronzeschmuck aus Olympia*, OlForsch 13 (Berlin, 1981), 88-93, especially n. 224. According to Boardman, however, this type of pin is "not hitherto met in Ionia, and rare enough in the rest of Greece" (*Emporio*, 223).
152. P.G. Warden, *The Metal Artifacts from Poggio Civitate (Murlo)* (Rome 1983), nos. 70-74, with discussion.
153. Jacobsthal, 120f.
154. *AfrIt* 4 (1931) fig. 21.

223 PINHEAD
Pl. 25; Fig. 4   77-727   F13/G13 2 2
L. 0.042; D. (disk) 0.016
Bronze. Broken in two. Large disk and four knobs separated by reels and decreasing in size going down shaft.

224 PINHEAD
Pl. 25; Fig. 4   77-1174   C13 1 4a
L. 0.023; D. (disk) 0.024
Bronze. Large disk topped by smaller disk knob below.

225 PINHEAD
Pl. 25; Fig. 4   73-1178   D16/17 1 3
L. 0.044; D. (disk) 0.012
Bronze. Disk, small knob, then six larger knobs in descending size order.

226 PIN
Pl. 25   77-1181a   C13 1 4a
L. 0.043; D. (disk) 0.011
Bronze. Disk head with raised upper edge, perhaps for inlay. Long shaft.

227 PIN
Pl. 25   77-1181b   C13 1 4a
L. 0.044
Bronze. Disk head similar to **226**. Part of matched set?

228 PIN
Not ill.   77-1183   C13 1 4a
L. 0.051
Bronze. Solid, spherical head.

229 PIN
Pl. 25   78-432   Stray
L. 0.024; D. (head) 0.016
Bronze. Square shaft conical head topped by small conical boss. Missing part of shaft.

The favorite type of pin at the Demeter Sanctuary was the straight pin with disk and knob head. Numerous varieties have been found.

Pins with disk-and-double-knob heads, similar to **207**, are common at Peloponnesian sites.[155] This type of pin has also been found in the Cyrenaica, in an early context at Cyrene,[156] and from a sixth-century context at Tocra.[157] Spherical pins with double collars, similar to **209**, are also found on the mainland.[158] More unusual is the pin with ribbed disk (**210**). It, too, is a mainland type,[159] although it is also paralleled at Tocra.[160] Pins with pomegranate heads similar to **214** are a favorite fifth-century type on the mainland,[161] although this unusual example, with glass inlay and socketed head, is probably later in date—Hellenistic, or perhaps Roman. Pins with conical heads are also later in date, Hellenistic judging by parallels from Macedonia and Delos.[162] Most of the disk- and knob-headed pins, however, are sixth century in date, or earlier; **208** with a vertically grooved knob, **210** with its biconical head, and **213** with multiple knobs and disk are all paralleled in early contexts at mainland sanctuaries.[163]

WHEEL-SHAPED PINHEAD?
230

230 PINHEAD?
Pl. 25; Fig. 4   74-854   C14 1 3
D. 0.035
Bronze. Wheel-shaped, with six spokes. Hole through center.

Pins with wheel-shaped heads are common in Italy and continental Europe during the Geometric and Orientalizing periods.[164] Wheels were also often used as pendants. A Late Bronze Age wheel from Cyprus was possibly used on a bronze stand or cart,[165] and wheels of this type are also found as decorative fittings on Italic tripods and stands.[166]

PIN CAPS
231 and 232

231 PIN CAP
Pl. 25   71-458   E11 3 3
H. 0.019; D. 0.023
Bronze. Solid top, hollow cylindrical collar with four holes. Juncture between top and collar articulated by two deep grooves.
Archaic.

232 PIN CAP
Pl. 25; Fig. 4   77-1087   C13 1 4b
H. 0.020; D. 0.013
Bronze. Solid dome-shaped, top decorated by small knob, hollow cylindrical collar with several large holes.
Archaic.

---

155. *Aegina*, pl. 14, fig. 52. *Argive Heraeum* 2, pl. 80.
156. From the First Artemisium: *AfrIt* 4 (1931) fig. 21.
157. *Tocra* 1, 158, nos. 15-22, fig. 73, considered by Boardman to be a Peloponnesian type. *Tocra* 2, F122-3, F125, F136-7 (iron), figs. 34-35, from Deposit I (620-590 B.C.) and Deposit III (565-520/510 B.C.): "the stratigraphy of this whole series suggests that this Orientalizing type might last in Greek land longer than has been suspected" (p. 77).
158. *Argive Heraeum* 2, no. 1551, pl. 92.
159. E.g., ibid., nos. 497-557, pls. 81-82. *Aegina*, pl. 114, fig. 41.
160. *Tocra* 1, 161, fig. 73.
161. Nauplion Museum inv. no. 786: Halieis Grave 11. 475-450 B.C., *ArchDelt* 31 (1976) A, 299, no. 72, pl. 72, with five other examples, nos. 73-77, p. 300, pl. 72. Also found in a votive deposit on the Halieis acropolis: S. Dublin, *Expedition* 11 (1969) 28. For a similar pinhead from Argos dating to the second quarter of the fifth century B.C.: *ArchDelt* 15 (1933-1935) 40, fig. 22.
162. Langaza: *JdI* 26 (1911) 204, fig. 16, found embedded in a wooden door in a Macedonian tumulus. Delos: *BCH* 100 (1976) 818, fig. 30.
163. **208**: *Argive Heraeum* 2, pl. 81, no. 502. **210**: *Argive Heraeum* 2, 62-71, pl. 78. *Aegina*, pl. 114, fig. 2. **213**: *Argive Heraeum* 2, 291-312, pl. 79. *Aegina*, pl. 114, fig. 42.
164. Jacobsthal, fig. 564.
165. V. Karageorghis, *RDAC* (1973), pl. 8, 10.
166. E.g., a fifth century Etruscan bronze "candelabrum," *Wealth of the Ancient World, The Nelson Bunker Hunt and William Herbert Hunt Collections* (Kimbell Museum, Fort Worth 1983), no. 31.

Both of these pinheads or caps are similar in having openwork collars. Fitted onto ivory or wooden pins, the bronze would have created a pleasing contrast with the lighter colored material of the shaft. Gold or electrum pins with heads in the form of a large domed box are similar in shape, although not in effect, to our plainer bronze examples. The gold pins of this type are thought to be the product of workshops at Ephesus.[167]

PIN FITTING
233

233 PIN FITTING
Pl. 26   76-1234   C11   1   2D
D. 0.067
  Bronze. Disk, hole through center.

Such simple bronze disks were probably used as fittings for pins; other examples are known from Cyrene.[168] Pin fittings of this type are common throughout the Mediterranean. In many cases, a number of disks may be threaded onto a single pin, and the disks often have decorated edges.

SILVER PIN
234

234 SILVER PIN
Pl. 26   71-774   D12/13   A   4
L. 0.071; D. (larger sphere) 0.010
  White, *Second Report*, 183 n. 58, pl. 95c.
  Silver. Shaft decorated with two hollow spheres, larger of which is ornamented with silver wire bent in omega shape. Mended from three fragments.
  Late 7th century B.C.

234a DISK
Pl. 26   71-771   D12/13   A   3
D. 0.016; Th. 0.003
  White, *Second Report*, 183 n. 58, pl. 95d.
  Silver. Hole through center, probably for attachment to pin shaft (**234**). Decorated on one side with filigree petals and concentric bands to form rosette.

This is the most spectacular pin from the Demeter Sanctuary, a beautifully preserved but fragile example in silver.
  Pins with spherical heads of bronze, and more rarely of silver or gold, are common from the Geometric period onwards. **234** with its double-sphered shaft is therefore not uncommon, although no exact parallels exist for the long, undecorated upper section of the shaft. It is likely that this upper section would have been fitted with a disk or spherical terminal, most likely the decorated rosette disk (**234**) found nearby. This disk is the perfect size for the pin shaft, and both pin and disk are decorated with filigree. When the two pieces are assembled, the resulting pin is very similar to Orientalizing pins from Perachora and the Argive Heraeum, particularly those with a separate rosette disk attached to the shaft.[169] **234** might be assigned plausibly to a late seventh century B.C. mainland workshop.

BONE AND IVORY PINS
235-237

235 IVORY PIN
Not ill.   73-781   C15/16   1   2
L. 0.068; Th. 0.005
  Ivory. Undecorated shaft, broken at both ends.
  Probably Roman.

236 BONE PIN
Pl. 26; Fig. 4   73-1187   D16/17   1   2
L. 0.074
  Bone. Elaborate lathe-turned shaft with reel moldings and narrow cylindrical terminal. Broken into three pieces and missing part of shaft.
  Probably Roman.

237 BONE PIN
Not ill.   74-778   D10/11   balk A-C (ext)   1
L. 0.073; D. 0.006
  Bone. Undecorated shaft and point. Broken at upper end.
  Probably Roman.

Two of these pins (**235** and **237**) are undecorated and may also have functioned as needles or other implements; they are probably Roman.[170] The more elaborate pin (**236**) is probably also Roman, although pins of this type are known from earlier contexts.[171] A number of otherwise lathe-turned or worked ivory and bone shafts found at Cyrene most likely belonged to small implements and have been catalogued elsewhere.[172]

BONE AND IVORY PIN TERMINALS
238 and 239

238 PIN CAP
Not ill.   69-5   2   1   2
L. 0.015
  Ivory. Dome-shaped with small knob and collar. Collar pierced horizontally for attachment.
  Probably Roman.

---

167. Jacobthal, figs. 267-268.
168. Three other examples: 76-1236, 78-436, 78-440.
169. Jacobthal, 21, nos. 98, 100. *Argive Heraeum*, no. 413, pl. 80.
170. Such pins were common at Corinth: *Corinth* 12, 279, pl. 118, no. 2295.
171. Halae acropolis (sixth century B.C.): *Hesperia* 9 (1940) 426, fig. 78, no. 22. From the Roman period at Delos: *Délos* 18, pl. 79, 668, nos. 1-2, said to be common at Roman sites (p. 247).
172. See chapter 4, 334-344.

239 PIN CAP
Pl. 26   78-758   F12/G12   wall cleaning   2
L. 0.016; D. 0.012
   Bone. Similar to **238**.
   Probably Roman.

Three dome-shaped ivory caps are similar to bronze pin caps (**231** and **232**).[173] These caps may have served as terminals for both fibulae and pins.

Like the bronze examples **231** and **232**, these caps are similar in shape to the "collar" beads (**53-57**), but differ in that they are considerably larger, decorated with a knob, and have a large neck hole. **238** and **239** are clearly meant to be placed on ivory, bone or wooden shafts.[174] Bone pinheads of this type are known from Delos.[175] Our examples are probably Roman.

BONE DISK PINHEADS
240-243

240 PINHEAD
Not ill.   71-524   E11   3   3
D. 0.016; Th. 0.007
   Bone. Convex, circular, burnt to gray color.

241 DISK
Pl. 26   77-106   C13   1   2
D. 0.028; Th. 0.003
   Ivory. Flat, small compass holes in center of each side, one side decorated with incised concentric line near edge.

242 DISK
Pl. 26   78-428   F14/G14   1   3
D. 0.035
   Ivory. Flat, pierced through center, decorated on one side with concentric circles and cable pattern.

243 PINHEAD
Not ill.   78-429   C17   Stray
D. 0.014; Th. 0.006
   Bone. Convex. Flat underside has central indentation, perhaps for attachment to pin shaft.

Several bone disks or bosses probably served as finials or terminals for ivory or bone pins.

Bone disk pinheads are common in the Orientalizing period and earlier. They are normally found in sanctuaries rather than tombs, for example at Perachora, Artemis Orthia, the Argive Heraeum, and Ephesus.[176] Most are decorated with patterns similar to **242**. The undecorated examples (**240**, **241**, and **243**) are too plain in form and decoration to attribute their place of origin, but they may very well be of local manufacture. The decorated example (**242**) may be an import; an incised rosette disk of shell is known from Lindos;[177] however, our decorated disk might be an import from the mainland, like the elaborate silver pin (**238**).

Like the spectacle fibulae, which form a group datable to the very beginning of the Demeter Sanctuary or earlier, the bone and ivory pins with top disks may have been "heirlooms," brought over by the earliest colonists and dedicated at the Sanctuary at a later date.

Bronze and ivory pins, like so many other objects of adornment, were a favorite type of dedication at the great Greek sanctuaries. In exceptional cases, pins even have dedicatory inscriptions—for example, a silver pin dedicated to Hera at the Argive Heraeum and a gilt bronze pin dedicated to Aphrodite on Paphos. In both cases, the pins are dedicated to goddesses, and the vast majority of Archaic pins from sanctuaries seem to have been dedications to goddesses.[178] No doubt the popularity of pins, fibulae, and other objects of female adornment as dedications at the Demeter Sanctuary at Cyrene results from a similar association between women dedicants and the cult of this goddess.

Rings
244-264

FINGER RINGS
244-259

244 RING
Not ill.   76-298   C12/13   1   2
D. 0.023; Th. 0.003
   Gold. Flat band, joined to form circle; join still visible. Bent.

245 RING
Pl. 27   77-1056   C13   1   Stray
D. 0.016; Th. 0.002
   Gold. Similar to **244**.

246 RING
Pl. 27   73-1230   C15/16   1   4
D. 0.021
   Silver. Small gold plug.

---

173. Not catalogued: 73-49, 73-149.

174. The caps differ from the beads in that they are pierced horizontally through one rather than both sides of the collar. The beads are pierced through for stringing; the caps are pierced through one wall only for doweling.

175. *Délos* 18, 241, figs. 267 and 268. Also: *AO* 227.
176. Jacobsthal, 12-13, 21, 35, no. 42.
177. *Lindos* 1, 128, pl. 13, no. 323.
178. For inscribed pins and the manner in which pins were dedicated at sanctuaries: Jacobsthal, 96-100.

247 RING
Pl. 27   74-305   D14   1   1
D. 0.021
  Silver. Gold plug. Identical to **246**.

248 RING
Pl. 27   77-1082   D15/E15   1   3
D. 0.016; Th. (band) 0.006
  Silver. Undecorated broad band. Hammered.

249 RING
Not ill.   76-229   C13/D13   1   6
D. 0.030; Th. 0.002
  Silver. Complete but crushed. Thin wire, drawplate markings visible.

250 RING
Not ill.   74-836   D12/13   F   3
L. 0.028
  Silver. Band, decorated with central groove and indentations along one edge. Broken and badly bent.

251 RING
Not ill.   76-1096   C12/13   1   3
D. 0.019; Th. 0.005
  Silver. Oval in cross section. Flattened oval bezel decorated with indented circles.

252 RING
Pl. 27   78-357   D14/E14   2   2
D. 0.025; Max. Th. 0.042
  Silver. Wide diamond-shaped bezel. Central axis of bezel decorated with three incised circles and two gold plugs. Bezel made separately, secured to ring by gold plugs at either end.

253 RING
Pl. 27   71-742   D12/13   B   4
D. 0.019; H. 0.012
  Bronze. Double coiled spiral projection.
  Sixth to fifth century B.C.

254 RING
Pl. 27   73-1059   D16/17   1   3
D. 0.022
  Bronze. Flattened band of metal. Each edge of band decorated with row of dots.

255 RING
Not ill.   71-745   D16/17   1   3
D. 0.050
  Bronze. Large with diamond-shaped bezel. Undecorated.
  Sixth to fifth century B.C.

256 RING
Pl. 27   74-1085   D12/13   F   3
D. 0.025
  Bronze. Diamond-shaped bezel decorated with incised diamond pattern, small hole in the center of diamond (for inset?).
  Sixth to fifth century B.C.

257 RING
Pl. 27   73-1194   C15/16   1   3
L. 0.014; D. of bezel 0.005
  Bronze. Thin. Part of band and entire bezel preserved. Cylindrical bezel set with red stone, probably carnelian.
  Probably Roman.

258 RING
Not ill.   74-843   D12/13   F   2B
D. 0.022; Th. 0.006
  Ivory. Complete.

259 RING
Pl. 27   77-676   F13/G13   2   2
D. 0.026; Th. 0.013
  Bone. Broad. Edges of outside surface grooved.

A variety of finger rings have been found. Two examples are gold (**244** and **245**), twenty-three silver (**246-252**, although only seven are included here), one bone (**259**), one ivory (**258**), and five bronze (**253-257**).

246 and **247** are unusual in having gold plugs set into them. The plugs are both functional and decorative: they join the ends of the band together and certainly would have been noticeable when the rings were polished.[179] Plain silver rings are more common.[180]

248 and **249** are characteristic of the simplest ring type, undecorated and only noteworthy because they are made of precious metal. Two manufacturing techniques were used: hammering sheet metal (**248**) and drawing wire (**249**). **250** is the only example of a silver band with simple linear decoration.

Both **251** and **252** have articulated bezels. The elaborate ring (**252**) uses the same bimetallic joining technique used to decorate **246** and **247**. Silver rings with diamond-shaped bezels similar to **252** are known from fifth century B.C. graves at Poteidia in northern Greece. **252**, however, is more precisely paralleled by a silver ring from Knossos with an oval bezel decorated with a gold plug and found in a Hellenistic context.[181] The Cyrene example, therefore, may date anywhere from the fifth to the second century B.C.

More elaborate rings, their bezels decorated with an incised or inset seal, are also known from the Demeter Sanctuary and are treated with the other seals and sealings rather than with the small finds.

Rings with spiral projections like **253** are known from Lindos, Thebes, Rhitsona, Olympia, Aegina, and the Argive Heraeum.[182] They are considered a common type during the Archaic and Classical periods.[183] **253** was probably not a finger ring and may have had some decorative function.

Rings like **254** are easily manufactured; they would have served as less expensive but personal dedications. Two other examples, similar to **254**, were also found at

---

179. For a more elaborate example of this technique: **252**.
180. Not catalogued: 71-396, 71-482, 71-769, 71-823, 71-824, 73-828, 74-835, 74-837, 74-839, 74-974, 76-238, 76-996, 77-1233, 77-241, and a single univentoried example excavated in 1974.

181. *Knossos* 134, no. 26. See also Boardman, *GGFR*, 417, top left, and pp. 157, 215 for discussion of this technique.
182. *Lindos* 1, 120-121, pl. 12, no. 278. Thebes: *JdI* 1-2 (1888) 363, 1 and m.
183. Blinkenberg, *JdI* 1-2 (1888) 363.

Cyrene.[184] Similar bronze rings have been found in late Roman contexts in Portugal,[185] but such a simple type of ring could have been popular in almost any period.

255 and **256** resemble the two silver rings with articulated bezels (**251** and **252**). Two bronze rings with articulated but undecorated bezels were also found.[186]

Ring **257** is the most unusual from the Demeter Sanctuary. Two iron finger rings were also found,[187] as well as a number of bone and ivory rings which might also have served as finger rings.

Two bone rings in addition to **259** were found at Cyrene.[188] Ivory rings of early date have been found at Perachora,[189] but our rings are too general in type to date precisely. They may be Hellenistic or Roman.

MISCELLANEOUS RINGS
260-264

260 RING
Not ill.   77-1125   C12/13   2   3
D. 0.011
Bronze. Thin, circular in cross section.

261 RING
Pl. 27   73-478   D12/E12   D   2
D. 0.017
Bronze. Circular in cross section.

262 RING
Pl. 27   73-786   E12/13   C   4
D. 0.032
Bronze. Heavy, circular in cross section. Cast.

263 DISK
Pl. 27   77-1126   C13   1   4b
D. 0.070; Th. 0.004
Bronze. Large. Slightly convex on one side.

264 RING
Pl. 27   71-747a   D12/13   A   3
D. 0.035
Bronze. Thick. Outer edge decorated with eight pairs of shallow grooves, creating bead-and-reel molding effect. Three iron plugs inserted into the ring at intervals. Hole for suspension. Cast.

A great number of bronze rings of assorted sizes were found in the Sanctuary. These are not finger rings. They are made from wire or thicker metal rods, and range in size from less than 0.010 to more than 0.070 m. in diameter. They are usually found singly, and do not seem to have been attached to anything. They are, therefore, neither furniture attachments, hardware fittings, nor buckles or toggles.

The large bronze disk (**263**) should probably be grouped with the rings, although it is difficult to say whether it was functional or decorative. It seems far too large to have been a fitting for a pin. Two other bronze disks have been found.[190]

A few representative examples of these rings have been included here. In exceptional cases, bronze rings which are clearly not finger rings may be decorated. Ring **264**, with its moldings and bimetallic decoration, must have been decorative. It is much too large and bulky to have been a finger ring, however, it could have been suspended from a chain as an amulet. It was found together with three undecorated bronze rings of similar size.

Four hundred and fifty-eight of these bronze rings have been found. More than two-thirds of them are smaller than twenty millimeters in diameter. Eleven iron examples have also been found; they are larger than the bronze rings and were undoubtedly functional rather than decorative. The bronze rings are found in virtually every part of the sanctuary, but they appear in particularly heavy concentrations in three areas: D12/13, D15/16, and D16/17 (for a full listing of findspots see Appendix I). Because of their contexts it seems likely that many of them date earlier than 500 B.C.

A similarly large number of bronze rings, also from a sanctuary context, is known from the Argive Heraeum, where more than five hundred and fifty examples were found.[191] There they were considered to be "decorative," the sort of things that would have been suspended from pins and fibulae or joined together in decorative chains. This practice was common in both Italy and Greece during the Iron Age. At Cyrene, fibulae and pins are much scarcer than bronze rings; however, the latter might have been used decoratively in other ways, for example attached to clothing or suspended from a variety of other ornaments. Bronze rings do seem to have been popular at other sites in the Cyrenaica. A mold for casting metal rings was found at Tocra and actual bronze rings were found there in stratified contexts dating to the Classical period.[192]

The large number of bronze rings from the Demeter Sanctuary is suggestive. They do not seem to have functioned as money or as a standard of value, since they differ widely in both size and weight, but they could have served as a kind of sanctuary "token," standardized in form, medium, and meaning, if not in size and weight. Given the value of metal, they would have been a substantial offering, and, more important,

---

184. Not catalogued: 74-260, 74-375, both from D16/17, 2, 3.
185. *Conimbriga* 7, pl. 31, nos. 143-145.
186. Not catalogued: 74-1021, 74-1174. Diamond-shaped bezels: Boardman *GGFR*, fig. 198k.
187. Not catalogued: 78-155, 78-156.

188. Not catalogued: 71-220, 76-398.
189. *Perachora* 2, 441, A265-287, pl. 187.
190. Not catalogued: 71-172, 76-1164.
191. *Argive Heraeum* 2, nos. 975-1524.
192. *Tocra* 2, 102, F177, pl. 51; 102, F179.

a personalized dedication of the sort that seems to have been popular at the sanctuary, particularly during its early periods.

Bronze rings then, would have been popular for a variety of reasons: first, because they were a convenient, substantial, but by no means lavish dedication; second, as was suggested by DeCou at the Argive Heraeum,[193] because these rings are objects of a personal nature, owned and possibly worn by the dedicant, but not necessarily requiring the same kind of sacrifice as the dedication of a favorite pin, or an heirloom such as an ivory spectacle fibula, making the bronze ring a convenient but more personal dedication than, say, a mass produced terracotta figurine; and finally, the rings may also have had symbolic value as dedications, either at Greek sanctuaries in general, or to Demeter specifically, perhaps having the kind of symbolic value for the Demeter cult at Cyrene that certainly existed for other types of offerings, for instance shells and shell amulets (see pp. 26-27, 62).

Summary

That jewelry and ornaments were among the most popular dedications at the site is shown by the quantitative breakdown of ornaments by type, Table 1. The figures are general, and the caveat mentioned at the beginning of this chapter still applies: some of the object types form a disproportionately large percentage of the sample due to the "disintegration" of larger objects into a number of smaller finds. For example, the dedication of a single necklace might have resulted in twenty or thirty separate finds: beads, pendants, and attachments. The figures are doubly misleading for the purpose of determining the actual number of dedications, since some types of objects, such as earrings, hair coils, pins, and fibulae, could have been dedicated either individually or in groups or pairs.

Most of our datable jewelry and ornaments can be assigned to the earlier phases of the sanctuary's history, and some entire classes of objects—the pins, pendants, beads, and fibulae—are predominantly Archaic in date. The custom of dedicating personal possessions, apparently the personal possessions of women, thus seems to have been the fashion early in the sanctuary's history. During the Hellenistic and Roman periods, jewelry dedications are rarer, but an occasional spectacular piece, for instance the Severan gold diadem (**38** and **39**), still turns up. This scarcity of later offerings does not necessarily signal change in the economic prosperity of the site, and may merely indicate a change in fashion. The degree to which the small finds reflect changes in the cult's prosperity will be known only when the entire range of finds is considered.

Those finds which can be identified as imports seem to come from three main areas, although most of the finds, for instance the beads and pendants, are types which had a broad distribution throughout the Classical world. A few classes of pendants, however, are attributable to regional workshops. The bone axe pendants (**86-89**) were probably produced during the Archaic period at a mainland workshop. The carnelian poppy-head pendants (**113-118**) are probably Egyptian and also early in date. Many of the miscellaneous pendant types, for example the heart amulets (**154-158**), are also of probable Egyptian manufacture.

Other types of ornaments are usually only more vaguely attributable to specific source areas. The hair coils, or spirals, are certainly an East Greek type, and may in fact be East Greek imports. Some of the fibulae, particularly the heavy example with multiple moldings (**202**), are also somewhat reminiscent of East Greek and Ionian examples. The spectacle fibulae (**192-198**), how-

TABLE 1:
JEWELRY AND ORNAMENT

ATTACHMENTS	18
BEADS	ca. 400*
PENDANTS	81**
BAND	1
BRACELETS	3
BUCKLES	2
BUTTONS	3
COILS (HAIR)	18
EARRINGS	9
FIBULAE	16
PINS	ca. 50
FINGER RINGS	40
BRONZE RINGS	458

*not including glass beads
**not including glass pendants

---

193. *Argive Heraeum* 2, 251 n. 3.

ever, although of a type found throughout the Mediterranean, may be local products. The metal pins are also ubiquitous, but a few examples resemble mainland types. One example in particular, the elaborate silver pin with rosette disk head (**234**), is almost certainly a Peloponnesian import.

Overall, the imports for this class of artifacts are fairly evenly divided among the mainland, East Greece, and Egypt.

The large number of bronze rings is worthy of note. These rings are included here under the rubric of jewelry and ornament mainly for the reason that, while their exact function remains uncertain, it does seem that at least the smaller examples may have been used decoratively, perhaps attached to pins or fibulae. Many of these rings, however, valued primarily for the worth of their metal, may have been manufactured expressly for use as dedications, as were molded terracottas.

III

Hardware and Tools

Hardware and tools are relatively few in number in comparison to the decorative pieces discussed in the preceding chapter. Several mundane utilitarian objects, such as hardware, utensils, tools, and implements were found. The discussion of these objects is divided into two parts: 1) hardware (**265-314**) and 2) implements and tools (**315-366**); in each section the objects are arranged alphabetically by type.

Hardware
265-314

The following entries provide a representative sample of the hardware, including attachments, bases or stands, chains, clamps, cotter pins, disks, hinges, nails, rivets, rods, and wire.

ATTACHMENTS
265-276

265 ATTACHMENT
Pl. 28   71-762   D12/13   A   3
L. 0.015; W. 0.011; Th. 0.003
 Bone. Plaque, roughly rectangular in shape. Cross-hatched decoration on both sides.

266 ATTACHMENT
Pl. 28   73-765   D12/E12   D   3
L. 0.019; W. 0.011; Th. 0.006
 Bone. Flat plaque, decorated on one side with incised guilloche. Broken at both ends.

267 ATTACHMENT
Pl. 28   76-448   F13/G13   1   2
L. 0.027; W. 0.012; Th. 0.004
 Ivory. Rectangular plaque with convex profile. Decorated with five grooves.

268 ATTACHMENTS (8)
Pl. 28   71-449   D12/13   4   3
D. 0.012; Th. 0.007
 Bronze. Eight disks joined together. Top and bottom disks decorated with embossed rosette pattern.

269 ATTACHMENTS (2)
Not ill.   71-470   D12/13   A   3
D. 0.012
 Bronze. Fragmentary disks, embossed with rosette pattern. Similar to **268**.

270 ATTACHMENTS (3)
Pl. 28   74-1141   F11   2   4
Max. L. 0.014
 Bronze foil. Three fragments decorated with embossed palmettes.

271 ATTACHMENT
Not ill.   74-275   D16/15   2   2
L. 0.038; W. 0.035
 Bronze foil. Undulating fragment. Nail hole in one corner.

272 ATTACHMENT
Not ill.   74-1127   D12/13   F   3
L. 0.021
 Bronze foil. Grooved on one side. No hole or sign of attachment, but possibly part of foil revetment.

273 ATTACHMENT
Pl. 28   74-852   C10/11   A   1
H. 0.036; D. (stem) 0.009
 Bronze. Rosette with thick stem. Large florid head made from folded foil.

274 ATTACHMENT
Pl. 28   76-1216   C11   1   1S
L. 0.035; W. 0.014; Th. 0.004
 Bronze. Rectangular plaque with a tang at one end. Decorated with cut-out design of two four-leaf clovers and two circles. Both top and bottom edge finished. One end broken.
 Roman.

275 ATTACHMENT
Not ill.   76-1213   C11   1   Stray
L. 0.016; W. 0.014; Th. 0.004
 Bronze. Rectangular plaque fragment similar to **274**. Broken at both short ends.
 Roman.

276 ATTACHMENT
Pl. 28   76-1218   C12/D12   G   2
L. 0.029; W. 0.014; Th. 0.004
   Bronze. Rectangular plaque similar to **274** and **275**. Openwork decoration consisting of seven holes. Tenon protrudes from one side.
   Roman.

Both the bone (**265-267**) and bronze (**268-276**) examples could have been applied to wooden furniture or to some type of cloth or leather garment.

The disks (**268**) are not pierced and therefore could not have been pinheads of the silver rosette disk (**234**). Now corroded together, the disks were probably once separate pieces. They may have been either for furniture or garment attachments and were possibly removed at some point and stacked together, perhaps when the original object was destroyed or damaged.

The fragments of bronze foil (**270-272**), sometimes pierced and with the actual brads and tacks preserved, were surely used as revetments for wooden furniture. **270** is a rare decorated example; more common are the plain types e.g., **271** and **272**.[1]

The unusual rosette (**273**) could have been attached to a metal vessel as easily as to wooden furniture.

274-276 are similar in size and decoration, and all are probably part of a larger piece. That they were attachments is clear from **276**, which still preserves a tenon. Most likely these plaques formed part of a slide bolt for a piece of furniture or a door, a type of arrangement common during the Roman period.[2]

BASE AND STAND
277 and 278

277 BASE
Pl. 28   71-178   E16   2   2
L. 0.060; W. 0.049; H. 0.039
   Iron. Fragment, preserving one corner. Originally square or rectangular. Breaks straight and very even, suggesting piece cut rather than broken. Leaf pattern on edge; recesses on top of base.
   Cast iron and therefore Roman in date.

278 STAND
Pl. 28   76-1207   C13/D13   1   7
L. of side 0.085; H. 0.024
   Bronze. Triangular, with three feet in form of lion's paws. Small skirt around all three sides. Edges decorated with cable pattern, skirt decorated with incised vertical lines (dentils?). Single hole in center of triangular top, perhaps for attachment of small statue or figurine.

Only one of each type were found. Both might have been used for small statuary.

CHAINS
279-281

279 CHAIN
Pl. 29   73-784   D10/11   C   C
L. 0.030; Th. 0.016
   Bronze. Braided wire.

280 CHAIN
Pl. 29; Fig. 5   76-1091   C12/13   F   5
L. 0.150; W. 0.032
   Iron. Two figure-eight bars of different sizes joined together by S-link.
   Archaic.

281 CHAIN
Pl. 29   71-347   D12/13   B   4
L. 0.250
   Iron. Massive. Four links: two large ring links and two smaller, longer figure-eight links. Similar to **280** but much heavier.
   Archaic.

The bronze chain (**279**) is a common type made by braiding wire; it is not very strong and may have been used decoratively. Very different are the two iron chains, which could date to as early as the Archaic period. A bar-and-ring iron chain is known from the First Artemisium at Cyrene;[3] a similar example was found at Tocra.[4] The chain links were forged rather than cast; therefore, the technology does not preclude an early date. On the basis of the Cyrenaican parallels, I would consider both iron chains (**280** and **281**) to be Archaic.

CLAMPS, FASTENERS, AND DOWELS
282-291

282 CLAMP
Pl. 29   71-460   D12/13   B   4
L. 0.041
   Bronze. Two plates joined by two rivets.

283 CLAMP
Pl. 29   71-523   E11   4   2
L. 0.049
   Lead. Two plates joined by two lead rivets. Fragment of pottery remains attached.

284 CLAMP
Not ill.   77-1194   C13   1   4a
L. 0.047
   Iron. Similar to **282** and **283**. One plate and part of two rivets preserved.

285 FASTENER
Pl. 29   74-383   C10/11   A   1
L. 0.044; W. 0.016
   Bronze. Rectangular sheet with fold line through middle and holes at either end. One rivet or tack head preserved. Perhaps a hinge for wooden furniture.

---
1. Not catalogued: 74-1103, 76-1210, 76-1222, 76-1223, 76-1228, 77-956, 78-243.
2. E.g., *Délos* 18, p. 250, fig. 289, pl. 79, 672. Jacopi, *Das Römerkastell Saalburg*, 473, fig. 75, pl. 45.

3. *AfrIt* 11 (1931) 199, fig. 23.
4. *Tocra* 1, 164, no. 71, fig. 77.

286 FASTENER
Pl. 29   74-1137   D12/13   F   3
L. 0.031; W. 0.012
Bronze. Strip with hole in one end rivet in other.

287 FASTENER
Pl. 30   76-326   C13/D13   1   7
L. 0.055; W. 0.016
Iron. Rectangular plate with rounded ends. Traces of rivets at each end.

288 CLAMP
Pl. 30   71-522   E11   3   3
L. 0.180; W. (ends) 0.060
Lead. Part of one corner missing.

289 STAPLE CLAMP
Pl. 30   74-307   C10/11   A beta   2
L. 0.064
Iron. Cased in lead. Broken.
Roman.

290 BAR
Pl. 30   77-458   D15/16   1   3
L. 0.016
Iron. Bar with cross piece. Probably a clamp or fastener.

291 TUBE
Pl. 30   74-384   F12   1   2
L. 0.023
Bronze. Splayed at one end and filled with lead. Possibly used as a clamp.

The clamps range from large architectural and structural types to small-scale pottery fasteners. Lead is the favorite metal, but iron and bronze clamps have also been found.

282-284 represent the most common clamp type made from two plates connected by rivets and probably used to mend pottery. Four more clamps of the same kind were found at the Demeter Sanctuary.[5] This style of pottery clamp, normally made of lead, was common throughout the Mediterranean from the Archaic to the end of the Roman period.[6]

The type of small clamp or fastener (**285-287**), a metal bar with nails or rivets at either end, is even simpler in design than **282-284**. Eleven other fasteners of this type have been found.[7]

Both the large fasteners (**288** and **289**) were probably used architecturally. **288** is a stone architecture clamp. **289** is undoubtedly half of a Roman staple clamp, a type also used for architectural purposes. The staple clamp would have spanned the joint between adjacent stone blocks. Each block would have had a lead filled hole to receive the clamp.

Two other bronze and lead objects, possibly clamps similar to **291**, were found at the Demeter Sanctuary.[8]

COTTER PINS
292 and 293

292 COTTER PIN
Pl. 30   73-1196   C15/16   1   4
L. 0.019
Bronze. Thin strip, rectangular in cross section.

293 COTTER PIN
Not ill.   77-1236   C13   1   4a
L. 0.021
Bronze. Similar to **292**. Broken at one end.

Altogether five cotter pins were found at the Cyrene Demeter Sanctuary.[9] All are similar and of a type common at most Classical sites.[10]

DISK
294

294 DISK
Pl. 30   74-1108   F9/10   A   2
D. 0.014; Th. 0.006
Lead. Thick, disk with large central hole.

294 was undoubtedly functional in nature.

FURNITURE HINGES, BOLTS, AND FITTINGS
295-302

295 HINGE
Not ill.   74-612   C10/11   A beta
L. 0.018; D. 0.021
Bone. Tube, with hole drilled transversally through both walls.
Roman.

296 HINGE
Pl. 30   76-743   Stray
L. 0.013; D. 0.019
Bone. Similar to **295**. Grooved on interior.
Roman.

297 PLAQUE HINGE
Pl. 30   71-337   E11   3   3
H. 0.03; Max. W. 0.03
Bronze. Bell-shaped plaque, rolled up to form tube at one end. Loop at opposite end.

298 HINGE
Pl. 30   74-341   E12/13   C   4
L. 0.031; W. 0.024; Th. 0.007
Bronze. Curved plate with two nail holes; hinge itself consists of heavy loop at top of plate. Made from two bronze sheets fused together.

---

5. Three bronze examples: 71-754, 74-820, 74-1017; and one example of lead: 74-14.

6. From an Archaic context: *Tocra* 1, 163, fig. 65, fig. 76, from Deposit III, level 7. From a Roman context: Francolise (Italy), Republican villa: M. Alwyn Cotton, *The Late Republican Villa at Posto, Francolise* (London 1979) fig. 18, no. 5.

7. Inventory nos. 73-405, 73-1182, 74-830, 74-274, 76-1208, 76-1239, 77-956, 77-1129, 77-1127, 73-1182, all of bronze; two iron examples: 76-912, 77-1201.

8. Similar to **291** but without the bronze casing: 73-147. A misshapen lead-filled bronze object was probably a similar clamp or dowel: 74-609.

9. Not catalogued: 73-1195, 74-1143, 77-1061.

10. E.g., five bronze examples from Lindos: *Lindos* I, 204, pl. 26, no. 636.

299 RING PULL
Not ill.   74-570   E12/13   E   2
L. (bolt) 0.024; D. (ring) 0.018
 Bronze. Ring attached to spike.

300 RING PULL
Not ill.   74-374   D16/17   2   3
D. (ring) 0.015
 Bronze. Similar ring and spike, but spike slightly longer than that of **299**.

301 RING BOLT
Pl. 31   76-1010   D12/13   F   4
L. 0.048
 Iron. Heavy ring attached to flat shaft-swivel. Swivel originally attached to wood by heavy nail.

302 RING BOLT?
Pl. 31; Fig. 6   73-1135   D12/E12   D   2-3
L. 0.096
 Iron. Spike, vertical eyehole in head, perhaps to accommodate ring or swivel hook.

295 and **296** may have served as hinges for small wooden containers. Similar bone hinges are known from the Republican villa at Francolise (Italy) and date to the second or first century B.C.[11] Our examples are surely Roman in date. On the other hand, two bone hinges from the Limenia deposit at Perachora are from a much earlier, Greek context.[12]

A triangular hinge similar to **297** is also known from a third century A.D. Roman context on Mallorca.[13]

298 is a much heavier and apparently more functional hinge than **297**. It would have been suitable for a heavy piece of furniture.[14]

299-301 are definitely examples of ring and bolt fittings. Both **299** and **300** are suitable for furniture; they were probably pulls for drawers or lids. **301** is undoubtedly heavy enough to have served as a door pull; it is certainly too large to be a furniture fitting. Less elaborate door pulls (ring and bolt types) are known from Roman contexts at Conimbriga in Portugal,[15] as well as from earlier contexts in both Greece[16] and Italy.[17]

NAILS AND SPIKES
303-308

303 TACK
Pl. 31   77-427   D15/16   1   2
L. 0.007
 Bronze. Small circular head.

304 NAIL
Pl. 31   77-960   D11/12   A
L. 0.037
 Bronze. Long shaft, medium-sized circular head.

305 NAIL
Pl. 31   74-270   E12/13   E   2
L. 0.025; D. (head) 0.010
 Bronze. Broad convex head.

306 NAIL
Pl. 31   73-359   SW sondage   1B   4
L. 0.023; D. (head) 0.019
 Bronze. Broad flat head.

307 SPIKE
Pl. 31   73-107   SW sondage   1B   3
L. 0.098; D. (head) 0.024
 Iron. Small head. Bent and corroded.

308 SPIKE
Pl. 31   73-196   SW sondage   1B   4
L. 0.053; D. (head) 0.024
 Iron. Broad head. Missing tip of shaft.

Approximately sixty bronze nails or tacks were found at the sanctuary. Four representative examples are catalogued here (**303-306**).

Although none are included here, iron nails are more common than bronze examples; more than eighty-five were unearthed. Most have a medium-sized head and a shaft approximately 0.025 long.

Occasionally, longer spikes with small heads are encountered. They were clearly made to penetrate wooden planks or beams.

RIVETS
309 and 310

309 RIVET
Pl. 31   71-450   D12/13   B   4
L. 0.018
 Bronze. Two large disk backers at either end.

310 RIVET
Pl. 31   74-1100   F-G 9/10   A   2
L. 0.010
 Lead. Large circular backers, one partially preserved.

Approximately a dozen rivets and rivet backers were found, some still imbedded in bronze sheeting.[18]

RODS AND BARS
311

311 ROD
Pl. 32   76-919   C11   1/2   3B
L. 0.114; Max. Th. 0.014
 Iron. Long. Slightly tapered at one end. Corroded.

Fifteen bronze and iron rods and bars were found. Most are broken and corroded making it impossible to

---

11. M. Alwyn Cotton, *The Late Republican Villa at Posto, Francolise* (London 1979) fig. 19, nos. 2-3.
12. *Perachora* 2, 447, A386-7, pl. 189.
13. Pollentia, Casa de los Dos Tesoros, habitation I.A. Arribas, M. Tarradell, and D. Woods, *Pollentia II, Excavaciones en sa portella Alcudia* (Mallorca, Excavaciones Arquelogicas en España no. 98, 1978).
14. Another bronze ring (74-1132) bears traces of an attachment of sheet bronze. It too may have served as a ring bolt.
15. *Conimbriga* 7, no. 243, pl. 50.
16. Two bronze examples: *Lindos* 1, 204, pl. 26, no. 637.
17. Montefortino: *MonAnt* 9 (1899) pl. 4, fig. 15.
18. Inventoried but not catalogued: 71-338, 71-423, 73-888, 73-1181, and 76-1249. All are bronze.

determine their original function. These are utilitarian objects, and clearly not dedications. Many of the rods could have served as architectural dowels or struts. One example has been catalogued here as representative of the type.

WIRE
312-314

312 WIRE
Pl. 32   74-973   D12/13   F   3
L. 0.019
Silver. Flattened in cross section.

313 WIRE
Pl. 32   76-1247   E13/14   1   1
D. 0.012
Bronze. Thin, curving to form loose ring.

314 WIRE
Pl. 32   76-1259   C12/D12   G   2
L. 0.025
Bronze. Two lengths twisted together.

Several fragments of bronze wire and a section of silver wire were found in the sanctuary. In most cases, the function of the wire is impossible to determine.

Three examples were chosen to illustrate the different techniques used to make the wire found at Cyrene: **312** was made by rolling and hammering, **314** was made by twisting two wires together to form a stronger strand or wire rope. **313** is exceptionally interesting because it bears the marks of having been pulled through a drawplate proving the use of the iron drawplate in the Roman period, the probable date of our wire judging by its context.

Implements and Tools
315-366

Implements and other utilitarian objects are not common; most examples are small utensils, namely, objects of personal nature such as spoons, styli, and needles. Also included are a number of bone and ivory handle fragments.

BRONZE IMPLEMENTS
315-318

315 IMPLEMENT
Pl. 32   71-468   D12/13   A   3
H. 0.037; W. 0.074; Th. 0.090
Bronze. Small implement with crescent-shaped blade, open center, and rectangular socket, now broken.

316 IMPLEMENT
Pl. 32   71-758   D12/13   3   4
H. 0.028; W. 0.032; Th. 0.011
Bronze. Small implement with short cylindrical blade, open center, and rectangular socket. Missing part of blade.

317 IMPLEMENT
Pl. 32   74-1140   D12/13   F   3
H. 0.041; W. 0.036; Th. 0.007
Bronze. Small implement. Short blade with two blunt projections, open center, cut-away rectangular socket. One corner of socket missing; traces of nail hole at this point.

318 AXE
Pl. 32   74-1020   D12/13   F   3
L. 0.031; W. 0.014; Th. 0.013
Bronze. Axe head with two triangular blades set at right angles to each other. Small central hafting hole.

Four bronze implements of uncertain type (**315-318**) were found within the Demeter Sanctuary. All are very small, seemingly more decorative than functional, and possibly ceremonial in nature.

315-317 are similar in having rectangular sockets openwork centers, and blades with two blunt projections. They resemble axes in form but the projections are blunt so that they may in fact imitate hammers. In any case, they are too small to have been functional. **318** is different in form, resembling a true pick-axe, although once again much smaller. An axe head from Calabria, inscribed with a dedication to Hera, is proof that such objects were suitable for dedication.[19]

BLADES
319-326

319 BLADE
Pl. 33   71-227   D12/13   B   4
L. 0.085; Max. W. 0.021; Th. 0.005
Iron. Curves to rounded point. Broken at wide end.

320 BLADE
Pl. 33   71-494   D12/13   A   3
L. 0.175; Max. W. 0.030; Th. 0.005
Iron. Long and tapered. Broken at both ends.

321 BLADE
Fig. 6   71-610   D12/13   A   3
L. 0.233; Max. W. 0.036; Th. 0.006
Iron. Long and tapered curving to a flat point. Two rivets for hafting at wide end.

---

19. Found in 1850 at S. Agata in Calabria: Walters, 27, no. 252.

322 BLADE
Fig. 6   76-345   C13/D13   1   6
L. 0.171
Long, thin and straight iron. Most of point preserved. Broken at wider end. Attached by corrosion to sherd of sixth century B.C. Corinthian pottery.

323 BLADE
Fig. 6   76-913   C13/D13   1   7
L. 0.060; Max. W. 0.011; Th. 0.004
Iron. Broken at both ends. Flat piece of ivory with bronze discoloration (part of an ivory and bronze haft?) attached at one end.

324 BLADE
Pl. 33   77-1063   C13   1   3a
L. 0.079; Max. W. 0.024; Th. 0.014
Iron. Flat, broken at both ends. Part of haft preserved: iron covered with wood, held in place by bronze ring secured by bronze rivet.

325 BLADE
Pl. 33   77-1192   C13   1   3a
L. 0.120; Max. W. 0.027; Th. 0.013
Iron. Flat, broken at narrow end and mended from two pieces. Two rivets for hafting at wider end.

326 BLADE
Fig. 6   77-1259   C13   1   3a
L. 0.087
Iron. Flat. Triangular point preserved.

Approximately thirty blades or blade fragments were found. All are of iron. A few representative and well-preserved examples are catalogued here.

Blades **319-323** are probably Archaic in date judging by their findspots. They should probably be considered dedications, given to the cult at a time when iron implements were valuable for their metal content. **324-326** may be later in date; and surely some of the thirty blades found in the sanctuary must have been lost, or discarded, or date from late in the sanctuary's history.

CHISELS
327-331

327 CHISEL
Fig. 6   71-516   D12/13   B   4
L. 0.11; Max. W. 0.035
Iron. Broad rectangular blade, narrow tang for hafting. Missing part of blade edge.

328 CHISEL
Pl. 34; Fig.   76-1001   D12/13   F   3
L. 0.134; W. 0.035; Th. 0.035
Iron. Blade rectangular in cross section and pointed. Handle cylindrical and solid enough to withstand impact. Possibly a chisel, but given weight and shape of blade, more likely some kind of wedge.

329 CHISEL
Fig. 7   77-1255   C13   1   3a
L. 0.199; W. 0.044; D. 0.045
Iron. Large, with broad flat blade. Solid cylindrical upper part shows signs of having been hammered.

330 CHISEL
Fig. 7   77-459   F13/G13   2   2
L. 0.063; W. 0.031
Iron. Small. Broad, short blade. Long thin tang or handle. Possibly an engraving tool.

331 CHISEL
Fig. 7   77-1261   C13   1   4a
L. 0.148; Max. W. 0.040
Iron. Flat blade tapering to square tang.

The five iron chisels that were found present a variety of types, ranging from the large, heavy chisel which might be better termed a wedge (**328**), through broad flat chisels suitable for rough working of stone or wood (**329** and **331**), and smaller chisels for finer woodworking or stonecarving (**327**), to the small chisel (**330**) which might be better termed an engraving tool. These are all tools that could have been used in the sanctuary for maintenance and upkeep of buildings or sanctuary decorations. It is less likely that they were dedications.

A Roman chisel from Conimbriga, also of iron, approximates the shape of **327** and **330**: broad flat blade with thin triangular tang for insertion into a wooden handle.[20] Such chisels were common during the Roman period.[21]

HOOKS
332 and 333

332 HOOK
Pl. 34   77-425   F13/G13   2   2
L. 0.061
Iron. Curving to sharp point. Shaft broken at top.

333 HOOK
Pl. 34   77-963   C13   1   2
L. 0.053
Lead. Square in cross section. Doubled over at top to form loop. Bottom of shaft curved to form shallow hook.

IMPLEMENTS OF BONE AND IVORY
334-344

334 HANDLE
Pl. 35   73-6   E12/13   C   2
L. 0.040; D. 0.011
Ivory. Cylindrical. Five bead-and-reel moldings. Pierced twice transversally.

---

20. *Conimbriga* 7, no. 25, pl. 2: called a "bedane" or cold chisel, suitable for stone carving.

21. E.g., *Délos* 18, 213, pl. 71,575.

335 STYLUS
Pl. 35; Fig. 7   73-1167   C15/16   1   2
L. 0.058; Max. W. 0.017; Th. 0.050
 Bone. Wide triangular bone blade with small cylindrical shaft. Blade pierced near narrow end. Shaft broken.
 Roman.

336 SPOON
Pl. 35; Fig. 7   74-306   C10/11   A (beta)   2
L. 0.055; D. of bowl 0.021
 Ivory. Long thin cylindrical handle, broken. Shallow bowl with 'omphalos.' Missing part of bowl.
 Roman.

337 HANDLE
Pl. 35   74-746   D11/12   1   4
L. 0.035; D. 0.012
 Ivory. Tubular, with multiple bead-and-reel moldings. Similar to **328**.

338 STYLUS
Pl. 35; Fig. 7   74-976   D12/13   F   3
L. 0.107; W. 0.020
 Bone. Wide flat blade. Pointed tapering shaft. See also **329**.
 Roman.

339 HANDLE
Pl. 35   76-733   C13/D13   2   2
L. 0.014; W. 0.009
 Ivory. Fragment, broken on three sides. Wide bead-and-reel moldings. Burnt.

340 HANDLE?
Pl. 35; Fig. 7   76-738   F13/G13   1   2
L. 0.024; W. 0.017; Th. 0.004
 Bone. Fragment. Probably part of cylindrical handle. Four transverse grooves near finished edge. Broken at one end, semi-circular in cross section. Hole (for attachment?).

341 CYLINDER
Pl. 35   77-406   F13/G13   2   2
L. 0.078; D. 0.034
 Bone. Wide collar at one end. Broken.

342 HANDLE
Pl. 35   77-1088   C13   1   4a
L. 0.035; D. 0.010
 Ivory. Cylindrical. Broken at one end. Finished end pierced for insert.

343 HANDLE
Pl. 35   78-241   F14/G14   1   1
L. 0.021; D. 0.008
 Ivory. Cylindrical. One end square in cross section. Grooved at square end. Hollow throughout.

344 IMPLEMENT
Pl. 35; Fig. 7   78-430   F15   1   2
L. 0.049
 Bone. Cylindrical shaft, flaring to rounded flat terminal with central hole. Broken at opposite end.

METAL IMPLEMENTS
345-351

345 HOOK
Pl. 36   73-358   SW sondage   1A   4
L. 0.011
 Bronze. Hollow tapered shaft (for insertion of wooden handle?) ending in small hook.

346 IMPLEMENT
Pl. 36   73-1180   D16/17   -   3
L. 0.095
 Bronze. Flat handle swelling to spatula-like terminal.

347 SPOON
Pl. 36   74-571   C10/11   A(B)   2
L. 0.076; Th. 0.005
 Bronze. Most of flat handle and small portion of bowl.
 Roman.

348 KOHL STICK
Pl. 36   77-533   D15/16   1   3
L. 0.108
 Bronze. Thin shaft with thickened rounded ends.

349 KOHL STICK
Not ill.   77-1188   C13   1   4b
L. 0.117; Th. 0.007
 Bronze. Rod with bulb at either end. Central portion decorated with reel moldings.
 Roman.

350 IMPLEMENT
Not ill.   76-154   C17   2   2
L. 0.066; W. (blade) 0.012
 Iron. Implement. Flat handle with triangular spatula-like blade.

351 HANDLE?
Pl. 36   73-1188   D12/E12   D   2
L. 0.022; W. 0.012; Th. 0.011
 Silver. Fragment of tube, broken at both ends. Filled with charcoal, probably remains of wooden handle.

Many of these implements are Roman in date, for example, the spoon (**336**), the styli (**335** and **338**), and many of the bone handles. Bone spoons are quite common as sanctuary dedications from the fifth century B.C. onward; they have been found at Delos,[22] Halae,[23] Tocra,[24] Lindos,[25] and at the Argive Heraeum,[26] to cite only a few examples. Even more common is the stylus; bone and metal examples abound at both Greek[27] and Italian[28] sites. A bone stylus from Perachora[29] is similar to **338** in having a wide flat blade or eraser. Another example from Perachora[30] has a pierced blade similar

---

22. *Délos* 18, 229, pl. 75, 603.
23. Bone spoon from temple area and acropolis: *Hesperia* 9 (1940) 426, fig. 78,20.
24. *Tocra* 2, F197, 122, pl. 53.
25. *Lindos* 1, no. 330.
26. *Argive Heraeum*, pl. 140.

27. Athens, Delphi, Eleusis, Argive Heraeum, Delos, Lindos, Sparta, Tanagra, and Thebes, as cited by Stubbings, *Perachora* 2, 446, with complete bibliography.
28. Marzabotto: *MonAnt* 1 (1890) 311, pl. 10, no. 7. Also, *MonAnt* 8 (1898) pl. 8, fig. 16.
29. *Perachora* 2, A336, A369, pl. 189.
30. Ibid., A358.

to **335**. Stubbings[31] has pointed out that the implement we call a "stylus" might also have been used as an ointment spreader, a pin, or a surgical implement. The bronze hook with shaft insert (**345**) is paralleled exactly at Olympia and Lindos.[32] The date of kohl stick **348** cannot be determined precisely from either its context or type. It is almost certainly pre-Roman and probably dates to the earliest use of the sanctuary.[33] Kohl stick **349**, on the other hand, is of a variety typical during the Roman period.[34] **351** probably belonged to a rather ornate type of implement. A silver sheet rolled to form a tube and with a hole near one end is known from the Classical period at Tocra.[35]

NEEDLES
352-356

352 NEEDLE
Not ill. 76-330 C13/D13 1 6
L. 0.062
Iron. Shaft tapers to point at one end, curves to small hook or eye at other end.

353 NEEDLE
Not ill. 76-1193 C15/16 1 2
L. 0.058
Iron. Similar to **346**.

354 NEEDLE
Not ill. 74-824 C10/11 A (B) 3
L. 0.070
Bronze. Bent. Small eye.

355 NEEDLE
Pl. 36 74-829 D10/11 balk A-C (ext) 1
L. 0.076
Bronze. Complete. Small eye.

356 NEEDLE
Pl. 36 77-1119 D15/16 2 2
L. 0.0125; Th. 0.005
Bone. Flattened end is pierced by rectangular eye, other end tapers to fine point.

Two iron implements (**352** and **353**) were probably needles. About a dozen bronze needles were found (**354** and **355** are the catalogued examples).[36] Bronze needles are also known from the First Artemisium at Cyrene[37] and are common dedications at Greek sanctuaries.

Four bone needles were uncovered, the one complete example (**356**) is included here.[38]

ADZE, HAMMER, AND PICK-AXE
357-359

357 ADZE
Not ill. 71-520 E2 1 5
L. 0.105; Max. W. (blade) 0.022
Iron. Flat triangular blade set at sharp angle to socket.

358 PICK-AXE
Pl. 36 71-521 D12/13 B 4
L. 0.285
Iron. Two blades on either side of socket hole. Short blade cylindrical and hammer-like. Long blade triangular and set at oblique angle (like blade of **357**).
Probably Roman.

359 HAMMER
Pl. 37; Fig. 7 77-1220 C13 1 4a
L. 0.166; W. 0.029
Iron. Shaped like a modern geologist's hammer. Short hammer end, square in cross section, and longer chisel-like blade.
Probably Roman.

The iron pick-axe (**358**) and hammer (**359**) are probably Roman in date. Both are standard types, paralleled at Delos.[39]

SICKLE
360

360 SICKLE
Pl. 37 76-441 C13/D13 1 7
L. 0.098
Iron. Fragment, missing point and haft.

SPINDLE WHORLS
361-364

361 SPINDLE WHORL
Pl. 37 77-1216 C13 1 4a
L. 0.012; D. 0.025
Dark gritty stone. Truncated cone.

---

31. Stubbings, ibid., 446.
32. *Lindos* 1, 136, no. 343, pl. 13. *Olympia* 4, pl. 23, no. 422.
33. For similar kohl sticks: J. Vandier d'Abbadie, *Les objets de toilette égyptiens au Musée du Louvre* (Editions des Musées Nationaux, 1972, 159-161, nos. 711, 712 and 717. Also, Petrie, *Objects*, pl. 23, nos. 41 and 42.
34. Petrie, *Objects*, pl. 23, no. 48, for example.

35. *Tocra* 2, F176, pl. 51. According to Boardman "...conceivably part of temple furniture..." (p. 1010).
36. Not catalogued: 73-854A and B, 73-1087, 74-577, 74-826, 74-827, 74-856, and 74-1129.
37. *AfrIt* 4 (1931) 197, fig. 21, no. 18.
38. Fragmentary bone needles: 73-781, 74-778, 78-240.
39. *Délos* 18, 213, pl. 70, no. 565.

362 SPINDLE WHORL
Not ill.   73-77   F12/13   C   2
H. 0.034
   Terracotta. Truncated cone. Orange fabric.

363 SPINDLE WHORL
Pl. 37   78-612   F14/G14   1   3
H. 0.032; Max. D. 0.036
   Terracotta. Beehive-shaped. Incised lines around circumference.

364 SPINDLE WHORL
Pl. 37   77-574   F13/G13   2   2
L. 0.026; D. 0.030
   Terracotta. Biconical. Deep vertical grooves at junction of two cones.

These are probably beads, but are catalogued here under the more common designation of "spindle whorl." Stone whorls are common at the Demeter Sanctuary at Knossos,[40] and are known in various media from most Greek sanctuaries.[41]

STRAINERS
365 and 366

365 STRAINER
Not ill.   76-1235   F13/G13   1   2
L. 0.044; W. 0.038; Th. 0.004
   Bronze. Fragments of thick bronze sheet punched with numerous holes.

366 STRAINER
Pl. 37   78-756   F14/G14   1   3
L. 0.038; W. 0.030; Th. 0.002
   Iron. Fragment.

In addition to the preceding strainers (**365** and **366**), the bronze frog (**17**) allows the reconstruction of an elaborate Etruscan funnel-strainer, an object far more sumptuous. The duck handle (**402**) is also worth noting here, since it seems to have formed part of a second elaborate strainer.

Summary

Large tools are rare at the sanctuary, and only one, the sickle (**360**), is agricultural in nature. The pick (**358**), adze (**357**), hammer (**359**), and chisels (**327-331**) would probably have been used for the daily upkeep of the sanctuary buildings and sculptures. It is also possible that some of these tools were dedications, perhaps offered because of the value of their metal; however, because of their relative scarcity here at Cyrene and at other Greek sanctuaries, that possibility seems less likely. Much of the hardware was certainly functional in nature, for instance the hinges (**295-298**), bolts (**299-302**), and clamps (**282-291**), although some of the smaller hardware might have formed part of larger, dedicatory objects, for example the small bone hinges (**295** and **296**, from wooden boxes or furniture?), the ring bolts (**299-302**), and the lead clamps (**283** and **285**) from pottery or stone vases. Many of the small implements were undoubtedly offerings, and are documented as such at other sanctuaries: the needles, spindle whorls, styli, and possibly some of the blades. Generally, the hardware and tools provide little chronological or contextual evidence. The finds are scattered around the site, and most of them are too generic in nature to allow for even rough dating.

---

40. *Knossos*, 120-121, nos. 42-52, pl. 80.
41. E.g., *Aegina*, 119, fig. 8 (beehive-shaped), and 119, fig. 7 (conical). *Corinth* 12, 175, pl. 77, no. 1214. A clay conical "weight" from Knossos, considered Protogeometric: *Knossos* 117, no. 19. For a varied assortment of spindle whorls of stone, terracotta, glass and bone: *Lindos* 1, nos. 348-402, pls. 13-14.

IV

Weapons

Few weapons were found and only three types are included in this small group of objects: arrowheads, sling pellets, and spear points.

ARROWHEADS
367-372

The seven bronze arrowheads from the Demeter Sanctuary are of several types; socketed, with triple blade and spur (Type A); socketed, with triple blade and barbs (Type B); socketed, with double blade and spur (Type C); and tanged with double blade and barbs (Type D).

TYPE A (Ill. 11)

367 ARROWHEAD
Not ill.   69-317   D13 (Area 2)   1   5
L. 0.035
  Bronze. Socketed, with transverse hafting hole, triple blade, and spur.

368 ARROWHEAD
Not ill.   73-885   D12/E12   D   2
L. 0.032
  Bronze. Socketed, with triple blade and spur.

Illustration 11

TYPE B (Ill. 12)

369 ARROWHEAD
Not ill.   73-1223   C15/16   1   5
L. 0.038
  Bronze. Socketed, with triple blade and barbs.

Illustration 12

TYPE C (Ill. 13)

370 ARROWHEAD
Not ill.   76-1211   C12/13   1   3
L. 0.019
  Bronze. Socketed, with double blade and spur.

Illustration 13

TYPE D (Ill. 14)

371 ARROWHEAD
Pl. 38   73-913   C15/16   1   1
L. 0.051
  Bronze. Tanged, with double blade and barbs.

372 ARROWHEAD
Not ill.   77-1130   D15/16   2   2
L. 0.043
  Bronze. Tanged, with double blade and barbs.

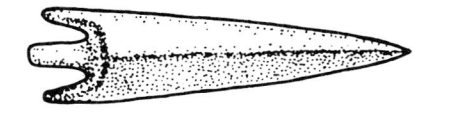

Illustration 14

The three triple-bladed examples (**367-369**) seem to be earlier in date than the tanged, double-bladed ones (**371** and **372**). They are common at most Greek sites from the Classical period onward,[1] for instance at Chios, Delos, Olympia, Lindos, and Aegina.[2]

The three other arrowheads (**370-372**) are of later date. Two are of bronze, and are tanged, double bladed, and barbed; one (**370**) is socketed. These types of arrowhead were common in the Hellenistic and Roman periods, although examples are known from Cyprus and Sicily as early as the fifth and fourth centuries B.C.[3] The type may be derived from Anatolia.[4] Double-bladed arrowheads are common at many Greek sites:

---

1. Richter, *Bronzes*, 407. Snodgrass, *Armour*, 146.
2. Chios: *Emporio*, 226, nos. 405-6. *Délos* 18, pl. 69. Olympia: *OlForsch* 1, 160f. *Lindos* 1, pl. 23, 606-7. *Aegina*, pl. 117,42.

---

3. Richter, *Bronzes*, 404. Snodgrass, *Armour*, 153.
4. *Emporio*, 226. *Boğazköy* 1, 31, 59, pls. 11,24,28. *BSA* 53-54 (1958-59) 131.

Lindos, Olympia, Delphi, Delos, Chios, and Aegina.[5] Iron examples are known from the first Artemisium at Cyrene.[6]

SLING PELLETS
373-375

373　SLING PELLET
Pl. 38　　74-1102　　F12　-　1
D. 0.014
  Lead. Slightly flattened on two sides.

374　SLING PELLET
Not ill.　　76-1012　　D12　balk　2
D. 0.018
  Lead. Similar to **373**.

375　SLING PELLET?
Pl. 38　　77-28　　D14/E14　1　2
D. 0.017
  Bronze. Solid ball.

Five lead pellets were found;[7] all are round or oval in shape. They most likely served as ammunition for slings.

SPEARHEAD POINTS
376-381

376　SPEARHEAD
Pl. 38　　77-1200　　F13/G13　1　2
L. 0.112
  Iron. Socketed, with leaf-shaped blade. Missing part of blade.

377　SPEARHEAD
Not ill.　　77-1257　　C13　1　4a
L. 0.119
  Iron. Similar to **376**. Missing most of blade. No midrib.

378　SPEARHEAD
Not ill.　　77-1202　　C13　1　4a
L. 0.098
  Iron. Socketed. Diamond-shaped blade, square in cross section tapering to fine point. Missing part of socket.

379　SPEARHEAD
Not ill.　　77-1256　　C13　1　3a
L. 0.159
  Iron. Socketed, with diamond-shaped blade. Square in cross section. Similar to **378**.

380　SPEARHEAD
Not ill.　　76-346　　F13/G13　1　2
L. 0.134
  Iron. Similar to **378**.

381　SPEARHEAD
Pl. 38; Fig. 7　　not inv.　　F9/10　G9/10
L. 0.207
  Iron. Long. Similar to **378**.

Eight spearhead points were discovered, all made of iron.[8] There are two types. The first type is socketed and has a broad, leaf-shaped blade (**376** and **377**). An example of this type of spearhead is known from Roman Portugal.[9] The second type (**378-381**) of spearhead is long, bolt-shaped and tapers to a thin point.

Summary

In all, only twenty-one objects from the sanctuary can be identified as weapons. None is precisely datable, and as a whole, the weapons do not come from any one specific context, although three of the spearheads were found not far apart in Area C13, Trench 1. Weapons were not uncommon dedications at Greek and Roman sanctuaries, but they may be considered male dedications. Therefore, their rarity at the Demeter Sanctuary may be due to reasons of cult. Weapons form, by far, the smallest class of objects from the excavation.

---

5. *Lindos* 1, pl. 23, 608. *Olympia* 4, pl. 64, nos. 1083-90. *Delphi* 5, 97, fig. 337, no. 484, fig. 338. *Délos* 18, 209, fig. 240. *Emporio*, 226, nos. 399-404. *Aegina*, 117, 45 (two-bladed, but socketed).
6. *AfrIt* 4 (1931) 197, no. 17, fig. 21.

7. Not catalogued: 71-567, 74-1099, 74-1107.
8. Two examples are too fragmentary to classify: 71-274 (D12/13,B,4) and 76-917 (F/G13,1,2).
9. *Conimbriga* pl. 17, no. 2.

V

Vessels

Included in this chapter are vessels in a variety of media, **382-473**. Many are fragmentary and complete profiles were almost never found. It is worth noting here that objects classified elsewhere in this study should be considered in conjunction with these vessels. The bronze lions (**23** and **24**) or the frog (**17**) probably served as attachments for metal vessels. The bases or stands (**277** and **278**), and strainers (**365** and **366**) which, although not strictly speaking containers and hence discussed in the chapter on hardware, are typologically related to the metal vases. The vessels are catalogued and discussed by medium: faience, metal, stone, ostrich egg, and *Tridacna* shell.

Faience Vessels
382-389

382 ARYBALLOS
Not ill.   77-728   D15/16   1   3
H. 0.030; W. 0.046
  Faience. Body fragment of globular aryballos. Decorated with reticulate incision. White core with blue glaze.
  East Greek.
  Archaic, 575-550 B.C.

383 ARYBALLOS
Pl. 39   76-734   F13/G13   1   3
H. 0.057; W. 0.042; Th. 0.013
  Faience. Body fragment of globular aryballos. Lower part decorated with reticulate incision; upper part (shoulder) undecorated. White core with traces of green glaze.
  East Greek.
  Archaic, 575-550 B.C.

384 ARYBALLOS
Pl. 39   77-677   D15/16   1   3
D. 0.033; H. 0.015
  Faience. Rim fragment and part of handle. White core with blue glaze.
  East Greek.
  Archaic, 575-550 B.C.

385 ARYBALLOS
Pl. 39   78-833   F11/G11   wall cleaning
D. 0.038; H. 0.016
  Faience. Rim fragment. Similar to **384**. Cream core with traces of green glaze.
  East Greek.
  Archaic, 575-500 B.C.

386 ARYBALLOS?
Pl. 39   76-525   C13/D13   1   7
Largest fragments 0.022 by 0.019
  Faience. Seven fragments of a vessel decorated with ribbing. Gray core with white glaze.
  East Greek.
  Archaic, 575-550 B.C.

387 LENTOID JAR
Pl. 39   76-527   F13/G13   1   2
H. 0.060; L. 0.061
  Faience. Two fragments of vessel with wide lenticular body and narrow neck. Shoulder area has three superimposed registers: a row of tongues, a row of dots, and another row of tongues. Traces of brown paint on decorated area.
  Egyptian or Egyptianizing.
  7th to 6th century B.C.

388 FLASK?
Pl. 39   78-829   F11/G11   wall cleaning
H. 0.034; D. (rim) 0.027
  Faience. Cylindrical neck with flaring rim. Traces of dark glaze or paint. From a flask?
  East Greek.
  Archaic.

389 FLASK
Pl. 39   78-649   1   1   3
H. 0.036
  Faience. Cylindrical neck fragment, probably from a flask. Two incised lines on rim. At base, squatting figure with hands raised to mouth, probably an ape. Little modeling of figure. Yellow core with no glaze preserved.
  East Greek?
  Archaic.

All the faience vessels are fragmentary. Most of the fragments are decorated with an incised, reticulate pattern and are from aryballoi.[1]

---

1. Inventoried but not catalogued: 74-611, 74-747, 76-526, 76-975, 76-977, 77-561 (all with reticulate decoration); 77-1109, 77-1171, 77-1239 (undecorated body fragments); and a number of fragments from faience vessels of unidentifiable shape: 71-193, 73-880, 77-230, 78-853, 78-854.

The globular aryballoi (**382-385**) belong to a group of vases with reticulate decoration of East Greek, probably Rhodian, manufacture. They are discussed by Webb and comprise her Group I.[2] All are comparable to East Greek clay aryballoi of similar shape and decoration. The faience examples have been dated by Webb to just after 575 B.C., on the basis of a comparable series of faience aryballoi decorated with the cartouches of Egyptian pharaohs.[3] Faience globular aryballoi are found in Archaic contexts in both Greece (almost exclusively on the islands) and Italy. In the Cyrenaica aryballoi with reticulate decoration are known from Tocra; one example is from a stratified context dating to ca. 590-565 B.C.[4]

386 was probably also a globular aryballos. The ribbed decoration places it in Webb's Group II, of East Greek manufacture and datable, like her Group I, to the second quarter of the sixth century B.C.[5]

387 includes fragments from a lentoid jar of Egyptian or Egyptianizing type, a class of vase known as a New Year's gourd or vessel that was probably made in Egypt[6] to hold Nile water, the "eau de jouvence" well attested in literary sources of later date. This type of vase was first manufactured in Egypt during the New Kingdom, but production continued well into the first millennium B.C. The Iron Age examples have elaborate plastic attachments on the neck and incised and painted decoration on the upper body and neck.[7] Lentoid jars of this type gained a wide distribution throughout the Mediterranean, Palestine, Cyprus, and Italy,[8] although not many examples have been found in Greece.[9] They are normally found in seventh-sixth century B.C. contexts.

Both **388** and **389** may be of Archaic East Greek manufacture. As noted in the discussion of the bronze ape (**25**), the motif of an ape holding a hand to its mouth has a wide diffusion in Greece and Etruria during the Archaic period.

Metal Vases
390-402

VESSELS
390-393

390 VESSEL
Pl. 39   73-801   E11/12   1   2
L. (rim) 0.025; H. 0.022
Bronze. Rim fragment of small vessel. Steep vertical sides. Straight rim decorated with a row of indented dots.

391 VESSEL
Pl. 39   74-1080   F11   2   2
L. 0.022; H. 0.016
Bronze. Fragment of vessel with right-angled, overhanging lip. Undecorated.

392 BOWL
Pl. 39   74-1089   D10/11   balk   1
L. 0.054; H. 0.013; Th. (rim) 0.003
Bronze. Rim fragment of shallow bowl. Small horizontal rim.

393 BOWL
Pl. 39   78-433   F14/G14   1   2
L. 0.018; H. 0.013; Th. (rim) 0.003
Bronze. Fragment of bowl. High vertical rim decorated with horizontal ridge.

Although fragments of sheet metal are not uncommon, recognizable metal vessel fragments are rare and restricted to a few rim fragments from small bronze vessels.[10] **390-393** provide a sample of the types from the excavation.

HANDLES
394-402

394 OMEGA HANDLE
Pl. 40   71-452   D11/12   A   3
W. (loop) 0.018; Th. (wire) 0.002
Bronze. Small.

395 OMEGA HANDLE
Not ill.   74-1026   C14   1   3
W. (loop) 0.040
Bronze.

396 OMEGA HANDLE
Not ill.   76-1249   D16/E16   1   1
L. 0.055
Bronze. Bent, but complete.

397 OMEGA HANDLE
Not ill.   77-430   D16/E16   1   2
W. 0.030
Bronze. Missing the small loop at one end.

398 HANDLE
Pl. 40   73-1096   C15/16   1   4
L. 0.128; Th. 0.016
Bronze. Thick horizontal handle, circular in cross section. Oval terminal at either end. Knob in center.

399 HANDLE
Pl. 40   77-271   D15/16   1   3
L. 0.025
Bronze. Fragment of spool handle.

---

2. Webb, 109-12, nos. 703-739. Also discussed by von Bissing, *Zeit und Herkunft* (1941) 18f, 79f.
3. Webb, 108, 114-115.
4. *Tocra* 1, 165, nos. 87-99. *Tocra* 2, 85, F162.
5. Webb, 112-113, nos. 740-750.
6. Called Naukratite by von Bissing (supra n. 2) 7 and by J. Vercoutter, *Les objets égyptiens et égyptisants du mobilier funeraire carthaginois* (1945), 11 n. 7.

7. E. Largarce and J. Leclant in *Excavations at Kition* II, *Objets égyptiens et égyptisants* (Nicosia 1974), 243.
8. M.E. Aubet, "Vasos egipcios en la necropolis de Etruria y Cartago," in *Simposio de colonizaciones* (Barcelona-Ampurias 1971: Barcelona 1974). Webb, 162 n. 15.
9. Kameiros: *ClRh* 4, 312, fig. 346; pp. 318-319, figs. 353-354, no. 36 (Tomb 177). Chios: *Emporio* 241-242, pl. 96, no. 592. Hogarth, *Ephesus* 208, pl. 44,6.
10. Inventoried but not catalogued: 74-1083, 74-1139, 76-1222, 76-1238, 77-1002, and 77-1249, all fragments of bronze vessels.

400 HANDLE
Pl. 40   73-1184   D16/17   1   3
L. 0.149
Bronze. Thin strip handle, rectangular in cross section. Edges of flat lower portion curve inward to form tube at top.

401 HANDLE
Not ill.   76-1123   C13/D13   1   7
L. 0.039; W. 0.020; Th. 0.002
Bronze. Fragment of flat handle. Traces of repoussé decoration.

402 DUCK HANDLE
Pl. 40   73-1186   D16/17   -   3
H. 0.148; Max. W. (shaft) 0.027; L. (bird's head) 0.041
Bronze. Flat handle terminating in duck or swan head. Lower part forms cut-out palmette. Incised decoration on outer surface of palmette terminal (lyre volute with upper and lower palmette) and on inner surface of upper section of handle (lyre volute with palmette terminals). Traces of three rivets preserved.
Magna Graecia.
5th century B.C.

394-397 are examples of the most common type of handle for metal vessels, a single loop made from thin bronze wire and shaped like an omega. They would have been fitted into bronze rings attached to small vessels. Omega handles of this type have been found on Lindos.[11]

402 is part of a large group of vertical handles with duck finials used for ladles and strainers. The earliest duck handles are Etruscan (seventh-sixth century B.C.), based upon Orientalizing models.[12] By the fifth century, duck-handled strainers and ladles were produced in Magna Graecia, and somewhat later in Greece,[13] remaining popular through the Roman period.[14] **402** is very close to a handle from a tomb at Cavallino (Lecce).[15] The Lecce example has the same cut-out palmette attachment with three rivets, the upper part of the handle and of the duck head are of exactly the same form, and there is also incised decoration in the form of lyre volutes and palmettes on both the interior and exterior of the handle. The Lecce handle can be dated to the early fifth century by its context; it and the Cyrene handle are from the same workshop, and probably of South Italian manufacture. Also attributable to this source of production is a handle in the Louvre with incised decoration,[16] and a handle from the second Artemisium at Cyrene.[17]

Because of the angle of the attachment terminal and the parallels with the Lecce strainer, we can safely say that our handle was part of a strainer rather than a ladle. Strainers are often found paired with a ladle in tomb contexts, and it is tempting to hypothesize that our strainer and the Artemisium handle formed part of a set of utensils imported from South Italy and dedicated at different Cyrenaic sanctuaries. That such ladles and strainers made good dedications or were actually used in cult practices at sanctuaries is known from other examples which bear dedicatory inscriptions.[18] In any case, **402** is of probable South Italian manufacture and of certain early fifth century date.

Stone Vessels
403-463

Of the many stone vessels which have been excavated most are closed shapes, almost exclusively alabaster alabastra.

ALABASTRA
403-413

403 ALABASTRON
Fig. 8   69-285/71-212   E11   1   2
D. 0.072; H. 0.101
White yellow-veined alabaster. Fragment preserving all of rounded base and profile of vessel's lower half.

404 ALABASTRON
Fig. 8   71-16/73-364   E11   1   1; D11/12   A   1;
E11/12   1   2
H. 0.066; D. (rim) 0.07; Max. D. (body) 0.014
White stone with brown veins. Four joining fragments from three different areas, preserving shoulder and most of neck.

405 ALABASTRON
Pl. 41; Fig. 8   71-436   E11   1   3
H. 0.045
Yellow alabaster. Fragment, preserving shoulder, neck, and much of lip.

---

11. *Lindos* 1, 219, no. 712-713, pl. 29.

12. The earliest example is from the Bernardini Tomb at Palestrina and thus of secure mid-seventh century date, see *MAAR* 3 (1919) 49, no. 30, pl. 26. For a sixth century duck-handled ladle see *Arte e civiltà degli Etruschi* (Turin 1967), no. 65, from Trevignano, Museo Nazionale di Villa Giulia Inv. no. TR7.

13. M. Zuffa, *StEtr* 28 (1960) 174. P.J. Riis, *From the Collection of the Ny Carlsberg Glyptothek* 2 (1938), 156. For the Greek duck handles, see *Olynthos* 10, pl. 50, nos. 613-617, 622.

14. For Roman examples, e.g., S. Tassinari, *Le vaseille de bronze romaine et provinciale au Musée des Antiquités Nationale* (Paris, 1975), nos. 41-43, pl. 10. A splendid example in silver, now in the Metropolitan Museum, is from Tivoli: F. Baratte, *Archéologie* 28 (1978) 73, 111.

15. P. Arias, *RömMitt* 76 (1969) 3, pl. 1.3, 4.3.

16. A. DeRidder, *Les bronzes antiques du Louvre* 2 (Paris, 1915) pl. 108, no. 3081.

17. L. Pernier, *AfrIt* 4 (1931) 214, fig. 40 on p. 219. Found with black-glazed and red-figure pottery and thus in a fifth century context. Almost identical in size (L. 0.147 m.) to our example.

18. A strainer found at Olympia bears the inscription: ἱαρον τὸ Διὸσ λεδρινον. See *ArchDelt* 19 (1964) 169, pl. 173 a and b.

406 ALABASTRON
Pl. 41   73-414   E11/12 Pit 3
D. 0.030; H. 0.016
White alabaster. Fragment, preserving neck and lip.

407 ALABASTRON
Fig. 8   76-988   F13/G13 1 2
D. 0.035; H. 0.087
Alabaster. Fragment, preserving rounded base and more than half of profile.

408 ALABASTRON
Pl. 41; Fig. 8   77-75/77-429   F13/G13 2 2
H. 0.124; D. 0.049
Alabaster, stained brown. Reconstructed from numerous fragments. Complete profile preserved: rounded base tapering up to sloping shoulder, vertical neck, and horizontal lip. Large lug on shoulder.

409 ALABASTRON
Pl. 41   77-108   F13/G13 2 2
H. 0.113; D. (est.) 0.048
Yellow-veined alabaster. Fragment, preserving base and partial profile, including lug on shoulder.

410 ALABASTRON
Fig. 8   77-154   F13/G13 2 2
H. 0.089
White alabaster. Fragment, preserving most of vessel lower half.

411 ALABASTRON
Fig. 8   77-307   F13/G13 2 2
H. 0.063; D. 0.042
Alabaster. Fragment, preserving shoulder, neck, and horizontal rim. One lug on shoulder.

412 ALABASTRON
Pl. 41   78-171   F14/G14 1 2
H. 0.051; D. (est.) 0.06
Yellow alabaster. Fragment, preserving part of shoulder and one lug.

413 ALABASTRON
Not ill.   71-805   E12 1 6
H. 0.089; W. 0.040
Alabaster. Small body fragment.

More than seventy-five additional alabastron fragments were found.[19] These represent at least forty separate vases. The alabastra range from small, almost miniature vases no larger than about ten centimeters in height, to large, thick-walled vessels such as **403**. All have the characteristic rounded base, vertical neck, and horizontal lip, and many have traces of lugs on the shoulder. The lugs, sometimes pierced, were no doubt used to suspend the vessels by means of a cord or thong.[20]

Many of our alabastra are of the curved-profile, round-bottomed type popular in the sixth and early fifth centuries B.C.,[21] and may be of Egyptian manufacture. Two fragments of alabaster alabastra, considered to be Egyptianizing, were excavated at Tocra.[22] Alabaster alabastra are common in tombs, both at Naukratis, where they are found along with alabaster bowls,[23] and at Alexandria.[24] They seem to have been exported from Egypt to East Greece, where they are common tomb offerings.[25] Alabastra are found in funerary contexts at Cyrene,[26] and are also depicted in Cyrenaic statuary,[27] held by aniconic figures, for example. Because of their funerary association, alabaster alabastra may have been considered appropriate offerings at the sanctuary; alternatively, they might have figured in the ritual aspects of sanctuary life.

LEKYTHOS
414

414 LEKYTHOS
Pl. 42   71-432   D11/12 A 3
H. 0.035; D. (rim) 0.034
Marble. Thin neck, with flaring conical lip. Trace of lug or handle at juncture of neck and lip. Probably a lekythos.

LEUTROPHOROS
415

415 LEUTROPHOROS
Not ill.   76-646   D16/17 2 3
H. 0.038; Th. (lip) 0.018
White marble. Tall narrow neck, with flaring concave sides and two-stepped lip. Probably a leutrophoros.

VASE
416

416 VASE
Pl. 42; Fig. 9   78-852   F11/G11 wall cleaning
H. 0.036; D. rim (est.) 0.045
Marble. Neck fragment, with carved relief decoration. Archaic?

---

19. Neck fragments: 71-537, 73-388, 76-214, 76-985, 77-851, 78-148, 78-246, 78-388, and five examples not inventoried. Base fragments: 71-65, 71-291, 71-437, 71-714, 71-805, 74-938, 76-986, 76-987, 76-1090, 77-155, 77-576, 78-162, 78-349, 78-351, 78-352, 78-359, 78-488, 78-755, 78-760, and three examples not inventoried. Body fragments: 74-648, 77-110, 77-225, 77-944, 77-1092, 78-96, 78-349, 78-352, 78-470, 78-488, 78-760, and twenty-eight examples not inventoried.

20. D. Amyx, *Hesperia* 27 (1958) 213.

21. *JdI* 87 (1972) 259.

22. *Tocra* 1, no. 98, two examples, very fragmentary and not illustrated. p. 166: "Egyptian alabastra like 98 are fairly common on

Greek sites especially in East Greece. There was a factory of them at Naukratis."

23. *Naukratis* 2, 29.

24. E. Breccia, *La necropoli di Suabti* (Cairo 1912), v. 2, pl. 60, no. 139.

25. E.g., *ClRh* 4, 107-108, fig. 96; 133, fig. 126. *ClRh* 5-6, 446, fig. 1.

26. East Necropolis, Cyrene, Tomb M5: A. Rowe, *Cyrenaican Expedition of the University of Manchester 1955, 1956, 1957* (Manchester 1959), pl. 27c.

27. Ibid., pl. 27a.

CUPS, BOWLS, OR PYXIDES
417-429

417 CUP
Pl. 42; Fig. 9   71-236   E11   2   2
H. 0.056; D. (at top) 0.070
  Medium-grained white marble. Foot and lower body of high-footed cup. Hollow flaring foot. Half-round molding marks juncture of foot and cup.

418 CUP
Pl. 42; Fig. 9   73-412   E11/12   1   2
H. 0.091; D. 0.075
  Fine-grained white marble. Foot and body of cup. Body has vertical, slightly concave sides. Bottom edge of body decorated with two horizontal grooves. Broken at lip. Hollow foot, slightly flaring, broken. Hawk's beak molding marks juncture of foot and body.

419 BOWL OR PYXIS
Pl. 42; Fig. 9   71-439   D11   1   2
H. 0.041; W. 0.035; Th. 0.007
  White marble. Rim and body fragment of small vessel with steep curving sides. Inset rim with slight overhang.

420 BOWL OR PYXIS
Pl. 42; Fig. 9   74-646   D16/17   2   3
H. 0.055; W. 0.038; Th. 0.018
  Marble. Rim and body fragment. Vertical wall, inset rim with sharp horizontal overhang.

421 CUP OR BOWL
Pl. 42; Fig. 9   74-946   F11   2   3
L. 0.074; H. 0.035
  Rim and body fragment. Marble. Rim has three sharply cut moldings on outside.

422 BOWL OR PYXIS
Pl. 42; Fig. 9   76-1017   D12   Balk   2
L. 0.053; H. 0.038
  Fine-grained white marble. Rim and body fragment. Curved sides and double offset lip with sharp horizontal overhang. Lathe-turned.

423 CUP OR PYXIS
Fig. 9   not inv.   D12/E12   D   3
H. 0.034
  Stone. Rim and body fragment. Steep vertical sides, inset rim with slight overhang.

424 PYXIS
Pl. 42; Fig. 10   71-39   E11   1   2
H. 0.058; D. (rim, est.) 0.09
  Medium-grained white marble. Fragment, preserving entire profile. Slightly convex side; inset lip with slight overhang, segmented foot.
  5th century B.C.

425 PYXIS
Fig. 10   71-538   E11   2   2
L. 0.055; D. (rim, est.) 0.09-0.10
  White marble. Fragment of foot and body. Similar to **424**, but segmented foot smaller.
  5th century B.C.

426 PYXIS
Pl. 42; Fig. 10   78-832   F11/G11   wall cleaning
L. 0.041; W. 0.025; Th. 0.009
  Marble. Fragment of small pyxis, preserving horizontal foot.

427 PYXIS
Pl. 42; Fig. 10   not inv.   E11/12   slope   1
H. 0.013; L. 0.057
  White marble. Fragment of small pyxis, preserving foot and base as well as beginning of vertical wall.

428 PYXIS
Fig. 10   not inv.   E12   1   5
H. 0.021
  Marble. Fragment, preserving vertical foot.

429 BOWL PYXIS
Pl. 43   71-712   E10/11 (Area 1)   1   1
D. (rim) 0.14; H. 0.05
  White marble. Thin stem at base, now broken. Rim of bowl forks and flares inward as well as outward.
  4th century B.C.

Stone cups are rare. Only two stemmed cups (**417** and **418**) could be identified. Two pyxides (**424** and **425**) are paralleled exactly by a stone pyxis from a fifth century B.C. tomb at Kameiros, Rhodes.[28] The elaborate bowl pyxis (**429**) would have had a high stemmed foot. An alabaster pyxis of similar shape, with inset bowl and outflaring rim, was found in a fourth century B.C. tomb on Rhodes.[29]

LIDS
430-432

430 LID
Pl. 43; Fig. 10   71-238   E11   3   2
L. 0.065; D. (est.) 0.12-0.14
  Marble. Thin circular lid with heavy molded lip.

431 LID
Pl. 43   78-828   F11/G11   W.C.
L. 0.029
  Marble. Three fragments of thin circular lid.

432 LID
Pl. 43   71-440   E11   3   2
L. 0.030; W. 0.025
  Marble. Fragment, preserving rim and part of vertical flange. Broken on interior.

430-432 might have covered any of vessels **419-428**.

BASINS
433-446

433 BASIN
Pl. 43; Fig. 10   71-62   E11   1   2
L. 0.085; W. 0.055
  Marble. Base fragment of shallow basin. Rectangular foot ribbed and sharply set off from body.

---

28. Tomb 27. Found with red-figure pottery of the first half of the fifth century B.C. *ClRh* 4, 108, fig. 26.

29. Tomb 17. *ClRh* 6-7, 465, figs. 18-19.

434 BASIN
Pl. 43   71-690   D12/13   A   4
L. 0.175; W. 0.165
Marble. Rim, body, and foot fragment of shallow basin. Similar to **433**.

435 BASIN
Pl. 43   71-67   F12   1   1
L. 0.175; W. 0.090
Marble. Fragment of a shallow basin, preserving part of rim and body. Horizontal rim.

436 BASIN
Pl. 43   71-438   E11   2   2
L. 0.095; W. 0.065; D. (est.) 0.22
White alabaster with broad white veins. Rim and body fragment of shallow basin with gently curving sides and horizontal rim.

437 BASIN
Fig. 11   77-524   E12/F12   balk   1
L. 0.013; H. 0.029
Rim and body fragment of shallow alabaster. Horizontal rim. Similar to **436**.

438 BASIN
Not ill.   78-810   F11/G11   1   2
L. 0.139; D. (est.) 0.023
White alabaster, stained brown. Fragment of shallow basin, preserving over a third of base, body, and small section of rim. Flat base, short sloping sides, large horizontal rim.

439 BASIN
Pl. 44   77-463   F13/G13   2   2
L. 0.172; H. 0.047
White marble. Thick, with shallow sides.

440 BASIN
Not ill.   77-467/77-1068   C13   1   1
L. 0.031; D. (est.) 0.040
Dark volcanic stone. Large and shallow, with triangular spout. Possibly a quern.

441 BASIN
Pl. 44   77-1221   F13/G13   2   2
L. 0.118; W. 0.085; Th. 0.032
White marble. Shallow, with flat bottom and gently sloping sides. Outside circumference decorated with two drafted horizontal grooves.

442 BASIN
Pl. 44   77-1222   F13/G13   2   2
L. 0.154; H. 0.040
White marble. Heavy and shallow. Similar to **441** but with slightly different profile. Same double drafted line. Mended in antiquity with lead clamp.

443 BASIN
Pl. 44   78-106   F14/G14   Test   2
L. 0.064
White marble. Rim fragment of shallow basin. Similar to **441**.

444 BASIN
Pl. 44; Fig. 11   78-650   G16/H16   1   1
L. 0.064

Alabaster. Fragment, large horizontal rim and small section of wall. Originally rectangular or square in shape.
Roman.

445 BASIN
Pl. 45   78-786   F11/G11   wall cleaning
L. 0.086; H. (basin) 0.044
Broad-veined alabaster, stained brown. Shallow rectangular or square basin. Fragment of rim, wall, and base. Flat bottom, straight wall, and wide horizontal rim. Similar to **444**.
Roman.

446 BASIN
Pl. 45   78-811   F11/G11   1   2
L. 0.108; H. (basin) 0.032
Alabaster. Shallow rectangular or square basin. Similar to **444**. Part of rim, body, and base.
Roman.

Second only to alabastra in popularity at the Demeter Sanctuary were shallow basins or bowls (**433-446**), perhaps because, like the alabastra, they may have played a role in sanctuary ritual. **435-438** are all circular with broad horizontal rims.

GRINDING INSTRUMENTS
447-450

447 SADDLE QUERN
Pl. 45   77-1118   C13   1   4a
L. 0.54; W. 0.17; Th. 0.085
Gray, igneous stone. Complete.
Probably Archaic.

448 SADDLE QUERN
Not ill.   79-18   Stray 1974
L. 0.105; W. 0.081; Th. 0.04
Limestone. Fragment, preserving only one end.
Probably Archaic.

449 SADDLE QUERN
Not ill.   71-74   F10/12 (N Terrace)   III   I
L. 0.33; W. 0.17; Th. 0.095
Gray, igneous stone (similar to **447**). Oval, with flat underside.
Probably Archaic.

450 GRINDER?
Pl. 45   78-1177   F14/G14   test   2
D. 0.096
Limestone. Large round sea stone, worn smooth. Possibly used as grinder.

Although many of the shallow basins could have been used as querns as well as receptacles, **447-450** provide actual evidence for what are certainly grinding instruments.

Greek to Roman saddle querns and other grinding instruments have been studied by White; the saddle querns (**447-449**) correspond to his Type I.A.a and are probably of Archaic date.[30]

---
30. D. White, *AJA* 67 (1963) 199-206. A few other fragments of what seem to have been querns have also been found, including a fragment of a possible rotary mill.

PESTLES
451 and 452

451 PESTLE
Pl. 45   76-633   C13/D13   2   1
L. 0.129; H. 0.086; Max. Th. 0.056
Marble. Nail and knuckle well defined. Chipped at one end. Hellenistic-Roman.

452 PESTLE?
Pl. 46   73-150   SW sondage   1B   3
L. 0.68; W. 0.040; Th. 0.031
Marble. Oblong. Similar to finger end of finger pestle, but no articulation of nail or finger joint.

Marble finger pestles similar to **451** are usually considered Roman. Finger pestles were extremely common throughout the Roman world, from England to Mesopotamia,[31] and are, for example, extremely common in the Roman levels at Delos.[32] They may have been in use earlier, however, even before the Hellenistic period. An example from Lindos, inscribed with a dedication to Athena, is dated to the fourth century B.C.,[33] and a finger pestle from Corinth was found in a cistern with objects dating to the fifth century B.C.[34] Clearly, although normally Roman, finger pestles can date to as early as the Hellenistic period. The example from Lindos provides good evidence for their use as dedications in Greek sanctuaries. In the Cyrenaica, finger pestles have also been found at Tocra.[35]

OFFERING TABLES OR TRAYS
453-456

453 OFFERING TABLE
Pl. 46   78-702   F12/G12   1
H. 0.069; D. (pres.) 0.0143
Alabaster. Table or offering stand. Flat top and cylindrical base. Top and base broken around all edges. Highly polished. Roman.

454 TRAY
Pl. 46   71/101/73-1290   E11   3   2; E11/E12   1   1
L. 0.195; W. 0.023; H. (base) 0.040. D. (depressions) 0.065-0.075
Alabaster. Rectangular, with five circular depressions and raised edge. Pedestal base with everted rim. Mended from four fragments and missing two corners of tray.
Roman.

455 TRAY?
Pl. 46   73-272   E11/12   slope   1
D. 0.060; H. 0.032
Alabaster. Pedestal base with everted rim. Similar to base of **454**.

456 TRAY
Pl. 47   71-210   F10   1   1
L. 0.10
Marble. Fragment of circular tray or platter, preserving rim and two shallow, circular depressions.

Offering tables or trays with depressions carved in the top surface are not uncommon at Hellenistic and Roman sites,[36] but I know of no exact parallels for our examples.

MEASURING STONE
457

457 MEASURING STONE
Not ill.   78-715   F13/14   1   1
L. 0.209; W. 0.025; Th. 0.044
Fine-grained marble. Flat slab. Upper and lower edges finished, side edges broken, roughly chiseled on underside. Two horizontal grooves divide top surface into three sections. Middle section pierced by three funnel-shaped holes of different sizes. Holes taper towards underside. Center hole fully preserved; other holes only partially preserved.

This measuring stone with three graduated funnel holes is only partially preserved, but was undoubtedly intended for small measures. A number of measuring stones from Delos have similarly graduated small openings.[37]

FEET
458-460

458 HIGH FOOT
Pl. 47; Fig. 11   74-343   C10/11   A (beta)   2
H. 0.028; D. 0.048
Limestone. Fragment of vase. Cylindrical pedestal foot, horizontal molding, and circular inset. Broken near bottom of foot.

459 FOOT?
Pl. 47; Fig. 11   74-647   F12   1   1
H. 0.059; D. 0.032
White marble. Solid cylindrical stem, flaring out horizontally. Broken at bottom. Possibly foot of vase.

460 FOOT
Pl. 47; Fig. 11   78-836   F11/G11   1   2
H. 0.040; Max. D. 0.036
White marble. Stem or foot of vessel. Solid cylinder, flaring horizontally. Broken at bottom.

---

31. H.L. Cleasby, *AJA* 40 (1936) 116. The distribution is also discussed by Deonna, *Délos* 18, 118.
32. *Délos* 18, 118, pl. 47.
33. *Lindos* 1, 748, no. 3229, pl. 152.
34. *Corinth* 12, 192.
35. *Tocra* 2, 122, nos. F205-6 (level 3), pl. 53.

36. For an offering tray with five circular cavities but otherwise not similar to our examples: *Délos* 18, 61, pl. 27. See also Deonna, *BCH* 58 (1934) 10.

37. For example, *Délos* 18, pl. 62, nos. 517, 521. Smaller rectangular tables or measuring stones similar to **457** but with differently shaped openings are also known: *Délos* 18, pl. 61, no. 513.

PALETTES
461 and 462

461 PALETTE
Pl. 47   71-165   F16   1   2
Block: L. 0.14; H. 0.036; W. 0.089; Lozenge: L. 0.111; W. 0.041; Th. 0.013
Plaster. Rectangular block with recess on top side. Flat lozenge fits into inset. Traces of red color on one side of lozenge.

462 PALETTE
Not ill.   73-310   F13/G13   1   2
L. 0.043; H. 0.023; W. 0.050
Slate. Rectangular, with raised edges. Broken, only one corner preserved. Short foot on underside of corner.

The two recessed blocks (**461** and **462**) were most likely used as palettes for grinding, preparing, or applying cosmetics. The plaster lozenge found within the recess of **461** is undoubtedly an applicator for some kind of powdered pigment, and traces of a reddish color can still be seen on one side. Both palettes are probably of Hellenistic or Roman date. The engraved *Tridacna* shells (**465-473**) are earlier examples of cosmetic palettes from the site.

MORTAR?
463

463 MORTAR?
Pl. 47   74-525   E12/13   E   1/2
L. 0.112; W. 0.164; Th. 0.062
Limestone. Square or rectangular with circular depression in center for grinding. Broken.

This vessel with a depression on one side probably served as a mortar.

Ostrich Eggshells
464

464 OSTRICH EGG CUP?
Not ill.   77-1232   C13   1   4a
L. 0.062
Ostrich eggshell. Large fragment, mended from six pieces. Undecorated.

Thirty-one fragments of ostrich eggshells were found.[38] They are probably all from vessels. The Cyrene ostrich eggshell fragments are from an Archaic context. All of them are undecorated. As at Tocra,[39] where they were found in Roman contexts, the Cyrene ostrich eggs were probably sawn in half and used as cups. Undecorated ostrich eggs are common at Greek sanctuaries,[40] but decorated examples are very rare.[41] Decorated ostrich eggs are also known from Orientalizing contexts in Etruria[42] and from Punic sites.[43]

Tridacna Shells
465-473

A number of undecorated examples have been found of which only two (**465** and **466**) are catalogued here.[44] Seven decorated fragments (**467-473**) were also found in the Demeter Sanctuary.

---

38. Inventoried but not catalogued: 78-159, 78-160, 78-161, 78-179, 78-217, 78-221, 78-222, 78-223, 78-245, and twenty-one other fragments which were not inventoried.
39. *Tocra* 2, F195. Level 2/3. "It was clear that the shells had been chipped into halves for use as cups." (p. 122) For use of shells as cups: B. Laufer, *Ostrich Egg-Shell Cups of Mesopotamia and the Ostrich in Ancient and Modern Times*, Field Museum of Natural History, Anthropology Leaflet no. 23 (Chicago 1923). For recent discussion: D. Reese, "The Kition Ostrich Eggshells," Appendix VIII(B) in V. Karageorghis, *Excavations at Kition* V, Part 2 (Nicosia 1985).
40. E.g., *Lindos* 1, 182, no. 563 (sixty-nine fragments). *Argive Heraeum* 2, 353.
41. *Naucratis* 1, 145, pl. 20.15. Chios: *Emporio* 243, no. 604, pl. 97.
42. M. Torelli, *StEtr* 33 (1965) 330-365. More recently: A. Rathje, "Oriental Imports in Etruria," in D. and F. Ridgway, *Italy Before the Romans* (New York 1977).
43. M. Astruc, *Cahiers de Byrsa* 6 (1956) 29-56. Idem, *Archivo de preistorica Levantina* 6 (1957) 47-112.
44. 76-970, 78-459, and six other pieces.

UNDECORATED *TRIDACNA*
465 and 466

465 *TRIDACNA*
Not ill.   76-213   E12/F12   Balk   2
L. 0.111
Shell. Fragment of *Tridacna squamosa* shell mantle. Undecorated.

466 *TRIDACNA*
Not ill.   78-632   F12/G12   vault A   surface
L. (larger piece) 0.082
Shell. Two fragments of *Tridacna squamosa*. Unworked.

ENGRAVED *TRIDACNA*
467-473

467 ENGRAVED *TRIDACNA*
Pl. 48   69-219   E10/11 (Area 1)   1   3
H. 0.075; W 0.080
White, *First Report*, 102, pl. XLIII,b.
Shell. Fragment, preserving part of right mantle. Exterior surface engraved: part of siren's hair, feathering of wing, and, in center of back, a partially preserved palmette.
7th century B.C.

468 ENGRAVED *TRIDACNA*
Pl. 48   71-657   F15   3   2
L. 0.107; W. 0.047
White, *Second Report*, 178, pl. XCIV,g,h. *Expedition* 17 (1975) 13, figs. 5, 6.
Shell. Large fragment, preserving head and right wing of siren. Exterior surfaced engraved; features of face, hair, and feathering of wing; lotus bud tendril on edge of wing (mantle). Underside undecorated.
7th century B.C.

469 ENGRAVED *TRIDACNA*
Pl. 49   71-789   C15/16   1   4
L. 0.065; W. 0.045
Shell. Fragment preserving part of mantle. Engraved on both interior and exterior surfaces. Exterior: feathering and part of siren's hair. Interior: lotus bud chain and most of seated sphinx, missing only head. Interior decorated on lower edge of mantle only.
7th century B.C.

470 ENGRAVED *TRIDACNA*
Not ill.   73-1136   C15/16   1   4
L. 0.078
Shell. Fragment preserving small section of mantle. Worn and weathered. Traces of engraving, mainly feathering. Pierced by lead plug.
7th century B.C.

471 ENGRAVED *TRIDACNA*
Pl. 49   74-750   C10/11   A (beta)   4
L. 0.060; W. 0.050
Shell. Fragment preserving part of mantle. Decorated with wing and back of siren and part of sphinx. Engraved feathering (siren) and haunch (cross-hatched circle), leg, and lower wing (sphinx).
7th century B.C.

472 ENGRAVED *TRIDACNA*
Pl. 49   77-207   F13/G13   2   2
L. 0.105; W. 0.055
Shell. Fragment preserving part of wing. Engraved feathering on exterior. Carved lotus and palmette chain on inside surface of bottom edge.

473 ENGRAVED *TRIDACNA*
Pl. 49   78-300   D14/E14   2   1
L. 0.047; W. 0.027
Shell. Fragment. Engraved feathering and lotus bud frieze. Worn and broken on all sides.
7th century B.C.

Engraved *Tridacna* shells have been found in most parts of the Mediterranean and Near East. The corpus now numbers well over one hundred examples from Mesopotamia, the Levant, Egypt, Ionia, the Greek mainland and islands, and even Etruria (a single example).[45] The origin of this widespread group of luxury objects is much discussed. Most recently, Stucky has stressed the Hittite and North Syrian elements of the decoration,[46] but the alternate theory of a Phoenician workshop still seems viable. More work will have to be done on the definition of North Syrian, Phoenician, and Phoenicianizing styles and iconography before the question can be resolved. Now, as the corpus of engraved *Tridacnas* grows larger, it becomes increasingly likely that we are dealing with more than one workshop. We are certainly not dealing with a single "cargo" of engraved shells and similar exotica traded from east to west along linear trade routes.[47]

The Cyrene *Tridacna* shells seem to be related to other decorated examples found at Greek island sites. **467**, with the palmette in the center of the siren's back, seems comparable to examples found on Samos.[48] The hair and face treatment of the siren on **468** is paralleled by another example from Samos.[49] The sphinx engraved on **471** is closely paralleled by a sphinx engraved on the interior of a shell said to be from the coast of Asia Minor.[50]

Decorated *Tridacna* shells seem to have been used as containers for cosmetics.[51] (It is worth noting again that two plaster trays from the sanctuary [**461** and **462**] might also have been used to hold cosmetics). The form of the carved shell was even imitated in Near Eastern stone palettes.[52] The Cyrene shells do not provide much

---

45. R. Stucky, *Dédalo* 19 (1974) 1-170. More recently: P. Amiet, "Tridacnes trouvés à Suse," *RAAO* 1976: 185-186. A. Rathje, "Oriental Imports into Iron Age Italy and Objects of the Orientalizing Period," paper presented at the Sixth British Museum Classical Colloquium, *Aspects of Italic Culture*, December 1982 (in press, Rome, Giorgio Bretschneider). D. Reese, "A New Tridacna Shell from Kish," *JNES*, in press.

46. R. Stucky, *Dédalo* 19 (1974) 86-89.

47. Ibid., 101.

48. Ibid., nos. 51-52.

49. Ibid., no. 56.

50. Ibid., no. 67.

51. Ibid., 96-99 with full bibliography.

52. C.M. Bennet, *Antiquity* 41 (1967) 197-201. Idem, *Levant* 9 (1977) 1-10.

new information about these objects, with the exception of **470**, which is pierced by a lead plug. The plug does not seem to be decorative, and is probably part of a lead clamp. The shell was broken just at this point, and the ancient mend shows that this shell, at least, was a prized object used over a period of time.

As a group, engraved *Tridacna* shells can now be securely dated to the seventh century B.C., with a date in the first half of the seventh century being most likely.[53] These shells, however, were durable objects which could have been used over a fairly long period of time. Given the traditional date of 631 B.C. for the founding of Cyrene, it seems possible that these shells were brought to Cyrene by the first colonists and dedicated at the Demeter Sanctuary as heirlooms. As we have seen, shells in general were considered particularly apt offerings at the sanctuary, and, in fact, *Tridacna* shells are normally found in Greece as dedications at sanctuaries of goddesses. Stucky has suggested that the shells were dedicated along with their contents, and that "the Greeks associated the contents of the shell with the female."[54]

The decorated shells from the Sanctuary of Demeter at Cyrene are an important addition to the corpus of engraved *Tridacnas*, and are significant because of their context and number. The seven examples, along with the single previously known example from the agora in Cyrene,[55] form one of the largest known groups, second only to the fourteen shells found on Samos and the nine shells from Lindos. The Cyrene find will thus radically affect any conclusions that can be reached from the distribution pattern of the finds.

Summary

The vessels form the most varied assemblage of small finds from the Demeter Sanctuary. They are made of faience, bronze, stone (including alabaster, basalt, marble, and a gray, igneous stone), possibly ostrich eggshell, shell, and even plaster. The forms include alabastra, aryballoi, bowls, basins, cups, lekythoi, lentoid vases, lids, plates, pyxides, trays, and even a number of shapes which are strictly speaking not vessels but implements: pestles, mortars, grinders, ladles, strainers, and even a measuring stone.

Chronologically, these vessels cover the entire duration of the sanctuary's history. Some of the pieces are clearly early, for instance the engraved *Tridacna* shells used as cosmetic palettes (**467-473**) are of seventh century date. The ostrich eggshell fragments may also be early, judging by the context of **464**, but ostrich eggshell vessels remained popular well into the Roman period. The faience aryballoi (**382-386**) can be dated fairly precisely to the second quarter of the sixth century, and the faience lentoid jar (**387**) is also of Archaic date. In sharp contrast to other classes of objects from the site, the stone vases (**403-463**) remained popular into the fourth century B.C. Two pyxides (**424** and **425**) can be dated to the fifth century, and a bowl-pyxis (**429**) has good fourth century parallels. Many of the alabastra (**403-413**) seem to be of relatively early date as well (sixth to fourth century B.C.). The bronze strainer, **402**, is also of Classical date.

The stone vessels are generally far harder to date precisely than the faience vases, but it is likely that many of them date to the Hellenistic and Roman periods. The offering trays (**453-456**), pestles (**451** and **452**), basins (**441-446**), and possibly some of the smaller stone vases seem likely candidates for dating to the later periods of the sanctuary.

Given the fragmentary nature of the assemblage, quantitative conclusions are dangerous, but given the wide variety of shapes represented and the large numbers of uncatalogued body fragments, vessels seem to have been popular dedications at the site; faience vases during the Archaic period, stone vases and vessels from the sixth century onward. If the evidence for ceramic vases and stone lamps discussed in other studies is also taken into account, then the vases as a whole overwhelmingly outnumber any other type of small find from the Demeter Sanctuary. In any case, the pestles, grinders, and mortars—implements and vessels used to process the fruit of the harvest—seem particularly apt finds for a Demeter Sanctuary. Many of the vessels, however, might not have been dedications but might have been used during the daily activities of the sanctuary.

Most of the vessels discussed in this chapter were imported to Cyrene, mainly from the eastern Mediterranean or Egypt. Marble and alabaster are not native materials to the Cyrenaica. The alabaster vases (**403-**

---

53. R. Stucky, *Dèdalo* 19 (1974) 90-99 and Rathje (see above, n. 45). The example from the agora in Cyrene (infra n. 55) has been used as evidence for a lower date, given a presumed *terminus post quem* of 631 B.C. for all the objects from the site. This terminus, however, need not apply if the shells are explained as heirlooms.

54. R. Stucky, *Dèdalo* 19 (1974) 96-99.
55. Ibid., no. 36. S. Stucchi, *BdA* 44 (1959).

413) are probably of Egyptian manufacture, as are most of the other stone vessels. At least one of the faience vases (**387**) is also Egyptian. The ostrich eggshell fragments (**464**) also derive from an African source. The origin of the *Tridacna* shells (**465-473**) is more of a problem. Although we cannot pinpoint the site where they were engraved, it is clear that they are imports from the east, perhaps brought to Cyrene by Ionian traders.

A smaller number of vases is of East Greek manufacture, certainly the faience aryballoi (**382-386**), and perhaps a few of the marble vases (**424**, **425**, and **429**) that are closely paralleled in Rhodian tombs of the Classical period. It is not entirely clear, however, whether these vases are of East Greek manufacture or if both the Cyrenaican and Rhodian examples are Egyptian imports. The bronze strainer with duck handle (**402**) is unusual in that it is an import from Magna Graecia, and thus a rare example of a trade connection between Italy and Cyrene, as is a similar ladle from the second Artemisium at Cyrene.

VI

Miscellaneous Finds

Included in this chapter are all objects which could not be easily grouped in the preceding sections (474-506). Within this diversified group of objects the largest group, numerically, is the weights.

Loom Weights
474-491

474 WEIGHT
Not ill.   76-397   C13/D13   1   7
H. 0.025
Stone. Spherical. Drilled through center.

475 WEIGHT
Pl. 50   76-980   C13/D13   2   1
L. 0.026; W. 0.026; Th. 0.025
Granite. Cube. Drilled for suspension.

476 WEIGHT
Pl. 50   77-597   F13/G13   2   2
L. 0.035; W. 0.030; Th. 0.017
Soft, pumice-like stone. Triangular. Drilled.

477 WEIGHT
Pl. 50   77-777   E12/F12   balk   3
L. 0.034; W. 0.023; Th. 0.006
Limestone. Oval. Drilled longitudinally.

478 WEIGHT
Pl. 50   74-273   D12/13   D   surface
H. 0.016; Max. D. 0.023
Bronze. Loaf-shaped.

479 WEIGHT
Pl. 50   76-1147   C12/13   1   3
D. 0.022
Bronze. Sphere with solid collar. Pierced on one side of collar. Very heavy, possibly filled with lead.

480 WEIGHT
Pl. 50   76-446   C11   2   1
H. 0.043; W. 0.018
Lead. Pyramidal. No suspension hole or loop.

PYRAMIDAL LOOM WEIGHTS
481-483

TYPE A (Ill. 15)

481 WEIGHT
Pl. 50   73-754   C15/16   1   4
H. 0.067
Terracotta. Pyramidal, tall. No markings. Dark orange fabric.

482 WEIGHT
Pl. 50   77-423   F13/G13   2   2
H. 0.051
Terracotta. Pyramidal. Marked with three vertical lines capped by horizontal line. Light brown fabric.

483 WEIGHT
Pl. 50   77-1021   F13/G13   1   wall sondage
H. 0.039
Terracotta. Pyramidal, small. Pierced twice. Burned orange fabric.

Illustration 15

SHELL-SHAPED LOOM WEIGHTS
484-486

TYPE B (Ill. 16)

484 LOOM WEIGHT
Not ill.   73-1206   E   10   balk
H. 0.053; W. 0.047; Th. 0.024
Terracotta. Trapezoidal, finger-made depressions on each flat side. Hole through center. Marked with two parallel lines on one side. Light orange fabric.

485 LOOM WEIGHT
Pl. 51   76-293   F13/G13   1   2
H. 0.050; W. 0.047; Th. 0.033
Terracotta. Shell-shaped. Similar to **484**. No markings. Light brown fabric.

486 LOOM WEIGHT
Pl. 51   77-1023   F13/G13   2   2
H. 0.054; W. 0.046; Th. 0.037
Terracotta. Shell-shaped. No depressions on flat sides and no markings. Brown fabric.

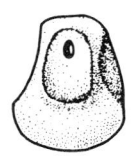

Illustration 16

DISK-SHAPED LOOM WEIGHTS
487-489

TYPE C (Ill. 17)

487 LOOM WEIGHT
Pl. 51   71-571   D12/13   B   2
D. 0.039
  Terracotta. Disk-shaped. Hole through center. Orange fabric.

488 LOOM WEIGHT
Pl. 51   73-762   C15/16   1   3
D. 0.038
  Terracotta. Similar to **487**.

489 LOOM WEIGHT
Not ill.   76-283   C13/D13   1   4
D. 0.032
  Terracotta. Disk-shaped. Much more spherical profile than **487**.

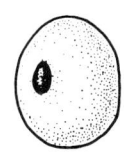

Illustration 17

CONICAL/BICONICAL LOOM WEIGHTS
490 and 491

490 LOOM WEIGHT
Pl. 51   76-151   C11   1   2
H. 0.073; Max. D. 0.040
  Terracotta. Conical. Pierced at top. Coarse buff fabric.

491 LOOM WEIGHT
Not ill.   73-1127   C15/16   1   3
H. 0.045; Max. D. 0.055; D. (base) 0.025
  Terracotta. Roughly biconical. Pierced at top. Flat, circular base. Coarse light orange fabric.

474-477 are all drilled and probably functioned as loom weights. A number of beach stones, some of them drilled, were also found.[1]

Terracotta weights, undoubtedly loom weights, were found in much greater abundance than other types of weights. There are three major types (see Ills. 15-17): Type A (Ill. 15) is pyramidal, Type B (Ill. 16) is shell-shaped, and Type C (Ill. 17) is disk-shaped. Twenty-eight loom weights of Type A were found,[2] represented here by **481-483**. Only seven examples of Type B were uncovered at the sanctuary[3] (**484-486** are representative), and seventeen examples of Type C were found[4] of which **487-489** are catalogued. A biconical loom weight from Knossos, similar to **491**, has been called a Cretan type[5] and comes from a Hellenistic context.

Astragals
492-501

BRONZE ASTRAGALS
492-499

492 ASTRAGAL
Pl. 52   71-514   D12/13   B   4
L. 0.024
  Bronze. Originally pierced near top edge. Hole plugged in antiquity and suspension loop fused onto bone.

493 ASTRAGAL
Not ill.   71-794   E11   3   3
L. 0.025
  Bronze. Long omega-shaped suspension loop. Complete.

494 ASTRAGAL
Not ill.   73-831   E12/13   C   4
L. 0.015
  Bronze. Hole through center.

495 ASTRAGAL
Pl. 52   74-847   D12/13   F   3
L. 0.028
  Bronze. Omega-shaped suspension loop, similar to **493**.

496 ASTRAGAL
Not ill.   74-1014   D12/13   F   3
L. 0.026
  Bronze. Hole through center. Burnt and corroded.

497 ASTRAGAL
Not ill.   74-1142   D12/13   F   3
L. 0.030
  Bronze. Omega-shaped suspension loop. Badly chipped and corroded. Found with three bronze collar beads.

498 ASTRAGAL
Pl. 52   77-1001   C13   1   3b
L. 0.019
  Bronze. Similar to **493**, but missing suspension loop.

499 ASTRAGAL
Not ill.   77-1052   C13   1   4b
L. 0.024
  Bronze. Hole through one end. Complete.

---

1. Other pierced stones, possibly weights: 76-17, 76-780, 78-301, 76-397, 76-983.
2. Not catalogued: 69-300, 71-143, 71-569, 72-702, 73-136, 73-176, 73-755, 73-1085, 74-124, 74-215, 74-614, 74-687, 76-151, 76-201, 76-470, 76-471, 76-473, 77-239, 77-424, 77-467, 77-571, 77-589, 77-1021, 77-1022, 78-611, 78-684.
3. Not catalogued: 69-332, 71-354, 73-1065, 74-688.
4. Not catalogued: 69-102, 71-153, 71-540, 73-85, 74-131, 74-707, 76-156, 76-197, 76-921, 77-237, 77-243, 77-597, 77-900, 78-768.
5. *Knossos*, 122, no. 54, pl. 80, from the Hellenistic levels at the Royal Road, Knossos.

BONE ASTRAGALS
500 and 501

500 ASTRAGAL
Not ill.   77-279   F13/G13   2   2
L. 0.033
Bone. Pierced. Stained brown and chipped.

501 ASTRAGAL
Pl. 52   77-996   F13/G13   2   2
L. 0.036
Bone. Similar to **500**. Pierced.

Both real astragals (**500** and **501**) and bronze imitations (**492-499**) were popular at the Demeter Sanctuary. Both bronze and real astragals seem to have had a number of uses in antiquity. Most often they were used as gaming pieces,[6] but they also seem to have been used for divination,[7] much in the way that any game of chance can be used to tell fortunes, foresee the future, etc. They were also popular in antiquity as votives,[8] perhaps because of their association with divination. Votive astragals of bronze can be quite large and are sometimes inscribed.[9] Astragals were also used as weights,[10] as tomb offerings,[11] and as ornaments on vases.[12] Our astragals were probably used as beads;[13] they are either pierced or have suspension loops; one astragal (**497**) was found with beads, suggesting that it had been strung on a necklace. Astragals, because of their use as gaming pieces, and because of their association with divination (and with the afterlife?), would have made appropriate amulets or talismans. Chronologically, astragals range from the Bronze Age through the Roman period. In antiquity, imitation astragals were manufactured from ivory, stone, terracotta, bronze, and glass.

Fish Vertebrae
502-504

502 FISH VERTEBRA
Pl. 52   71-192   E16   2   2
D. 0.028; Th. 0.016
Bone. Pierced through center.

503 FISH VERTEBRA
Not ill.   74-1175   C10/11   A(B)   2
D. 0.015; Th. 0.009
Bone. Similar to **502**, but smaller and not pierced.

504 FISH VERTEBRA
Not ill.   76-974   C12/D12   G   3
D. 0.022; Th. 0.010
Bone. Similar to **503**.

These fish vertebrae (**502-504**), which might have been used as gaming pieces, or strung as amulets or beads, are related to the astragals (**492-501**).

Eight of these vertebrae were inventoried. They normally would have served as gaming pieces but the examples, in which the central hole has been enlarged or smoothed, e.g., **502**, might also have been used as buttons or beads. Fish vertebrae are known from a number of Classical sites;[14] they are sometimes imitated in bronze and gold.[15]

Gaming Die
505

505 DIE
Pl. 52   not inv.   E13/F13   a   Stray
L. 0.021
Limestone. Slightly asymmetrical cube. Marked one through six with bull's-eyes. Sequence 1:6, 2:5, and 3:4 opposite each other. Worn and chipped.
Roman.

Dice numbered from one to six with engraved circles and bull's-eyes are known from the Roman period.[16] **505** now has a propensity to overwhelmingly shoot the number six, but this may be the result of wear and chipping. The possibility exists, however, that it was originally intended to be "loaded."

---

6. Deubner, *AA* 1929: 272.
7. Picard, *RA* 1935: 126 n. 3.
8. *Lindos* 1, 749. D. Reese, "The Kition Astragali," Appendix VIII(C) in V. Karageorghis, *Excavations at Kition* V, Part 2 (Nicosia 1985).
9. Pezard and Pottier, *Catalogue des antiquités de Susienne* (1926), 117, no. 234, from the Temple of Apollo Didymaion at Susa.
10. *Délos* 18, 332 n. 13. *ÖJh* 10 (1907) 127, pl. 6.
11. As at Kameiros, *ClRh* 4: 175, fig. 187. *ClRh* 6-7, 328, fig. 74, no. 51. *Délos* 18, pl. 93, fig. 818, 1-6.
12. *BCH* 37 (1913) 427. *Délos* 18, 332 n. 14.
13. See also *Corinth* 12, 22, pl. 100, no. 1755. Halae: *Hesperia* 9 (1940) 418, fig. 61, no. 10. Stubbings in *Perachora* 2, 447, A376, pl. 189. *Délos* 18, 332, pl. 93, figs. 821-824.
14. *Perachora* 2, A331-A333, pl. 188. Troy: Schliemann, *Ilios* (New York 1881), 432. *Ephesus* 192, pl. 36. *Délos* 18, 331, pls. 818, 819. Rhodes: *ClRh* 6-7, 328, fig. 74, no. 51.
15. V. Karageorghis, *Excavations at Kition I. The Tombs* (1974), pl. 20, dated to Period III (600-450 B.C.).
16. For a similar example, W. Hornbostel, *Kunst der Antike* (Mainz 1977), 494, no. 442, with bibliography.

Stone Tool
506

506 CHIPPED STONE TOOL
Not ill.   73-347   E12/13   C   4
H. 0.061; W. 0.040; Th. 0.016
Light brown flint. Roughly triangular, with two worked edges. Little sign of wear except at point, now dull. Unworked reverse.

This blade is a rather perplexing find at a Classical sanctuary. Paleolithic and Neolithic sites abound in the area around Cyrene, and chipped stone tools often wash out from these sites. It is possible that this tool was found and recognized as an artifact in antiquity, something mysterious, perhaps even magical, which would have made it a suitable offering to the goddess. Alternately, and more likely, it could have become inadvertently mixed in with earth used to build, terrace, or alter the sanctuary in its many phases of construction.

Shells
507-510

507 COWRIE
Pl. 52   74-984   D12/13   F   3
L. 0.022
Shell *Erosaria (Cypraca) spurca*. Not pierced or worked.

508 COWRIE
Pl. 52   76-383   F13/G13   1   2
L. 0.070
Shell. *Cypraca tigris*. Large. Intact and unworked.

509 BIVALVE
Pl. 52   76-742   F13/G13   1   2
W. 0.040
Shell. *Acanthocardia tuberculata*. Ribbed bivalve. Unworked. Worn and chipped.

510 LIMPET
Pl. 52   76-297   F13/G13   1   2
D. 0.038
Shell. *Patella*. Intact and unworked.

We have seen that actual shells and fossilized shells were often used as pendants at the Demeter Sanctuary, and imported *Tridacna* shells were carved and used as vessels. In addition, unpierced and unworked shells of various types were also found.

A number of other cowries,[17] bivalves,[18] and another limpet shell[19] were found, as well as numerous broken shells, pieces of mother-of-pearl, and snail shells.[20] Shells were considered suitable dedications to Astarte on Cyprus,[21] and were often placed in tombs on Rhodes.[22] As discussed above, they seem to have been considered particularly appropriate as offerings at the Cyrene Demeter Sanctuary.

---

17. Not catalogued: 74-841, 76-302, 76-529, 76-972, 77-1121, 77-287, 77-112, and one example not inventoried.
18. Not catalogued: 76-741, 78-263.
19. Not catalogued: 77-645.
20. Not catalogued: 78-99, 78-146, 78-147, 78-244, 78-567, 78-757.

21. V. Karageorghis, *Kition* (1976), pl. 20. Period III, Astarte Temple. See also: D. Reese, "The Shells," in I. Nicolau, "Excavations at the Eastern Necropolis of Amanthou in 1984," *RDAC* (1985); and D. Reese, "Recent and Fossil Shells," in D. Soren, ed., *The Sanctuary of Apollo Hylates at Kourion, Cyprus* (Tuscon 1987) 72-79.
22. *Clara Rhodos* 4, figs. 181, 269.

Appendix I

Find Spot Index

AREA	TRENCH	STRATUM	CAT. NO	APPROX. DATE
1	1	3	389	Archaic
2	1	2	25	Archaic
			238	Probably Roman
C10/11	A	1	167	Roman?
			273	
			285	
C10/11	A,β		295	Roman
C10/11	A,β	2	168	Roman
			289	Roman
			336	Roman
			458	
C10/11	A,β	3	5	6th century B.C.
C10/11	A,β	4	471	7th century B.C.
C10/11	A(B)	2	347	Roman
			503	
C10/11	A(B)	3	354	
C11	1	1S	274	Roman
C11	1	2	20	
			490	
C11	1	2D	233	
C11	1	Stray	275	Roman
C11	1/2	3B	311	
C11	2	1	480	
C12	1	4a	8	Archaic
C12/13	1	2	138	
			197	Archaic
			218	
			244	
C12/13	1	3	17	6th century B.C.
			96	Probably Archaic
			132	Probably Archaic
			162	
			251	
			370	
			479	

AREA	TRENCH	STRATUM	CAT. NO	APPROX. DATE
C12/13	1	4	7	6th century B.C.
			131	Probably Archaic
			190	Probably late 7th or 6th century B.C.
C12/13	2	3	260	
C12/13	F	5	280	Archaic
C12/D12	G	2	276	Roman
			314	
C12/D12	G	3	37	
C12/D13	G	3	133	Probably Archaic
			184	Probably 6th century B.C.
			188	Probably late 7th or 6th century B.C.
			504	
C13	1	1	440	
C13	1	2	241	
			333	
C13	1	3a	324	
			325	
			326	
			329	
			379	
C13	1	3b	155	Archaic
			498	
C13	1	4	15	
C13	1	4a	11	Archaic
			14	Archaic
			57	Archaic
			64	Archaic
			99	From Archaic context. Archaic (6th century B.C.)
			136	Probably Archaic
			140	
			160	Archaic
			166	Archaic
			191	Probably late 7th or 6th century B.C.
			224	
			226	
			227	
			228	
			284	
			293	
			331	
			342	
			359	Probably Roman
			361	
			377	
			378	
			447	Probably Archaic
			464	

AREA	TRENCH	STRATUM	CAT. NO	APPROX. DATE
C13	1	4b	12	6th century B.C.
			46	From undisturbed Archaic context
			65	Archaic
			115	Archaic
			116	Archaic
			117	Archaic
			157	Archaic
			186	
			232	Archaic
			263	
			349	Roman
			499	
C13	1	stray	245	
C13/D13	1	3	103	Probably Archaic
			137	
C13/D13	1	4	489	
C13/D13	1	6	24	Archaic
			181	Probably 6th century B.C.
			182	Probably 6th century B.C.
			249	
			322	
			352	
C13/D13	1	7	51	
			97	
			187	
			189	Probably late 7th or 6th century B.C.
			194	Possibly 6th century B.C.
			195	Possibly 6th century B.C.
			219	
			278	
			287	
			323	
			360	
			386	Archaic, 575-550 B.C.
			401	
			474	
C13/D13	2	1	451	Hellenistic-Roman
			475	
C13/D13	2	2	339	
C14	1	3	230	
			395	
C14	1	4	90	Probably Archaic
C14/D14	1	2	75	Archaic
C14/D14	2	2	60	
			62	
			68	Archaic
			98	Archaic (6th century B.C.)
C15/16	1	1	371	

AREA	TRENCH	STRATUM	CAT. NO	APPROX. DATE
C15/16	1	2	235	Probably Roman
			335	Roman
			353	
C15/16	1	3	18	
			257	Probably Roman
			488	
			491	
C15/16	1	4	123	Probably Archaic
			148	
			164	
			200	Archaic
			246	
			292	
			398	
			469	7th century B.C.
			470	7th century B.C.
			481	
C15/16	1	5	21	Probably Late 7th-Early 6th century B.C.
			369	
C15/D15	1B	4	149	
			205	
C15/D15	1B	5	170	
C17	1	2	172	Roman
C17	2	2	350	
C17	Stray find		243	
D10/11	Balk	1	392	
			237	Probably Roman
D10/11	Balk A-C (ext)	1	355	
D10/11	C	C	279	
D11	1	2	419	
D11/12	1	3	95	Probably Archaic
			178	Probably 6th century B.C.
			201	Probably Archaic
D11/12	1	4	337	
D11/12	1	Stray	130	Probably Archaic
D11/12	A		304	
D11/12	A	1	404	
D11/12	A	3	153	
			394	
			414	
D12	2	2	113	Archaic
D12	A scarp	3	2	6th to 5th century B.C.
			3	6th century B.C.
D12	Balk	2	374	
			422	
D12/13	1	4	108	Probably Archaic
D12/13	3	4	316	

AREA	TRENCH	STRATUM	CAT. NO	APPROX. DATE
D12/13	4	3	268	
D12/13	A	3	79	Archaic
			86	7th or early 6th century B.C.
			93	Probably Archaic
			120	Probably Archaic
			183	Probably 6th century B.C.
			234a	
			264	
			265	
			269	
			315	
			320	
			321	
D12/13	A	4	118	Archaic
			208	
			234	Late 7th century B.C.
			434	
D12/13	A	9	88	7th or early 6th century B.C.
D12/13	B	2	92	Probably Archaic
			487	
D12/13	B	4	22	Archaic
			53	Archaic/Classical
			70	Archaic
			101	
			102	Probably Archaic
			121	Probably Archaic
			122	Probably Archaic
			154	Archaic
			209	
			253	6th to 5th century B.C.
			281	Archaic
			282	
			309	
			319	
			327	
			358	Probably Roman
			492	
D12/13	D	Surface	23	Archaic
			478	
D12/13	F	1	139	
D12/13	F	2a	217	
D12/13	F	2B	258	
D12/13	F	3	9	Archaic
			10	Archaic
			13	7th to 6th century B.C.
			29	Archaic
			30	Archaic
			43	Archaic
			47	Classical
			48	Classical

AREA	TRENCH	STRATUM	CAT. NO	APPROX. DATE
			50	
			52	
			55	Archaic
			56	Archaic
			63	Archaic
			73	Archaic
			80	Archaic
			82	Archaic
			84	Archaic
			87	7th or early 6th century B.C.
			89	7th or early 6th century B.C.
			91	Probably Archaic
			106	Archaic
			107	
			111	
			112	
			114	Archaic
			127	
			128	Probably Archaic
			129	Probably Archaic
			145	
			146	
			151	
			152	Probably Archaic
			156	Archaic
			159	Archaic
			161	
			169	Archaic or Classical
			177	Probably 6th century B.C.
			179	Probably 6th century B.C.
			180	Probably 6th century B.C.
			202	Probably Archaic
			206	
			215	
			250	
			256	6th to 5th century B.C.
			272	
			286	
			312	
			317	
			318	
			328	
			338	Roman
			495	
			496	
			497	
			507	
D12/13	F	4	71	Archaic
			134	Probably Archaic
			216	
			301	
D12/13	F	4/5	54	Archaic/Classical
D12/13	F	e	76	Archaic

AREA	TRENCH	STRATUM	CAT. NO	APPROX. DATE
D12/E12	D	2	193	Archaic
			261	
			351	
			368	
D12/E12	D	2-3	302	
D12/E12	D	3	4	6th century B.C.
			58	Archaic
			81	Archaic
			150	
			175	Probably 6th century B.C.
			266	
			423	
D12/E13	D	3	125	Probably Archaic
D13 (Area 2)	1	5	367	
D14	1	1	247	
D14/E14	1	2	185	Probably 6th century B.C.
			375	
D14/E14	2	1	473	7th century B.C.
D14/E14	2	2	252	
D15/16	1	2	104	Probably Archaic
			147	
			221	
			222	
			303	
D15/16	1	3	45	
			59	
			83	Archaic
			85	Archaic?
			135	Probably Archaic
			290	
			348	
			382	Archaic 575-500 B.C.
			384	Archaic, 575-550 B.C.
			399	
D15/16	2	2	356	
			372	
D15/E15	1	2	61	
D15/E15	1	3	119	
			248	
D16/15	2	2	271	
D16/17		3	346	
			402	5th century B.C.
D16/17	1	2	163	
			192	Archaic
			236	Probably Roman
D16/17	1	3	225	
			254	
			255	6th to 5th century B.C.
			400	

AREA	TRENCH	STRATUM	CAT. NO	APPROX. DATE
D16/17	2	2	36	Archaic
			49	Classical
D16/17	2	3	300	
			415	
			420	
D16/17	2	4	214	
D16/17	7	1	19	
D16/E16	1	1	220	
			396	
D16/E16	1	2	397	
D17/16			124	Probably Archaic
D17/16	1	3	199	Archaic
			213	
E10	Balk		484	
E10	Balk	2	40	Roman
E10	Balk	3	44	
E10/11 (Area 1)	1	1	429	4th century B.C.
E10/11 (Area 1)	1	3	467	7th century B.C.
E11	1	1	404	
E11	1	2	33	Archaic
			403	
			424	5th century B.C.
			433	
E11	1	3	110	Probably Archaic
			405	
E11	2	2	417	
			425	5th century B.C.
			436	
E11	2	3	16	
E11	3	2	430	
			432	
			454	Roman
E11	3	3	1	6th century B.C.
			6	6th century B.C.
			72	Archaic
			74	Archaic
			78	Archaic
			100	Probably Archaic
			211	
			231	Archaic
			240	
			288	
			297	
			493	
E11	4	2	283	
E11/12	1	1	454	Roman
E11/12	1	2	390	
			404	
			418	

AREA	TRENCH	STRATUM	CAT. NO	APPROX. DATE
E11/12	Pit	3	406	
E11/12	Slope	1	427	
			455	
E11/D11	Balk	2	212	
E12	1	3	210	Archaic
E12	1	5	94	
			176	Probably 6th century B.C.
			428	
E12	1	6	413	
E12/11	Slope	1	41	Roman
E12/13	C	2	334	
E12/13	C	3	26	7th century B.C.
E12/13	C	4	262	
			298	
			494	
			506	
E12/13	E	1	42	Roman
E12/13	E	1/2	463	
E12/13	E	2	38	
			39	Severan
			66	Archaic
			299	
			305	
E12/13	E	3	109	Probably Archaic
			126	Probably Archaic
E12/F12	Balk	1	437	
E12/F12	Balk	2	465	
E12/F12	Balk	3	477	
E13/14	1	1	313	
E13/F13	a	Stray	505	Roman
E15	3	3	34	Archaic
E16	2	2	277	Roman
			502	
E2	1	5	357	
F9/10	A	2	294	
F-G 9/10	A	2	310	
F10	1	1	456	
F10/12 (N Terrace)	III	I	449	Probably Archaic
F11	2	2	391	
F11	2	3	421	
F11	2	4	270	
F11/G11		1	173	Roman
F11/G11		2	174	Roman
F11/G11	1	2	438	
			446	Roman
			460	

AREA	TRENCH	STRATUM	CAT. NO	APPROX. DATE
F11/G11	Wall cleaning		385	Archaic, 575-500 B.C.
			388	Archaic
			416	Archaic?
			426	
			431	
			445	Roman
F12		1	373	
F12	1	1	435	
			459	
F12	1	2	291	
F12/13	C	2	362	
F12/G12	1		453	Roman
F12/G12	Vault A	Surface	466	
F12/G12	Wall cleaning	2	239	Probably Roman
F13	1	3	203	Archaic
F13/14	1	1	457	
F13/G13	1	2	28	Probably Roman
			35	Archaic
			67	Archaic
			143	
			196	Archaic
			267	
			340	
			365	
			376	
			380	
			387	7th to 6th century B.C.
			407	
			462	
			485	
			508	
			509	
			510	
F13/G13	1	3	383	Archaic, 575-550 B.C.
F13/G13	1	Wall sondage	483	
F13/G13	2	2	31	Archaic
			32	Archaic
			69	Archaic
			77	Archaic
			141	
			142	
			144	
			198	Possibly 6th century B.C.
			223	
			259	
			330	
			332	
			341	
			364	
			408	

AREA	TRENCH	STRATUM	CAT. NO	APPROX. DATE
			409	
			410	
			411	
			439	
			441	
			442	
			472	
			476	
			482	
			486	
			500	
			501	
F14/G14	1	1	343	
F14/G14	1	2	105	Probably Archaic
			165	
			393	
			412	
F14/G14	1	3	242	
			363	
			366	
F14/G14	Test	2	171	
			443	
			450	
F15	1	2	344	
F15	3	2	468	7th century B.C.
F16	1	2	461	
F16	1	3A	207	
F9/10	A	2	294	
F9/10 G9/10			381	
G16/H16	1	1	444	Roman
SW sondage	1B	3	307	
SW sondage	1B	4	306	
			308	
	Stray find		27	Probably Roman
	Stray find		229	
	Stray find		296	Roman
	Stray find 1974		448	Probably Archaic
Surface			158	Archaic
SW sondage	1A	3	204	
SW sondage	1A	4	345	
SW sondage	1B	3	452	

Appendix II

Concordance of Catalogue Numbers with Excavation Inventory Numbers

Inv. No.	Cat. No.	Inv. No.	Cat. No.	Inv. No.	Cat. No.
N.I.	158	71-438	436	71-750	122
N.I.	381	71-439	419	71-751	183
N.I.	423	71-440	432	71-753	22
N.I.	427	71-449	268	71-755	208
N.I.	428	71-450	309	71-758	316
N.I.	506	71-452	394	71-762	265
69-1	25	71-454	121	71-763	86
69-5	238	71-455	154	71-767	93
69-219	467	71-458	231	71-772	118
69-285	403	71-459	6	71-774	234
69-317	367	71-460	282	71-788	94
69-486	467	71-465	78	71-789	469
71-16	404	71-468	315	71-792	153
71-39	424	71-470	269	71-794	493
71-62	433	71-494	320	71-798	211
71-67	435	71-514	492	71-799	16
71-74	449	71-516	327	71-804	210
71-90	113	71-520	357	71-805	413
71-101	454	71-521	358	71-821	71
71-146	33	71-522	288	71-822	73
71-165	461	71-523	283	71-825	110
71-178	277	71-524	240	73-6	334
71-192	502	71-538	425	73-77	362
71-210	456	71-549	34	73-107	307
71-212	403	71-561	79	73-150	452
71-227	319	71-562	92	73-196	308
71-236	417	71-563	102	73-233	40
71-238	430	71-520	299	73-237	41
71-272	69	71-571	487	73-272	455
71-275	207	71-610	321	73-286	26
71-285	1	71-657	468	73-330	2
71-287	120	71-690	434	73-331	3
71-329	100	71-712	429	73-332	212
71-337	297	71-738	53	73-341	298
71-347	281	71-740	209	73-353	204
71-421	176	71-742	253	73-358	345
71-432	414	71-745	255	73-359	306
71-436	405	71-747A	264	73-364	404

Inv. No.	Cat. No.	Inv. No.	Cat. No.	Inv. No.	Cat. No.
73-412	418	73-1262	149	74-847	495
73-414	406	73-1263	150	74-848	90
73-478	261	73-1264	125	74-849	151
73-686	192	73-1290	454	74-852	272
73-722	76	73-1293	205	74-854	230
73-746	163	74-79	42	74-857	5
73-754	481	74-122	36	74-858	80
73-762	488	74-170	38	74-902	152
73-765	266	74-270	305	74-903	56
73-779	164	74-271	49	74-915	156
73-781	235	74-272	23	74-946	421
73-784	279	74-273	478	74-967	55
73-786	262	74-275	271	74-968	111
73-801	390	74-305	247	74-969	177
73-802	19	74-306	336	74-970	178
73-831	494	74-307	289	74-971	50
73-885	369	74-343	458	74-973	312
73-889	148	74-374	300	74-976	338
73-890	18	74-380	214	74-977	29
73-892	81	74-383	285	74-984	508
73-913	370	74-384	291	74-1014	496
73-915	193	74-401	27	74-1020	318
73-1059	254	74-403	65	74-1022	201
73-1090	175	74-450	39	74-1026	395
73-1096	398	74-525	463	74-1050	47
73-1127	491	74-561	126	74-1063	179
73-1131	4	74-571	347	74-1080	391
73-1135	302	74-612	295	74-1081	184
73-1136	470	74-613	167	74-1085	256
73-1140	44	74-615	109	74-1087	112
73-1167	335	74-646	420	74-1089	392
73-1178	225	74-647	459	74-1096	43
73-1180	346	74-743	114	74-1100	310
73-1183	199	74-746	337	74-1102	373
73-1184	400	74-750	471	74-1108	294
73-1186	402	74-760	106	74-1222	127
73-1187	236	74-762	82	74-1123	109
73-1188	351	74-763	194	74-1124	13
73-1191	21	74-764	87	74-1125	91
73-1192	123	74-778	237	74-1126	215
73-1193	353	74-794	75	74-1127	273
73-1194	257	74-824	354	74-1128	146
73-1196	292	74-829	355	74-1130	48
73-1206	484	74-831	145	74-1134	9
73-1224	213	74-833	84	74-1135	128
73-1225	124	74-836	250	74-1136	216
73-1230	246	74-840	95	74-1137	286
73-1231	200	74-843	258	74-1138	10
73-1233	368	74-844	168	74-1140	317
73-1261	170	74-846	159	74-1131	270

Inv. No.	Cat. No.	Inv. No.	Cat. No.	Inv. No.	Cat. No.
74-1142	497	76-951	108	76-1259	314
74-1144	202	76-968	138	77-75	408
74-1145	217	76-971	139	77-77	198
74-1146	129	76-974	504	77-96	68
74-1149	161	76-979	30	77-106	241
74-1152	206	76-980	475	77-108	409
74-1153	52	76-988	407	77-112	141
74-1159	72	76-989	96	77-154	410
74-1160	62	76-990	180	77-207	472
74-1175	503	76-991	188	77-229	104
76-151	490	76-993	51	77-252	221
76-154	350	76-994	97	77-268	185
76-213	465	76-995	189	77-271	399
76-229	249	76-1001	328	77-279	500
76-283	489	76-1010	301	77-307	411
76-293	485	76-1012	374	77-381	32
76-297	511	76-1017	422	77-406	341
76-298	244	76-1045	190	77-423	482
76-301	103	76-1046	74	77-425	332
76-310	462	76-1047	88	77-427	303
76-326	287	76-1048	37	77-429	408
76-330	352	76-1091	280	77-430	397
76-345	322	76-1095	181	77-449	222
76-346	380	76-1096	251	77-453	98
76-348	195	76-1097	182	77-454	58
76-349	196	76-1129	130	77-458	290
76-383	509	76-1130	131	77-459	330
76-397	474	76-1131	132	77-463	439
76-399	197	76-1132	133	77-467	440
76-438	187	76-1138	70	77-495	59
76-441	360	76-1147	480	77-524	437
76-446	479	76-1151	54	77-530	45
76-448	267	76-1207	278	77-533	348
76-469	67	76-1209	162	77-574	364
76-525	386	76-1211	371	77-582	144
76-527	387	76-1213	275	77-597	476
76-528	137	76-1214	20	77-645	142
76-633	451	76-1220	7	77-646	31
76-646	415	76-1221	89	77-676	259
76-732	66	76-1223	401	77-677	384
76-733	339	76-1226	17	77-689	77
76-734	383	76-1227	134	77-715	83
76-738	340	76-1228	219	77-727	223
76-739	143	76-1229	220	77-728	383
76-740	28	76-1231	24	77-730	85
76-742	510	76-1224	233	77-745	135
76-749	35	76-1235	365	77-746	61
76-911	218	76-1247	313	77-760	304
76-913	323	76-1248	203	77-777	477
76-919	311	76-1249	396	77-795	60

Inv. No.	Cat. No.	Inv. No.	Cat. No.	Inv. No.	Cat. No.
77-963	333	77-1181a	226	78-173	105
77-996	501	77-1181b	227	78-241	343
77-1001	498	77-1183	228	78-300	473
77-1021	483	77-1188	349	78-301	165
77-1023	486	77-1189	46	78-357	252
77-1046	157	77-1192	323	78-428	242
77-1052	499	77-1194	284	78-429	243
77-1053	64	77-1200	376	78-430	344
77-1055	115	77-1202	378	78-432	229
77-1056	245	77-1210	160	78-433	393
77-1063	324	77-1216	361	78-489	502
77-1064	155	77-1220	359	78-612	363
77-1068,		77-1221	441	78-632	466
77-467	440	77-1222	442	78-649	389
77-1082	248	77-1232	464	78-650	444
77-1083	11	77-1234	63	78-702	453
77-1085	186	77-1235	117	78-714	507
77-1087	232	77-1236	293	78-715	457
77-1088	342	77-1237	136	78-756	366
77-1108	116	77-1240	57	78-758	239
77-1114	14	77-1242	99	78-786	445
77-1118	447	77-1249	15	78-807	173
77-1119	356	77-1255	329	78-808	174
77-1120	119	77-1256	379	78-810	438
77-1124	12	77-1257	377	78-811	446
77-1125	260	77-1259	326	78-828	431
77-1126	263	77-1261	331	78-829	388
77-1130	372	77-1266	147	78-832	426
77-1154	169	78-40	172	78-833	385
77-1172	140	78-74	171	78-836	460
77-1173	191	78-106	443	78-852	416
77-1174	224	78-117	450	79-18	448
77-1180	166	78-171	412		

Appendix III

Bronze Rings

Area			Inv. No.	Area			Inv. No.
1	2	1	69-156	C13	1	2	77-26
2	1	2	69-81	C14	1	2	74-808
			69-205				74-816
2	1	5	69-250	C14	1	4	74-807
2	2	2	69-302				74-817
3	1	2	69-80				74-1001
			69-83	C15/16	1	surface	73-295
			69-85	C15/16	1	1	73-400
			69-88				73-430
			69-182	C15/16	1	2	73-429
C10/11	A(A)	4	74-563	C15/16	1	3	73-259
C10/11	A(B)	2	74-564				73-497
C10/11	A(B)	6	74-814				73-613
C11	1	2	76-1170				73-614
			(10 examples)				73-615
C12	1	2	77-773	C15/16	1	4	73-507
			77-847				73-649
			77-849				73-736
			77-878				73-882
C12	1	3A	77-998	C15/16	1	5	73-1052
			77-1000	C17	1	2	78-100
C12	1	3B	77-1001	D10/11	C	3	73-787
C12	1	4A	77-1133	D10/11	C	5	74-265
			77-1175	D10/11	C	6	74-269
			77-1176	D11	1	3	71-469
			77-1177				71-484
			77-1179	D12	1	3	71-341
			77-1248	D12	2	2	71-90
C12	1	4B	77-1060	D12	A scarp	3	73-207
			77-1128	D12/13	A	1	71-513
			77-1132	D12/13	A	2	71-180
			77-1134				71-766
C12/13	1	2	76-1159	D12/13	A	3	71-183
			76-1163				71-184
C12/13	1	3	76-1193				71-221
C12/13	1	4	76-1155				71-397
C12/13	2	1	76-1198				71-398

Area	Inv. No.	Area	Inv. No.
	71-399		74-1010
	71-456		74-1012
	71-467		74-1013
	71-483		74-1015
	71-508		74-1016
	71-509		74-1018
	71-607		74-1019
	71-646		74-1024
	71-651		74-1154
	71-747a		74-1161
	71-747b (3 rings)		74-1162
D12/13 A 4	71-647		74-1164
	71-648		74-1165
	71-650		74-1166
D12/13 B 1	71-447		74-1168
D12/13 B 2	71-182		74-1169
	71-510		74-1170
	71-550		74-1171
D12/13 B 4	71-268		74-1172
	71-269		74-1173
	71-270		74-1179
	71-464	D12/13 F 4	76-1152
	71-466		76-1180
	71-511	D14 1 1	71-569
	71-512	D14 1 3 (see B)	74-810
	71-551	D15/16 1 2	77-255
	71-552		77-256
	71-553		77-270
	71-554		77-273
	71-606		77-274
	71-645		77-275
	71-649		77-310
	71-743		77-336
	71-744		77-339
	71-746	D15/16 1 3	77-269
	71-748		77-337
	71-749		77-338
D12/13 F 2	71-1004		77-499
D12/13 F 3	74-805		77-500
	74-811		77-534
	74-819		77-536
	74-851		77-577
	74-1000		77-695
	74-1002		77-696
	74-1003		77-697
	74-1005		77-698
	74-1006		77-699
	74-1007		77-700
	74-1008		77-701
	74-1009		77-774

Area	Inv. No.	Area	Inv. No.
D16 west wall of sanctuary	71-605	E12/13 E 3	74-815 74-812
D16/17 A 2	76-1154	E13 Balk 2	76-1197
D16/17 A 3	76-1202	E13/14 1 1	76-1247
D16/17 2 2	74-264	E13/14 1 2	74-1163
	74-267		74-1167
	74-268		76-1153
D16/17 2 3	74-256		76-1194
	74-257		76-1201
	74-258		76-1204
	74-259	E14/15 1 1	76-1172
	74-260	E14/15 1 2	76-1162
	74-261		76-1173
	74-370		76-1187
	74-371	E14/15 1 3	76-1189
	74-372	E15 1 2	76-1174
	74-374		76-1199
	74-562	E15 1 4	76-1190
D16/17 2 4	74-266	E15 2 2	76-1181
	74-369		76-1182
	74-373		76-1185
	74-376	E15 2 3	76-1160
	74-566		76-1176
	74-567		76-1177
D16/17 - 2	73-730		76-1178
D16/17 - 3	73-731		76-1179
	73-733		76-1184
	73-734	E16 1 2	71-222
	73-1058		77-776
	73-1059	E16 1 5	77-909
D16/17 - 4	73-829	E16 2 topsoil	71-88
	73-1119	E16 2 1	71-109
E10 Balk 2	73-194	E16 2 2	71-131
E11 3 2	71-130		71-170
E11 3 3	71-283		71-171
	71-448		71-172
	71-793		71-173
	71-802	F12 - 2	74-366
E11/12 slope 1	73-213	F14/15 1 2	78-572
E12 1 2	71-339	F15 cleanup 1	78-101
	71-340	F15 1 -	78-435
E12 1 3	71-803	F16 1 2	71-50
E12/13 C 2	73-117		71-51
E12/13 C 4	73-786		71-52
E12/13 E 2	74-253		71-87
	74-262		71-89
	74-263		71-110
	74-364		71-111
	74-365		71-112
	74-565	F16 2 1	78-189

Area	Inv. No.	Area	Inv. No.
F16/17 1 1	78-41	D15/E15 1 2	77-999
	78-42	D15/E15 1 3	77-1178
	78-102	D15/E16 1 3	77-448
G15 1 1	78-626	D16/E16 1 1	77-428
G15 1 2	78-627	D16/E16 1 2	76-1158
	78-738		76-1171
C12/D12 G 3	76-1165	F10/G10 1 1	78-816
C13/D13 1 3	76-1156	F10/G10 1 2	78-844
	76-1200	F11/G11 wall	
C13/D13 1 5	76-1167	cleaning 1	78-763
C13/D13 1 7	76-1166	F12/G12 wall	
	76-1169	cleaning 2	78-819
	76-1203	F13/G13 1 2	76-1183
C13/D13 2 1	76-1188		76-1191
C14/D14			76-1205
sondage, cleanup	77-309		76-1206
	77-450	F13/G13 wall	
C15/D15 - 1	73-883	sondage 1	77-958
C15/D15 - 2	73-881	F13/G13 wall	
	73-1072	sondage 2	77-957
C15/D15 - 4	73-1073	F14/G14 1 2	78-191
	73-1074		78-319
C15/D15 1B 4	73-1260		78-320
D12/E12 D 2	73-478		78-321
	73-725		78-322
	73-1133		78-434
D12/E12 D 2A	73-1088		78-437
	73-1089		78-480
D12/E12 D 3	73-727	F14/G14 1 3	78-475
	73-728		78-570
	73-729		78-571
	73-887	F14/G14 test 2	78-194
D13/E13 1 2	76-1196	F15/G15 1 1	78-190
D13/E13 1 4	76-1195		78-192
D14/E14 1 2	77-27		78-193
	77-177	F15/G15 1 2	78-843
	77-178	G16/H16 1 1	78-741
D14/E14 2 1	78-573	SW sondage 1 1	73-42
	78-625		73-43
	78-739	SW sondage 1 2	73-18
	78-742	SW sondage 1A 2	73-41
D14/E14 2 2	78-471		73-45
	78-472		73-49
	78-473	SW sondage 1A 3	73-44
	78-474	SW sondage 1A 4	73-152
	78-569	SW sondage 1B 3	73-106
	78-574		73-129
	78-575		73-131
	78-740		73-146
	78-743	SW sondage 1B 4	73-206
	78-818		73-215

Part II

Glass

I

Glass

Core-formed Glass
1-71

The group of core-formed glass vessels to which these fragments belong was not made before ca. 550 B.C. Some of the examples listed here come from the late sixth century and possibly earlier; none is likely to date later than ca. 400 B.C., with the possible exception of some of the fragments with thread combed in inverted festoons, and most are probably not later than ca. 450 B.C. Rhodes has been suggested as a principal source of these perfume containers during this period, but others (rare at Cyrene) must have been made in Italy.

The selection catalogued here was made from a group of nearly 600 recovered fragments, but not 600 vessels. Many of the fragments must belong together, as in **20** and **21**, though not necessarily joining. This is the largest concentration of core-formed glass yet found in Cyrenaica. Most were of blue glass; a disproportionate number of white and red fragments are included here. **1-3** come from an alabastron type dating to the last quarter of the sixth century B.C., judging from the context of comparable examples from Olbia[1] and Delphi.[2] **6** has a sealing-wax red body, a relatively common color for alabastra. There is one in the Royal Ontario Museum,[3] and others in the British Museum, one of which came from a grave at the Fikellura cemetery, Kameiros, datable to ca. 450-400.[4] The color of **7**, white opaque, is also relatively common and probably early.[5]

Neither the amphoriskoi nor aryballoi can be closely dated; nevertheless, they must be placed in the late sixth or fifth century.

Fragments of two oinochoai (**20** and **21**), made up of joining fragments found over several seasons, are closely matched by two in the British Museum that come from graves at the Fikellura cemetery of Kameiros, datable to ca. 460-440 B.C.[6] A trademark of this group is the added dot at the base of the handle, imitating the rivet attachment of a metal oinochoe. Other examples of this group are in the British Museum,[7] the Corning Museum of Glass,[8] Kassel,[9] the Bologna Museo Civico,[10] and the Oppenlander collection,[11] and one was once on the London art market.[12]

29 is of interest in that undecorated vessels of aquamarine color are uncommon. Harden, following Fossing, cites only four alabastra which could be of the shape to which the fragmentary **29** belongs.[13]

Five fragments (**31-35**) with thread combed into "inverted festoons" are difficult to date closely. **31** could come from an alabastron of a type datable from the late sixth to the mid-fifth century. **32-35** could belong to a group of core-formed vessels later than the others from Cyrene, post 400 B.C.

ALABASTRA
1-7

BLUE BODY (1-5)

1 Pl. 1 69-240 E10/11 (Area 1) 1 4
Max. P.W. 0.033; Max. P.H. 0.032
  Combed white threads on center of body; plain white threads above and below.

---

1. Voscinina 1967, 557, pl. 120:1.
2. I. Konstantinou, *ArchDelt* 20 (1965) B:2 "Chronika," 303, pl. 358.
3. Hayes 1975, 9, no. 7, pl. 1.
4. Harden 1981, 69, no. 129, pl. IX.
5. See, for example, Harden 1981, 62-64, nos. 85-96, pl. VIII.
6. Harden 1981, 98, nos. 258, 261, pl. XIV.
7. Harden 1981, 98, nos. 259, 260 (both from Rhodes), no. 262 (without provenance), pl. XIV.
8. Goldstein 1979, 126, no. 261.
9. Spartz 1967, no. 3, pl. 2.
10. Notarianni 1979, 18, nos. 2-3.
11. von Saldern *et al.* 1974, 55, no. 127.
12. *Catalogue of the Constable-Maxwell Collection of Ancient Glass*, Sotheby Parke Bernet and Co., London, 4-5 June, 1979, 20 n. 8.
13. Two are in the British Museum and two in Berlin. See Fossing 1940, 59; Harden 1981, 61-62, nos. 83-84, pl. VIII.

2   Pl. 1   73-537   E10   balk S   3
Max. P.W. 0.030; Max. P.H. 0.045
    Lower body. White threads.

3   Pl. 1   71-780   E11   3   3
Max. P.W. 0.030; Max. P.H. 0.965; D. rim 0.030; D. mouth 0.013;
    White, *Second Report* 192, pl. XCV,g.
    Rim, neck, upper body, and handle lug. Unmarvered white thread on rim, white on neck, combed orange and white threads on body.

4   Pl. 1   71-400   D12/D13   B   4
Max. P.W. 0.020; Max. P.H. 0.026
    Orange threads only?

5   Pl. 1   76-127a   C12/D12   G   3
Max. P.W. 0.038; Max. P.H. 0.053
    Grooved body. Combed light blue and orange threads.

RED BODY (6)

6   Pl. 1   71-782   E12   1   5
Max. P.W. 0.020; Max. P.H. 0.015; D. body est. 0.030
    Bottom of body. Greenish thread.

WHITE BODY (7)

7   Pl. 1   74-464   F12   2
Max. P.W. 0.027; Max. P.H. 0.036; Th. 0.003
    Center of body. Combed blue thread.

AMPHORISKOI
8-16

BLUE BODY (8-14)

8   Pl. 2   71-532   F15   3   2
Max. P.W. 0.037; Max. P.H. 0.056; Th. 0.002
    Combed orange and light blue threads on body; orange above, orange and light blue below.

9   Pl. 2   73-679   D17/16   3
Max. P.H. 0.031; D. rim 0.028
    Neck and one handle. Unmarvered white thread on rim, white on upper shoulder.

10 Pl. 2   73-901   C15/16   1   3
Max. P.W. 0.036; Max. P.H. 0.030
    Neck and shoulder. White and yellow thread.

11 Pl. 2   73-935   D17/16   3
Max. P.W. 0.040; Max. P.H. 0.026; D. rim 0.024
    Rim, neck, shoulder, and handles from shoulder to below rim. Light blue thread on rim, orange thread on shoulder.

12 Pl. 2   73-1170   E10   balk   3
Max. P.W. 0.027; Max. P.H. 0.039
    Lower neck, shoulder, upper body, and base of handle. Body grooved. White thread on neck and upper shoulder, white and broad orange threads combed on body, white trim on dark blue handle.

13 Pl. 2   76-247   C13/D13   1
Max. P.W. 0.023; Max. P.H. 0.023
    Shoulder with handle stub. Body grooved. White thread on lower neck; combed white and yellow threads on body.

14 Pl. 2   76-464   F13/G13   1   2
Max. P.W. 0.034; Max. P.H. 0.051
    Grooved lower body and button base. Combed white thread on body, white below, traces of unmarvered white thread on base.

WHITE BODY (15 and 16)

15 Pl. 2   73-910   C15/16   1   5
Max. P.W. 0.022; Max. P.H. 0.038; Th. 0.008
    Shoulder and upper body. Thick purple thread combed into wavy zigzag pattern.

16 Pl. 2   73-985   C15/16   1   5
Max. P.W. 0.032; Max. P.H. 0.024; Th. 0.008
    Part of shoulder. Thick purple thread.

ARYBALLOI
17-19

BLUE BODY (17-19)

17 Pl. 3   73-1097   D17/16   3
Max. P.W. 0.038; Max. P.H. 0.042
    Part of shoulder and body. Orange and light blue threads.

18 Pl. 3   74-74   D10/11   C   5
Max. P.H. 0.023; D. (body) 0.047
    Shoulder and upper body. Broken handle stubs orange and light blue.

19 Pl. 3   74-121   D16/17   2   3
Max. P.W. 0.044; Max. P.H. 0.042; Th. 0.003
    Grooved shoulder and body, and orange handle. Combed threads light blue (and orange?, now missing), orange above, orange and light blue below. Handle orange.

OINOCHOAI
20-22

BLUE BODY (20-22)

20 Pl. 3   73-1098; 76-371   D16/17   1   3;
                                F13/G13   1   2
Max. P.H. 0.033; D. body 0.061; D. handle 0.018
    Shoulder, body, and handle. Orange thread on shoulder, combed orange and light blue thread on body, orange spot at base of handle.

21 Pl. 3   73-1139a; 73-705; 74-115; 77-395
              D16/17   3   4
Max. P.H. 0.084; D. foot 0.036
    Shoulder, body, and foot. Orange thread on shoulder, combed orange and light blue thread on body, light blue between two orange threads below. Unmarvered orange thread on foot.

22 Pl. 3   73-1139b   D16/17   1   3
Max. P.H. 0.040; D. body (est.) 0.055
    Three joining fragments.

SHAPE UNCERTAIN
23-38

The following examples were too fragmentary to allow exact shape determinations. It is certain that they all come from one of the our preceding shapes—alabastra, amphoriskoi, aryballoi, or oinochoai.

BLUE BODY (23 and 24)

23 Pl. 4   73-916   D12/E12   D   1
Max. P.W. 0.020; Max. P.H. 0.020; Th. 0.003
  Probably an alabastron.

24 Pl. 4   73-1099   D16/17   1   3
Max. P.W. 0.042
  Probably an amphoriskos body.

WHITE BODY (25)

25 Pl. 4   73-585   D12/E12   D   3
Max. P.W. 0.023; Max. P.H. 0.020; Th. 0.003
  Probably an alabastron. Blue-green thread.

RED BODY (26 and 27)

26 Pl. 4   76-886   E15   2   2
Max. P.W. 0.012; Max. P.H. 0.018
  Aryballos or oinochoe shoulder. Orange thread.

27 Pl. 4   77-116   C13   1   surface
Max. P.W. 0.016; Max. P.H. 0.007
  Neck and shoulder.

BLUE-GREEN BODY (28 and 29)

28   74-110   D16/17   2   3
Max. P.W. 0.025; Max. P.H. 0.037; Th. 0.002
  No threads.

29 Pl. 4   73-688   D16/17   1   3
Max. P.W. 0.014; Max. P.H. 0.022
  Possibly an amphoriskos brownish blue-green glass. Green thread.

"INVERTED FESTOON" THREAD (30-34)

30 Pl. 4   73-712   C15/16   1   4
Max. P.W. 0.021; Max. P.H. 0.030; Th. 0.002
  Light blue body, white threads.

31 Pl. 4   73-716   C15/16   1   3
Max. P.W. 0.011; Max. P.H. 0.028; Th. 0.005
  Light blue body, white and orange threads.

32 Pl. 4   73-610   C15/16   1   3
Max. P.W. 0.014; Max. P.H. 0.021; Th. 0.002
  Light blue body, white and orange threads.

33 Pl. 4   77-555   C14/D14   2   2
Max. P.W. 0.015; Max. P.H. 0.012; Th. 0.003
  Dark opaque black or purple body, threads combed.

34 Pl. 4   73-848   D16/17   1   3
Max. P.W. 0.020; Max. P.H. 0.035
  Possibly an alabastron. Body color uncertain, orange threads.

OTHER, POSSIBLY LATER, FRAGMENTS (35-38)

35 Pl. 4   77-553   F13/G13   2   2
Max. P.W. 0.025; Max. P.H. 0.024
  Rim and neck. Blue body, broad white thread.

36 Pl. 4   76-601   C13/D13   2   1
Max. P.W. 0.026; Max. P.H. 0.014; Th. 0.003
  Amphoriskos or oinochoe neck and shoulder.

37 Pl. 4   77-447   F13/G13   2   2
Max. P.W. 0.033; Max. P.H. 0.039; Th. 0.004
  "Hydria" or amphoriskos tall neck, shoulder, and upper body. Blue body, orange and blue-green threads.

38 Pl. 4   71-261   D12/D13   B   4
Max. P.W. 0.040; Max. P.H. 0.019; Th. 0.005
  Short neck. Blue body, broad orange thread.

PENDANT
39

Ram-head pendants with coloring similar to the example from the Demeter Sanctuary (**39**) are in the Palermo and Syracuse Museums from Birgi and Megara Hyblaea, respectively, and are dated to the late sixth or early fifth century B.C.[14] Another is in the British Museum.[15] Although the type is thought to run as late as the early third century, there is no reason the Cyrene pendant could not date to the fifth century. Other examples, in the Ashmolean Museum and the Petrie Collection of the University of London, come from Deve Huyuk and Yehudiyeh, respectively.[16]

39 Pl. 5   74-80   D16/17   2   2
P.L. 0.022
  Ram-head pendant. Blue head. White for ears, white threads on horns, orange for mouth and nostrils, orange and black for eyes. Hole in neck left by rod over which object was made.

EYE BEADS
40-56

Fifty-nine eye beads were recovered, only seventeen of which are catalogued here. The earliest are the

---

14. A. G. Spano, *SicArch* 12 (1979) 39, nos. 25, 27, 29, fig. IV, pls. II and VII.
15. Harden 1981, 152, no. 438, pl. XXVIII.

16. M. Seefried, *Les Pendentifs en verre sur noyau des pays de la Méditerranée antique* (École Française de Rome 1982), 135-136, type EIIa.

canonical and common "eye" bead with either a green or turquoise matrix (**40-45**), or an orange or "yellow" matrix (**46-49**). Beads of both colors have blue and white eyes. The eyes occur in a single row, in two tiers, or in a combination of both schemes. More than twice as many green ones were found (thirty-four green, sixteen orange), but since the orange glass is generally less well preserved, there originally could have been more of that color. The beads were fashioned on a rod, the eyes of contrasting colors marvered into the surface of the matrix. The beads of this group are unlikely to have been made earlier than the mid-sixth century when the core-formed vessels to which they are linked by color were first made. Tomb 7, an early fifth century burial from the south necropolis at Sambuca, Monte Adranone, Sicily, yielded eight orange/yellow and sixteen green/blue examples.[17] Tombs at Muschovitza and Arabadzigskala, Bulgaria, both dated to the second quarter of the fifth century B.C. by Attic black-glazed pottery, yielded similar beads.[18] Margaret Guido has discussed the orange type, noting the range of deposits from the sixth to the first centuries B.C.[19]

One complete (**52**) and four fragmentary beads (**53**) of "Arras Type II" were recovered. Margaret Guido's suggestion that beads of this type originated in the eastern Mediterranean is probably correct, but her assertion that they first made their appearance in the eighth or seventh century is based on evidence that can no longer be substantiated.[20]

Dan Barag drew attention to three tombs, containing core-formed vessels, which are dated by their excavators to the late seventh or early sixth century.[21] Two of them, those at Meqabelein near Amman[22] and Beth Shean[23] contained beads of Arras Type II, and it is on this basis that Guido dated the early beads. Donald Harden, however, disputes these early dates, arguing that the tomb groups cited by Barag are incorrectly dated and that core-formed vessels of the type found in them made their first appearance only in the mid-sixth century.[24] Resembling **53**, the beads from the Meqabelein tomb, therefore, are probably no earlier than the second half of the sixth century.[25]

Among the examples cited by Guido, those in the Musée des Antiquités Nationales at Saint-Germain-en-Laye from Bussy-le-Chateau (Marne) and Bergeres-les-Vertus (Marne) and datable to the La Tene I period, 475-300 B.C., are now published in an exhibition catalogue.[26] Others, not cited by Guido, come from a late fifth-century burial at Aleria, Corsica.[27] Guido notes that beads of this general type are found in contexts down to the first century B.C.[28]

40 Pl. 5   76-180   C13/D13   1   1
D. 0.017
Large. Green matrix. Five white eyes, each with three blue circles and a blue center.
One other example was found.

41 Pl. 5   76-182   Stray
D. 0.009
Green matrix. Four white eyes, each with one blue circle and a blue center.
Seven others were found.

42 Pl. 5   73-529   C15/16   1   4
D. 0.008
Green matrix. Three white eyes with blue centers.
Three others were found.

43 Pl. 5   73-694   D16/17   1   3
D. 0.010
Green matrix, four pairs of white eyes, each with two blue circles and a blue center.
Eight others were found.

44   74-116   D16/17   2   4
D. 0.006
Green matrix. Two large white eyes, two pairs of small ones, all with blue centers.
Two others were found.

45 Pl. 5   77-254   F13/G13   2   2
D. 0.010
Green matrix, one large white eye, three pairs of small ones, each eye with a blue center, and a blue circle.
Seven others were found.

46 Pl. 5   76-829   C11   1   4
D. 0.014
Large. Yellow matrix. Four pairs of white eyes, each with a blue circle and a blue center.
One other was found.

47 Pl. 5   73-936   D16/17   1   3
D. 0.010
Yellow matrix. Four pairs of white eyes, each with a blue circle and a blue center.
Two others were found.

48 Pl. 5   74-117   D16/17   2   4
D. 0.006
Yellow matrix. Three big white eyes, one pair of small ones, all with one blue circle and blue center.
Five others were found.

---

17. Agrigento Museum inv. 11458, unpublished.
18. B. Filow, *Die Grabhügelnekropole bei Duvanlij in Südbulgarien* (Sofia 1934), 82-97, fig. 121, no. 27; pp. 127-142, fig. 165, nos. 20 and 21.
19. Guido 1978, 50-51. A summary of selected findspots and dates is given in Czurda-Ruth 1979, 193-195.
20. Guido 1978, 47.
21. D. Barag, *'Atiqot* (English Series) V (1966) 58-59.
22. G. Lankester Harding, *QDAP* 14 (1950) 44-48.
23. N. Tsori, *The Bulletin of the Department of Antiquities of the State of Israel* 5/6 (1957) 17 (in Hebrew).
24. Harden 1981, 60, 161-163.
25. G.L. Harding, *QDAP* 14 (1950) 45, no. 32, pl. XV:3.
26. Soprintendenza Archeologica di Roma, *I Galli e l'Italia* (Rome 1978), 50, nos. 85-86.
27. J. and L. Jehasse, *La nècropole prèromaine d'Alèria (1960-1968)*, *Gallia* supplement 25 (Paris 1973), 421, no. 1643, pl. 162.
28. Guido 1978, 47.

49 Pl. 5   73-675   D16/17   1   3
D. 0.009
  Yellow matrix. Three white eyes with blue centers.
  Four others were found.

50 Pl. 5   73-589   D16/17   1   2
D. 0.0095
  Blue matrix. Seven white eyes with blue centers.

51 Pl. 5   73-485   C15/16   1   4
D. 0.010
  Blue matrix. Four white eyes.
  Two others were found.

52 Pl. 5   76-1056   E15   2   4
D. 0.023
  Large cylindrical bead. Blue matrix. Three tiers of white eyes, twenty-one in all, with blue centers.

53 Pl. 5   77-1090   D15/E15   1   3
Max. P.H. 0.039
  Fragmentary bead, larger than preceding (**52**). Blue matrix. Six tiers of eyes of light color, probably white but glass gone, with blue centers remaining as stalks.
  Three smaller fragments of similar beads were found.

54   73-545   Stray
Max. P.H. 0.020
  Same as **53**.

55   76-304   D16/E16   1   4
Max. P.H. 0.020
  Same as **53**.

56   76-170   C11   1   2
Max. P.H. 0.023
  Same as **53**, but only four tiers of eyes.

BEAD WITH THREADS
57

57 Pl. 5   76-901   D11   balk   2a
Max. P.L. 0.014; D. 0.006
  Cylindrical. Dark (black?) opaque matrix. Single white thread spirally wound around its length.

PLAIN BEADS
58-63

DOUGHNUT SHAPED (58-61)

Undecorated greenish blue, yellow, and blue beads must be comparable in date to those with eyes.

58 Pl. 5   77-267   D15/16   1   2
D. 0.011
  Greenish blue.
  Twelve others were found.

59 Pl. 5   77-328   D15/16   1   2
D. 0.014
  Yellow.
  Twelve others were found.

60 Pl. 5   77-917   C13   1   2a
D. 0.014
  Blue.
  Approximately sixty others were found, some as small as 0.004 in diameter.

61 Pl. 5   77-1111   C13   1   4b
D. 0.016
  Translucent blue. Roman in date?

OVOID (62 and 63)

62 Pl. 5   73-672   D16/17   1   3
P.L. 0.020; D. 0.010
  Blue opaque.

63 Pl. 5   77-216   D15/16   1   2
P.L. 0.017; D. 0.008
  Green opaque.

MELON OR LOBED BEADS
64-68

Melon beads were found in the debris of a glass factory, at Rhodes, of ca. 3rd century B.C. date.[29] Margaret Guido mentions others from a third-century B.C. site at St. Étienne-au-Temple, now in the Musée des Antiquités Nationales at Saint-Germain-en-Laye.[30]

64 Pl. 6   73-601   D16/17   1   3
P.L. 0.016; D. 0.020
  Blue opaque.

65 Pl. 6   76-521   E13/14   1   2
P.H. 0.012; D. 0.018
  Blue opaque.

66 Pl. 6   73-696   D16/17   1   3
P.H. 0.018; D. 0.015
  Natural translucent green, bubbly.

67 Pl. 6   76-242   C13/D13   1   4
P.L. 0.016; D. 0.015
  Natural translucent green, bubbly.

68 Pl. 6   73-586   D16/17   1   2
Max. P.L. 0.017; Max. P.W. 0.030
  Natural translucent green. Lobes edged with blue glass. One-third preserved.

RODS
69-71

Objects of this shape (**69-71**), usually twisted rods of glass and approximately 0.16-0.22 m. in length, are found all over the Roman Empire in first-century A.D. contexts.[31] They first appear in Tiberian contexts and continue through the end of the century.[32] Examples

---

29. G. D. Weinberg, *ArchDelt* 24, Part A (1969) pl. 76a.
30. Guido 1978, 100.

31. Isings 1957, 94-95. A selected survey of findspots is given in Czurda-Ruth 1979, 207-209.
32. G. Cairoli, *NSc* (1979) 32, fig. 19.

looped at one end have been found in Syria,[33] Cyprus,[34] and elsewhere.

69 Pl. 6   77-1110   D15/16 2 2
Max. P.L. 0.035; D. rod 0.006
Looped end of a twisted rod. Natural green.

70   77-323   C10/11 A 2
Max. P.L. 0.022; D. rod 0.006
Center of a twisted rod. Natural green.

71 Pl. 6   74-597   Stray
Max. P.L. 0.029
Flattened, butt end of a twisted rod. Natural green.

Cast Glass
72-98

The cast glass can be separated into two principal groups: 1) opaque, which includes polychrome mosaic, monochrome opaque, and banded glass; 2) translucent, which includes ribbed and plain bowls, wheel-turned, some with engraved interior grooves.

OPAQUE
72-81

All the mosaic glass is of Roman date, with the possible exception of **72** which may be late Hellenistic, late second or first century B.C. **73** is from a deep bowl with offset rim. A complete example in purple glass with mosaic spots is in the Metropolitan Museum; there is also one of polychrome banded glass in the Museum at Pula, Yugoslavia, from the necropolis at Carano, Porto di Bado, near Nesactium.[35] A fragment of a gold-band bowl of this shape was found in the Athenian Agora, inv. G33. **75** is from a shallow dish. Complete examples of this type of dish are in the Yale University Art Gallery,[36] in the Metropolitan Museum,[37] and on the European art market.[38] Dishes with this profile also occur in emerald green glass of a type found at Pompeii and elsewhere.

79 appears to be from a gold-band alabastron, a type with a wide distribution in Italy, Greece, Asia Minor, Cyprus, Syria, and Egypt.[39]

MOSAIC (72-78)

72 Pl. 6   73-720   C15/16 1 3
Max. P.W. 0.025; Max. P.H. 0.013; Th. 0.002
Thin-walled bowl? Tesserae: blue with yellow spirals, purple with white spirals.

73 Pl. 6; Fig. 1   73-425   D12/E12 D 2
Max. P.H. 0.043; D. 0.15
Deep bowl. Tesserae: dark purple with red circle containing white dot on blue ground. Individual tesserae separated by white borders.

74 Pl. 6   69-218   D13 (Area 2) 2 1
Max. P.W. 0.025; Max. P.H. 0.022; Th. 0.002
Possibly from the same object as the preceding.

75   73-488   C15/16 1 3
Max. P.L. 0.044; D. (est.) 0.18
Two nonjoining fragments from flat-bottomed dish with double convex rim molding. Mosaic elements discolored, but most have red or yellow circle; a few with blue matrix with yellow spirals. One fragment preserves the base formed by a thick thread of green glass.

76   74-714   D12/13 F 2b
Max. P.L. 0.038
Bowl? Purple or blue tesserae with white swirls. Coarse.

77   74-589   D12/13 F 1
Max. P.W. 0.019; Max. P.H. 0.040; Th. 0.004
Possibly from the same object as **76**.

78 Pl. 6   73-1031   E10 balk 1
Max. P.W. 0.016; Max. P.H. 0.010; Th. 0.003
Shape uncertain. Blue green ground with white dots.

BANDED (79)

79 Pl. 6   73-512   C15/16 1 4
Max. P.L. 0.025
Alabastron. Gold band (gold missing) with green and white flanked by blue.

MONOCHROME (80 and 81)

Opaque white and red glass was employed for a wide variety of shapes in the late first century B.C. and the first century A.D.

---

33. S. Abdul Hak, *JGS* 7 (1965), 34, fig. 23.

34. Hayes 1975, 158, no. 656b, fig. 21; *The Swedish Cyprus Expedition* IV:3 (Stockholm 1956), 174, fig. 51, nos. 15 and 17, fig. 62:6; *Glass at the Fitzwilliam Museum* (Cambridge 1978), 50, no. 96.

35. Metropolitan Museum of Art, 13.224; Pula: A. Gnirs, *Pola, ein Führer durch die antiken Baudenkmäler und Sammlungen* (Vienna 1915), 135, fig. 86.

36. Matheson 1980, 20, no. 54.

37. Smith 1957, 82-83, no. 134.

38. Kunsthaus Zürich, *Sammlung E. und M. Kofler-Truniger* (Zurich 1974), 47, no. 459, pl. 36; sale catalogue, Christie, Manson & Woods Ltd., London, 5 March 1985, lot 183.

39. A. Oliver, Jr. *JGS* 9 (1967) 20-21; *Revue Archéologique de l'Oise* 18 (1980) 9-13.

80 Pl. 6; Fig. 1   73-386   C15/16   1   1
Max P.L. 0.030; D. (est.) 0.15
   White opaque bowl. Interior groove at angle of rim to body. Exterior angled and offset.

81 Pl. 6   74-605   C10/11   2
Max. P.L. 0.016
   Red opaque cup base fragment with ring foot exhibiting the usual green surface corrosion.

TRANSLUCENT, MONOCHROME
82-96

RIBBED (82-86)

The common ribbed bowls found all over the Mediterranean and western Europe during the time of the early Empire range in date from the late first century B.C. to nearly the end of the first century A.D.[40] Although the diameters of the five pieces described here (**82-86**) cannot be calculated, it is evident that they all belong to deep rather than shallow bowls. The exteriors of their rims are not ground or polished. Ten scrappy fragments, not catalogued here, were also found: two brown, three pale blue, and five natural green.

82 Pl. 7   73-379   C15/16   1   2
Max. P.W. 0.039; Max. P.H. 0.034; Th. 0.004
   Brown. One groove on interior. Small ribs. Rim not preserved.

83 Pl. 7; Fig. 1   74-320   C10/11   A   1
Max. P.W. 0.020; Max. P.H. 0.046; Th. 0.10
   Natural green. No grooves. Bold ribs.

84 Pl. 7; Fig. 1   76-373   E13/14   1   2
Max. P.W. 0.37; Max. P.H. 0.048
   Natural green. Two grooves on interior. Bold ribs.

85 Pl. 7   77-758   Stray
Max. P.W. 0.039; Max. P.H. 0.035; Th. 0.007
   Colorless. One groove on interior. Small ribs. Out-turned rim.

86   74-320   C10/11   A   4
Max. P.W. 0.020; Max. P.H. 0.020; Th. 0.010
   Dark aquamarine.

PLAIN, RELATED TO RIBBED BOWLS (87-94)

Wheel-turned bowls without ribs, but with horizontal grooves on the interior (and sometimes the exterior), began to be made at a much earlier period than the ribbed bowls, but all of the Cyrene fragments belong to the late group contemporary with the ribbed bowls, late first century B.C. to at least the mid-first century A.D. Colors and arrangements of grooves are identical.[41] All fragments except one (**91**) appear to belong to deep bowls. Some lack grooves (**93, 94**). Eighteen scrappy fragments, not catalogued here, were also found: two colorless, the rest brown or natural green.

87 Pl. 7   77-1017   D15/E15   1   1
Max. P.W.; 0.016; Max. P.H. 0.017
   Intentional dark blue. Two grooves on the interior.

88 Pl. 7; Fig. 1   74-499   C10/11   A (beta)   3
   Brownish green. Two pairs of grooves on the interior.

89 Pl. 7; Fig. 1   74-595   C14   1   2
Max. P.W. 9.943; Max. P.H. 0.039; D. (est.) 0.130
   Pale greenish brown. Two grooves on interior.

90 Pl. 7; Fig. 1   78-284   C17   2   1
Max. P.W. 0.029; Max. P.H. 0.029; D. (est.) 0.100
   Colorless. One groove on interior.

91   Stray 1973
   Shallow bowl. Natural blue green. Groove on interior directly at rim.

92   Stray 1973
D. (est.) 0.110
   Brown. No grooves.

93 Pl. 8; Fig. 1   74-487   C10/11   A (beta)   3
D. (est.) 0.120
   Natural green. No grooves.

94 Pl. 8; Fig. 1   71-233   E12   1   5
D. (est.) 0.100
   Colorless. No grooves.

UNDECORATED, NOT RELATED TO THE PRECEDING (95 and 96)

Fragments of cast and wheel-cut bowls, but without significant additional decoration and of a type unrelated to the preceding, were are also found at Cyrene (**95 and 96**). They date to the middle and second half of the first century A.D. The group is colorless and probably represents fine quality tableware from Egypt.

Fragmentary examples similar to those from Cyrene have been found in England at Fishbourne,[42] at Corbridge,[43] and at Conimbriga, Portugal.[44] Glass of this type was much more widespread than these selected, published examples imply.

95 Pl. 8; Fig. 1   74-730   C14   1   4
Max. P.W. 0.073; Max. P.H. 0.045; D. (est.) 0.170
   Bowl. Colorless. Out-turned rim, groove on upper surface. Thickening ridge below rim at one point must signify edge of handle.

96 Pl. 8; Fig. 2   76-907   C13/D13   2   2
D. (est.) 0.170
   Bowl. Colorless. Out-turned rim.

---

40. Grose in *Muse* 13 (1979), 61-63; comparable fragments have been found at Sidi Khrebish, Benghazi: Price 1985, 291-292, fig. 24.2, nos. 14-22.

41. Ibid., 1979, 63-65; for similar fragmentary bowls from Sidi Khrebish, Benghazi see Price 1985, 291, 294, fig. 24.3, nos. 27-34.

42. Harden and Price 1971, 331-332, nos. 25-26, fig. 138.

43. D. Charlesworth, *Archaeologia Aeliana* n.s. 37 (1959) 39-40, fig. 3.

44. Alarcão 1965, 78, no. 106, pl. IV.

Blown Glass
97-173

Glass blowing is thought to have been invented in the mid-first century B.C., but no blown fragments from Cyrene can be attributed to an object from that early a date. Some pieces, however, may well have been made in the late first century B.C.

Apart from several fragments from bottles blown into square molds with a bottom design (considered here with the free-blown glass), only one fragment comes from what we normally consider a mold-blown vessel, one fashioned with fully decorated molds (**97**). All others are free-blown and have been catalogued by shape, and within shape, by manner of decoration. First are open shapes: bowls; dishes; cups with ribbing and wheel-cut decoration; undecorated rims, rims with added threads, and folded rims (including those with corrugated trimming); cup handles without rims; and bases (folded, tubular, solid, and otherwise fashioned). Second are closed shapes: square bottles (bottle handles and bases), flasks, and unguentaria.

The glass has not been separated according to color (i.e., natural green, intentionally colored, or colorless), although an effort has been made to put like colors together within each shape group.

MOLD-BLOWN
97

97, the only fragment from a mold-blown vessel, comes from a flask in the form of a bunch of grapes. The overall curve of the remaining "wall" is concave on the side that the "grapes" are convex, but this seeming contradiction of shape occurs on grape flasks in New Haven,[45] in Leiden,[46] and on a fragment from Heddernheim.[47] Its date is probably second century A.D.

97 Stray 1973
Max. P.L. 0.025
Bunch of grapes flask. Intentionally blue.

Open Shapes
98-160

RIBBED BOWLS
98 and 99

Ribbed bowls of blown glass, with or without a marvered thread wound many times around the body, are found all over the Roman Empire in contexts from ca. A.D. 25-100.[48] Examples of blue, and natural green glass without threads are not unusual.

98 Pl. 8 73-326 C15/16 1 2
Max. P.W. 0.042
Bottom. Intentional blue.

99 Pl. 8 74-412 C10/11 A 1
Max. P.W. 0.042
Side. Natural green.

BOWLS AND CUPS WITH WHEEL-CUT LINEAR AND FACETED DECORATION
100-109

In this section are some of the finer fragments from Cyrene, all from the first century A.D.

100, a bowl with strigillated grooves, belongs to a small group of open shapes from Cologne, Begram in Afghanistan, and Fishbourne, England, all of colorless glass with fine grooves, and all dating from the second half of the first century A.D.[49]

102 and **103** come from beakers cut with a regular pattern of hollow hexagonal facets, a style of cutting that flourished in the last quarter of the first century A.D.

---

45. Matheson 1980, 104, no. 278.
46. *Oudheidkundige Mededelingen* 44 (1963) 109, no. 18.
47. Welker 1974, 119, no. 275, pl. 23.

48. W. Pfeffer and T. E. Haevernick, *SaalbJb* 17 (1958) 76-88; T. E. Haevernick, *JRGZM* 14 (1967) 153-166; Czurda-Ruth 1979, 43-47.
49. Harden and Price 1971, 334, for references.

104-107 have knocked off rims. **106** is placed here, even though no linear decoration is visible, because it was made in the same fashion as the others, with rim left rough, and because some complete vessels have pairs of lines engraved low on the body. Intentionally blue cups of the same shape as **106** are probably of mid-first century A.D. date. A complete specimen is in Aquileia;[50] another, with a pair of engraved lines, was formerly in the R. W. Smith collection.[51]

106 comes from a cup of the sort found in the west in mid-first-century (Claudian-Neronian) contexts. Compare, for example, one from Vindonissa, Switzerland.[52]

100 Pl. 9; Fig. 2   76-121   D16/17   A   2
D. (est.) 0.100
 Bowl. Colorless. On exterior: pair of engraved lines at rim, another below, curved grooves on body.

101 Pl. 9; Fig. 2   76-122   C11   1   2
Max. P.L. 0.054; D. (est.) 0.120
 Bowl. Colorless. On exterior: groove at rim, another below.

102 Pl. 9; Fig. 2   73-1105   C15/D15   1B   4
Max. P.L. 0.027
 Beaker. Colorless. Row of hollow, hexagonal facets.

103 Pl. 9; Fig. 2   73-1108   E10 balk   3
Max. P.W. 0.043; Max. D. 0.043
 Beaker. Colorless. Horizontal groove at bottom, two tiers of hexagonal facets preserved above.

104 Pl. 9; Fig. 2   73-1109   E10 balk   3
D. (est.) 0.06
 Cup. Colorless. Thin walled. Three lines on exterior.

105 Pl. 9; Fig. 2   73-227   E10 balk   2
D. (est.) 0.07
 Cup. Intentional blue. No linear cutting.

106 Fig. 2   77-545   F13/G13   2   2
Max. P.W. 0.018; Max. P.H. 0.025; D. (est.) 0.09
 Cup. Natural green. Thick walled. Broadly engraved groove.

107 Pl. 9; Fig. 2   77-1160   C12/13   2   3
D. (est.) 0.075
 Cup. Natural green. Abraded line low on exterior.

108 Pl. 9   73-1041   C15/D15   1B   3
Max. P.W. 0.020; Max. P.H. 0.023
 Bowl. Natural green. Pair of grooves. Rim not preserved.

109 Pl. 10; Fig. 2   74-451   C10/11   A   3
Max. P.H. 0.046; Max. D. 0.073
 Base and lower part of cup. Natural green. Indented bottom. Abraded line on body, 0.045 above bottom.

UNDECORATED CUPS OR BOWLS: ROUNDED, FIRE-POLISHED RIMS
110 and 111

110 and **111** come from two relatively undistinguished bowls of natural green glass dating probably not earlier than the second century A.D. In addition to those catalogued, many other similar fragments were found.

110 Pl. 10; Fig. 3   73-612   C15/16   1   2
D. (est.) 0.12
 Cup. Natural green.

111 Pl. 10   74-732   D11/12   1   2
Max. P.W. 0.037; Max. P.H. 0.024; Th. 0.005
 Cup. Natural green.

CUPS AND BOWLS: RIMS WITH THREADS ON EXTERIOR
112-118

A thread of glass was added to many cups and bowls, about a centimeter below the rim, as a decorative feature and perhaps also to catch drips. This feature, widespread in Roman glass, first appeared early in the second century A.D. Cups with rim profiles appearing similar to **112-114** have been found at a Roman frontier fort in Northumberland built ca. A.D. 128 and abandoned ca. A.D. 139-142.[53] The type was still being made in the third century. An out-turned rim, as on **117** and **118**, occurs on a fragment from Conimbriga, Portugal.[54]

CUPS, RIMS WITH THREAD ON EXTERIOR (**112-116**)

112 Fig. 3   73-427   D12/E12   D   2
D. (est.) 0.065
 Almost colorless. Thread not pronounced.

113 Pl. 11; Fig. 3   77-1162   D15/16   2   2
D. (est.) 0.08
 Pale yellow green. Two turns of a thread, irregular.

114 Pl. 11; Fig. 3   76-764   C14/D14   1   2;
D. (est.) 0.09   D12/13   F   2
 Pale yellow green. Thickened rim.

---

50. Calvi 1968, 73, no. 176, pl. 11, fig. 5.
51. Smith 1957, 131, no. 250, later on the art market, *Sotheby Parke Bernet*, New York, 20-21 November 1975, lot 462, ill.
52. L. Berger, *Römische Gläser aus Vindonissa* (Basel 1960), 44, no. 100, pl. 7:100, pl. 17:14.

---

53. D. Charlesworth, *JGS* 13 (1971) 34-36, fig. 102, where other examples are cited.
54. Alarcão 1965, 85, no. 118, pl. IV.

115 Pl. 11; Fig. 3   77-1161   D15/16   2   2
D. (est.) 0.045
Pale yellow green.

116 Pl. 11; Fig. 3   76-374   C12/13   1   2
D. (est.) 0.07
Colorless.

BOWLS, RIMS WITH THREAD ON EXTERIOR
(**117** and **118**)

117 Pl. 11   73-424   C13   1   1
D. (est.) 0.19
Natural green. Out-turned, thickened rim.

118 not inv.   C14/D14   1   1;2
D. (est.) 0.10
Colorless. Out-turned rim.

BOWLS WITH FOLDED RIMS
119-123

Folded rims first appear in the late first century B.C. as the obvious solution for strengthening the edge of the glass.[55] They remain common throughout the Roman period. None of the following five fragments (**119-123**) has a profile of the sort with corrugated trimming.

119 Pl. 11; Fig. 3   Stray 1973
D. (est.) 0.18
Natural green. Tubular fold.

120 Pl. 11; Fig. 3   74-900   D12/13   F   2B
D. (est.) 0.15
Natural green. Large fold.

121 Pl. 11   74-496   C10/11   A   2
D. (est.) 0.19
Natural green. Out-turned rim.

122 Pl 11; Fig. 3   74-488   C10/C11   2
Max. P.W. 0.026; D. (est.) 0.15
Natural green. Flange beyond fold.

123 Pl. 12; Fig. 3   74-600   D11/12   1   2
Max. P.W. 0.049; D. (est.) 0.12
Colorless. Out-turned rim.

BOWLS WITH FOLDED RIM AND CORRUGATED TRIMMING
124-134

Corrugated trimming first appears on rims in the second half of the first century A.D. Examples from the third quarter of the century are cited by Clasina Isings, but the folded rims are not necessarily of the same contours as those published here.[56] The colors of a dish, in Berlin, of dark blue glass with opaque white trimming are also suggestive of a date in the third quarter of the century.[57] An example from Nahal David in the Judean Desert came from a context of A.D. 132-135,[58] and one from Tipasa, Algeria, was found with coins of Marcus Aurelius and Lucius Verus, A.D. 161-180.[59] I know of no specific evidence to indicate the survival of corrugated trimming into the third century.

124 Pl. 12   76-61   D16/17   A   3
D. (est.) 0.22
Natural green.

125 Pl. 12   73-902   D12/E12   D   2
D. (est.) 0.18
Colorless?

126 Pl. 12   76-60   D16/17   A   3
D. (est.) 0.15
Natural green.

127 Pl. 12   74-739   D12/13   F   2b
D. (est.) 0.15
Natural green.

128 Pl. 12   73-381   C15/16   1   4
D. (est.) 0.14
Natural green.

Several fragments of folded rims must come from similar bowls.

129 Pl. 12   73-453   C15/16   1   1
130 Pl. 12   76-63   D16/17   A   2
131 Pl. 13   76-78   C11   1   1
132 Pl. 13   76-90   C11   1   2
133 Pl. 13   74-596   D11/12   1
134 Pl. 13   76-88   C11   1   2

DISH AND CUP WITH OTHER TYPES OF FOLDED RIMS
135 and 136

135, of colorless glass, has a flanged rim with a double fold and may well come from a type of dish found at Tipasa, Algeria in a tomb in use from Trajanic to Antonine times[60] and also in a cave in the Judean desert dated no later than A.D. 135.[61]

136 could come from the rim of a modiolus (the shape suggested for a similar fragment from Heerlen,

---

55. D. Grose, *JGS* 19 (1977) 17-20, fig. 1:10.
56. Isings 1957, 59, form 43.
57. Platz-Horster 1976, 61, no. 115.
58. D. Barag, *IEJ* 12 (1962) 210, fig. 4.
59. Lancel 1967, 94, no. 195, pl. X:4. See also D. Barag in Y. Yadin, *The Finds from the Bar Kokhba Period in the Cave of Letters* (Jerusalem 1963), 105 n. 13.
60. Lancel 1967, 88, no. 175, pl. IX:4.
61. *Bulletin des Journées Internationales du Verre* 2 (1963) 109 and 112, fig. 70.

the Netherlands)[62] or from a bowl comparable to one from Magdalensberg.[63]

135   Stray
D. (est.) 0.15
Colorless. Flanged rim, double fold.

136   Fig. 4   C12/13   1   2
D. (est.) 0.12
Natural green. From a modiolus or a bowl.

RIMS FORMED BY A DOUBLE FOLD
137-140

The four fragments published here (**137-140**) come from rims, not bases. Several fragments of this sort from Ostia have been published as bases by Maria Paola Moriconi.[64] The Ostia fragments are dated to the late first century A.D., not before the time of Domitian, when the Terme del Nuotatore at Ostia were built. A bowl with double folded rim from Ashdod, Israel, is thought by Dan Barag to be from the second or third century.[65]

137   C13   1   2
D. (est.) 0.13
Pale green. Double tubular fold.

138   Pl. 13   74-489   C10/11   A   2
Max. P.W. 0.018; Max. P.H. 0.005
As **137**.

139   Pl. 13   77-120   C13   1   1
D. (est.) 0.12
Natural green. No edge preserved.

140   Pl. 13   74-995   F9/10; G9/10   A   3
Max. P.W. 0.009; Max. P.L. 0.046
Natural green blue. No edge preserved.

CUP HANDLES
141-144

141 and **142** are from handles of skyphoi of a type placed in the first century A.D. as early as the Augustan period, but continuing late in the century.[66] Both tall and short varieties of this skyphos are known, but is not possible to say from which variety these handles come.

143, a handle with part of the vessel wall featuring a tubular double fold below the upper attachment, was one of a pair of handles from a different kind of skyphos represented by stemmed examples in Corning[67] and Aleppo,[68] and a squat one in Warsaw.[69]

144, a bipartite ring handle, could come from a modiolus, the one-handled cup common in the first century.[70] The rim fragment (**138**) could also come from a modiolus, or it could be one of a pair of ring handles from a skyphos type found in Aquileia.[71]

141   not inv.   C12/13   1   1
Skyphos handle. Light blue glass.

142   Pl. 13   74-992   F9/10; G9/10   A   3
Max. P.W. 0.013; Max. P.H. 0.020; Th. 0.009
Skyphos handle. Natural green.

143   Fig. 4   Stray
D. (est.) 0.09
Handle and part of wall of skyphos. Colorless. Double fold in wall below upper attachment of handle.

144   Pl. 13   74-322   C10/11   A   2
Max. P.W. 0.014; Max. P.L. 0.063
Bipartite ring handle of cup. Natural green.

BASES
145-160

152-155, with solid ring feet, may well belong to cups of the type from which rims **112-114** come. **147** is comparable in size and shape to a base from Nida-Heddernheim dated to the late first or early second century A.D.[72] **145** and **146** are from shallow dishes. **149**, one of four catalogued fragments with a tubular ring foot, resembles Isings form 42, a bowl, examples of which date to the first and second centuries A.D.[73] **157** is from a glass with four indented sides, a feature common on glasses of the first century A.D., especially in Cyprus.[74] **159**, a base with a separately made blown foot, is not likely to be earlier than the second century A.D., though this method of providing a foot begins in the late first century A.D.[75]

---

62. C. Isings, *Roman Glass in Limburg* (Groningen 1971), 73, no. 60, fig. 19.

63. Czurda-Ruth 1979, 65, no. 524, pl. 3, where in the text one of Tiberian date is cited as being published in *Cambodunum Forschungen* I, 1953, 79, fig. 9:22.

64. A. Carandini *et al.*, *Le Terme del Nuotatore: Ostia II, Studi miscellanei del seminario di archeologia e storia dell'arte greca e romana*, 16 (Rome 1970), 79, pl. XVI, nos. 248 and 249.

65. D. Barag, *'Atiqot* 7 (1967) 37, 73, fig. 16, no. 16.

66. Isings 1957, 55-56, form 39; Czurda-Ruth 1979, 54-56

67. 61.1.7; Smith 1957, 123, no. 218.

68. *Bulletin des Journées Internationales du Verre* 3 (1964) 35-36, no. 5, fig. 15.

69. *Bulletin des Journées Internationales du Verre* 2 (1963), 52-53, fig. 47.

70. J. H. C. Kern, *ArchCl* 8 (1956) 58-63; Isings 1957, 52-53, form 37.

71. Calvi 1968, no. 60, pl. 7, fig. 1.

72. Welker 1974, 42, no. 95, pl. 6.

73. Isings 1957, 58.

74. A. Oliver Jr. *RDAC* (1983) 251.

75. Harden and Price 1971, 352, s.v. no. 69.

FOLDED BASE (145-147)

145 Pl. 14   73-850   E10   balk   3
Max. P.L. 0.075; D. (est.) 0.15
Colorless. Large fold. Although it looks like a rim, curve is reversed.

146 Pl. 14; Fig. 4   76-524   C11   2   2SE
Max. P.L. 0.035; D. (est.) 0.09
Colorless. Large fold.

147 Pl. 14; Fig. 4   77-1091   D15/16   2   2
D. (est.) 0.05
Natural green. Splayed foot. Pontil mark.

TUBULAR FOOT (148-151)

148 Pl. 14   73-608   D16/17   1   1
D. (est.) 0.05
Natural green. Thread on exterior concentric with foot. Pontil mark.

149 Pl. 14   76-80   D16/17   A   2
D. (est.) 0.005
Natural green.

150 Pl. 14   76-62   E13/14   1   2
Natural green. Angled wall beyond foot.

151 Pl. 14   76-71   D16/17   A   2
Natural green. Angled wall beyond foot.

SOLID RING FOOT (152-156)

152 Pl. 14   76-1062   C14/D14   1   2B
Natural green. Pontil mark.

153 Pl. 15   77-1165   D11   1   2
Natural green.

154 Pl. 15   76-111   C11   1   1
Natural green.

155 Pl. 15   76-120   C11   1   2
Colorless. Thin walled. Not thickened at center. Pontil mark.

156 Pl. 15; Fig. 4   76-124   C12/D12   G   1
D. (est.) 0.18
Natural green. Center not preserved. The foot is not a rod as in **152-155**, but wedge-shaped merging with the bottom of the glass.

BOTTOM INDENTED FOR STABILITY (157)

157 Pl. 15   76-66   D16/17   A   1
Natural green. From base of cup with four indented sides.

FLATTENED FOLD AS FOOT (158)

158 Pl. 15   74-492   F11   1   1
Natural green. No pontil mark.

SEPARATELY MADE, BLOWN FOOT (159)

159 Pl. 15; Fig. 4   77-918   D15/16   2   1
Natural green.

"TOED" BASE (160)

"Toed" bases similar to **160**, mostly colorless as here, have been found at Dura-Europos,[76] Karanis,[77] Kourion in Cyprus,[78] and at many other sites. They have traditionally been dated on slim evidence to the second and early third century A.D.

160 Pl. 16   76-766   D13/E13   1   2
D. 0.035
Colorless.

Closed Shapes: Bottles, Flasks, and Unguentaria
161-173

Included here are all fragments that can be associated with closed shapes, though some of the preceding bases might belong to such shapes. Dorothy Charlesworth considered that in the East, square bottles like **161** were made from the mid-first through the mid-third centuries A.D.[79] **162** and **163** are the upper parts of strap handles from bottles. Thick-walled, natural green unguentaria like **166** were made in the first and second centuries; a similar one in Berlin is dated a century too late.[80] An unguentarium of this general shape was found in a burial of the first century A.D. near Tyre.[81] Another, from Dura-Europos, could well date from the late first or early second century.[82] **167** is from a "test-tube" unguentarium of a type common from the first through the fourth centuries.[83] The profile of **169** indicates a first century date as does the intentional blue color of **171**.

---

76. Clairmont 1963, 50-52, pl. V.
77. Harden 1936, 219 and 229, nos. 682 and 708.
78. A. Oliver, Jr., *Glass from Kourion*, forthcoming.
79. D. Charlesworth, *JGS* 8 (1966) 31.
80. Platz-Horster 1976, 67, no. 126.
81. J. Hajjar, *BMBeyr* 18 (1965) 66, no. F 351, pl. XVII.
82. Clairmont 1963, 135, no. 687, pl. XXXV.
83. Isings 1957, 41, Form 27.

SQUARE BOTTLE
161

161 Pl. 16; Fig. 4   76-168   D16/17   A   3
P.W. 0.055
Natural green. Molded bottom showing large circle with four satellite circles in corners.

BOTTLE HANDLES
162 and 163

162 Pl. 16   76-209   C11   1   2
P.W. of strap 0.045
Handle fragment with neck. Natural green.

163 Pl. 16   74-108   D16/17   2   2
P.W. of strap 0.035
Natural green.

FLASKS WITH FUNNEL NECKS
164 and 165

164 Pl. 16; Fig. 4   74-738   D11/12   1   2
D. (rim) 0.070
Colorless. Rib on underside of rim.

165 Pl. 17; Fig. 4   73-392   C15/16   1   2
D. (rim) 0.055
Colorless. Rounded rim.

UNGUENTARIA
166-171

166 Pl. 17   74-93   D16/17   2   3
Max. P.H. 0.058; D. 0.043
Body and lower neck of thick-walled unguentarium. Natural green.

167 Pl. 17   76-123   C11   1   2
Max. P.H. 0.025
Lower body of piriform unguentarium. Natural green.

168 C11   1   2
D. (base, est.) 0.090
Lower body.

169 Pl. 17   74-410   C10/11   A   1
Neck and shoulder of a thin-walled example. Natural green.

170 Pl. 17   74-875   F11   2   3
Neck and shoulder.

171 not inv.   F12   2
Neck of tall unguentarium. Intentional blue.

GLASS WITH APPLIED DECORATION
172 and 173

Glass fragments with raised points, like **172**, have been found at Dura-Europos, which suggests a date before the mid-third century A.D.[84] The fragment from Cyrene could be from a funnel-necked flask similar to one in Berlin.[85] **173** is from a bottle or cup. Comparable decoration, though found in the fourth century, began as early as the first century A.D.

172 Pl. 17   74-580   D11/12   1   2
Max. P.W. 0.030
Bottle with points or projections. Natural green.

173 Pl. 17   74-779   F11   2   2
Max. P.W. 0.054
Cup or bottle. Pale yellow-green glass. Thick thread applied in a wavy pattern.

Summary

The glass from the Sanctuary of Demeter and Persephone at Cyrene can, for the most part, be divided into two chronological and typological groups: 1) core-formed glass bottles and opaque beads from the late 6th to the early 4th century B.C. (**1-71**); 2) cast and blown glass from the late first century B.C. through the second century A.D. (**72-173**). No glass need necessarily be dated later than the late second century A.D., although some of the types assigned to the late first and early second century could well have been made at a later period. The rare and quite fine example of a mold-formed, carved glass head (**174**) is discussed in detail by Jennifer Price in Appendix I (see pp. 102-103).

---

84. Clairmont 1963, 51-53, pl. VI.

85. Platz-Horster 1976, 86, no. 172. M. C. Calvi in *Atti del convegno internazionale per il XIX centenario della dedicazione de "Capitolium" e per il 150° anniversario della sua scoperta Brescia 27-30 settembre 1973* (Brescia 1975), 210, fig. 9.

Appendix I

The Glass Head from the Sanctuary of Demeter and Persephone at Cyrene 174
by Jennifer Price

CONTEXT
73-165; C17, 1B, 4 Pottery and lamp dump containing objects dating from sixth century B.C. to late first century B.C., early.

Maximum Dimensions: PH. 0.052; W. 0.034; D. Shaft at top 0.012; Th. (through wall of shaft) 0.0045; Th. (through face) 0.019. m.

DESCRIPTION
Fragment, perhaps from unguent bottle or votive statuette, showing part of female head, and part of rim and neck with conical cavity on back. Greenish colorless.

Exterior surfaces smooth and slightly pitted, surfaces in shaft very rough. Strain cracks visible on neck and inside shaft. Milky and multicolored iridescence.

Quality of glass very good; only a few small round bubbles visible.

Upper part of narrow vessel or object with female head carved in relief. Surviving fragment shows right side of face and neck expanding outward, having broken in vertical line down center of face to left of nose and below chin. Details of face, such as chin, mouth, nose, eye, eyebrow and hairstyle clearly defined. Hair parted in center, arranged around two elaborate 'topknots' with grooves on top surfaces, one above right eye and smaller one at side of the head. Rest of hair upswept above right ear, and no hair indicated below ear or at back of the vessel. Area behind face contains a vertical shaft which tapers inward from top to the bottom of surviving fragment. Fine wheel cut line runs from back of smaller 'topknot' to back of piece, and continues as diagonal groove round outside of neck.

The piece was either formed in an open or closed mold or carved from a solid piece of glass The final details were produced by carving, drilling, grinding, and polishing the surfaces. The shaft behind the face was probably drilled out with a bow drill, using a solid-pointed bit.

DISCUSSION
It is difficult to establish an exact chronological and cultural setting for this fragment, partly because the context in which it was found cannot be closely dated, and also because the form and decoration of the fragment itself appear to be without many parallels in ancient glass. Nonetheless, the color and quality of the glass, the technique of manufacture, and the detail of the decoration may be compared with other vessels and objects, and if these are taken together they provide some information about the likely date and provenance of the piece.

The object is made of fine quality colorless glass with a pale greenish tint that is probably noticeable only because of the great thickness of the fragment. It would be interesting to establish if the nearly colorless glass is the result of care taken in selecting the raw materials, or if a decolorant such as antimony or manganese was used, but this information is not available at present. The color and quality of the glass is comparable to that of the colorless Hellenistic vessels of the Canosa group produced in the third and second centuries B.C., fragments of which have been found at Sidi Khrebish, Benghazi, in Cyrenaica,[1] as well as at sites in southern Italy, Sicily, and elsewhere in the eastern Mediterranean region.[2]

Several methods of manufacture could have been employed. In theory it might have been possible to produce the vessel by core-forming, and then by carving, grinding, and polishing the surfaces to achieve the final shape; however, the absence of any vestige of core material in the hollow shaft, or of

---

1. Price 1985, 290, fig. 24.1, 7-9.

2. Harden 1968A; Oliver 1968, 50; von Saldern 1975, 41, figs. 11-13; Grose 1981, 62-5. Grose 1982, 23-4, fig. 2c.

elongated or distorted bubbles and black specks in the glass, indicate that this was not the process used.

It is much more probable that the piece was produced either by cold-cutting, that is, by carving, grinding, and polishing a block of glass into the required shape, or by casting and cold-cutting, that is, by forming the shape in an open or closed mold and then working up the final details afterward. The finished surfaces have been completely ground and polished, so that it is not now possible to establish which production method was employed.[3]

The rough surfaces and tapering form of the vertical shaft behind the head indicate that this was drilled out, probably by using a bow-drill with a solid-pointed bit, although the heavy grinding marks associated with rotary abrasion using a tubular drill are not present.[4]

The method of manufacture of the Cyrene fragment is similar in many respects to that of a group of glass alabastra produced at several periods within the first millennium B.C. These vessels are not common at any time, although they are associated with a group of cast monochrome vessels found in many parts of western Asia and the eastern Mediterranean region from the eighth century B.C. onward. Many of them were open vessels, such as bowls, while others were closed forms, often with heavily ground interior surfaces. Most of the pieces were made in pale greenish or colorless glass, though yellow-brown, purple, and deep blue vessels were also produced.

The earliest group of this glass, which includes the Sargon Vase, a squat alabastron with a carved inscription on the exterior and heavy grinding marks on the interior, was produced during the later eighth or seventh century B.C. and may well be of Phoenician workmanship.[5] These vessels are mostly found in western Asia on Assyrian sites, though some examples are known from other parts of the Mediterranean world. Other alabastra also occur in later contexts. Some, which were in use from the mid-seventh to sixth century B.C. at sites in the eastern Mediterranean region and Italy, may have been produced in western Asia,[6] and a few date from the Achaemenid period in the fifth or fourth century B.C.[7]

The methods of manufacture employed in the production of the Cyrene piece were those used to make open vessels for most of the first millennium B.C., though it is difficult to be certain when these techniques went out of use, as so few closed vessels have survived. At present, the weight of the evidence implies that very few examples were manufactured in this way during the period, and it seems unlikely that many were produced by casting and cold-carving after the middle of the first century B.C. The invention of glass blowing brought about great changes in the glass industries of the ancient world, although a wide variety of cast or sagged[8] monochrome and polychrome mosaic forms were manufactured during the first century of the Roman Empire.

Little glass sculpture has survived from the ancient world. Most of the early pieces are from Egypt, where glass sculpture cast and carved in the round was produced at various times in the Dynastic and Ptolemaic periods.[9] The earliest known example is a small blue glass head of Amenhotep II (1436-1411 B.C.) in the Corning Museum of Glass,[10] and the latest probably dates from the first century B.C. or slightly later.[11] Most of glass sculptures are royal heads or figures of deities, and none of them resembles the Cyrene fragment.

A small number of pieces of glass sculpture, such as the small opaque light blue head of Augustus in Cologne,[12] are known in the early Roman Empire, but few are female representations, and none comes from a vessel or object with a hollowed interior. The female portrait head in opaque blue glass in the Metropolitan Museum of Art, dated to the first or second century A.D., is thought to come from north Africa,[13] and may be compared with the Cyrene piece in that the hair has a central parting; however, the details of the hairstyle and face are quite different, and the New York piece comes from a much larger object. Similarly, at Tolmeita in Cyrenaica there is a fragment of marble sculpture dated to the second century A.D. that shows the head of Cleopatra with a centrally parted and swept back hairstyle and an elephant headcovering,[14] but the details of design as well as the scale of the two pieces differ considerably.

CONCLUSIONS

The discussion above shows that the date, place of manufacture and decoration of this piece are quite uncertain, though because of its method of production, it seems likely to belong to the Hellenistic period at the latest and may perhaps have come from Egypt in light of the apparently long-standing tradition of glass sculpture there.

---

3. These methods of glassmaking have been examined and discussed on several occasions in recent years. For example, see Schuler 1959; Harden 1968B, 51-2; Goldstein 1979A, 33-4; Cummings 1980, 11-8; Barag 1985, 30-2.
4. Charleston 1964, 84-6, discusses methods of drilling glass.
5. Harden 1968B, pl. V, A and B; von Saldern 1970, no. 17, fig. 17; Barag 1985, no. 26, fig. 2, pl. 3, col. pl. B.
6. von Saldern 1970, nos. 48-53, 54a; Barag 1985, no. 44.
7. von Saldern 1970, no. 54, Barag 1985, no. 45.

---

8. See Cummings 1980, 23-44, for explanation and discussion of this production method.
9. Cooney 1960, 11-31.
10. Goldstein 1979B.
11. Cooney 1960, 31, fig. 23.
12. Doppelfeld 1965-6.
13. Metropolitan Museum of Art 59.11.8; Smith 1957, 115, no. 189.
14. Fabbricotti 1985, 226, pl. 18.IV,2.

Appendix II

Find Spot Index

AREA	TRENCH	STRATUM	CAT. NO.	APPROX. DATE
C10/11	2	-	81	late 1st century B.C.-1st century A.D.
			122	Roman
C10/11	A	1	83	late 1st century B.C-late 1st century A.D.
			99	A.D. 25-100
			169	1st century A.D.
C10/11	A	2	70	1st century A.D.
			121	Roman
			138	late 1st century A.D.
			144	1st century A.D.
C10/11	A	3	109	1st century A.D.
C10/11	A	4	86	late 1st century B.C to late 1st century A.D.
C10/11	A,β	3	88	late 1st century B.C. to mid-1st century A.D.
			93	late 1st century B.C. to mid-1st century A.D.
C11	1	1	131	2nd half of 1st century A.D.
			154	
C11	1	2	56	mid-6th century B.C.
			101	1st century A.D.
			132	2nd half of 1st century A.D.
			134	
			155	
			162	
			167	1st-4th centuries
			168	
C11	1	4	46	mid-6th century B.C.
C11	2	2SE	146	
C12/13	1	1	141	1st century A.D.
C12/13	1	2	116	2nd century A.D.
C12/13	1	2	136	
C12/13	2	3	107	1st century A.D.
C12/D12	G	1	156	
C12/D12	G	3	5	late 6th or 5th century B.C.
C13	1	1	117	2nd century A.D.
			139	late 1st century A.D.
C13	1	2	137	late 1st century A.D.
C13	1	2a	60	
C13	1	4b	61	Roman?
C13	1	surface	27	late 6th or 5th century B.C.
C13/D13	1		13	late 6th or 5th century B.C.
C13/D13	1	1	40	mid-6th century B.C.
C13/D13	1	4	67	3rd century B.C.

AREA	TRENCH	STRATUM	CAT. NO	APPROX. DATE
C13/D13	2	1	36	late 6th or 5th century B.C.
C13/D13	2	2	96	mid- to late 1st century A.D.
C14	1	2	89	late 1st century B.C. to mid-1st century A.D.
C14	1	4	95	mid- to late 1st century A.D.
C14/D14	1	1;2	118	2nd century A.D.
C14/D14	1	2	114	2nd century A.D.
C14/D14	1	2B	152	
C14/D14	2	2	33	post 400 B.C.
C15/16	1	1	80	late 1st century B.C and 1st century A.D.
			129	2nd half of 1st century A.D.
C15/16	1	2	82	late 1st century B.C-late 1st century A.D.
			98	A.D. 25-100
			110	2nd century A.D.
			165	
C15/16	1	3	10	late 6th or 5th century B.C.
			31	late 6th to mid-5th century B.C.
			32	post 400 B.C.
			72	late 2nd or 1st century B.C.
			75	Roman
C15/16	1	4	30	late 6th or 5th century B.C.
			42	mid-6th century B.C.
			51	
			79	Roman
			128	2nd half of 1st century A.D.
C15/16	1	5	15	late 6th or 5th century
			16	
C15/D15	1B	3	108	1st century A.D.
C15/D15	1B	4	102	last quarter of 1st century A.D.
C17	1B	4	174	Hellenistic?
C17	2	1	90	late 1st century B.C. to mid-1st century A.D.
D10/11	C	5	18	late 6th or 5th century B.C.
D11	1	2	153	
D11	balk	2a	57	
D11/12	1		133	2nd half of 1st century A.D.
D11/12	1	2	111	2nd century A.D.
			123	Roman
			164	
			172	mid-3rd century A.D.
D12/13	B	4	4	late 6th or 5th century B.C.
			38	
D12/13	F	1	77	Roman
D12/13	F	2	114	2nd century A.D.
D12/13	F	2b	127	2nd half of 1st century A.D.
			76	Roman
D12/13	F	2B	120	Roman
D12/E12	D	2	73	Roman
			112	2nd century A.D.
			125	2nd half of 1st century A.D.
D12/E12	D	3	25	late 6th or 5th century B.C.
D13	(Area 2) 2	1	74	Roman
D13/E13	1	2	160	2nd and early 3rd century A.D.
D15/16	1	2	58	
			59	
			63	

AREA	TRENCH	STRATUM	CAT. NO	APPROX. DATE
D15/16	2	1	159	2nd century A.D.
D15/16	2	2	69	1st century A.D.
			113	2nd century A.D.
			115	
			147	1st or early 2nd centuries A.D.
D15/E15	1	1	87	late 1st century B.C. to mid-1st century A.D.
D15/E15	1	3	53	mid-6th century B.C.
D16/17	1	1	148	
D16/17	1	2	50	mid-6th century B.C.
			68	3rd century B.C.
D16/17	1	3	20	460-440 B.C.
			22	late 6th or 5th century B.C.
			24	
			29	
			34	post 400 B.C.
			43	mid-6th century B.C.
			47	
			49	
			62	
			64	3rd century B.C.
			66	
D16/17	2	2	39	late 6th or early 5th century B.C.
			163	
D16/17	2	3	19	late 6th or 5th century B.C.
			28	
			166	1st and 2nd centuries B.C.
D16/17	2	4	44	mid-6th century B.C.
			48	
D16/17	3	4	21	460-440 B.C.
D16/17	A	1	157	1st century A.D.
D16/17	A	2	100	2nd half of 1st century A.D.
			130	
			149	1st and 2nd centuries A.D.
			151	
D16/17	A	3	124	2nd half of 1st century A.D.
			126	2nd half of 1st century A.D.
			161	mid-1st to mid-3rd centuries A.D.
D17/16	3		9	late 6th or 5th century B.C.
			11	late 6th or 5th century B.C.
			17	
D12/E12	D	1	23	
D6/E16	1	4	55	mid-6th century B.C.
E10	balk	1	78	Roman
E10	balk	2	105	1st century A.D.
E10	balk	3	12	late 6th or 5th century B.C.
			103	last quarter of 1st century A.D.
			104	1st century A.D.
			145	
E10	balk S	3	2	last quarter of 6th century B.C.
E10/11	(Area 1)1	4	1	last quarter of 6th century B.C.
E11	3	3	3	last quarter of 6th century B.C.
E12	1	5	6	450-400 B.C.
			94	late 1st century B.C. to mid-1st century A.D.

AREA	TRENCH	STRATUM	CAT. NO.	APPROX. DATE
E13/14	1	2	65	3rd century B.C.
			84	late 1st century B.C to late 1st century A.D.
E13/14	1	2	150	
E15	2	2	26	late 6th or 5th century B.C.
E15	2	4	52	mid-6th century B.C.
F11	1	1	158	
F11	2	2	173	1st-4th centuries A.D.
F11	2	3	170	
F12	2		7	late 6th or 5th century B.C.
			171	1st century A.D.
F13/G13	1	2	14	late 6th or 5th century B.C.
			20	460-440 B.C.
F13/G13	2	2	35	post 400 B.C.
			37	late 6th or 5th century B.C.
			45	mid-6th century B.C.
			106	mid-1st century A.D.
F15	3	2	8	late 6th or 5th century B.C.
F9/10; G9/10	A	3	140	1st century A.D.
			142	
stray 1973			91	late 1st century B.C. to mid-1st century A.D.
			92	
			97	2nd century A.D.
stray 1973?			119	Roman
stray			41	mid-6th century B.C.
			54	
			71	1st century A.D.
			85	late 1st century B.C to late 1st century A.D.
			91	
			143	
stray?			135	no later than A.D. 135

Appendix III

Concordance of Catalogue Numbers with Excavation Inventory Numbers

Inv. No.	Cat. No.	Inv. No.	Cat. No.	Inv. No.	Cat. No.
	136	73-586	68	74-110	28
	137	73-589	50	74-115	21
	168	73-601	64	74-116	44
N.I.	118	73-608	148	74-117	48
N.I.	171	73-610	32	74-121	19
N.I.	141	73-612	110	74-320	83
stray	143	73-672	62	74-322	144
stray	135	73-675	49	74-410	169
69-218	74	73-679	9	74-412	99
69-240	1	73-688	29	74-451	109
71-233	94	73-694	43	74-464	7
71-261	38	73-696	66	74-487	93
71-400	4	73-705	21	74-488	122
71-532	8	73-712	30	74-489	138
71-780	3	73-716	31	74-492	158
71-782	6	73-720	72	74-496	121
73-stray	97	73-848	34	74-499	88
73-stray	92	73-850	145	74-580	172
73-stray	91	73-901	10	74-589	77
73-stray?	119	73-902	125	74-595	89
73-165	174	73-910	15	74-596	133
73-227	105	73-916	23	74-597	71
73-326	98	73-935	11	74-600	123
73-379	82	73-936	47	74-605	81
73-381	128	73-985	16	74-714	76
73-386	80	73-1031	78	74-730	95
73-392	165	73-1041	108	74-732	111
73-424	117	73-1097	17	74-738	164
73-425	73	73-1098	20	74-739	127
73-427	112	73-1099	24	74-779	173
73-453	129	73-1105	102	74-875	170
73-485	51	73-1108	103	74-900	120
73-488	75	73-1109	104	74-992	142
73-512	79	73-1139a	21	74-995	140
73-529	42	73-1139b	22	74-1190	86
73-537	2	73-1170	12	76-60	126
73-545	54	74-108	163	76-61	124
73-585	25				

Inv. No.	Cat. No.	Inv. No.	Cat. No.	Inv. No.	Cat. No.
76-62	150	76-247	13	77-267	58
76-63	130	76-304	55	77-323	70
76-66	157	76-371	20	77-328	59
76-71	151	76-373	84	77-395	21
76-78	131	76-374	116	77-447	37
76-80	149	76-464	14	77-545	106
76-88	134	76-521	65	77-553	35
76-90	132	76-524	146	77-555	33
76-111	154	76-601	36	77-758	85
76-120	155	76-764	114	77-917	60
76-121	100	76-766	160	77-918	159
76-122	101	76-829	46	77-1017	87
76-132	167	76-886	26	77-1090	53
76-123	167	76-901	57	77-1091	147
76-124	156	76-907	96	77-1110	69
76-127a	5	76-1062	152	77-1111	61
76-168	161	76-1086	52	77-1160	107
76-170	56	77-116	27	77-1161	115
76-180	40	77-120	139	77-1162	113
76-182	41	77-216	63	77-1165	153
76-209	162	77-254	45	78-284	90
76-242	67				

Part III

Faunal and Human Skeletal Remains

I

Faunal Skeletal Remains From Cyrene

Introduction

The skeletal remains from the Sanctuary of Demeter and Persephone at Cyrene include both animal and human bones. The animal bones, which are discussed in the first chapter of this section, include just under 2500 bones and fragments recovered from 26 different excavation units at the site. The human skeletal material includes the remains of two immature individuals. These skeletons are described in detail in the second chapter of this section.

The Faunal Remains from the Sanctuary of Demeter and Persephone

INTRODUCTION

During the past twenty years, studies of faunal remains have played an increasingly important role in archaeological interpretation. Archaeozoologists have focussed primarily on the analysis of animal bones recovered from settlement sites, since bones discarded as domestic rubbish can provide information on patterns of animal husbandry, hunting practices, and diet. Considerably less attention has been paid to animal bones recovered from ceremonial and religious sites. This is unfortunate, as studies of animal bones from ceremonial sites can provide information on the nature of animal sacrifices, on ritual feasting, and on the role of animals in ancient religion. It was with these aims in mind that we undertook the analysis of the animal bones from the sanctuary of Demeter and Persephone at Cyrene, Libya.

The sanctuary consecrated to Demeter and Persephone is located outside the ancient walls of Cyrene, across the steep Wadi Bel Gadir, and opposite the city's agora. Excavations at the site were carried out between 1969 and 1981 under the direction of Professor Donald White of The University Museum, University of Pennsylvania. These excavations traced the development of the sanctuary from its establishment at around 600 B.C. to its destruction in the third or fourth century A.D.[1]

There are few previous detailed studies of faunal remains from sanctuaries of Demeter and Persephone. Jarman[2] provided a brief analysis of the animal bones from the sanctuary of Demeter at Knossos, while Reese[3] is currently engaged in the study of the fauna from the sanctuary of Demeter and Kore at Corinth. The large and well preserved faunal collection from the Sanctuary at Cyrene is therefore of critical importance to our understanding of the cult of Demeter and Persephone.

COMPOSITION OF THE FAUNAL ASSEMBLAGE

The faunal collection from the sanctuary includes 2494 animal bones and fragments, of which approximately 30% could be identified to species. The animals identified include domestic sheep (*Ovis aries*), domestic goat (*Capra hircus*), domestic pig (*Sus scrofa*), domestic cattle (*Bos taurus*), domestic dog (*Canis familiaris*), and domestic chicken (*Gallus gallus*) (Table 1). Two equid (*Equus* sp.) bones which could not be identified to species were also recovered from the sanctuary.

---

1. D. White, *The Extramural Sanctuary of Demeter and Persephone at Cyrene, Libya: Background and Introduction to the Excavation* (Philadelphia, 1984).
2. M.R. Jarman, "Chapter IX: Preliminary Report on the Animal Bones," *Knossos: The Sanctuary of Demeter* (London, 1973, J.N. Coldstream, ed.) 177-179.
3. D. Reese, personal communication.

Since not all bones of sheep and goats can be distinguished at the species level,[4] we have included an undifferentiated sheep/goat category. Nearly two-thirds (64%) of the caprine bones from Cyrene could not be identified to the species level and were included in the sheep/goat category. Of the bones which could be identified, over half were the remains of sheep. In contrast, at the nearby Roman town of Berenice[5] horn core and metrical evidence indicates that goats were the more common species. The numbers of identifiable sheep and goat bones at Cyrene are so small, however, that any estimates of the relative importance of the two species should be treated with caution.

Higher order taxonomic categories were used to classify the Cyrene animal bones that could not be identified to species. These include small artiodactyl (sheep-, goat-, or pig-sized), large artiodactyl (cattle-sized), and a general large mammal category which may include equid as well as cattle remains.[6] Since the vast majority of the identifiable animal bones from Cyrene are those of pigs, it is likely that the majority of the non-diagnostic small artiodactyl fragments represent pigs, rather than sheep and goats. The large artiodactyl bones are almost certainly those of cattle, as no other large artiodactyl was identified from the Cyrene faunal assemblage.

Many of the Cyrene animal bones are in very fragmentary condition, and only about one-third could be fully identified. Nearly half (49.6%) are unidentified fragments of mammal, bird, and fish bone which could not even be assigned to higher order taxonomic categories. One reason for the high proportion of unidentifiable bone is that faunal assemblage included a substantial number of immature pigs (see the section on aging, below), whose bones would have been particularly susceptible to destruction by weathering, carnivore gnawing, and the like.[7] In addition, the extensive earthquake activity in the Cyrene area may have further fragmented the animal bones.

A major goal of faunal analysis is the assessment of the relative importance of each species at a site. Unfortunately, there is no consensus among faunal analysts as to the most appropriate quantification technique.[8] Methods most commonly used to calculate taxonomic abundance include the fragment count or NISP (number of identified specimens per taxon) method,[9] the minimum number of individuals (MNI) technique,[10] and the relative frequency (RF) method.[11] In order to provide a large enough sample to estimate the relative importance of the different animals at Cyrene, the bones from all the excavation units have been pooled. The Appendix to this chapter lists the bones identified in each excavation unit. Table 2 presents the species ratios for cattle, sheep/goat,[12] and pigs calculated using the MNI[13] and fragment count methods of estimation. Relative frequencies for the Cyrene animal bones were calculated in three ways (Table 3): 1. overall relative frequencies based on all major skeletal elements, 2. relative frequencies excluding the most common and least common skeletal elements (relative frequencies minus first and last), and 3. relative frequencies excluding the most common and least common 25% of the anatomical elements (relative frequency quartiles).[14] These three methods are abbreviated as RF, RF-(F&L), and RF (1/4iles), respectively, in Table 3.

The most striking aspect of the Cyrene faunal assemblage, regardless of the method of quantification used, is that pigs are by far the most commonly represented animals, making up nearly 80% of the identified faunal remains (Fig. 1). Sheep and goats together account for only about 15% of the bones, while cattle are extremely rare, making up less than 5% of the Cyrene faunal collection. The high proportion of pigs

---

4. Distinctions between sheep and goat bones were drawn following the guidelines of J. Boessneck, H.H. Muller, and M. Teichert, "Osteologische Unterschiede Zwischen Schaf (*Ovis aries* Linné) und Ziege (*Capra hircus* Linné)," *Kühn Archiv* 78 (1964) 1-129.

5. G. Barker, "Economic Life at Berenice: The Animal and Fish Bones, Marine Molluscs and Plant Remains," *Excavations at Sidi Krebish Benghazi (Berenice), Supplement to Libya Antiqua* V vol. 2 (1982) 16.

6. These higher order categories are defined by R.T. Jones, *Computer Based Osteometric Archaeozoology* (Ancient Monuments Laboratory, Department of the Environment, London, n.d.).

7. See, for example, C.K. Brain, "Hottentot Food Remains and Their Bearing on the Interpretation of Fossil Bone Assemblages," *Scientific Papers of the Namib Desert Research Station*, No. 32. Brain's ethnoarchaeological investigations have shown that long bones with unfused epiphyses, i.e., those from immature animals, are less likely to survive that those with fused epiphyses.

8. A review of the problems associated with the estimation of taxonomic abundance is provided by D.K. Grayson, "On the Quantification of Vertebrate Archaeofaunas," *Advances in Archaeological Method and Theory*, vol. 2 (New York, 1979, M.B. Schiffer, ed.) 199-237; for a more detailed discussion of the issue, see D.K. Grayson, *Quantitative Zooarchaeology* (Orlando, 1984).

9. A. Gautier, "How Do I Count You, Let Me Count the Ways? Problems of Archaeozoological Quantification," *Animals in Archaeology: 4. Husbandry in Europe* (Oxford, British Archaeological Reports, International Series, 227, 1984, C. Grigson and J. Clutton-Brock, eds.) 237-251.

10. T.E. White, "A Method of Calculating the Dietary Percentage of Various Food Animals Utilized by Aboriginal Peoples," *American Antiquity* 18 (1953) 396-398.

11. D. Perkins, "A Critique on the Methods of Quantifying Faunal Remains from Archaeological Sites," *Domestikationsforschung und Geschichte der Haustiere* (Budapest, 1973, J. Matolcsi, ed.) 367-369.

12. For purposes of quantification, this category includes identifiable sheep and goat bones plus indeterminate sheep/goat fragments.

13. We have used the minimum number of individuals technique described by A.S. Gilbert and P. Steinfeld, "Faunal Remains from Dinka Tepe, Northwestern Iran," *Journal of Field Archaeology* 4 (1977) 333.

14. A discussion of the different relative frequency methods is provided by B. Hesse and D. Perkins, "Faunal remains from Karatas-Semayuk in Southwest Anatolia: An Interim Report," *Journal of Field Archaeology* 1 (1974) 149-156.

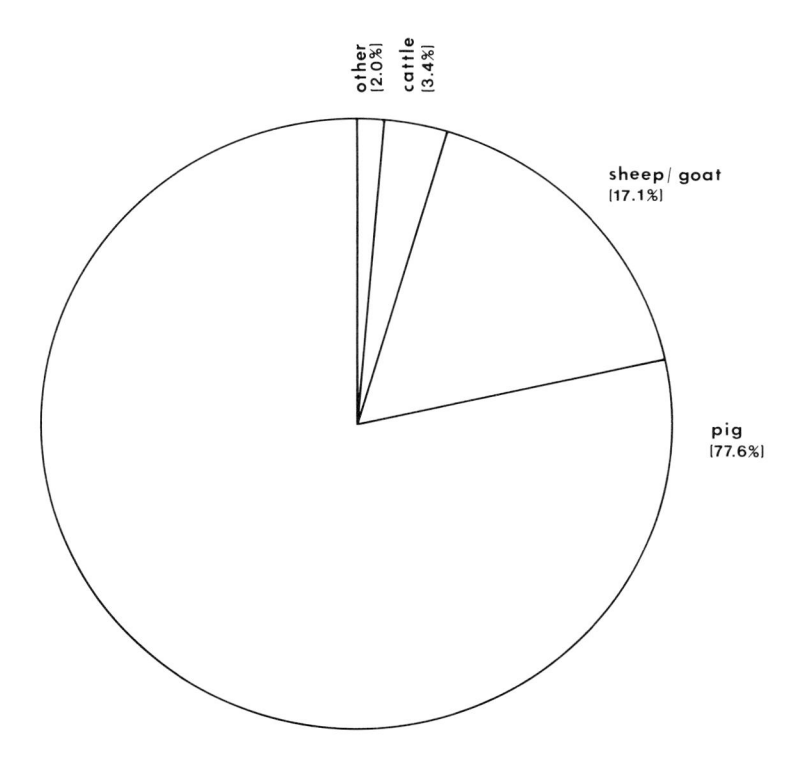

Figure 1. Relative importance of the animal species identified from the Sanctuary of Demeter and Persephone at Cyrene, Libya. These proportions are based on fragment counts.

at Cyrene is undoubtedly due to the fact that pigs are associated with the cult of Demeter and Persephone. At the Roman town of Berenice, also located in Cyrenaica, sheep and goats were the most commonly slaughtered stock animals.[15] Moreover, sheep and goats are far better adapted to the local grazing conditions in Cyrenaica than pigs are. The high proportion of pigs in the Cyrene faunal assemblage clearly reflects the significance of the pig to the cult of Demeter and Persephone. What we see at Cyrene is a faunal assemblage whose composition is structured by ritual rather than economic principles.

Body part distributions for cattle, sheep/goat, and pigs are presented in Table 4. These have been grouped into major anatomical categories—head, forelimb, hindlimb, feet, loose teeth, and trunk (body)—in Table 5. Tables 4 and 5 indicate that there are major differences between species in body part frequencies. The pig bones include a high proportion of hindlimb elements, while the sheep and goat remains include a higher proportion of forelimb bones. Loose teeth and foot bones are relatively more common among the sheep/goat remains, while the pig remains include a higher proportion of cranial bones. There are too few cattle bones for detailed anatomical analysis.

AGING EVIDENCE

The data on ages at death can provide additional evidence for the ritual use of pigs at Cyrene. Age determinations can be based on two methods: 1. the degree of epiphyseal fusion of the long bones, and 2. the state of dental eruption and wear on the mandibular teeth. In an immature animal, the epiphyses (ends) of the long bones are separated from the diaphyses (shafts) by cartilaginous zones. When bone growth is completed, these zones ossify, and the epiphyses and diaphyses fuse together. Since these epiphyses fuse in a set sequence for each animal species, the state of epiphyseal fusion can be used to estimate the age at death of an archaeological specimen. Similarly, the

---

15. Barker (above n. 5) 13.

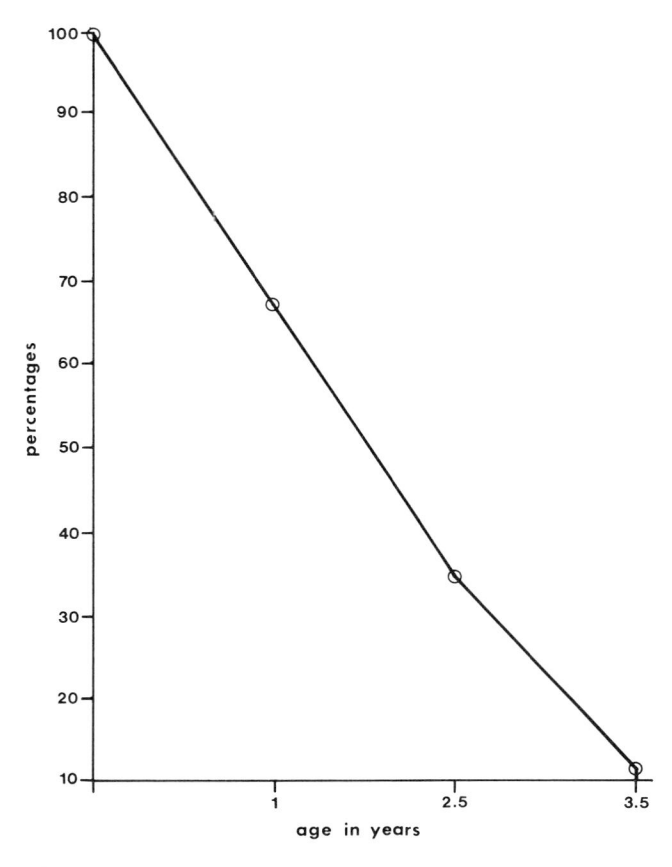

Figure 2. Ages at death for the Cyrene pigs based on epiphyseal fusion of the long bones, following Silver (1969). Note that most of the pig bones recovered from the Cyrene excavations were from subadult animals.

state of eruption or degree of wear on each tooth in a mandible (lower jaw) can be recorded. The overall pattern of dental eruption and wear can be used to estimate the age at death of the specimen. Since an animal's teeth continue to wear throughout its lifetime, dental wear can be particularly useful in distinguishing between mature and elderly individuals.

The evidence for epiphyseal fusion of the long bones (Table 6)[16] indicates that one third of the Cyrene pigs were killed during the first year of life (Fig. 2). Nearly two thirds were killed by two and one half years, and only about 11% survived to three and one half years of age.

Analyses of ages at death based on dental eruption and wear produce similar results. Relative ages at death were calculated following the method developed by Grant.[17] Using this method, the state of dental eruption or wear is recorded for each tooth in a mandible. The sum of the scores for the first, second, and third molars provides a relative age estimate or "mandible wear stage" for the jaw. Twenty-two mandibles from Cyrene were sufficiently complete to allow estimation of age at death. The distribution of mandible wear stages for the Cyrene pig mandibles is shown in Figure 3.

Figure 3 indicates that pigs of all ages from neonatal to mature are present in the Cyrene faunal assemblage. The vast majority of the pigs, however, were killed during the first two years of life (indicated by mandible wear stage less than or equal to 20). No elderly pig jaws were present in the faunal sample, and only two of the mandibles showed wear on the third molars.[18] The **predominance of younger animals (Plate 1A), including a number of suckling pigs, probably resulted from the choice of younger animals as sacrificial victims.**

---

16. Ages of fusion follow I.A. Silver, "The Aging of Domestic Animals," *Science in Archaeology* (New York, 1970, D. Brothwell and E. Higgs, eds.) 283-302.

17. A. Grant, "Appendix B: The Use of Tooth Wear as a Guide to the Age of Domestic Animals—A Brief Explanation," *Excavations at Portchester Castle. Volume 1: Roman* (London, 1975, B. Cunliffe, ed.) 437-450.

18. A pig's third molar comes into wear at about the time the animal reaches bodily maturity.

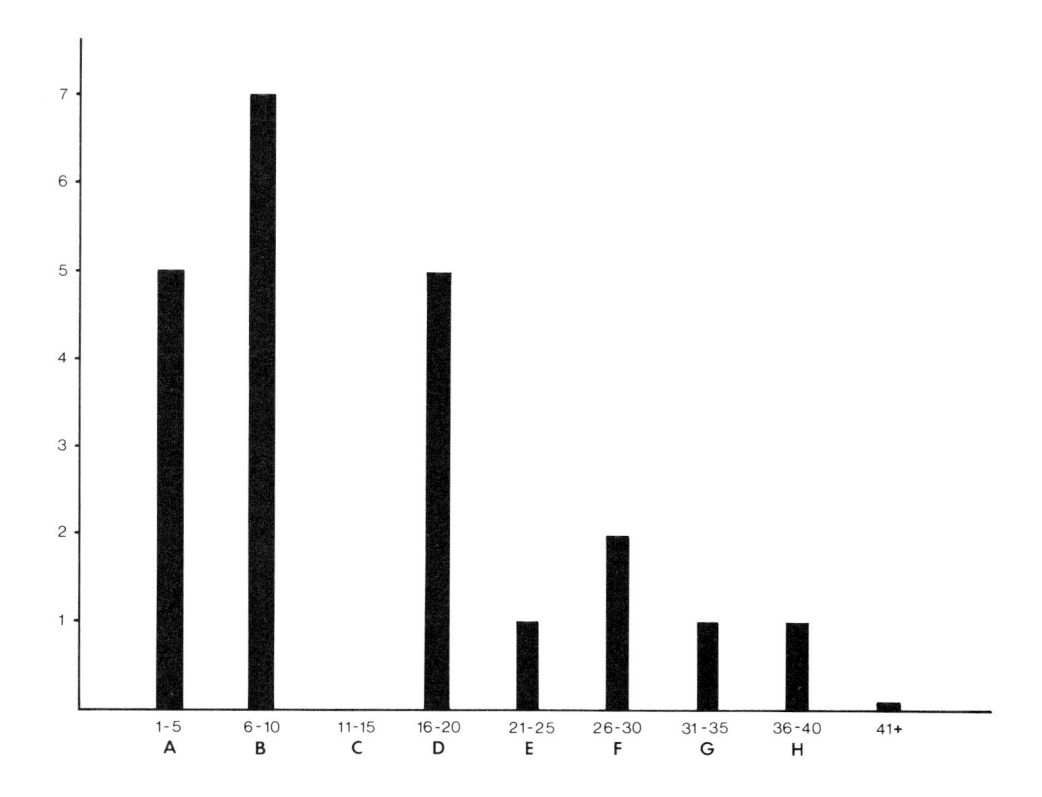

Figure 3. Mandible Wear Stages (MWS) for pigs from Cyrene (n = 22). A (MWS 1-5), B (MWS 6-10), C (MWS 11-15), D (MWS 16-20), E (MWS 21-25), F (MWS 26-30), G (MWS 31-35), H (MWS 36-40).

Only limited aging evidence is available for the cattle and sheep and goats from Cyrene. Only eight cattle bones could be scored for epiphyseal fusion, and all were from mature animals. The epiphyseal union data for sheep and goat long bones is shown in Table 7. Unlike the Cyrene pigs, the majority of the sheep and goats appear to have been more than two years old at death. Over 95% of the Cyrene caprines survived the first year, and about two-thirds survived to two years of age. The sample is too small to indicate what proportion of sheep and goats survived to more than three years of age. There is no clear difference between sheep and goat kill-patterns. Nevertheless, the limited aging evidence for sheep, goats, and cattle indicates that these animals were killed at much older ages than the Cyrene pigs were.

BUTCHERY

The distribution of butchery marks on bones can also tell us something about the ritual use of pigs at the sanctuary of Demeter and Persephone. Definite butchery traces appeared on 32 identifiable pig bones, approximately 6% of the total pig sample excluding teeth. The vast majority of the butchery traces (21 of 32) appear on the bones of the pig forelimb, especially the humerus (Plate 1B) and scapula. Half the butchered scapulae showed knife cuts, probably made during meat removal; the others were chopped to produce joints of hams. Butchery marks on the humerus are often found on the distal portion of the midshaft. Most are knife cuts, and corresponding cut marks are seen on the anterior (dorsal) portion of the proximal radius. Chop marks are also seen on the shafts of the radius, humerus, and ulna. These chop marks indicate that the forelimb was chopped into joint-sized pieces, and the cut marks indicate that the meat was subsequently removed from the bones. It is therefore reasonable to assume that the forequarters of pig may have been used in ritual feasting at the site.

The hindlimbs of the Cyrene pigs seem to have been treated in a very different manner. Butchery marks on hindlimb bones are extremely rare. One area of the site, in particular,[19] produced a concentration of pig hindlimb elements, primarily femora and pelves. Nearly all the bones were from young animals, and none was butchered. These bones were found with a large quantity of charcoal and ash. These hindlimb bones may represent an offering or offerings rather than the debris from ritual feasts.

Only two skull fragments showed butchery marks. One skull had been axially split, probably for the removal of the brain. Another cranial fragment showed chop marks at the base of the skull resulting from decapitation. The single butchered mandible showed knife cuts along the ventral margin, possibly from removal of the tongue.

Butchery traces on pig foot bones are also relatively rare. Those found on the calcaneus and astragalus probably resulted from the removal of the feet.

Only 11 butchered sheep and/or goat bones were discovered. As is the case with the pig, butchery marks on forelimb elements, especially the humerus, predominate. Although the sheep/goat sample is too small for detailed butchery analysis, the types of butchery traces identified do not differ appreciably from those found on pig bones. Among the butchered sheep/goat bones is an axially split lumbar vertebra, indicating that the right and left halves of the carcass were separated as part of the butchery process.

MEASUREMENTS

Unfortunately, only a small number of the Cyrene animal bones could be measured. As noted above, the majority of the Cyrene pig bones were immature and therefore unmeasurable. The only pig bone which could be measured with any consistency was the distal humerus (see Table 9).[20] The distal breadth of the Cyrene pig humeri (mean = 36.3 mm.) is typical of Roman period domestic pigs in general. A two-tailed Student's t-test was used to compare the mean distal humeral breadth for the Cyrene pigs to the Berenice[21] distal humeral breadth. The difference between the two means was not statistically significant. Since no complete long bones were recovered, no shoulder height estimates could be calculated for the Cyrene pigs.

Very few measurable sheep, goat, and cattle bones were recovered from Cyrene. A single complete cattle metatarsal, 215.0 mm in length, provides a shoulder height estimate[22] of 117.2 cm. A withers' height estimate of 66.7 cm is provided by a goat metacarpal (116.0 mm long).

Conclusion

The study of the fauna from the sanctuary of Demeter and Persephone at Cyrene confirms the importance of pigs to the cult of these two goddesses (Plate 1C). Analyses of the ages at death and butchery marks seen on these pig bones indicate that pigs may have been used both as sacrificial animals and in ritual feasting. The analysis of animal bones from additional ritual sites will allow us to study variations in ritual practice within individual cults and to study the relationship between the ritual uses of animals and their uses for everyday, non-ritual purposes.[23] It is through comparisons between secular and ritual uses of animals that we can begin to understand the true importance of animals in the ancient world.

---

19. Archaeological context F14/G14, TR. 1, ST. 4.
20. Distal humeral breadth (Bd) as defined by A. von den Driesch, "A Guide to the Measurement of Animal Bones from Archaeological Sites," *Peabody Museum Bulletin* 1 (1976) 76-77.
21. Barker (above n. 5) 46. Mean, range, and standard deviation were calculated from Barker's raw data.
22. Shoulder height estimates for cattle metapodia are based on Fock's factors; those for goat bones are based on Schramm's factors. See A. von den Driesch and J. Boessneck, "Kritische Anmerkungen zur Widerristhohenberechnung aus Langenmassen vor-und fruhgeschichtlicher Tierknochen," *Saugetierkundliche Mitteilungen* 22 (1974) 325-348.
23. See, for example, P. Crabtree, "Dairying in Irish Prehistory: The Evidence from a Ceremonial Center," *Expedition* 28 (1986) 59-62.

TABLE 1
TOTAL SPECIES REPRESENTED

Species	No. of Fragments	% of Total	% of Subtotal
Cattle	26	1.04	3.37
Sheep	21	.84	2.72
Goat	14	.56	1.81
Sheep/Goat	97	3.89	12.56
Pig	599	24.02	77.59
Equid	2	.08	.26
Dog	7	.28	.91
Fowl (Chicken)	1	.28	.78
Subtotal	772	.28	.78
Small Artiodactyl	466	18.68	
Large Artiodactyl	3	.12	
Large Mammal	15	.60	
Unidentified Mammal	1235	49.52	
Unidentified Fish	2	.08	
Unidentified Bird	1	.04	
Total	2494		

TABLE 2
SPECIES/ANATOMY DISTRIBUTION

	Cattle	Sheep/Goat	Pig
Head			
Skull	2	1	43
Horn Core	0	1	—
Maxilla	0	1	12
Mandible	03	52	
Hyoid	0	0	0
Atlas	0	0	4
Axis	0	0	1
Forelimb			
Scapula		6	23
Humerus	1	18	44
Radius	2	15	17
Ulna	0	1	19
Hindlimb			
Sacrum	0	0	11
Innominate	0	2	37
Femur	0	2	91
Patella	0	0	2
Tibia	1	13	33
Fibula	—	—	9
Feet			
Carpals	0	0	1
Tarsals	0	1	0
Astragalus	0	7	5
Calcaneus	1	2	11
Metacarpals	0	5	22
Metatarsals	1	7	19
Metapodials	0	1	15
1st phalanx	2	9	7
2nd phalanx	3	0	2
3rd phalanx	2	1	4
Sesamoids	0	0	0
Teeth			
Maxillary	6	21	21
Mandibular	1	6	39
Tooth fragments	0	3	12
Body			
Vertebrae	2	5	21
Ribs	1	1	18
Total	26	132	599

TABLE 3
ANATOMICAL GROUPINGS FOR CYRENE FAUNA

	Cattle N	Cattle %	Sheep/Goat N	Sheep/Goat %	Pig N	Pig %
Head	2	7.70	6	4.55	112	18.70
Forelimb	4	15.38	40	30.30	103	17.20
Hindlimb	1	3.85	17	12.88	183	30.55
Feet	9	34.62	33	25.00	90	15.03
Teeth	7	26.92	30	22.73	72	12.02
Body	3	11.54	6	4.55	39	6.51
Total	26		132		599	

TABLE 4
COMPARISON OF MNI AND FRAGMENT COUNT
METHODS OF QUANTIFICATION

	Fragment Count N	Fragment Count %	MNI N	MNI %
Cattle	26	3.43	1	1.79
Sheep/Goat	132	17.44	9	16.07
Pig	599	79.13	46	82.14

TABLE 5
RELATIVE FREQUENCIES OF THE CYRENE FAUNAL REMAINS

Species	RF	RF-(F & L)	RF (1/4 ILE)
Cattle	.33	.30	.31
Sheep/Goat	2.72	2.46	1.97
Pig	16.25	14.31	13.83*
	Proportion	Proportion	Proportion
Cattle	1.71%	1.76%	1.92%
Sheep/Goat	14.09%	14.41%	12.23%*
Pig	84.20%	83.83%	85.85%*

* based on middle 60%

TABLE 6
EPIPHYSEAL UNION DATA FOR CYRENE PIGS

Early Fusing Epiphyses (1 year)	No. Unfused	No. Fused
Distal Humerus	7	15
Proximal Radius	6	5
Proximal 2nd Phalanx	1	1
Total = 35	14	21
	(33.3%)	(66.7%)
Middle Fusing Epiphyses (2-2½ yrs.)		
Distal Metapodial	23	16
Proximal 1st Phalanx	2	3
Distal Tibia	10	1
Proximal Calcaneus	7	2
Total = 64	42	22
	(65.5%)	(34.4%)
Late Fusing Epiphyses (3-3½ yrs.)		
Proximal Humerus	3	0
Distal Radi	4	1
Proximal Ulna	4	1
Distal Ulna	2	0
Proximal Femur	29	4
Distal Femur	24	2
Proximal Tibia	4	1
Total = 79	70	9
	(88.6%)	(11.4%)

TABLE 7
EPIPHYSEAL UNION DATA FOR CYRENE SHEEP AND GOATS

Early Fusing Epiphyses (approx. 1 yr.)	No. Unfused	No. Fused
Distal Humerus	1	12
Proximal Radius	0	8
Total = 21	1	20
	(4.8%)	(95.2%)
Middle Fusing Epiphyses (approx. 2 yrs.)		
Distal Metapodial	1	5
1st Phalanx	1	6
Distal Tibia	5	3
Total = 21	7	14
	(33.3%)	(66.7%)
Late Fusing Epiphyses (approx. 3 yrs.)		
Distal Radius	0	1
Proximal Ulna	0	1
Proximal Calcaneus	0	1
Total = 3	0	3

TABLE 8
DISTRIBUTION OF BUTCHERY MARKS ON CYRENE PIG AND SHEEP/GOAT BONES

	Pig	Sheep/Goat
Skull	2	0
Mandible	1	0
Vertebrae	0	1
Scapula	6	1
Humerus	12	3
Radius	2	1
Ulna	1	0
Innominate	1	1
Femur	1	1
Metapodia	1	0
Astragalus	2	1
Calcaneus	3	1
1st Phalanx	0	1
Total	32	11

TABLE 9
COMPARISON OF DISTAL HUMERAL BREADTHS FOR CYRENE AND BERENICE PIGS

	Cyrene	Berenice
Mean Distal Humeral Breadth	36.26	36.59
Ranges	33.5-38.3	33.3-40.1
Standard Deviation	1.63	2.06
Number of Measurements	10	10

All measurements in millimeters

II

Human Skeletal Remains From Cyrene

Introduction

The human skeletal material from Cyrene consists of the remains of two individuals. The most complete individual is estimated to be about three to three and a half years of age and is represented by most of the cranium and mandible along with many postcranial elements. This immature skeleton will be discussed in detail. There are, however, fragmentary remains of a second individual which appears to be a well developed fetus or full term infant, given the size and development of the bones. This individual is also represented by cranial and postcranial elements.

Given the very young age at death of both of these individuals, the skeletons are in relatively good condition. For example, the fetal (term infant) skeleton has 10 almost complete associated ribs (a very friable skeletal element). The three year old child's skeleton was difficult to reconstruct, however, since the bones were impregnated with plastic during excavation, and in several cases gauze was glued to the surface of very fragmentary or fragile bone. It was difficult to clean the matrix and gauze from these fragile bones, and much surface detail was obliterated. On several postcranial bones and areas of the cranium, removal of the gauze would have resulted in the destruction of the bone. In these instances, the bone was not cleaned.

Individual I

This individual is represented by most of the cranium and mandible. The major missing portion of the cranium is in the mid-facial area. The missing parts include the orbital process of the maxilla, a portion of the anterior part of the aveolus of the maxilla, and also part of the palate, ethmoid, vomer, nasal conchae and the lesser wing of the right sphenoid. Both zygomatic arches are missing as are small pieces of bone from the parietals, frontal, temporals, and occipital. The crypts of both sides of the upper permanent 2nd molars are open and these teeth have been lost. Given the age and therefore the thinness of the cranial bones of this individual, the skull is reasonably complete. There is another problem, however, in reconstructing this particular specimen. All of the cranial bones have been pressure distorted since the time of burial. As a consequence, no good bony connection can be made along suture lines. In addition, much of both the internal and external surface of the bone has been eroded away. It is difficult, therefore, to see any surface detail on the bone or any bone pathology such as cribra orbitalia—a non-specific stress indicator.

Most of the post-cranial skeleton of this individual is also present. The remains are very fragmentary and several bones (e.g. scapula and ilium) were coated with gauze and glue during excavation. These bones are impossible to reconstruct given the fragility of these elements. Both clavicles are present, as are very fragmentary scapulae, the ilium, pubis and ischium of the right side (although labelled left), part of the sacrum, and very fragmentary elements of the vertebral column. Ribs are also present from both right and left sides. Most of the limb long bones are present. These include: right and left femora, radii, and ulnae, left tibia, left fibula, right proximal humerus and left distal humerus. Parts of both hands and feet are present. These include phalanges, metacarpals and metatarsals, but no carpals and tarsals.

AGING

The age estimate for this human skeleton from Cyrene is based upon the degree of development of the dentition. Although x-rays of crown and root development of the permanent dentition were not taken, it was possible to estimate the age of this specimen fairly accurately. The entire deciduous dentition is present minus the left lower canine, right lower first incisor, and both right and left upper first incisors. These teeth have been lost post-mortem based on characteristics of the aveolus. The entire deciduous or milk dentition therefore was originally present. An absolute minimum age can be assigned based on this information alone since the last tooth to erupt in the child's dentition is the deciduous second premolar between approximately one and three quarters to two and one half years of age.

Further information, however, can be added based on several teeth which have fallen out of the alveolus (crypt) but have not been lost. The upper right second deciduous premolar has fully formed roots; this occurs at about three years of age. The degree of wear on the tooth, which is slight but distinct, indictes that the deciduous second premolars were in occlusion for some period of time.

The degree of crown development of some of the permanent teeth can also be ascertained. A second lower lateral incisor and canine are outside the crypt along with two upper teeth, a left central incisor and first molar. The crown of the first molar is totally formed as is the beginning of the root system. The upper central incisor crown enamel is about two-thirds completed and, taken in conjunction with the first molar, indicates a dental age of about three to three and one half years. This accords with the enamel development of the lower second incisor and the lower canine.

Still visible in the crypt are the lower right and left first and second molars and the upper right first molar. The degree of crown development cannot be estimated for these teeth without an x-ray, but the development of these teeth also suggests a dental age of about three to three and one half years. This age estimate is similar to that published previously.[1] A list of the measurable dentition is given in Table 10.

The degree of development of the vertebrae also supports this age estimate. The two halves of the arches of the vertebrae fuse between the ages of 1 and 3 years. In some of the more complete vertebrae the arch halves have fused, but the line of fusion is not yet obliterated. The arches of the vertebrae present have not yet fused to the centrum or body of the vertebrae. This fusion occurs between the ages of three to seven years.[2] The degree of vertebral fusion, therefore, is in line with an age estimate of about three to three and one half years for this individual.

The degree of development of the epiphyses of the other post-cranial bones can also be used as an aging index, but these elements are not usually found in most archaeological contexts and are not present in this case.

PATHOLOGY

Macroscopic dental defects, usually termed hypoplasia, can be seen in the forms of bands, pits, or discolorations on the teeth. These dental defects are a general indicator of stress. The total effect of stress on an individual tooth depends upon the timing of the stress, the degree of crown development of the tooth and possibly the type of tooth. While precise estimation of stress times was not attempted, there appears to be continuous stress or series of stresses affecting this individual over the entire time period of the development of the permanent dentition. The crowns of all the permanent dentition are riddled with bands of hypoplasia extending from the tip of the crown to the junction of the crown and root on the first molars and to the last formation of enamel on the other permanent teeth.

No other pathologies were seen on the skeleton. This may be due to the fragmentary nature of the bone. The eroded surface of the cranial bones of Individual I makes it impossible to identify certain pathologies, such as cribra orbitalia.

Individual II

The cranial remains of this fetal skeleton are very fragmentary. They consist of several undiagnostic pieces of what seem to be portions of the skull vault: the parietals, temporals, frontal and occipital. It is impossible to distinguish these fragments further because of the size of the pieces and also because much of the surface detail has been eroded away.

The post-cranial skeletal element distribution is interesting. A scapula, clavicle, 10 almost complete ribs, humerus, ulna, radius, femur and tibia are present. All of these are right side bones. The reason for this side distribution is not known. A manubrium, a mid-line bone element, is also present.

---

1. D. White, "Excavations in the Sanctuary of Demeter and Persephone at Cyrene—Sixth Preliminary Report," *Libya Antiqua* XV-XVI (1978-1979) 182-83.

2. W. Bass, *Human Osteology* (Missouri, 1971) 77.

TABLE 10
INDIVIDUAL I FROM CYRENE:
DENTAL MEASUREMENTS

Deciduous Dentition

	Left		Right	
Lower	MD	BL	MD	BL
i1	4.75	3.80	—	—
i2	4.85	4.10	4.90	4.15
c	—	—	6.80	5.70
dpm1	8.25	7.00	8.10	7.10
dpm2	10.45	8.70	10.45	8.80
Upper	MD	BL	MD	BL
i1	—	—	—	—
i2	5.05	4.85	5.00	4.85
c	6.65	4.90	6.70	4.85
dpm1	6.85	8.75	6.95	8.80
dpm2	8.75	10.15	8.80	10.20

Measurable Permanent Dentition

Lower	MD	BL	MD	BL
I2	—	—	6.25	—
C	—	—	6.70	—
Upper	MD	BL	MD	BL
I1	9.50	—	—	—
M1	10.50	12.20	—	—

All measurements are in millimeters

Conclusion

Our conclusions based on the analyses of the human bones from Cyrene are in agreement with those published in the preliminary report.[3] The bone fractures were definitely produced post-mortem since these breaks show no evidence of splintering which is the product of fresh bone breakage. This does not refute the idea that the skeleton of Individual I was buried and the individual suffocated during the earthquake which affected the area. It does not appear, however, that the individual was actually killed by falling debris, at least in any way which would affect bone.

Two minor points mentioned in the preliminary report need to be updated. When the skeletons were cleaned it was clear that a tibia and fibula were present from Individual I. In the report it was noted that the lower leg segments were not present for this individual. The lower limb segments are present but only unilaterally, and they were probably not identified because they are fragmentary and were also covered in matrix and gauze.

The second discrepancy between our analyses and the preliminary report is in the number of individuals represented by the skeletal remains. The initial report stated that there were remains of three individuals, and the third individual was a two-to three-year old child. We think that this third individual was represented by a left zygomatic which was separated from the bones of Individual I. This zygomatic bone articulates with the cranium of Individual I although this bone was not preserved in the same way as the rest of the skeleton.

Finally, a scapula of a young pig is present along with several fragments of bone which are too large to be part of Individual II. We are not sure if these extra fragments are human. It seems likely that all this skeletal material has been extensively disturbed since the fetal (or near term) skeleton is represented by only right side bones and the carpal and tarsal bones of Individual I are missing.

---

3. D. White (above n. 1).

Appendix I

Key to Abbreviations

PIG	pig	FEM	femur
CATTLE	cattle	PAT	patella
S/G	Sheep/goat	TIB	tibia
SHEEP	sheep	CAR	carpal
GOAT	goat	TAR	tarsal
SAR	small artiodactyl (sheep/goat or pig-sized)	MC	metacarpal
LAR	large artiodactyl (cattle-sized)	MT	metatarsal
OXO	large mammal (cattle or equid)	MP	metapodial
SKL	skull	APH	1st phalanx
HC	horn core	CPH	3rd phalanx
MAX	maxilla	FIB	fibula
MAN	mandible	AST	astralagus (talus)
ATLAS	1st cervical vertebra	CAL	calcaneus
AXIS	2nd cervical vertebra	UTEETH	upper or maxillary teeth
SCAP	scapula	LTEETH	lower or mandibular teeth
HUM	humerus	TFRAG	tooth fragment
RAD	radius	VERTS	vertebrae
ULN	ulna	RIBS	ribs
OC	os coxae (innominate)	LFRAG	long bone fragment
SACR	sacrum		

C10/11   A   4

	PIG	CATTLE	S/G	SHEEP	GOAT	SAR	LAR	OXO	OTHER
SKL	2								
HC									
MAX	1								
MAND									
ATLAS	1								
AXIS									
SCAP	3								
HUM	1								
RAD									
ULN	2								
OC									
SACR									
FEM									
PAT									
TIB									
CAR									
TAR									
MC	1								
MT									
MP									
APH									
BPH									
CPH									
FIB	1	-	-	-	-	-	-		
AST									
CAL									
UTEETH									
LTEETH									
TFRAG									
VERTS	1								
RIBS	1					1		1	
LFRAG									

UNIDENTIFIED MAMMAL FRAGMENTS = 0

C10/11   A   REMOVAL UNDER STELE

	PIG	CATTLE	S/G	SHEEP	GOAT	SAR	LAR	OXO	OTHER
SKL									
HC									
MAX									
MAND	1								
ATLAS									
AXIS									
SCAP									
HUM					1				
RAD									
ULN	1								
OC									
SACR									
FEM									
PAT									
TIB									
CAR									
TAR									
MC									
MT	1								
MP									
APH									
BPH									
CPH	1								
FIB		-	-	-	-	-	-	-	-
AST	1								
CAL									
UTEETH									
LTEETH	1								
TFRAG									
VERTS									
RIBS									
LFRAG									

UNIDENTIFIED MAMMAL FRAGMENTS = 1

C10/11   A(B)   6

	PIG	CATTLE	S/G	SHEEP	GOAT	SAR	LAR	OXO	OTHER
SKL									
HC									
MAX	1								
MAND				1					
ATLAS									
AXIS									
SCAP									
HUM	1				1				
RAD	1								
ULN									
OC									
SACR									
FEM									
PAT									
TIB									
CAR									
TAR									
MC									
MT	1								
MP									
APH									
BPH									
CPH	1								
FIB		-	-	-	-	-	-	-	-
AST									
CAL	1								
UTEETH			2						
LTEETH									
TFRAG									
VERTS	1								
RIBS									
LFRAG									

UNIDENTIFIED MAMMAL FRAGMENTS = 0

C14 — 2

	PIG	CATTLE	S/G	SHEEP	GOAT	SAR	LAR	OXO	OTHER
SKL									
HC									
MAX									
MAND									
ATLAS									
AXIS									
SCAP									
HUM	1								
RAD			1		1				
ULN									
OC									
SACR									
FEM	1								
PAT									
TIB									
CAR									
TAR									
MC									
MT	1								
MP	1								
APH									
BPH									
CPH									
FIB		-	-	-	-	-	-	-	-
AST	1								
CAL									
UTEETH									
LTEETH	2		1						
TFRAG									
VERTS									
RIBS									
LFRAG									

UNIDENTIFIED MAMMAL FRAGMENTS = 0

C17 2 1

	PIG	CATTLE	S/G	SHEEP	GOAT	SAR	LAR	OXO	OTHER
SKL									
HC									
MAX									
MAND									
ATLAS									
AXIS									
SCAP									
HUM	3		1						
RAD			1	1					
ULN									
OC									
SACR									
FEM									
PAT									
TIB	1								
CAR									
TAR									
MC									
MT	1	1							
MP	1								
APH				1					
BPH									
CPH									
FIB	-	-	-	-	-	-	-	-	
AST									
CAL									
UTEETH									
LTEETH									
TFRAG									
VERTS									
RIBS						3		2	
LFRAG								1	

UNIDENTIFIED MAMMAL FRAGMENTS = 8

C14 1 4

	PIG	CATTLE	S/G	SHEEP	GOAT	SAR	LAR	OXO	OTHER
SKL									
HC									
MAX	1								
MAND	6								
ATLAS									
AXIS	1								
SCAP	5			1					
HUM	1			2					
RAD									
ULN									
OC									
SACR									
FEM									
PAT									
TIB	3								
CAR									
TAR									
MC	1				1				
MT	3								
MP	1								
APH									
BPH									
CPH									
FIB		-	-	-	-	-	-	-	
AST									
CAL	1								
UTEETH									
LTEETH			1						
TFRAG									
VERTS	1								
RIBS	1						1		
LFRAG									

UNIDENTIFIED MAMMAL FRAGMENTS = 0

C17 2 2

	PIG	CATTLE	S/G	SHEEP	GOAT	SAR	LAR	OXO	OTHER
SKL	6		1						
HC									
MAX	2								
MAND	7								
ATLAS	1								
AXIS									
SCAP	5					1			2 CHICKEN
HUM	10		1			1			
RAD	2			1					
ULN	2								1 CHICKEN
OC									
SACR						1			
FEM	2								
PAT									
TIB	5		1			1			
CAR									
TAR									
MC	3	1							
MT									
MP			1						
APH	3				1				
BPH									
CPH				1					
FIB	1	-	-	-	-	-	-	-	-
AST									
CAL	2								
UTEETH	7		3						
LTEETH	14		1						
TFRAG	5								
VERTS	3		2			1			
RIBS		1				15			
LFRAG									

UNIDENTIFIED MAMMAL FRAGMENTS = 156
UNIDENTIFIED BIRD FRAGMENT = 1

C13/D13 1 4

	PIG	CATTLE	S/G	SHEEP	GOAT	SAR	LAR	OXO	OTHER
SKL	1								
HC									
MAX									
MAND	3								
ATLAS									
AXIS									
SCAP									
HUM	2		3						
RAD									
ULN									
OC									
SACR									
FEM									
PAT									
TIB			1						
CAR									
TAR									
MC									
MT	1				1				
MP									
APH									
BPH									
CPH									
FIB		-	-	-	-	-	-	-	-
AST									
CAL			1						
UTEETH			1						
LTEETH									
TFRAG									
VERTS						2			
RIBS						5			
LFRAG						1			

UNIDENTIFIED MAMMAL FRAGMENTS = 0

D10/11 C 5

	PIG	CATTLE	S/G	SHEEP	GOAT	SAR	LAR	OXO	OTHER
SKL									
HC									
MAX									
MAND									
ATLAS									
AXIS									
SCAP	1								
HUM									
RAD			1	1					
ULN			1						
OC									
SACR									
FEM									
PAT						1			
TIB									
CAR									
TAR									
MC	1								
MT									
MP	1								
APH									
BPH									
CPH									
FIB	-	-	-	-	-	-	-	-	
AST									
CAL									
UTEETH									
LTEETH									
TFRAG									
VERTS									
RIBS						2			
LFRAG								1	

UNIDENTIFIED MAMMAL FRAGMENTS = 0

D11/12 1 3

	PIG	CATTLE	S/G	SHEEP	GOAT	SAR	LAR	OXO	OTHER
SKL									
HC									
MAX									
MAND			1						
ATLAS									
AXIS									
SCAP									
HUM									
RAD	2			1					
ULN	1								
OC	1								
SACR									
FEM									
PAT									
TIB									
CAR									
TAR									
MC									
MT	1			1					
MP	2								
APH				1					
BPH		1							
CPH									
FIB		-	-	-	-	-	-	-	-
AST									
CAL									
UTEETH			1						
LTEETH									
TFRAG									
VERTS		1							
RIBS	2								
LFRAG									

UNIDENTIFIED MAMMAL FRAGMENTS = 0

D12/13 F 3

	PIG	CATTLE	S/G	SHEEP	GOAT	SAR	LAR	OXO	OTHER
SKL	2	1							
HC									
MAX									
MAND	4								
ATLAS									
AXIS									
SCAP		1	1			1*			
HUM	3								
RAD	1								
ULN									
OC									
SACR									
FEM									
PAT									
TIB	1		2						
CAR									
TAR									
MC					1				
MT	2								
MP	1								
APH									
BPH		1							
CPH									
FIB	1	-	-	-	-	-	-	-	-
AST					1				
CAL									
UTEETH		1							
LTEETH	2								
TFRAG									
VERTS	1								
RIBS	1					2			
LFRAG									

UNIDENTIFIED MAMMAL FRAGMENTS = 0
* PIG SIZED

D15/16 1 3

	PIG	CATTLE	S/G	SHEEP	GOAT	SAR	LAR	OXO	OTHER
SKL	3								
HC									
MAX									
MAND	5								
ATLAS									
AXIS									
SCAP	2		1						
HUM	2	1	2						1 DOG
RAD									
ULN	2								
OC									
SACR									
FEM									
PAT									
TIB			1						
CAR									
TAR									
MC			1						
MT									
MP	1								
APH									
BPH									
CPH									
FIB	-	-	-	-	-	-	-	-	
AST									
CAL									
UTEETH			1						
LTEETH	1								
TFRAG									
VERTS		1	1						
RIBS						1			
LFRAG								1	

UNIDENTIFIED MAMMAL FRAGMENTS = 0

D16/17 2 4

	PIG	CATTLE	S/G	SHEEP	GOAT	SAR	LAR	OXO	OTHER
SKL									
HC									
MAX									
MAND	1								
ATLAS									
AXIS									
SCAP	1								
HUM	2								
RAD	2								
ULN									
OC									
SACR									
FEM									
PAT									
TIB			1						
CAR									
TAR									
MC	2								
MT	1								
MP									
APH									
BPH									
CPH									
FIB		-	-	-	-	-	-	-	
AST	1								
CAL									
UTEETH			2						
LTEETH	1								
TFRAG									
VERTS									1 FISH
RIBS						1			
LFRAG									

UNIDENTIFIED MAMMAL FRAGMENTS = 2

D13/E13 BALK 2

	PIG	CATTLE	S/G	SHEEP	GOAT	SAR	LAR	OXO	OTHER
SKL									
HC									
MAX									
MAND									
ATLAS									
AXIS									
SCAP									
HUM									
RAD									
ULN									
OC									
SACR									
FEM									
PAT									
TIB									
CAR									
TAR									
MC									
MT									1 EQUID
MP									
APH									
BPH									
CPH									
FIB	-	-	-	-	-	-	-	-	
AST									
CAL									
UTEETH									
LTEETH									
TFRAG									
VERTS									
RIBS									
LFRAG									

UNIDENTIFIED MAMMAL FRAGMENTS = 0

BONES IN SOIL OFF BEDROCK, 1.00 M. TO SW CORNER OF E11/12 BUILDING

	PIG	CATTLE	S/G	SHEEP	GOAT	SAR	LAR	OXO	OTHER
SKL									
HC									
MAX									
MAND									1 DOG
ATLAS									
AXIS									
SCAP									
HUM									
RAD									
ULN									
OC									1 EQUID, ISCH
SACR								1	
FEM									
PAT									
TIB									
CAR									
TAR									
MC									
MT									
MP									
APH									
BPH									
CPH									
FIB	-	-	-	-	-	-	-	-	
AST									
CAL									
UTEETH			1						
LTEETH									
TFRAG									
VERTS									
RIBS									
LFRAG						1			

UNIDENTIFIED MAMMAL FRAGMENTS = 1

E13/14 1 2

	PIG	CATTLE	S/G	SHEEP	GOAT	SAR	LAR	OXO	OTHER
SKL	2								
HC									
MAX	1								
MAND	2								
ATLAS									
AXIS									
SCAP	2		2						
HUM	1		1						
RAD		1	2			2			
ULN	1								
OC									
SACR									
FEM									
PAT									
TIB	2		2						
CAR									
TAR									
MC	1								
MT	1		1						
MP	2								
APH					1				
BPH	1								
CPH	1								
FIB	2	-	-	-	-	-	-	-	-
AST									
CAL	1								
UTEETH	6		1						
LTEETH	6								
TFRAG	1								
VERTS	1					1			
RIBS						9	2		
LFRAG						1			

UNIDENTIFIED MAMMAL FRAGMENTS = 73

E16 1 2

	PIG	CATTLE	S/G	SHEEP	GOAT	SAR	LAR	OXO	OTHER
SKL									
HC									
MAX									
MAND	1								
ATLAS									
AXIS									
SCAP									
HUM									
RAD									
ULN									
OC									
SACR									
FEM	1								
PAT									
TIB									
CAR									
TAR									
MC	1								
MT									
MP									
APH	1								
BPH									
CPH									
FIB		-	-	-	-	-	-	-	-
AST									
CAL									
UTEETH			1						
LTEETH									
TFRAG									
VERTS						1			
RIBS			1						
LFRAG									

UNIDENTIFIED MAMMAL FRAGMENTS = 4

E16 1 5

	PIG	CATTLE	S/G	SHEEP	GOAT	SAR	LAR	OXO	OTHER
SKL									
HC									
MAX									
MAND									
ATLAS									
AXIS									
SCAP									
HUM									
RAD									
ULN									
OC									
SACR									
FEM									
PAT									
TIB									
CAR									
TAR									
MC	1								
MT									
MP									
APH			1						
BPH									
CPH									
FIB		-	-	-	-	-	-	-	-
AST									
CAL									
UTEETH									
LTEETH									
TFRAG									
VERTS									
RIBS									
LFRAG									

UNIDENTIFIED MAMMAL FRAGMENTS = 1

F13/G13 2 2

	PIG	CATTLE	S/G	SHEEP	GOAT	SAR	LAR	OXO	OTHER
SKL	1								
HC					1				
MAX	1								
MAND	3								
ATLAS									
AXIS									
SCAP									
HUM	2								
RAD	1								
ULN									
OC									
SACR									
FEM	1		1						
PAT									
TIB	3								
CAR									
TAR									
MC	1				1				1 DOG
MT									1*
MP	2								
APH		1							
BPH									
CPH									
FIB	-	-	-	-	-	-	-	-	
AST				1					
CAL									
UTEETH		3							
LTEETH	1								
TFRAG									
VERTS									1 FISH
RIBS						1			
LFRAG								1	

UNIDENTIFIED MAMMAL FRAGMENTS = 0
* CHICKEN TARSO-METATARSUS

F14/G14 1 5

	PIG	CATTLE	S/G	SHEEP	GOAT	SAR	LAR	OXO	OTHER
SKL									
HC									
MAX									
MAND									
ATLAS									
AXIS									
SCAP									
HUM									
RAD									
ULN									
OC	17								
SACR	4								
FEM	42								
PAT									
TIB									
CAR									
TAR									
MC									
MT									
MP									
APH									
BPH									
CPH									
FIB		-	-	-	-	-	-	-	-
AST									
CAL									
UTEETH									
LTEETH									
TFRAG									
VERTS						6			
RIBS	5					75			
LFRAG									

UNIDENTIFIED MAMMAL FRAGMENTS = 252

F14/G14 TEST 1

	PIG	CATTLE	S/G	SHEEP	GOAT	SAR	LAR	OXO	OTHER
SKL									
HC									
MAX	1		1						
MAND	1								
ATLAS									
AXIS									
SCAP	1								
HUM			3			1			
RAD			1						
ULN									1 CHICKEN
OC									
SACR									
FEM	3								
PAT									
TIB	2	1	3						
CAR									
TAR									
MC	2								
MT				2					
MP									
APH				1					
BPH									
CPH									
FIB	-	-	-	-	-	-	-	-	
AST	1								
CAL	1	1							
UTEETH	2								
LTEETH									
TFRAG	1								
VERTS	2					2			
RIBS	1					6		1	
LFRAG						1			

UNIDENTIFIED MAMMAL FRAGMENTS = 15

F14/G14 TEST 2

	PIG	CATTLE	S/G	SHEEP	GOAT	SAR	LAR	OXO	OTHER
SKL	21	1				1			
HC									
MAX	3								
MAND	15								
ATLAS	2								
AXIS									
SCAP	3					P			
HUM	12		3			1			
RAD	7		3	1					1 DOG
ULN	10								1 DOG
OC	11		1						1 RODENT
SACR	3								
FEM	18					2			
PAT	1								
TIB	7		2			1		1	
CAR	1								
TAR			1						
MC	6								
MT	6		2						
MP	5								
APH	1	1			1				
BPH	1	1							
CPH	3	1							
FIB	4	-	-	-	-	-	-	-	
AST			2		1				
CAL	5			1					
UTEETH	5	1	4						
LTEETH	10		2						1 DOG
TFRAG	5		3						
VERTS	5		2			15	1	3	
RIBS	3					228			
LFRAG						1		1	

UNIDENTIFIED MAMMAL FRAGMENTS = 583

F15 1 2

	PIG	CATTLE	S/G	SHEEP	GOAT	SAR	LAR	OXO	OTHER
SKL	4								
HC									
MAX	1								
MAND	2		1						
ATLAS									
AXIS									
SCAP			1						
HUM	3								
RAD						1			
ULN									
OC									
SACR									
FEM			1						
PAT									
TIB	8								
CAR									
TAR									
MC									
MT									
MP									
APH	2			1					
BPH									
CPH									
FIB		-	-	-	-	-	-	-	-
AST	1								
CAL	1								
UTEETH	1		3						
LTEETH	1	1	1						
TFRAG									
VERTS	2					2		1	
RIBS						30			
LFRAG						1			

UNIDENTIFIED MAMMAL FRAGMENTS = 49

AREA 2 1, BENEATH 19 ARCHITECTURAL BLOCK

	PIG	CATTLE	S/G	SHEEP	GOAT	SAR	LAR	OXO	OTHER
SKL									
HC									
MAX									
MAND									
ATLAS									
AXIS									
SCAP									
HUM									
RAD	1								
ULN									
OC			1						
SACR									
FEM									
PAT									
TIB	1								
CAR									
TAR									
MC	1		1						
MT									
MP	1								
APH									
BPH									
CPH									
FIB		-	-	-	-	-	-	-	-
AST				1					
CAL									
UTEETH									
LTEETH									
TFRAG									
VERTS	1								
RIBS									
LFRAG									

UNIDENTIFIED MAMMAL FRAGMENTS = 1

F13/G13 WALL SONDAGE

	PIG	CATTLE	S/G	SHEEP	GOAT	SAR	LAR	OXO	OTHER
SKL									
HC									
MAX									
MAND	1								
ATLAS									
AXIS									
SCAP									
HUM									
RAD									
ULN									
OC	2								1*
SACR									
FEM	2								
PAT									
TIB									
CAR									
TAR									
MC	1								
MT	1								1**
MP									
APH					1				
BPH									
CPH									
FIB		-	-	-	-	-	-	-	
AST					1				
CAL									
UTEETH		1	1						
LTEETH									
TFRAG									
VERTS							1		
RIBS	1								
LFRAG									

UNIDENTIFIED MAMMAL FRAGMENTS = 0
* DOG ISCHIUM
** CHICKEN TARSO-MT

F14/G14 1 4

	PIG	CATTLE	S/G	SHEEP	GOAT	SAR	LAR	OXO	OTHER
SKL	1								
HC									
MAX									
MAND1									
ATLAS									
AXIS									
SCAP									
HUM									
RAD									
ULN									
OC	6								
SACR	4								
FEM	21								
PAT	1								
TIB									
CAR									
TAR									
MC									
MT									
MP									
APH									
BPH									
CPH									
FIB		-	-	-	-	-	-	-	-
AST									
CAL									
UTEETH									
LTEETH									
TFRAG									
VERTS	4					6			
RIBS	2					24			
LFRAG						4			

UNIDENTIFIED MAMMAL FRAGMENTS = 88

F14/G14 1 5

	PIG	CATTLE	S/G	SHEEP	GOAT	SAR	LAR	OXO	OTHER
SKL									
HC									
MAX									
MAND									
ATLAS									
AXIS									
SCAP									
HUM									
RAD									
ULN									
OC	17								
SACR	4								
FEM	42								
PAT									
TIB									
CAR									
TAR									
MC									
MT									
MP									
APH									
BPH									
CPH									
FIB		-	-	-	-	-	-	-	-
AST									
CAL									
UTEETH									
LTEETH									
TFRAG									
VERTS						6			
RIBS	5					75			
LFRAG									

UNIDENTIFIED MAMMAL FRAGMENTS = 252

Arabic Summary

فقرات العمود الفقري . وتوجد الجمجمة والفك الاسفل ومعظم عظام الهيكل مابعد الجمجمة من هذا الهيكل العظمي ، ومهما يكن الا ان عظام الرسغ وعظام العقب والقصبة اليمنى والشظية وبعض العظام الاخرى مفقودة . وتشير تيجان الاسنان الدائمة (للطفل رقم ١) الى نقص في النمو ، مؤشر نقص غير محدد . ولا توجد اعراض امراض اخرى ، وربما يكون سبب ذللها ، على أى حال ، طبيعة العظام المكسرة .

أما بقايا عظام (الطفل رقم ٢) فهي عبارة عن مجموعة كسر . وتشمل كسرا من سقف الجمجمة ، وجزء من عظم القص ولوح الكتف ، والترقوة ، وعظم العضد ، وعظم الكعبرة ، وعظم الزند ، وعظم الفخذ ، وعظم القصبة من الجانب الايمن . كما يوجد ايضا حوالى عشرة اضلاع كاملة من الجهة اليمنى ويعود هذا الهيكل الى جنين أو طفل حديث الولادة .

يشير دليل تحديد أعمار الحيوانات الذي بني على أساس التحام العظام الطويلة وعلى نمو الاسنان وتآكلها ، الى ان الغالبية العظمى من خنازير قوريني قد ذبحت خلال السنتين الاوليتين من عمرها . وفي المقابل يبدو أن غالبية الابقار ، والضأن والاغنام قد عاشت حتى سن النضج .

كانت علامات الذبح واضحة على عظام ٣٢ خنزير من قوريني . وشوهدت غالبية علامات القطع على عظام الاطراف الامامية ، خاصة عظم العضد . وكانت علامات القطع على عظام الاطراف الخلفية نادرة . ويشير هذا الدليل الى أن الارباع الامامية ربما كانت قد استخدمت في اعياد الطقوس الدينية ، في حين أن الارباع الخلفية للخنازير ربما تمثل طقوسا نذرية . وبالرغم من اكتشاف عظام ١١ خروفا وماعزا مذبوحا ، تبين العظام نموذج ذبح مشابه بما في ذلك كثرة علامات القطع على عناصر الاطراف الامامية .

تدل قياسات اقصى عظم العضد لخنازير قوريني على أنها مشابهة لعظام الخنازير المعاصرة من موقع بير نيبقي في ليبيا .

وتشمل العظام البشرية من قوريني بقايا هيكلين عظميين لطفلين . وبقدر عمر الهيكل العظمي الكامل (فرد رقم ١) بحوالي ٣ الى ٣$\frac{1}{2}$ عام وارتكز هذا التقدير على أساس درجة تطور نمو الاسنان وعلى درجة التحام

بقايا الهياكل العظمية من قوريني

بام ج.ر كرابترى وجانيت م.مونج

تشمل بقايا الهياكل العظمية من قوريني عظاما حيوانية وبشرية . واكتشف حوالى ٢٥٠٠ عظم وقطعة عظم حيوانية من ٢٦ مربع في الموقع . وتضم الهياكل العظمية البشرية بقايا عظام طفلين صغيرين .

تضم مجموعة العظام من قوريني ٢٤٩٤ عظم وقطعة عظم حيوانى التى أمكن تصنيف ٣٠٪ منها تقريبا الى النوع . واشتملت العظام المصنفة على بقايا الضأن المستأنس ، الماعز المستأنس ، الخنزير المستأنس ، الابقار المستأنسة ، الكلاب المستأنسة ، الدجاج المستأنس ، وعدد صغير من عظام الحمر الوحشية التي لم يكن في الامكان تصنيفها الى النوع . وكانت عظام الخنزير اكثر المعثورات شيوعا ، بحيث شكلت حوالى ٨٠٪ من عظام الحيوانات المصنفة . وبلغت نسبة عظام الضأن والماعز ١٥٪ من مجموع العظام المصنفة ، في حين كانت عظام الابقار قليلة جدا وشكلت أقل من ٥٪ من العظام المصنفة وتوضح النسبة العالية لعظام الخنزير في قوريني أهمية الخنزير بالنسبة لعبادة ديمتير وبيرسيفوني .

المحتملة تشير الى تاريخ في العصر الهيلينستي ،واستخدم الصب والنحت البارد قليلا بعد معرفة نفخ الزجاج في منتصف القرن الاول ق.م. ولعل هذا المثال النادر من النحت الزجاجي كان قد صنع في مصر حيث عمل صب ونحت الزجاج اثناء عصر الاسرات والعصر الهيلينستي .

فلا يمكن تأريخ اى كسر من الزجاج المنفوخ من الحرم المقدس قبل أواخــــر القرن الاول ق.م. وجميع ال ٧٩ مثال من قورينا (٩٧ - ١٧٥) هي من طراز النفخ الحر باستثناء ٩٧ وهي اناء نفخ بالقالب على هيئة عنقود عنب. ورتبت بقية النماذج في هذه المجموعة حسب الشكل وتبعا لطراز الزخــرف ضمن كل شكل. وجاءت الاشكال المفتوحة أولا وشملت اقداحا وكؤوسا (٩٨ - ١٦٠) ، وتضمنت الاشكال المغلقة زجاجات ، قوارير ، ويوجوينتاريا (١٦١ - ١٧٣) ولم نحاول تقسيمها حسب اللون الا ان الالوان المتشابهة قد وضعت مع بعضها ضمن كل مجموعة أشكال.

عثر على الرأس الزجاجي (١٧٤) في حفرة المسارج والفخار التـــي احتوت على مخلفات تؤرخ من القرن السادس الى أواخر القرن الاول ق.م. ومن المحتمل ان الكسرة جزء من زجاجة مرهم أو مثالة نذرية. وشكل الرأس اما في قالب مفتوح أو مغلق ، أو نحت من كتلة زجاج صلبه. واضيفت التفاصيـــل بواسطة ونحت ، وثقب وطحن وصقل السطوح. ومن الصعب تحديد تأريخ ومكـان صناعة هذه القطعة ، وقرينها له مدى تاريخي واسع ، ويبدو أنه لايوجـــد قرين مشابه لها من حيث الشكل والزخرف. ويوجد القليل جدا من الامثلـــة الباقية لاعمال النحت المصنوعة من الزجاج. ويبدو ان طرق الصناعـــــة

على شكل بطيخ أو فصوص (٦٤ - ٦٨) ، وقضبان (٦٩ - ٧١) .

وتتكون أغلبية الأواني من الزجاج الازرق ، وتم ادخال عدد غير متكافئ من الزجاج الاحمر والأبيض في هذا الكاتالوج . ويتكون خرز العين من الزجاج الاخضر والبرتقالي بشكل أساسي .

قسمت قطع الزجاج المصبوب (٧٢ - ٩٨) الى قسمين رئيسيين :

معتم (٧٢ - ٨١) يتضمن متعدد الالوان ، فسيفساء ، معتم أحادى اللون ، محزم والشفاف (٨٢ - ٩٦) يشمل اللف على العجلة ، المضلع ، والاقداح العادية . وترجع جميع قطع الفسيفساء (٧٢ - ٧٨) الى العصر الرومانى باستثناء قدح من العصر الهيلينستي (٧٢) . والزجاج المعتم أحادى اللون (٨٠ و ٨١) أما أحمر أو أبيض اللون ، ويؤرخ في أواخر القرن الاول ق.م. حتى القرن الاول الميلادى . واكتشفت الاقداح المضلعة (٨٢ - ٨٦) في انحاء منطقة البحر المتوسط وغرب اوروبا ابتداء من اواخر القرن الاول ق.م. وحتى نهاية القرن الاول الميلادى تقريبا . وأما مجموعة الاقداح العادية من الحرم المقدس (٨٧ - ٩٤) فقد نقش عليها من الداخل خزوز أفقيه (وأحيانا من الخارج) وهي معاصرة للاقداح المضلعة .

وبالرغم من ان نفخ الزجاج ربما اخترع في منتصف القرن الاول ق.م. ،

زجاج من حرم ديميتر وبيرسيفوني المقدس

من قورينـــــــــــــــــا

أندرو أوليفـــــــر

يتضمن هذا الفصل ١٧٤ نموذجا من الزجاج من موقع الحرم المقدس للالهه ديميتر وبيرسيفوني في قورينا . ويمكن تأريخ هذه المجموعة حوالــي ٥٥٠ - ٤٠٠ق.م. ويقسم الزجاج الى ثلاثة أقسام رئيسية استنادا الى أسلوب التقنيه : التشكيل اليدوى ، الصب ، والنفخ . وليس من السهل ان ينسجم الرأس الزجاجي (١٧٤) مع هذه المجموعات ، كما أشارت ج. برانيس فـــي شرحها لهذا الرأس في ملحق رقم ١ ، وربما كان هذا الرأس قد عمل بواسطة القالب أو نحت من كتلة صلبة .

وجرى اختيار النماذج الزجاجية ذات التشكيل اليدوى (١ - ٧١) من بين مايقرب من ستمائة كسرة ، وتمثل هذه النماذج أكبر مجموعة مكتشفـــة من زجاج التشكيل اليدوى من اقليم برقه ، وتشمل أشكالا من الألباســـــــرا (١ - ٧) ، أمفوريسكوى (٨ - ١٦) ، آريبالوى (١٧ - ١٩) ، اوينوكوى (٢٠ - ٢٢) ، كسر من أشكال غير معروفة (٢٣ - ٣٨) ، دلاية (٣٩) ، خرز عين (٤٠ - ٥٦) ، خرزة مع خيط (٥٧) ، خرز عادى (٥٨ - ٦٣) ، خـــرز

تحاول مواد الكتالوج ان تتبع الشكل العام الذى استخدم في الدراسات السابقة من هذه السلسلة . وتتضمن رقم الكتالوج الذى أعطى لها في هذه الدراسة ، رقم جرد الحفريات ، نوع المادة ، رقم المربع الذى وجد فيه الاثر ، مرجع اللوحة أو الشكل ، ويعطي السطر الثاني الابعاد ، يتبعها وصف مختصر . واذا سبق ان نشرت المادة فتعطى مراجع ببليوجرافية في بداية وصف الكتالوج . وتقدم مقارنة عقب المواد من طراز مشابهة . وتزود في نهاية كل فصل النتائج الاولية وعدد المعثورات التي وجدت ، دليل التأريخ ومكان الصناعة المحتمل .

وعلى سبيل المثال ، الدلايات واحدة من اكبر المجموعات من حيث تنوع الطرز ، وقسمت الى عدد من المجموعات حسب الطراز ورتبت أبجديا . وفي المقابل قسمت الاواني الفخارية اولا قسمة فرعية حسب الوسيلة وبعدها قسمت حسب الشكل . والاستثناء الرئيسي الوحيد لهذا الترتيب الوظيفي هو الفصل الاول ، الذى يتناول المثالات الطينية ، الذى جمع كل أمثلة الاشكال الحيوانية والانسانية الكاملة . وعمل هذا من اجل الملاءمة ، بما انه من الصعب في الغالب تحديد الوظيفة الاصلية للمثالة الطينية . وربما يكون البعض دلايات ، والآخر ملحقات او زخارف بينما ماتزل البقية مجرد مثالات طينية نذرية . وايضا تتبع النقد المعقول بأن الفن الرمزى يجب أن يعامل على انفراد ، وذلك سباب تتعلق بالطراز ولانه ربما يكون للمثالات الطينية معنى رمزيا او تمثيليا هاما .

ودخل في الكتالوج نقاش للوظيفة والتأريخ ، مصدر الصناعة ، والمحيط الذى وجد فيه الاثر . وعادة يتبع نقاش من هذا النوع كل مجموعة رئيسية من المعثورات . ومن اجل معرفة التاريخ العام للموقع ، اعمال التنقيب وملخصات الطبقات يطلب من القارىء الرجوع الى المجلد الاول ضمن سلسلة حرم ديمتير المقدس .

المألوف والضروري لدراسات من هذا النوع . وان اي طريقة اختيار طبيعي ان تكون عشوائية ، وان التعصب الطبيعي لحالة الحفظ والتنقيب والبحث العلمي سوف تؤثر على النتيجة بالضرورة . وسوف تهمل بعض المواد ، على سبيل المثال الحديد ، لان المواد الحديدية غالبا ماتكون بحاله رديئة بحيث لايسهل تصنيفها .وايضا يوجد ميل لتأكيد الاثارة والخاصية على حساب الدنيوية .

وكان المعتقد الاولي عند محاولة تنظيم عدد وافر من العثورات المتنوعة بأن الوظيفة هي العامل الحاسم . وعند دراسة مادة من محيط ديني ان وظيفة المادة أو الشيء ، وظيفته كما يراها المقدم ، الذي يقرر معناها كتقدمة نذرية . وان تقسيمات عشوائية اكثر من خلال الوسيلة أو الصناعة سوف يخفي هذا المظهر الاساسي . ولهذا السبب نظمت المعثورات الصغيرة في هذا الكتالوج حسب وظائفها . ورتبت في فصول يحتوي كل فصل على فئة كبيرة من المواد ـ المثالات الطينية ، المجوهرات والحلى ، والادوات المعدنية والمعدات ، الاسلحة ، الاواني ومواد متفرقة . وضمن كل فصل رتبت المعثورات حسب طراز الاثر وتحت العنوان الفرعي للطراز ، وفي حالة أنواع المعثورات الاكبر ، فقد قسمت الى مجموعات يسهل التحكم فيها .

عدد قليل من المعثورات ، على سبيل المثال ، أصداف الترايداكنــــا المنحوتة (٣٦٧ - ٤٧٣) ، ذو أصل واضح من شرق البحر المتوسط ولعلها وصلت الى قوريني ، أما عن طريق الاستيراد المباشر أو بواسطة تجار مـــن شرق اليونان .

يوجد لدينا مثالين مستوردين غير عاديين من ايطاليا :
مفصلة على شكل ضفدع مصنوعة من البرونز من أنبوب (١٧) ، ومقبض برونزى لمصفاة على شكل بطة (٤٠٢) ربما صنعتا في ماجنا كرايكا . كلاهما مــن العصر الكلاسيكي ، والى جانب مغرفة برونزية من الارتيميزيوم الثاني فـي قوريني فأنهما يعتبران شهادة على الروابط التجارية القليلة مع العـزب في القرن الخامس ق.م .

الكاتالـــوج

ان عدد المعثورات التى يضمها هذا الكتالوج كبير ، ووجد بعض طرز المعثورات بكميات كبيرة . ويتصف هذا الكتالوج بكونه يشمل نموذجا أكثر من كونه شاملا . ولا يوجد متسع ولا حاجة بأن يتم تسجيل نموذج لكل الطراز ، ولذلك فقد تضمن نموذجا لكل طراز (امكن تصنيفه) عثر عليه ويمكــن ان يعطي انطباع كامل للمجموعة بأسرها ، مع الاخذ في الاعتبار التوضيــــح

في مواقع أثرية عديدة ، ويلاحظ ان المواد المستوردة من اليونان مبكرة جدا ، وتؤرخ في نهاية القرن السابع او السادس ق.م.

تشمل المواد المستوردة من شرق اليونان مثالات من الخزف المزخرف (٢٩ - ٣٥) وأواني (٣٨٢ - ٣٨٩) والقرد البرونزي (٢٥) ، واثنان من الأسود البرونزية (٢٢ و ٢٤) ، العديد من علب المجوهرات المصنوعة من الحجر ، ودبوس برونزي (٢٠٢) ربما تكون من أصل أيوني . وجميع هــذه المواد تؤرخ في العصر القديم ، باستثناء علب المجوهرات التي يمكن ان تعود الى العصر الكلاسيكي .

وتضم المواد المصرية الضفدع البرونزي (١٦) ومثالة الصقر (١٣) ، ودلاية كوزة الخشخاش المعمولة من العقيق الاحمر (١١٣ - ١١٨) دلايات القلب والوجه (١٥٤ - ١٥٨ و ١٥٩ و ١٦٠) ، وابريق المصنوع من الخزف (٣٨٧) ، وأواني الألباسترا (٤٠٣ - ٤١٣) ، بعض الاواني المصنوعة من الحجر ، وكذلك كسر قشر بيضة النعام (٣٦٤) .

وبالرغم من أن المواد المذكورة ليست أكبر من حيث العدد الكلي ، فان المواد المصرية تشكل أكبر مجموعة متنوعة من حيث الطراز والمواد المصنوعة منها . ومرة ثانية نجد ان معظم المعثورات تؤرخ في فترة أقدم .

الكلاسيكي ومابعد .

ويمكن تقسيم المواد المستوردة الى ثلاث مجموعات رئيسية : اليونان ، شرق بلاد اليونان ، مصر ، أو متأثرة بمصر . وتبدو هذه المجموعات الثلاث موزعة بالتساوى تقريبا .

المواد المستوردة من اليونان جاءت من شبه جزيرة البيلوبونيز في معظمها . وتشمل الكبش المعمول من العاج (٢٦) الذى لايوجد خلاف على أنه من صنع ورشة عمل في شبه جزيرة البيلوبونيز . ومن الجائز من نفس المصدر أساس طرازه ، مثالة غير عادية في شكل سيدة من البرونز (٢١) . وينطق نفس الشيء على دلايات في شكل سيدة (١٠٦ و ١٠٧) وان دلايات الفأس المزدوجة العاجية (٨٦ - ٨٨) بالاضافة الى نماذج مشابهة وجدت في توكره جميعها ايضا مستوردة من اليونان ، ويوجد لها قرائن قريبة فيجميع انحاء شبه جزيرة البليوبونيز . وامتازت بتوزيع أوسع من الاكباش العاجية . وربما تكون الدبابيس العاجية (١٩٢ - ١٩٨) مستوردة أيضا ، ومهما يكن ،ان كلا من دبابيس قوريني والنماذج التي وجدت في توكرة مختلفة عن طرز اليونان كي تدل على احتمال كونها صناعة محلية ، ولعل عدد كبير من الدبابيس البرونزية ايضا كان من انتاج شبه جزيرة البيلوبونيز حيث يوجد لها قرائن

ان المعثورات في العصر الكلاسيكي أكثر ندرة . وتشمل خرز ثنائي المخروط (٤٧ - ٤٩) ، مفصلة برونزية على شكل ضفدعة (١٧) ، بعض الخواتم الفضية والبرونزية (على سبيل المثال ٢٥٥ و ٢٥٦)، مقبض مغرفة من البرونز (٤٠٢) ، وعلب مجوهرات من الحجر (٤٢٤ ، ٤٢٥ ، ٤٢٩) .

ان المعثورات التي تنسب الى العصرين الهيلينستي والروماني نسبيا أقل اذا أخذنا في الاعتبار طول هذه الفترة الزمنية . وتشمل التاج الذهبي (٣٨ و ٣٩) ، الورديات الفضية (٤٠ - ٤٢) ، الأساور العاجية (١٦٧ و ١٦٨) ، زرائر عظمية (١٧٢ - ١٧٤) ، خاتم برونزي (٢٥٧) ، خواتم عاجية وعظمية (٢٥٨ و ٢٥٤) ، قاعدة معدنية (٢٧٧) ، بروش برونزي ، دسر ، مفاصل برونزية وعظمية (٢٩٥ - ٢٩٧) ، العديد من المسامير ، أصابع يد الهاون الحجري (٤٥١ و ٤٥٢) ، وبعض الأواني الحجرية الأقل أهمية . والكثير من الأدوات المعدنية ذات الوظائف الأكثر والأدوات ، والوسائل ، وماشابه ذلك ، وبالرغم من أنها غير مؤرخة بدقة ، فهي تتبع للمجموعة الأخيرة هذه .

وفيما يخص التأريخ فان الصورة واضحة : تقدمات نذريه غنية خلال العصر القديم ، وتقدمات أقل غنى ، وأقل كمية أو عددا ، منذ بداية العصر

يحتمل أنها من القرن السادس بدلا من السابع ق٠م٠ مثالات الخزف المزخرف (٢٩ - ٣٥) ، دلايات الفأس العاجية (٨٦ - ٨٩) ، دلايات هلالية (٩٨ و ٩٩) دلاية ورقة نبات (١٠٨) ، دلايات قلب (١٥٥ - ١٥٨) ، لفات الشعر (١٧٥ - ١٨٦) ، القرطان (١٨٨ - ١٩١) ، دبابيس المعدن (١٩٩ - ٢٠٣) ، العديد من دبابيس البرونز ، أواني الخزف المزخرف (٣٨٢ - ٣٨٩) ، والعديد من الأواني الحجرية ٠ ومجموعة متنوعة أكبر تعزى الى العصر القديم على أساس الطراز أو المحيط الذى وجدت فيه ، العديد من المثالات البرونزية (١- ٢٥) قناع من الفضة (٣٦) ، ورديه قرص من الفضة (٤٣) ، خرز مستدير (٦٣ - ٦٨) ، خرز كروى (٧٠ - ٧٧) ، خرز انبوبي (٧٨ - ٨٣) ، دلايات بقرية (٩٠ و ٩١) ، دلايات مخروطية (٩٢ - ٩٧) ، دلايات عاجية على شكل نقطة (١٠٠ - ١٠٥) ، دلايات في شكل سيدة (١٠٦ - ١٠٧) ، دلايات ذهبية على شكل أسد (١٠٩ و ١١٠) ، دلايات صدفية (١٢٠ - ١٣٦) ، والعديد من طرز أدوات الزينة بما في ذلك الخواتم البرونزية ٠

ومعثورات أخرى تؤرخ عادة اما في أواخر العصر القديم أو العصر الكلاسيكي مثل خرز القلادة (٥٣ - ٥٨) دلاية الزهرية (١٥٢) و أواني الألباسترا المعمولة من الألباستر (٤٠٣ - ٤١٣) ٠

عن الحقيقة التي تقبل الجدل بأن المعثورات القديمة تزيد في العدد بشكل كبير عن جميع المعثورات مجتمعة . واما ان الحرم المقدس كان غني جدا أو أكثر شعبية في العصر القديم ، والا تغير نمط التقدمات مع مرور الزمن . وهذا الاحتمال الأخير بأن تقدمات المجوهرات أو مثالات الطين المشوى قد استبدلت في مرحلة لاحقه بتقدمات عن أنواع أخرى يمكن أن يؤخذ به على ضوء جميع المعثورات التي وجدت في الحرم المقدس .

ربما يسبق تاريخ أقدم المعثورات التاريخ التقليدى لتأسيس المستوطنة الاغريقية في قوريني . وهذا هو حال أصداف ترايداكنا المنحوتة (٤٦٧ – ٤٧٣) ، التي يبدو أنها زخرفت في النصف الأول من القرن السابع ق.م. ومع أن الكبش المصنوع من العاج (٢٦) غير مؤرخ بدقة مثل الاصداف ، الا أنه يعود الى فترة مبكرة ، وبالتأكيد القرن السابع ، ويمكن أن يعود الى نهاية القرن . وان ولاية " كوزة الخشخاش " المعمولة من العقيق الأحمر (١١٣ – ١١٨) ، ودبوس العاج (١٩٢ – ١٩٨) ، وبعض الدبابيس المعدنية ، وعلى سبيل المثال ، الدبوس الذهبى (٢٣٤) الذى يؤرخ في نهاية القرن السابع ق.م. جميعها مبكرة أيضا .

ومن المعثورات التي تؤرخ في العصر القديم بصورة مؤكدة ، مع أنه

الملاحظة الهامة التي يمكن ان تقال عن طبيعة المعثورات المجمعة بصفة عامة هي الكثرة الغالبة للمواد التي كان من الواضح أنها ممتلكات شخصية ، ومواد ذات قيمة جمالية كبيرة على مايبدو . المثالات الطينية ، والمجوهرات وأدوات الزينة الشخصية ومواد أخرى مشابهة ذات جودة عالية مثل صدفه ترايداكنا الملونه كانت أكثر التقدمات انتشارا ، في العصور المبكرة بصورة خاصة . ولهذا السبب فقد تكونت المواد في هذه المجموعة في الغالب من تلك المواد التي ترتبط عادة مع الأصناف ذات الجودة العالية مثل : العاج والعظم والبرونز والفضة والذهب وصدف بيض النعام ، وأصداف البحر في مقابل الحديد والرصاص والطين المشوى أو الخشب . وعلى نحو لايمكن انكاره ، ان هذه الصورة الى حد ما نتيجة تغيير الحفظ ، وعلى أى حال ، حتى عندما نأخذ في الاعتبار حالة الحفظ الرديئة مثل المواد المعدنية فان المواد العملية تشكل نسبة مئوية قليلة ضمن المجموعة . وأيضا أن هذه المواد العملية مثل الأدوات أو الأدوات المعدنية التي يبدو أنها لم تكن نذورا في طبيعتها يرجح أن يكون تاريخها في نهاية الحرم المقدس .

المجموعة الكبرى والأكثر تحديدا من المواد الأثرية تعود الى العصر القديم ، ويرجع هذا نسبيا الى طبيعة المعثورات الصغيرة ، ولكنه ينتج

١٩

المعثورات الصغرى

ن. جريجوري جوردن

يتضمن هذا الكاتالوج ٥١٠ صنفا من المعثورات ممثلة لما يزيد عن ٤٠٠٠ لقية وجزء من اللقية التي جمعت تحت اسم المعثورات الصغرى. وعملية الجمع هذه متغايرة الخواص وتحتوي على الكثير من المواد التي تعود الى مجموعات من المواد المشابهة نشرت في مكان آخر من هذه السلسلة المخصصة الى حرم ديميتر وبيرسيفوني خارج أسوار المدينة في قوريني. ولذا ان التعميم والنتائج حول نوع أي مادة واحدة هو عمل محدود حتى تتوفر المعلومات من الدراسات الاخرى. وعلى سبيل المثال ، يمكن مناقشة الاواني فقط عندما يؤخذ في الحساب الدليل على الفخار الخشن ، الاواني الملونة ، الاسرجة والزجاج ، استثنيت بعض أنواع المواد الاثرية من هذه الدراسة لأنها استحقت اهتماما خاصا ، ومثال ذلك المسكوكات والاحجار الكريمة المحفورة بالرغم من أنها أيضا " معثورات صغيرة " وان صفة الجمع العشوائي المقدمة في هذه الدراسة هامة كي نتذكرها لأن النتائج التي تم التوصل اليها هنا يجب أن تعدل وتصحح حسب الدليل الاضافي الذى قدم فى منشورات الحرم المقدس الأخرى.

ARABIC SUMMARY

الوفاة الفعلية .

اكتشفت البقايا المبعثرة للطفل حديث الولادة ، التى تعود أساسا الى الجانب الايمن ، بجانب جمجمة طفل الثلاث سنوات. ولماذا بقيت هذه الأجزاء من الهيكل العظمي فقط وكيف عرف طفل صغير جدا طريقة الى الحرم المقدس تمثل مشكلة أثرية محيرة ، بما أنه لم تكتشف بقايا انسان كبير صاحب الطفل . ومهما يكن ، ان التربة الى الجنوب مباشرة من الطفلين تقع أسفل خط سكة الحديد التي وضعها فريق البعثة ولم يسبق ان نقب فيها . ولا بد أن الوالد أو الوالدة المفقود مازال تحت خط سكة الحديد أو أنه بقي حيّ أثناء الزلزال . ومن الصعب تفسير كيف أن عظام الجنين قد سلمت من الاختلاط مع عظام والدته ، وذلك هو السبب في اعتقادى أن بقايا العظام تعود بدلا من ذلك الى طفل حديث الولادة . وان فقدان الجانب الايسر من الجسم ربما تكون ببساطة نتيجة دفن غير عميق على أرض منحدرة ، وجرفت المياه بقايا الجسم أو حملت بعيدا . وعلى أى حال ، ان الحالتين تمثلان البقية الضئيلة للسكان الذين احتشدوا في قديم الزمان في هذا الحرم المقدس وتدل حداثة سنهما على بلاغة مزدوجة بارتباطهما مع نهايته الاليمة.[25]

* ملاحظة : انظر هوامش النص باللغة الانجليزية للاطلاع على الهوامش التى وردت في هذه الترجمة .

زلزال ٣٦٥ ميلادية . وكان الجثمان قد سقط على ظهره والرأس متجهة الى الغرب . ونتج عن حشر الرأس في فجوة ضيقة أنه ضغط الى الامام بحيث ان ارتكزت الذقن على الصدر . وامتدت الذراع اليمنى بشكل مواز لجانب الجسم ، في حين امتدت الذراع اليسرى فوق الحوض . ولم تكتشف اية بقايا للملابس أو أى شكل من أشكال الأردية . ولم يعثر المنقبون على أى دليل لوجود حفرة حول الجثمان كي تشير الى انه كان قد دفن على وجه السرعة داخل تجويف من رديم الزلزال . وبدلا من ذلك ، اذا حكمنا من خلال الطريقة غير المطابقة للعادات التي وضع فيها الجثمان بين الكتل الحجرية المستعملة في البناء ، يبدو ان الجثمان قد دفن بطريقة عرضية ونخمن بأن الطفل قليل الحظ قد سقط على ظهره داخل الشق الموجود في الجدار ، اما دائخ أو فاقد الوعي ، وعندها اختنق تحت رديم الزلزال المتحرك وبقي الرأس وجزء كبير من الجسم ، وان حقيقة عدم اظهار اجزاء الجسم لآثار نخر من القوارض أو أى نوع من الوحوش الكاسرة يعطينا سببا آخر للاعتقاد بأن الجسم لم يبق مدة طويلة مكشوفا للهواء بعد الموت . وان أى كسر في العظام قد حدث عندما جفت العظام وتفسر بشكل أفضل بسبب ضغط التراب لمدة طويلة من الزمن بدلا من الصدمة عند لحظة

الطمس النهائي لمعالم الحرم المقدس قد نتجت بسبب كارثة عـــام ٣٦٥ ميلادية ، ولذلك فان قطعتي الزجاج المتأخرتين (كاتالوج أوليفـر ١٦٧ و ١٧٣) يرجعان الى القرن الاول والقرن الرابع الميلاديين ، بينما صفائح الذهب الرومانية المتأخرة (كتالوج وردن ٣٧ و ٣٩) يؤرخا في فتــــرة لاتزيد عن أوائل القرن الثالث الميلادى .

وأخيرا نتناول الهياكل العظمية البشرية التي نشرتها ج . مونج ، واحد منها كان لطفل يبلغ من العمر ثلاثة أو ثلاثة ونصف أعوام في حيـن أن الهيكل الآخر وصفته بأنه أما جنين أو طفل كامل . وعكس الملاحظـات التي نشرت سابقا التي اعتبرت البقايا المبعثرة من الهياكل على أنها لثلاثة اشخاص[٣٣]، فان مونج توضح بأنها لطفلين فقط . ويتضمن التقرير غير المنشور لموسم ١٩٧٩ وصفا مفصلا لظروف اكتشافهما التي يمكن تلخيصهــا كالتالي[٣٤]، وجد الهيكلان على مسافة ٣٠رام الى الشمال من نقطة تقاطـع خطوط الشبكية ف و ١٢ (شكل ٠٠٠) وقع جثمان الطفل الاكبر في شق غيـر عميق نتج عن انقسام بسبب عنف الزلزال الذى أسقط الكتل الحجرية الضخمـة من السور المساند من العصر الامبراطورى المتأخر ت ٢٠ (شكل ٠٠٠) وفي وقت اكتشافه كانت بقاياه مدفونة في الطبقة الاولى تحت رديم خفيف مــن

١٥

بالاضافة الى تراكم مكثف لجميع انواع الفخار القديم بما في ذلك الفخار اللاكوني والأتيكي الأسود ، ومن جهة أخرى فان المعثورات الزجاجية التي وجدت فيها كانت قليلة نسبيا . وكما ورد كثيرا ان هذه الحفرة غير مفيدة للمقارنة كي تفسر الاستعمالات الاصلية التي استخدمت فيها اللقى الاثرية المختلفة في الحرم المقدس .

تركز الاهتمام في النقاش السابق على المعنى الذى تضمنته المعثورات المبكرة أكثر من المعثورات المتأخرة . وعلى الرغم من أن هذه الحقيقة لعل قراء هذه السلسلة على علم برأى د. روجرز الذى يقول ان زلزال عام ٢٦٢ ميلادية والذى يعزى اليه الدمار المبدأى للحرم المقدس في الواقع لم يحدث في قوريني وان الدمار كان بسبب زلزال عام ٣٦٥ ميلادية . وسيقال الكثير حول وجهة النظر الهامة هذه عندما تنشر المسكوكات واعمال النحت والاسرجة والعمارة في الفترة المتأخرة ، وفي الوقت الحاضر لم ينبثق من دراسة كل من وردن وأوليفر ما يعوض عن اعتقادنا بأن النشاطات في الحرم المقدس قد انتهت بشكل كبير عند منتصف القرن الثالث الميلادى وان هذا الوضع قد نتج عن زلزال . وكذلك نعتقد أنه جرت محاولة محدودة لتنظيف الحرم المقدس المتوسط بعد عام ٢٦٢ وان

١٤

تعيقها نتائج كثرة المباني المتأخرة الى جانب عدم استكمال اعمال التنقيب ، فقد كانت المنطقة قد ضمت ثلاثة ومن المحتمل أربعة مبان منفصلة[21]، تعود الى العصر القديم وأوائل العصر الكلاسيكي من تطوير الحرم المقدس ، وان السؤال عن سبب وجود اعداد كبيرة من كسر الفخار القديم في الجزر وشرق اليونان في هذه المنطقة من الموقع في مقابل نماذج بسيطة من الفخار اللاكوني وفخار الطراز الأسود الاتيكي ربما يكون له علاقة بعدم تحديد وظيفة هذه المباني حتى الآن . وان مربع س ١٠ /١١ ، أ ، (شكل ٠٠٠) الذى يقع الى الجنوب مباشرة من البوابة التذكارية من العصر الامبراطوري (س ٢٠) وعلى مسافة قصيرة الى الغرب من مبنى (س ٢) قد اكتشف فيه عددا كبيرا من كسر الزجاج ، ومهما يكن تظهر هذه الكسر الزجاجية في الطبقة العليا الرومانية المتأخرة ولا علاقة مباشرة لها مع أى من المباني المجاورة ، بما في ذلك البوابة، ولا تدلنا أى شيء عن استعمال الزجاج . وأخيرا ان الحفرة التي توجد خلف الجدار المساند (ت ١٠) الذى يفصل الحرم المقدس المتوسط عن الحرم المقدس السفلى (شكل ٠٠٠٠ ، ف ١٣/ج ١٣ ، أو ٢ ، ف ١٤/ج ١٤ ، ١) قد احتوت على عدد كبير من المعثورات الصغيرة المتنوعة التي درستها وردن

من منطقة السور والمحيطة بحفرة س ١٨ .

ان اكبر كمية من المعثورات المتنوعة من القرنين السادس والخامس ق.م. والتي تمثل دلايات وحيوانات صغيرة من البرونز قد جاءت من المربعات د ١٢/١٣ ، ب و د ١٢/١٣ ، ف (شكل ٠٠٠) ، التي تقع بين الجدار غير منتظم الحجارة الذى يعود الى العصر القديم (ت ١) وآخر من أواخر العصر القديم وأوائل العصر الكلاسيكى والمبانى س ٢ و س ٤ [17]. واكتشف في نفس المناطق كميات غير عادية من الاحجار الكريمة ذات النقوش الجميلة والجعران[18] بالاضافة الى كسر فخارية مستوردة من شرق اليونان والجزر[19] واكتشفت ايضا اعداد كبيرة من المعثورات الصغيرة والمتنوعة في المنطقة المفتوحة (س ١٣، ١) الى الغرب من مبنى س ٤ الذى أثبت مرة ثانية أنه مصدر غني للفخار القديم من شرق اليونان والجزر[20]. وجاءت نسبة كبيرة من ٤٥٨ من الخواتم البرونزية التـي احصاها وردن من د ١٢/١٣ ،ف ،وكذلك من د ١٥/١٦ ، ١ ، الى الجنوب من بيت العبادة القديم س ٦ ، والمنطقة المجاورة (د ١٦/١٧ ، ١) التي ارتبطت فيما بعد مع حجرة التخزين الهيلينستية س ١١ التي سبق شرحها وبالرغم من حقيقة الفهم المعقول للمباني المبكرة في هذا القطاع

١٢

الفخارية خارج سور الحرم المقدس من العصر الامبراطورى المبكر والتي احتوت على كميات كبيرة من أواني الطعام والشراب الهيلينيستيه[16] ومهما يكن فقد وجد في هذه الحفرة كمية قليلة نسبيا من الزجاج الهام فيما عدا الرأس الزجاجي الذى جرت مناقشته في ملحق ا . وهذه الحقيقة تجعل من غير المحتمل ان يكون للزجاج من مربعات د ١٧/١٦ و سي ١٦/١٥ أى علاقة مع طقوس تناول الطعام والتي بطريقة أخرى يثبتها الفخار المكتشف من هذه الحفرة ان حجرة التخزين س ١١ التي تعود الى العصر الهيلينستي ولاتزال تنتظر النشر في المجلد القادم من هذه السلسلة، لم تحفر بالكامل بل يبدو ، كما يدل الاسم ، أنها استعملت لاغراض يومية (منفعية) بدلا من الاغراض الدينية . وعلى أية حال فان المعثورات الزجاجية التي يشار بأنها جاءت من الطبقة الثانية من مربعات د ١٧/١٦ الثلاثة قد كانت جزءا من رديم الزلزال ولا علاقتها مع وظيفة الحجرة . ومن جهة أخرى ، ربما كانت المعثورات الزجاجية من الطبقة الثالثة جزءا من مخبأ للأدوات المصنوعة بما في ذلك مثالات الطين المشوى التي خزنت في حجرة س ١١ . وان الجواب النهائي لمسألة أين وكيف استعمل الزجاج سيمكن معرفته اذا جرى المزيد من أعمال التنقيب في الربع الجنوبى الغربي

وهناك حلقة مفقودة في فهمنا للزجاج تتعلق بطريقة ترتيبه الاصلية ضمن الحرم المقدس ، وعلى سبيل المثال ان وجود الكسر الزجاجية في مربع ١٣ في / ١٣ ج ١ ، ٢ خلف الجدار المساند ــ ت ١٠ من العصر الامبراطورى المبكر لايدلنا على أى شىء لانه ، كما رأينا سابقا ،لم يكن في الاستطاعة معرفة مصدر ًاو مصادر محتويات هذه الحفرة . واذا كانت المصنوعات الزجاجية تعرض كتقدمات نذرية داخل أى من بيوت العبادة المفصلة ، فلا يوجد هناك أى دليل من كنافة وجود الكسر الزجاجية كى تشير الى أى من البيوت الستة في الحرم المقدس التي استعملت لذلك الغرض[15]، باستثناء غرفه س ١١ التي سبق مناقشتها . وربما انه من الجدير بالملاحظة أنه لم تكتشف أى أوانٍ زجاجية لا على أو قرب المقاعد الحجرية التي امتدت خلف بيوت العبادة المنفصلة س ٥ و س ٧ .

كانت أكبر أماكن تركيز الزجاج في الموقع في مربعى د ١٧/١٦،(شكل ٠٠٠) بجوار حجرة التخزين س ١١ ومربع س ١٦/١٥ الذى يرتبط مع بيت النبع ف ٢ . وبعبارة أخرى فقد اكتشفت المجموعتان في المنطقة العامة من القسم العلوى للحرم المقدس وفي زاويته الجنوبية الغربية، وبذلك فانهما يحيطان بالحفرة (س ١٨) التي دفنت فيها الاسرجة والاوانى

مرة أخرى بالنسبة لمكان الأصل ، لم تسفر أعمال التنقيب في الكشف عن أى دليل خارجي يساعد في تقرير المكان الذى صنع فيه الزجاج ، ولا يقرتح أوليفر صناعة محلية لأى من الاوانى التي وردت في الدراسة واكتشفت كسرة زجاج واحدة أثناء أعمال التنقيب التي قامت بها جامعة ميتشجان في أبولونيا في الستينات ، ولكن هذا الدليل وحده لايثبت شيئا ، ومن جهة أخرى ، ان العثور على ورش تصنيع الزجاج يحير الكثيرون لكنها نظريا يمكن ان تقام في أى مكان . واذا أعتبرنا كمية الزجاج المكتشف من الحرم المقدس ، يمكن للمرء أن يتعجب ، من الواضح عكس الحكمة السائدة[13]، ان لم يكن على الاقل أصل بعض الامثلة المصبوبة والمنفوخة من المدن الخمس . ومن الواضح ان الحرم المقدس مكان غير مناسب كى يقام فيه ورشة لتصنيع الزجاج ، ولكن الأرض ذات المصاطب[14] شرق البوابة التذكارية في القسم العلوى من الحرم المقدس (س ٢٠) ربما كانت مكان مناسب لبيع لوزام المعبد مثل أوانى الطبخ والأكل والشرب ، المثالات الطينية والبرونزية ، والاوانى الزجاجية الى المتعبدين الذين يزورون المعبد . وعندما يتعجب المرء ان لم يكن يصنع عدد قليل من هذه الاوانى في هذا المكان أيضا .

٩

مجموعة ٢٤٩٤ من العظام التي درستها كرابتري ومونج هو عظمه دجاجة . مالم تحترق بقايا عظام الطيور في النار ، أو أنها دفنت في مكان لم يجرى التنقيب فيه في الحرم المقدس حتى الآن ، أو أنها حملت الى المنازل للاستهلاك[11]،فان نماذج الحيوانات من الذهب والبرونز والعاج والخزف المزخرف (بالاضافة الى الطيور تتضمن قرد ، أسود ، أوعال ، وضفادع) لم يكن لها علاقة مباشرة مع الحيوانات الحية التي قدمت بصورة دورية كنذور الى الالهة المقيمة مع الاستثناء الوحيد العرضي للاغنام[12].

ولعل المكان الاصلى قد لعب دورا في هذه العملية ، واذا أنتجت التقدمات النذرية محليا ، كما كان الحال بالتأكيد في كثير من التقدمات النذرية للحيوانات المصنوعة من الطين المشوى التي اكتشفت في الحرم المقدس ولم تنشر بعد ،وربما أنها بيعت في منطقة مجاورة للحرم المقدس، فان وجوها يمكن تفسيره على أس توفرها كأى معنى ديني . ولعل هذا هو التفسير الوحيد الذى نحتاجه بسبب الوفرة النسبية لنماذج الطيور الداجنة البرونزية ، التي يبدو أنها كانت تصنع محليا ، وكذلك ندرة وجود نماذج برونزية مستوردة تمثل القرد ، الضفدعة ، الأسد ، والصقر أسد من الخزف المزخرف ، وعل وصقر ، وعل من العاج .

التي جرى التنقيب فيها في الحرم المقدس . ومن جهة أخرى اكتشف عـــدد من المذابح الحجرية المحمولة يتراوح حجمها من حوالي ٩٠ر٠م ارتفـــاع الى الحجم الصغير ثيمياتيريا ولاتزال تنتظر النشر في المستقبل . ولابد أن أكبر المذابح المحمولة ، التي يوجد منها أقل من دزينه ، كانــــت تستعمل للقرابين المحروقة من لحم الحيوان ، ومن حيث الطراز لم تتسع لتضحية الحيوانات المستمرة وعلى نطاق كبير . ولا نعرف أين كان أصــل الحفرة التي وجدت خلف جدار الحرم المقدس المتوسط ، من الواضح أنهــــا جاءت من مكان آخر من الحرم المقدس ، ربما من القسم الذى لم ينقب حتى الآن في القسم العلوي من الحرم المقدس الاعلى ، حيث ربما كانت توجـــد مذابح الرماد المفقودة هذا اذا وجدت في الأصل .

أما بالنسبة لتصوير نماذج الحيوانات فقد عثر على اعداد وافرة من تماثيل نذريه لخنازير من الحجر والطين المشوى[١٠]، من المدهش الى حـد ما ، انها لم تعمل من المعدن أو المواد الأخرى التي درســـها وردن . وتصور نذور معمولة من البرونز حيوانات صغيرة منفصلة مثل البط والاوز والحمام ، وصورت الطيور الجارحة في مثال لصقر واحد من البرونـــز . وحتى الآن ان مثالا واحدا لبقايا الطيور الذى أمكن التعرف عليه مــــن

المجلد الاول من هذه السلسلة ، حيث يعتقدان أنها تشكل 77ر6٪ من بقايا الحيوانات التي أمكن التعرف عليها[5]، بالاضافة الى ذلك لاحظت المؤلفتان آثار عملية الذبح ، ويعتقدان أن هذا يقدم برهانا قويا على ممارسة طقوس الاحتفالات الدينية[6]. وفي أغلب الامثلة تظهر آثار الذبح على الأرجل الأمامية ، في حين يندر أن تظهر آثار القطع أو الفصل على الارجل الخلفية . وان الاجزاء الخلفية ، تتكون في الأساس من الفخذ والحوض ، كانت ترمى في حفرة مختلطة مع الفحم والرماد في مربع ف 14/ج 14 خلف جدار الحرم المقدس المساند ت 10 من أوائل العصر الامبراطوري (شكل ....)[7]، ويؤيد هذا النتيجة القائلة بأن حيوان القربان الرئيسي في الحرم المقدس كان يقسم الى أجزاء بصورة دورية تحفظ اما للأكل أو لحرقها ان لم يكن لدفنها المقدس (طقس الحزن)[8]، وبالاضافة الى ذلك فقد القيت الاجزاء المميزة في حفر منفصلة داخل الحرم المقدس . ولعلنا نشاهد نفس الطريقة تمارس في حرم ديميتر المقدس من العصر الهيلينستي الذي اكتشف حديثا على تل ميتيليني حيث استطاع ريس أن يميز كثرة أجزاء الخنزير الخلفية بين بقايا الحيوانات التي اكتشفت حتى الآن[9]، ومهما يكن فلم تشيد مذابح للرماد ، بصورة دائمة أو من الحجر ضمن الاجزاء

الأكبر من المواد المشابهة التي خزنت حسب المنطقة ، والمربع والطبقة ولكنها لم تسجل لوحدها ضمن كتالوج[2]. وهذا هو الحال بالضبط مع نماذج من المعدن والصدف وبعض أنواع مثالات الطين المشوى والى درجة أقل الزجاج . ومن جهة أخرى ، وبدون استثناء فلم يسجل أي من بقايا الهياكل العظمية ضمن كتالوج ولكن بدلا من ذلك فقد عزلت بعد العثور عليها وجمعت حسب المنطقة والمربع والطبقة داخل أكياس كي ترسل الى فيلادليفيا فيما بعد .

وكما هو الحال في المجلدين الثاني والثالث في هذه السلسلة ، فقد ضمن مؤلفوا هذا المجلد ملحقا للمواد التي سجلت في الكتالوج نظمت حسب المنطقة ، المربع ، الطبقة ، رقم الكتالوج ، والتأريخ[3]. والغرض الرئيسي من الملاحق توضيح الحدود الزمنية لكل موضوع طبقا لكل نوع ، وفي آخر الأمر فان هذه المعلومات سوف تدخل في ملحق رئيسي كي يمكن من تأريخ المراحل المعمارية والسكنية في الموقع[4]. ووجودهما هنا يجب أن يخدم في تذكير القارئ بأن جميع المواد المختارة للدراسة لها أهمية قرينية تفوق أهميتها كقطع منفردة .

وتقدم لنا مثلا بقايا الحيوانات والنماذج التي عملت لها . وفي حالة بقايا الحيوانات تؤكد دراسة كرابتري ومونج الملاحظات التي وردت في

مايمكنه أن يتوقعه المرء تحت ظروف وضعت عوائق رئيسية لشحن بقايا طبيعية .

وكانت دراسة اوليفر للزجاج المكتشف من الموقع محدودة بالوقت أكثر من حجم النموذج النهائي . ومن حسن الحظ كان في الامكان تكملة ملاحظاته عام ١٩٧٧ من خلال مذكرات أخذها م. مكليلان ، الذى نقب في قوريني في موسمي ١٩٨٧و ١٩٧٩ ، وكمختص في الزجاج القديم ، فان مكليلان ساهم في عدد من الابواب في كتالوج الزجاج الحالي وكذلك شارك في مراجعة الكثير منه . وندين بالشكر الى ج. برايس ، عضو الفريق العلمي لجمعية الدراسات الليبية في حفرياتها في سيدى خريبيش ، الذى وافق على نشر الرأس الزجاجى الهام الذى يشكل موضوع ملحق رقم ١ في فصل الزجاج . وفي الختام ، اذا أخذنا فى الاعتبار كثرة المعثورات المتنوعة ، فان مشروع الابحاث هذا محظوظ جدا بأن استطاع ب . ج . وردن أن يخصص موسم كامل لدراستها في قوريني وجاء ذلك في نهاية العمل الميداني بدلا من أن يكون فى وقت أبكر .

تقوم دراسات الكثير من الزجاج والمعثورات الصغيرة المتنوعة على المواد التي سجلت بأنها "لقية" بعد اكتشافها ، وهذا يعنى من حيث النتيجة العملية انه احتفظ بسجل لأبعادها الثلاث ضمن كل محيط أثرى منفصل ، حدد بالمنطقة "و "المربع " و "الطبقة" ١ واختيرت بعض النماذج كأمثلة للنماذج

٤

مقدمة المحرر

يدين مشروع أبحاث قوريني بالكثير الى الزملاء الذين أخذوا على عاتقهم دراسة المعثورات التي يحتويها هذا المجلد . تمكن ب . ج . وردن ، الذى يكتب عن المعثورات الصغيرة من الحرم المقدس ، من قضاء آخر موسم تنقيب في قوريني عام ١٩٨١ حيث درس عددا كبيرا من اللقى الاثرية المتنوعة بينما تمكن أ . أوليفر من قضاء أقل من عشرة أيام عام ١٩٧٧ كي يدرس الزجاج . وعلى سبيل المقارنة البعيدة نجد أن ب . كرابترى و ج . مونج كان عليهن أن يتعاملن مع نماذج من عظام الحيوانات التي أحضرت الى متحف الجامعة من ليبيا لغرض الدراسة . وبناء على ذلك لم يشارك أي منهن في التنقيب الاثرى الفعلي عن المادة التى تقع ضمن دراستهن التخصصيه ، ولذا لايتحملن مسؤلية طبيعة النماذج المتغيرة والتي وافقن على التعامل معها . وعلى سبيل المثال لو تواجدت المتخصصتان في دراسة الهياكل العظيمة اثناء أعمال التنقيب في الموقع ، فان مجموعة بقايا الهياكل العظمية كانت قد عملت على أسس أكثر دقة ونظاما ، وهذا بالتالي كان سيجعل بين أيديهن مجموعة مختارة أوسع . وفي ظل الوضع القائم ، ومع ان نماذج الهياكل العظمية الحالية لاترقى الى المستوى المثالى ، فانها تمثل أحسن

الخلاصة بالعربية في هذا المجلد وفي المجلد الثالث . وفي الختام أقدم شكري الخاص الى الاستاذ الدكتور آلان مارن من قسم علوم دراسات الانسان في جامعة بنسلفانيا الذي قام بتحليل بقايا الهياكل البشرية من الموقع ثم خطط لتنفيذ العمل النهائي على نموذج من الحيوانات الكاملة من قبــل طالبتيه السابقتين بام كرابتري وجانيت مونج ، اللتان هما بالطبع مؤلفتا الدراسة الحاضرة .

دونالد وايت

قسم البحر المتوسط

متحف الجامعة

كلمـة شكـر

مرة أخرى بصفتى رئيس تحرير هذه المجلدات يسرنى أن أشكر ، بالنيابة عن نفسى وعن المؤلفين الأربعة ، جامعة بنسلفانيا ، متحف الجامعة ، ومدير المتحف الدكتور روبرت ه . دايسون ، وذلك لتقديمهم الدعم المادى السخى اللازم لهذا الكتاب ، والذى تمت طباعته من الألف الى الياء دون أى مساعدة مالية خارجية . ولكن كارن فيلوشى ، منسقه المطبوعات الاكاديمية فــي المتحف ، تستحق منا جزيل الشكر حيث نقلت ما بدأ مجرد دعم نظرى كــى يصبح حقيقة أدبيه . وصدور هذا الكتاب بالكامل يعود الى نشاطها وحكمـــة ادارتها للقسم المالى وقسم التحرير والقسم الفنى والمسؤليات الشخصية التـى التى دون محاله تكتنف مشروعا تعاونيا من هذا النوع . وان آن بونـــد وجيورجيانــــــا جريتز بيرجر ، ومرة اخرى أنيتا ليبمان ، عضوات فى الماضى والحاضر فى قسم المطبوعات فى المتحف ، قد ساهمن بقدراتهــــن الفردية ولهذا نقدم لهن شكرنا العظيم ، وان الورقات الاخيرة الواضحـــة والمفيدة في هذا الكتاب وكما هو الحال فى المجلدين الثانى والثالث مــن مجلدات قورينى ، فهى من عمل الدكتور كارل بيتز ، الدكتور جمال الحرامى من قسم الآثار فى جامعة الرياض وصديق قديم لمتحف الجامعة ساهم فى ترجمــة

Figures and Plates

PENDANTS								WARDEN FIGURE 1

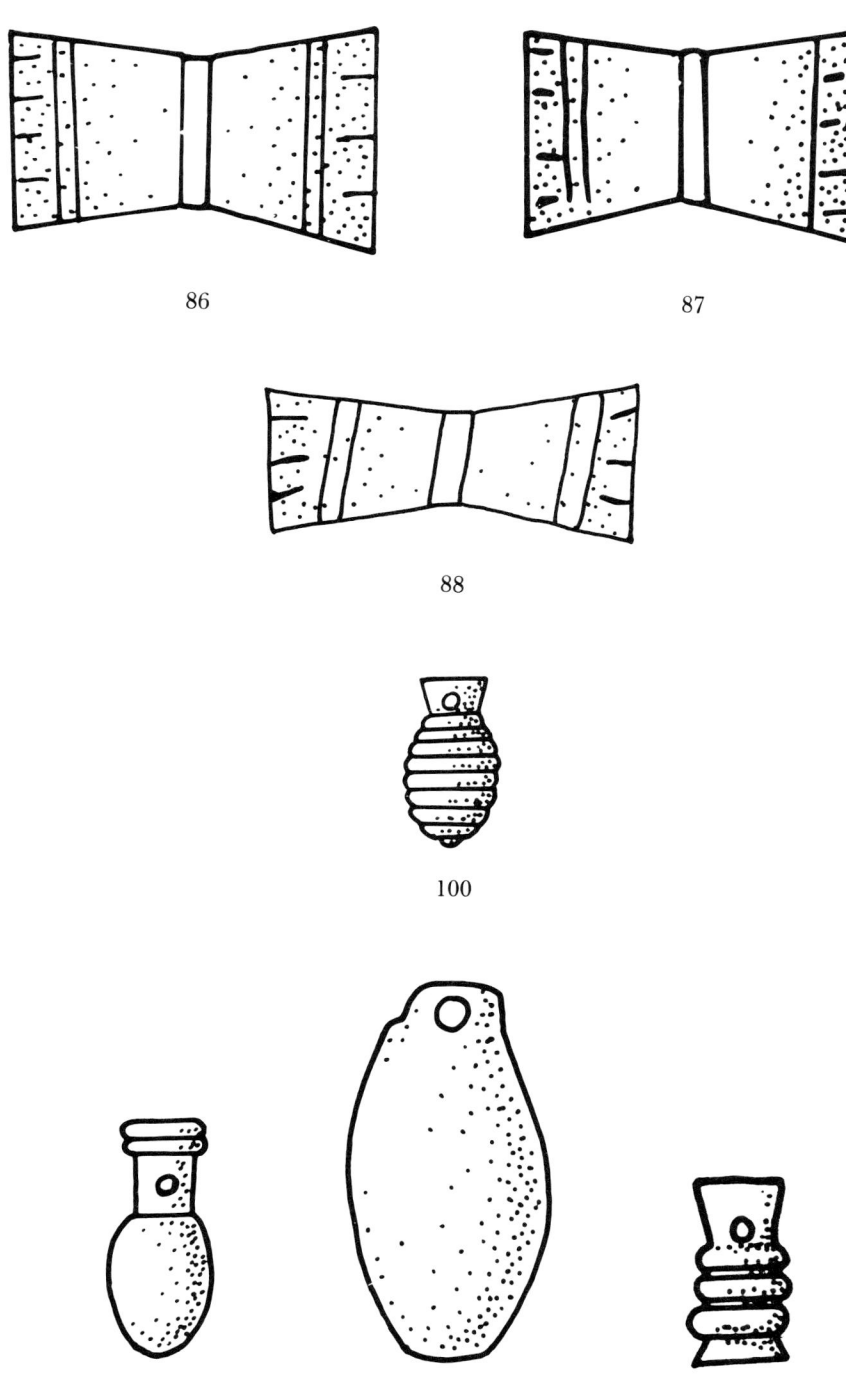

86

87

88

100

101			104			105

2:1

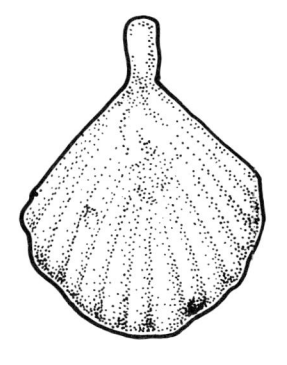

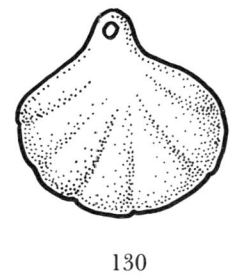

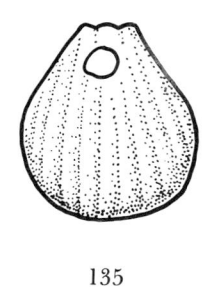

WARDEN FIGURE 2   *SHELL PENDANTS*

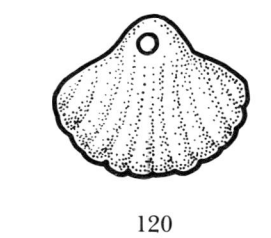

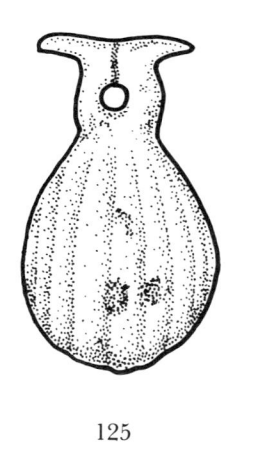

120

123

125   126   127

129   130   135

1:1

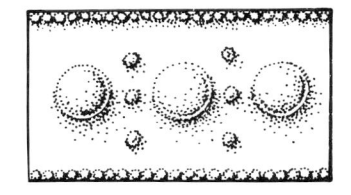

JEWELRY *WARDEN FIGURE 3*

166

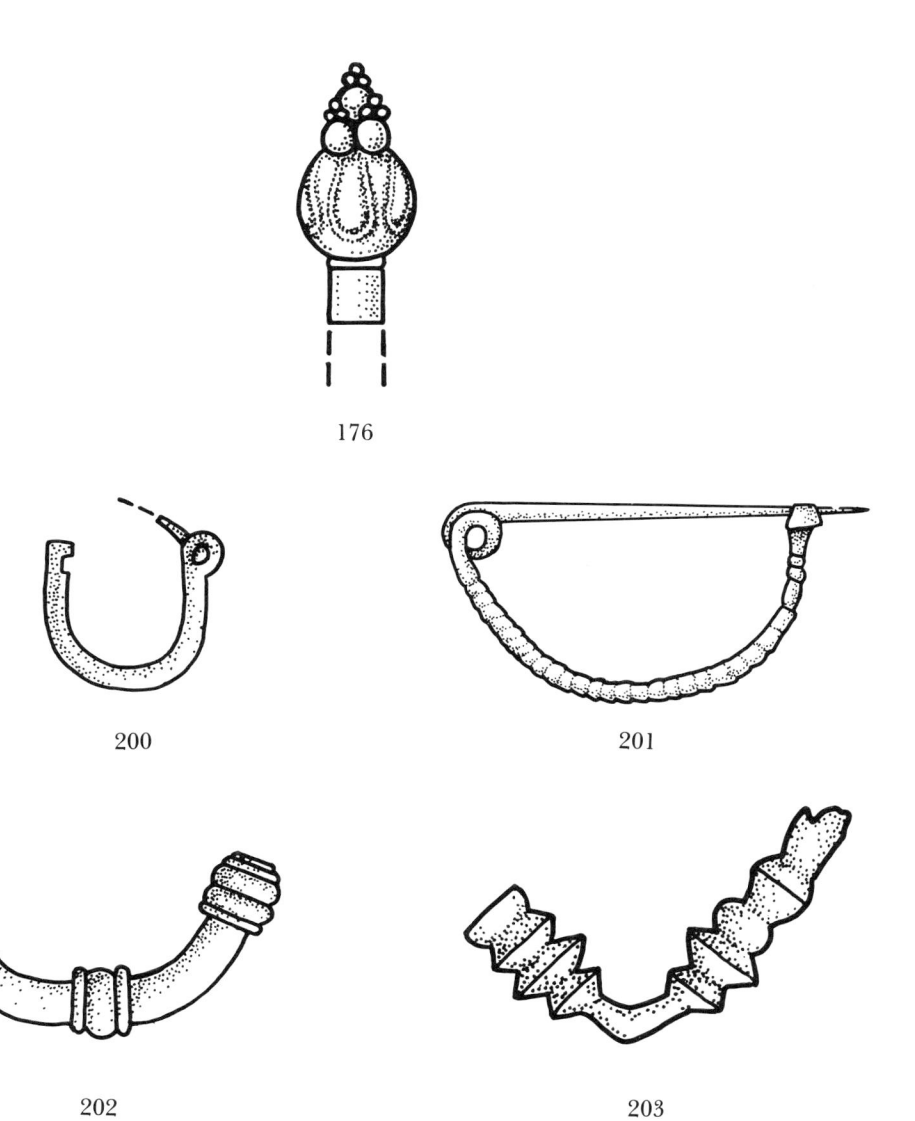

176

200 201

202 203

1:1
176- *2:1*

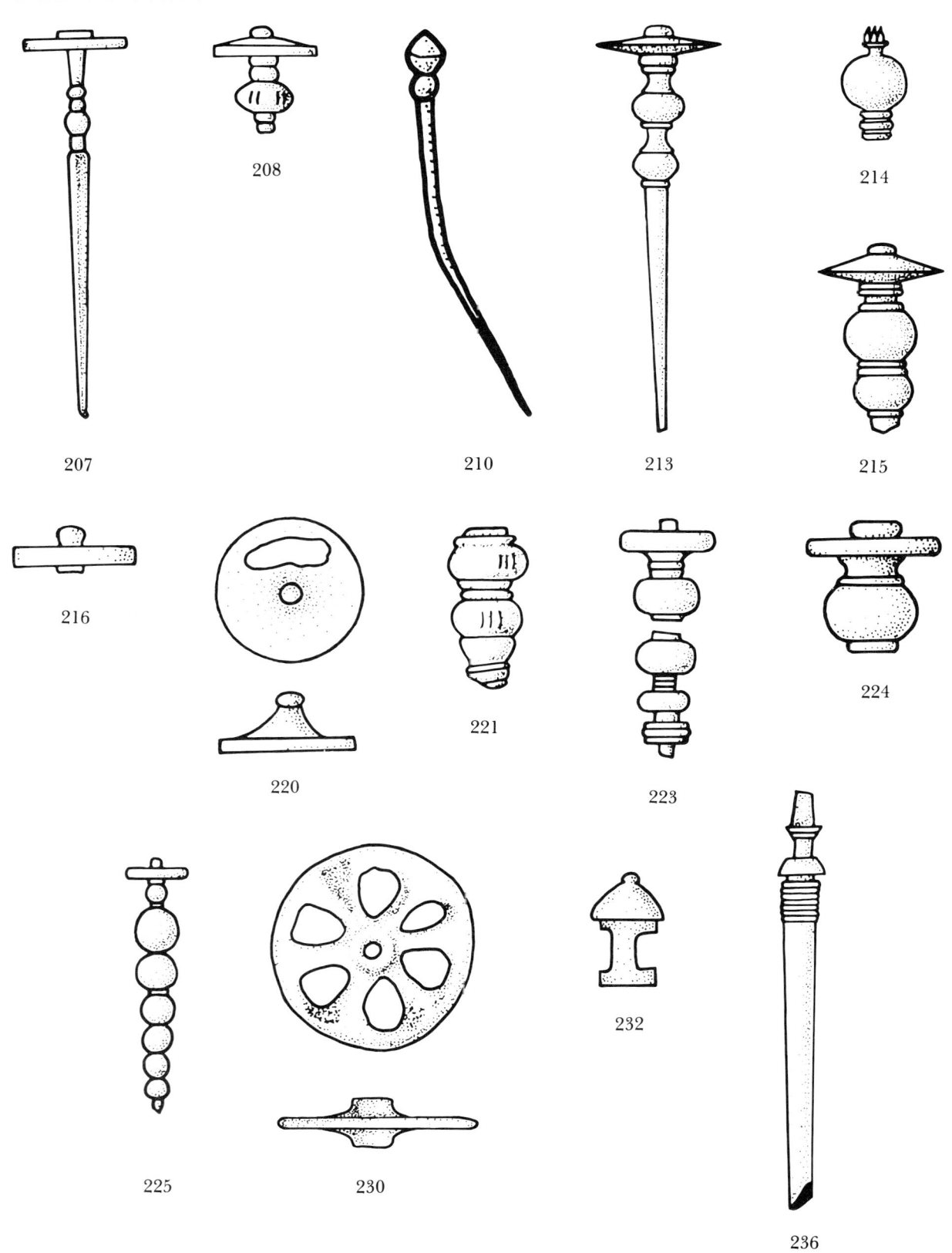

WARDEN FIGURE 4　　　　　　　　　　　　　　　　　　　　　　　　　　　　　　PINS

207　　208　　210　　213　　214

　　　　　　　　　　　　　　　　　　215

216　　220　　221　　223　　224

225　　230　　232　　236

1:1

CHAIN WARDEN FIGURE 5

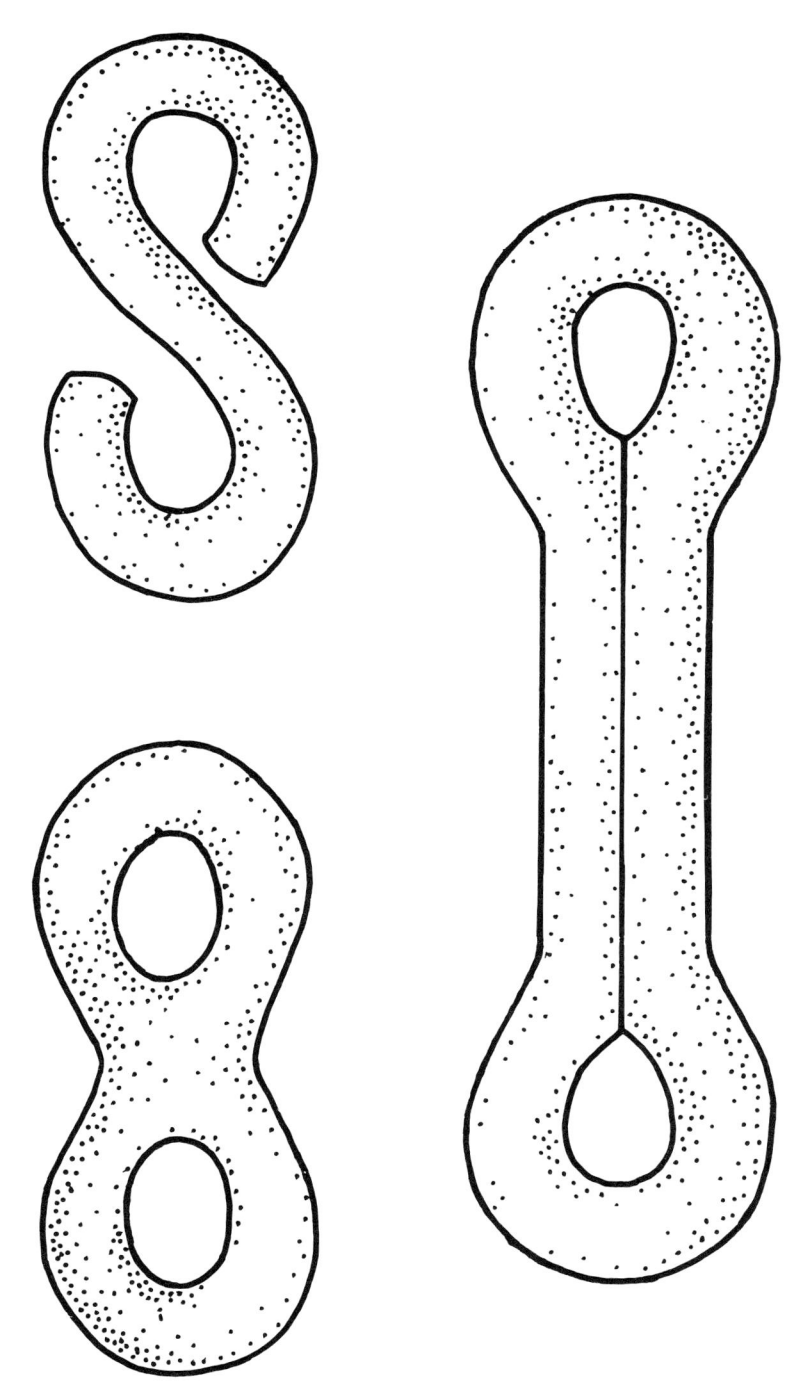

280

1:1

WARDEN FIGURE 6   MISCELLANEOUS IRON IMPLEMENTS

302

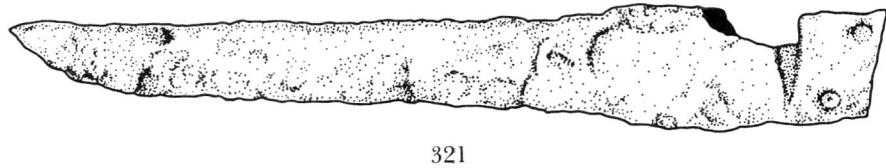

321

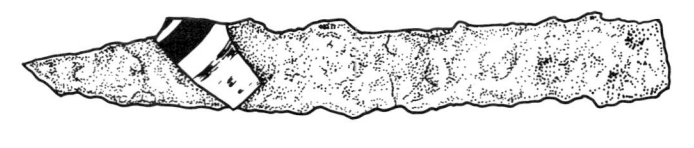

322

323 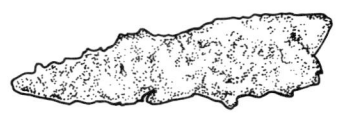   326

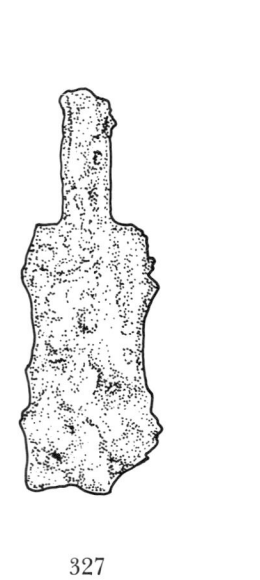

327 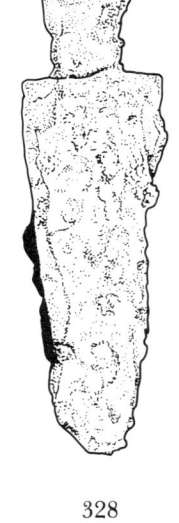   328

2:1

MISCELLANEOUS IMPLEMENTS   WARDEN FIGURE 7

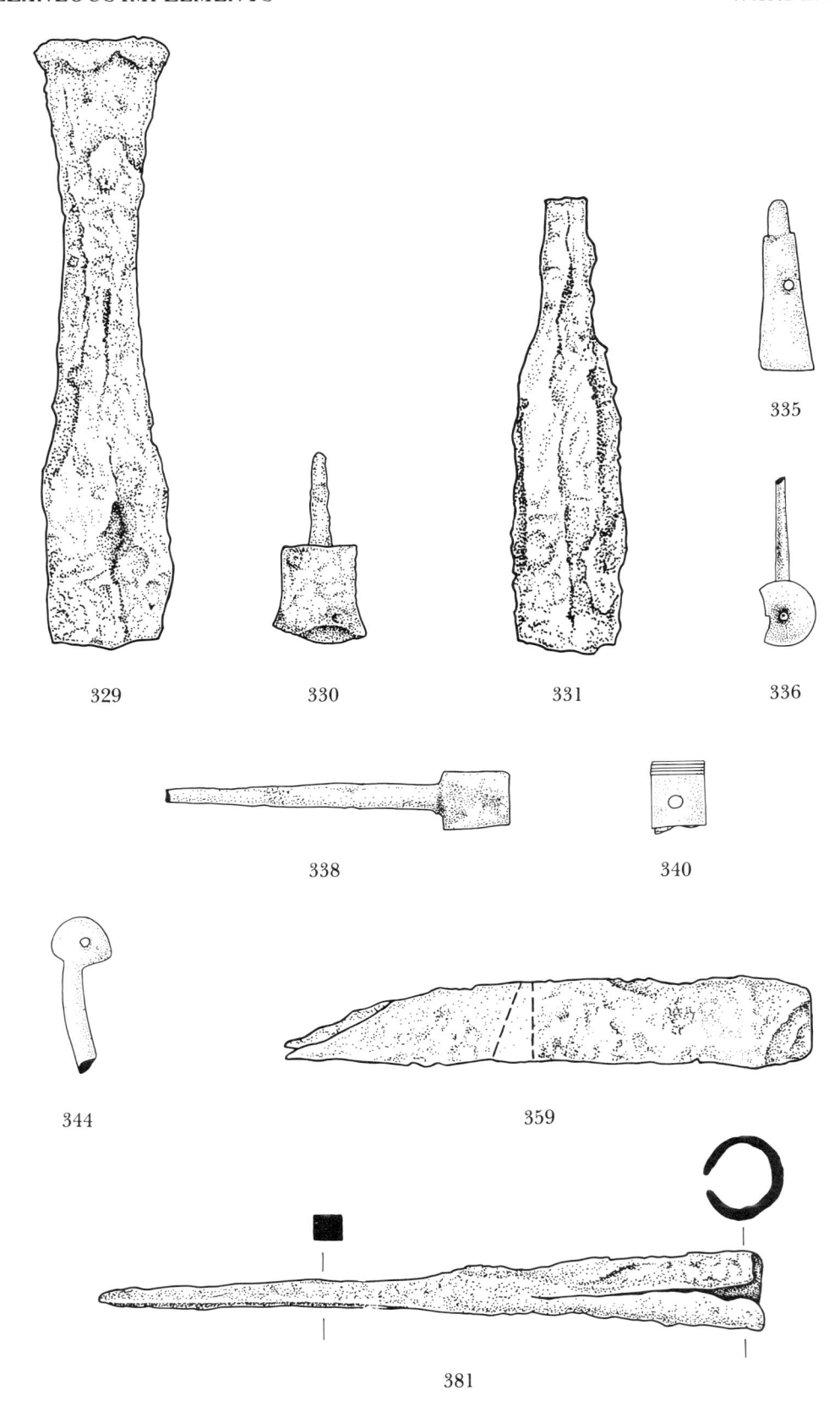

329   330   331   335

336

338   340

344   359

381

1:2

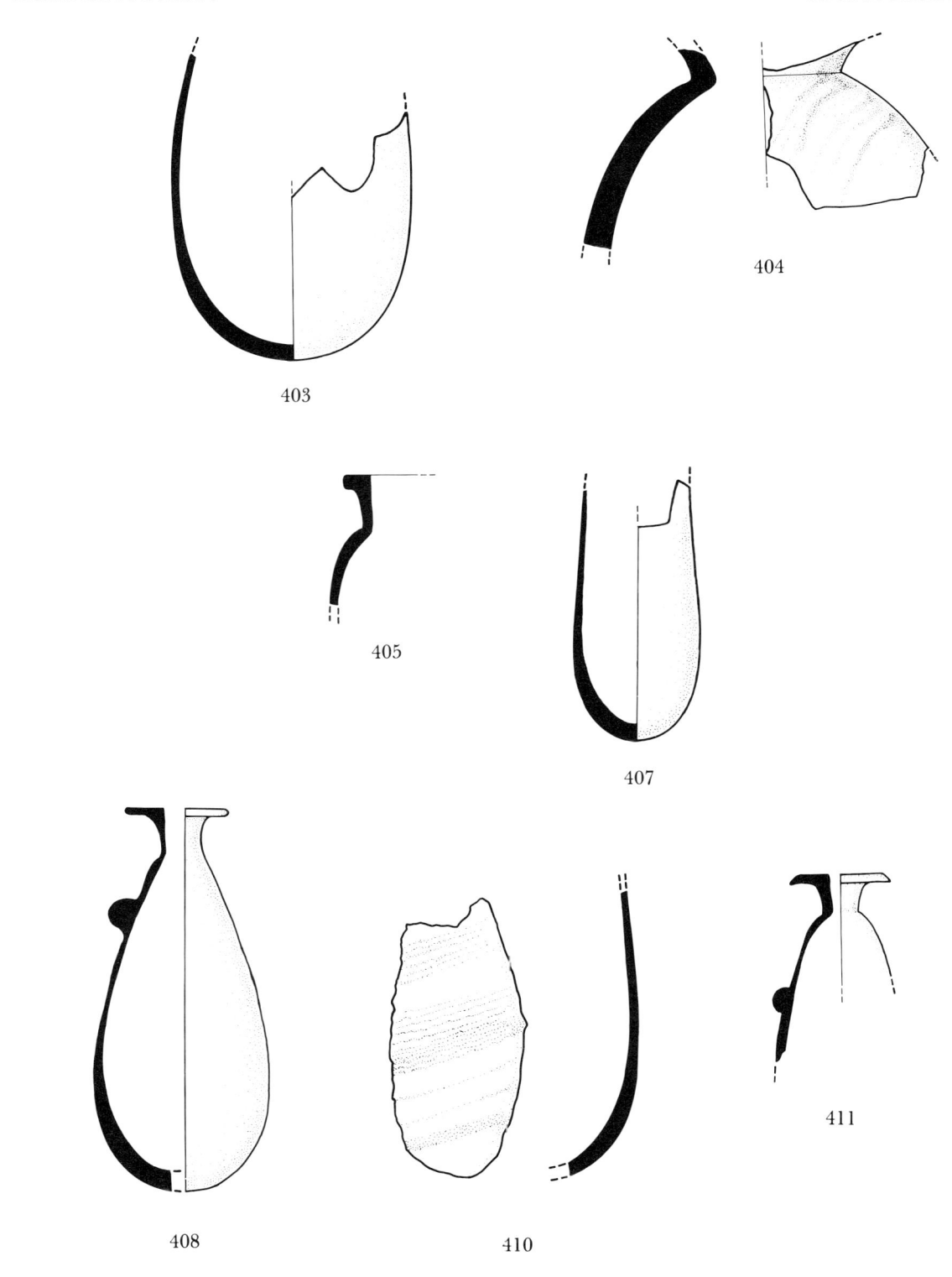

WARDEN FIGURE 8 STONE ALABASTRA

403

404

405

407

408 410 411

1:2

416
417
418
419
420
421
422
423

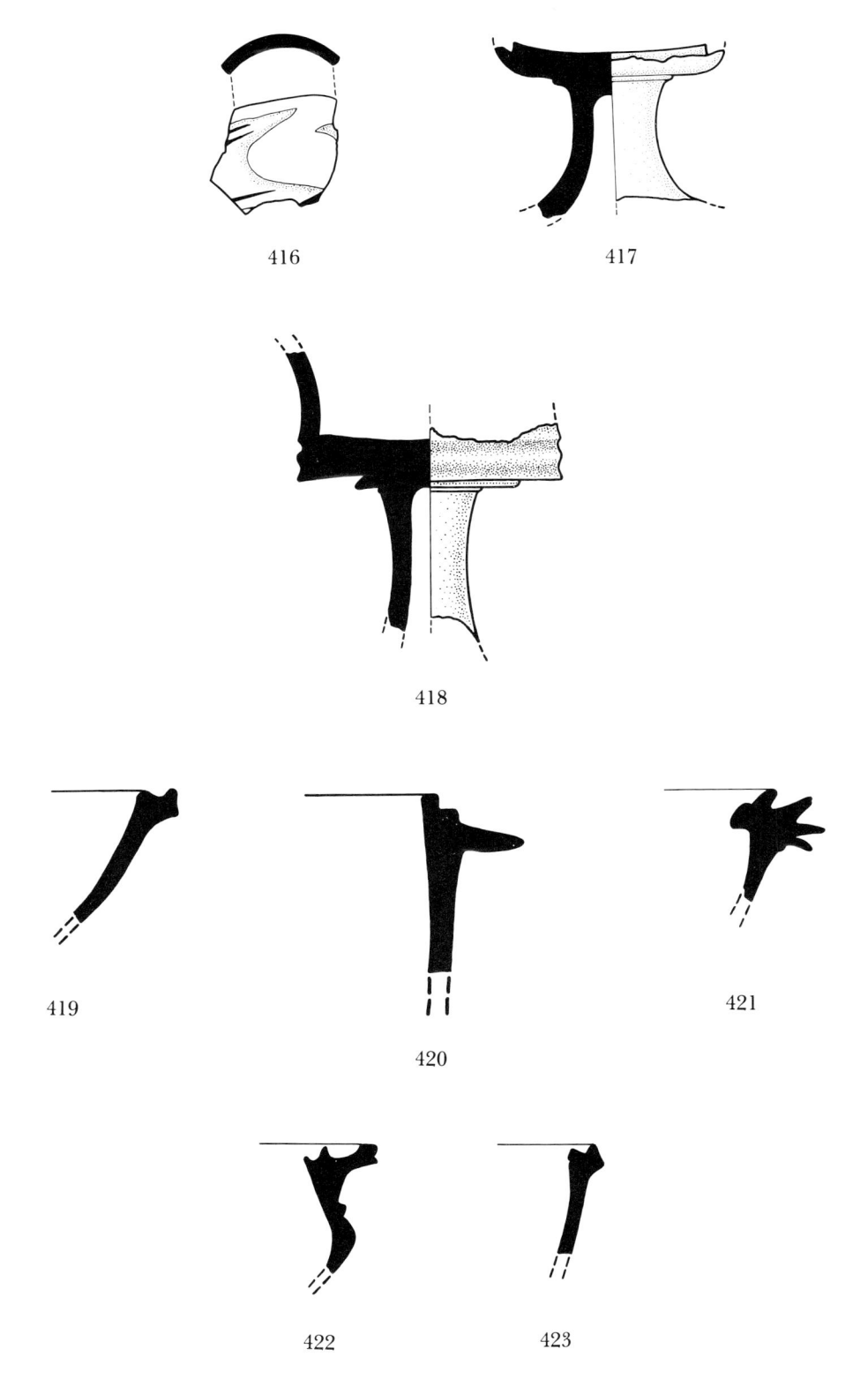

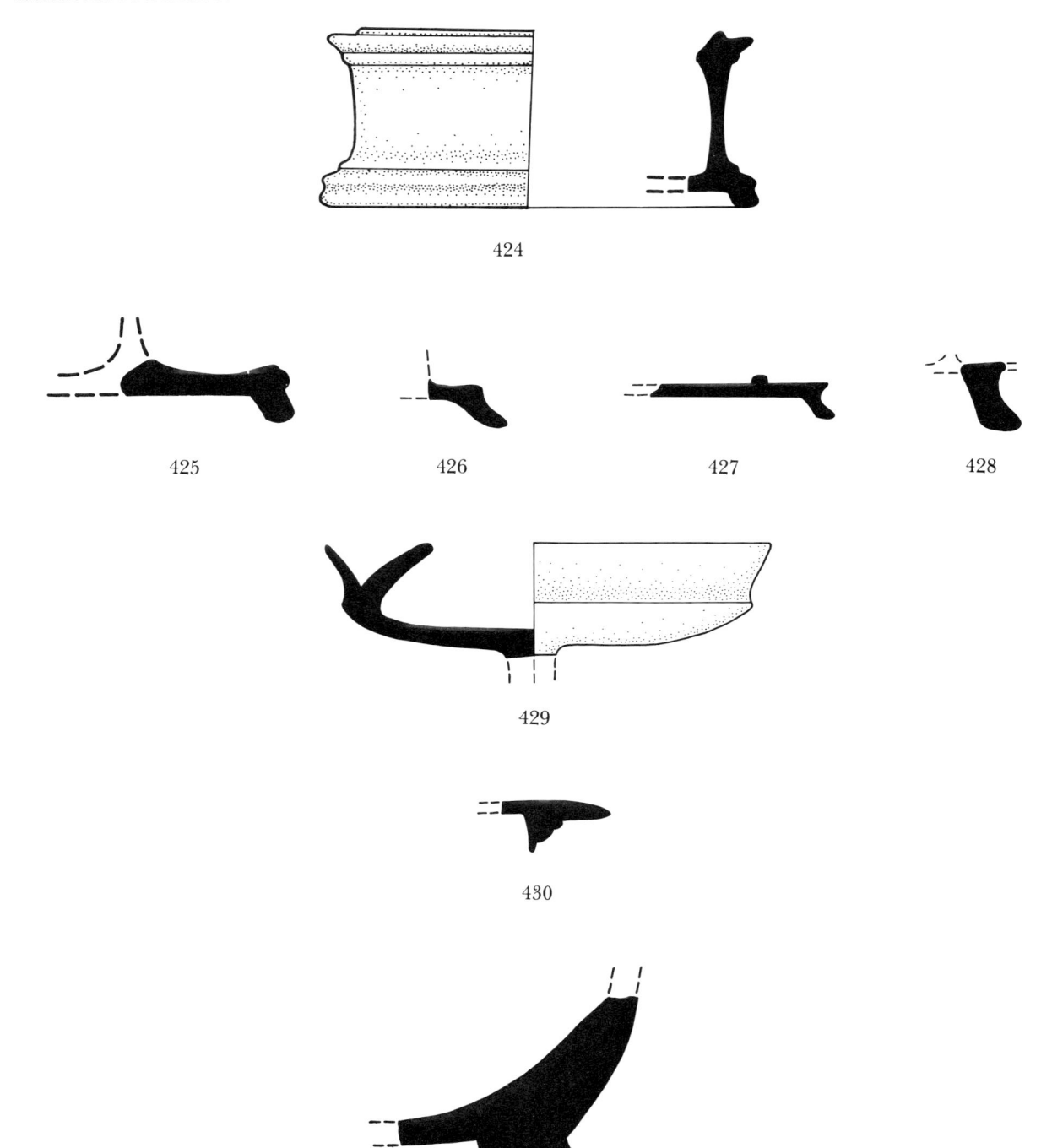

WARDEN FIGURE 10 MARBLE

424

425 426 427 428

429

430

433

1:2

437

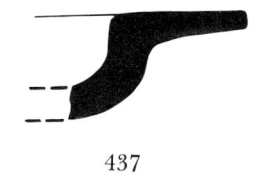

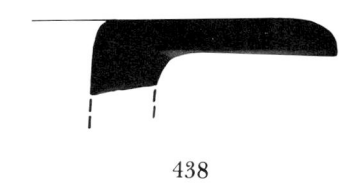

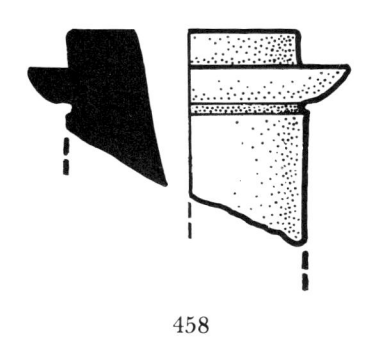

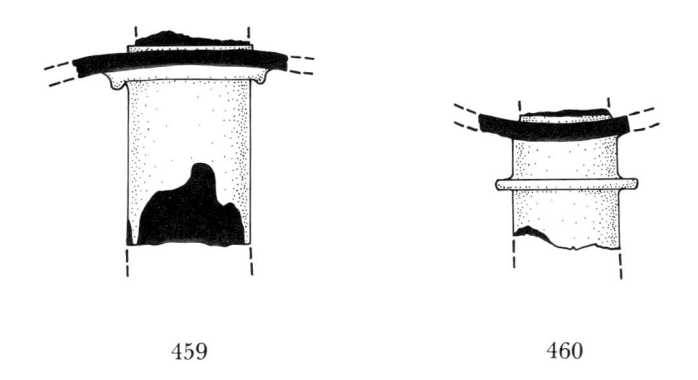

438

458

459 460

FIGURINES
WARDEN PLATE 1

1

2
3

3:2

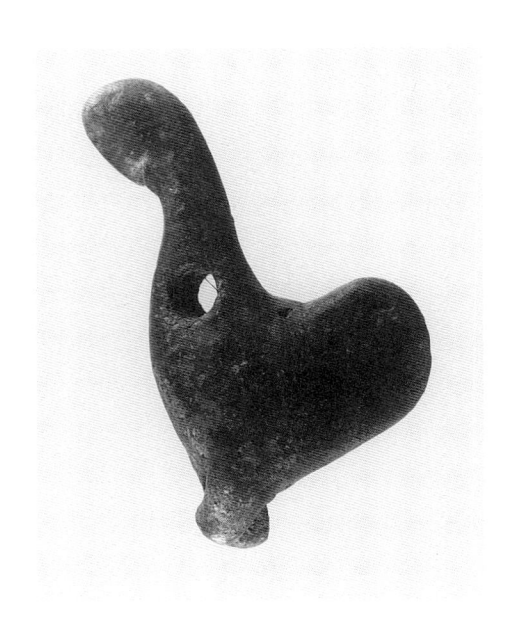

WARDEN PLATE 2 FIGURINES

4

5

6

7

FIGURINES   *WARDEN PLATE 3*

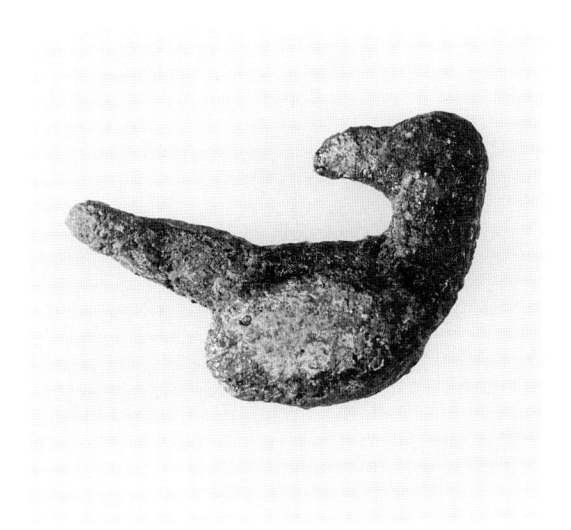

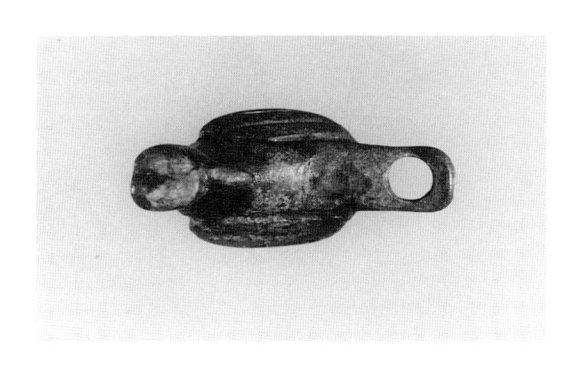

8

9

10

11

WARDEN PLATE 4

FIGURINES

12

13

14

15

3:2

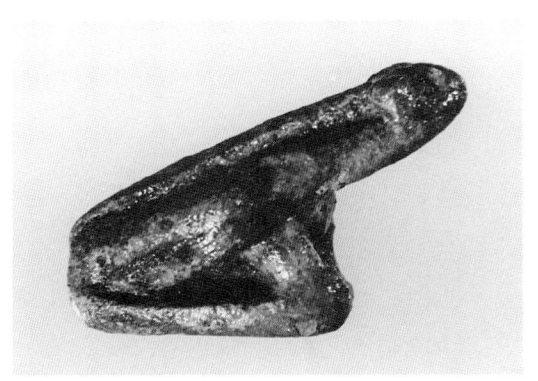

FIGURINES WARDEN PLATE 5

16

17

WARDEN PLATE 6　　　　　　　　　　　　　　　　　　　　　　　　FIGURINES

18

19

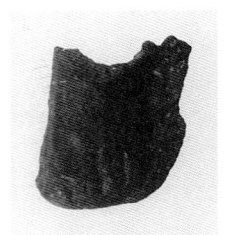

20

3:2

FIGURINES

WARDEN PLATE 7

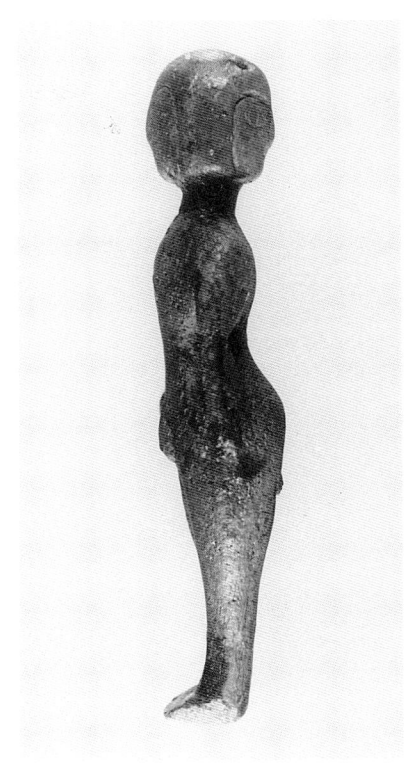

21

22

WARDEN PLATE 8 *FIGURINES*

23

24

25

3:2

FIGURINES *WARDEN PLATE 9*

26

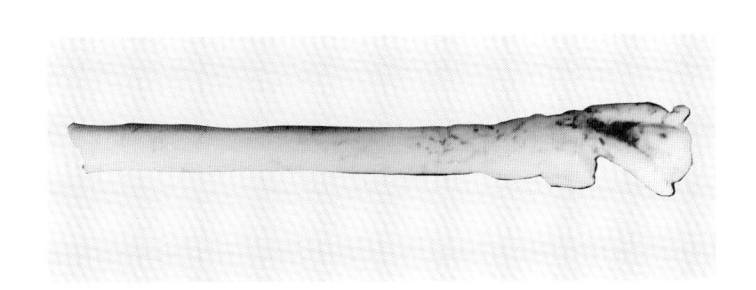

27

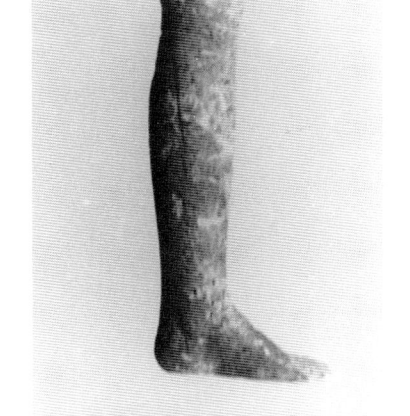

28

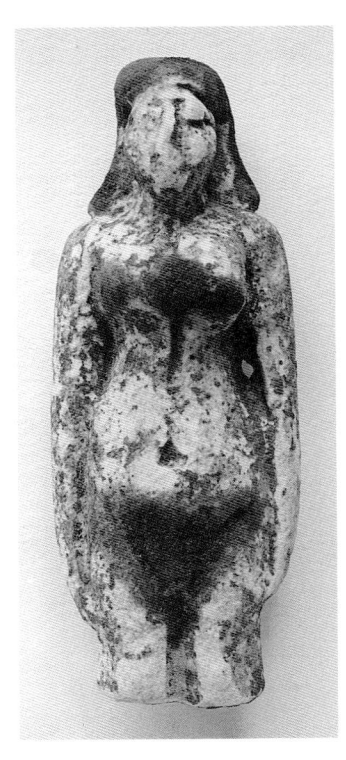

29

3:2

WARDEN PLATE 10 FIGURINES

30

31

32

FIGURINES
WARDEN PLATE 11

33

34

35

3:2

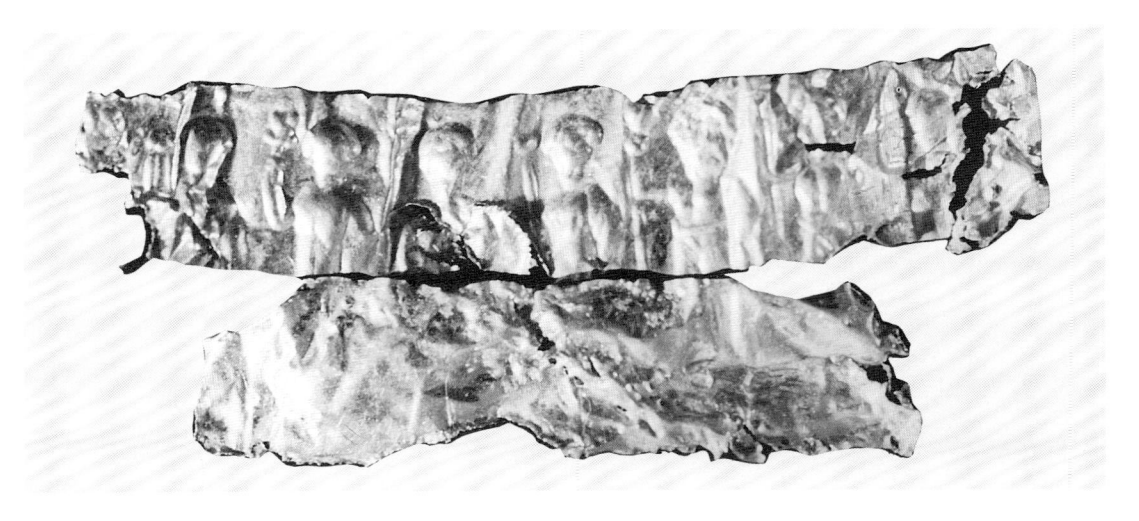

WARDEN PLATE 12   JEWELRY AND ORNAMENTS

36

38

39

3:1

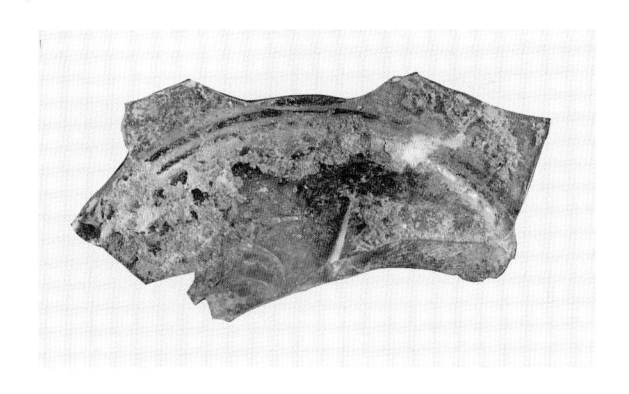

JEWELRY AND ORNAMENTS WARDEN PLATE 13

40

41

43

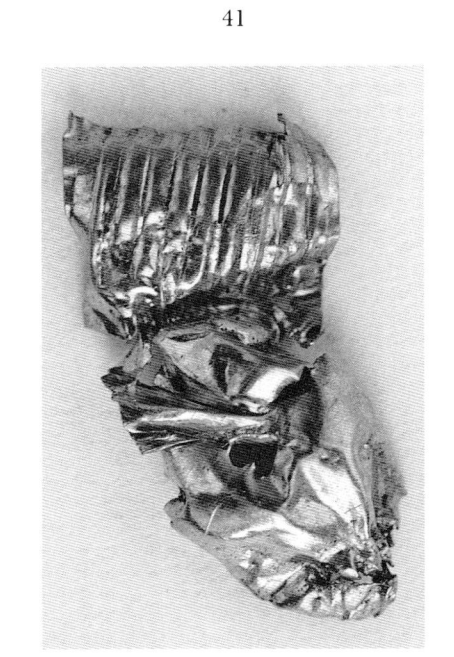

44

45

46

4:1

WARDEN PLATE 14   JEWELRY AND ORNAMENTS

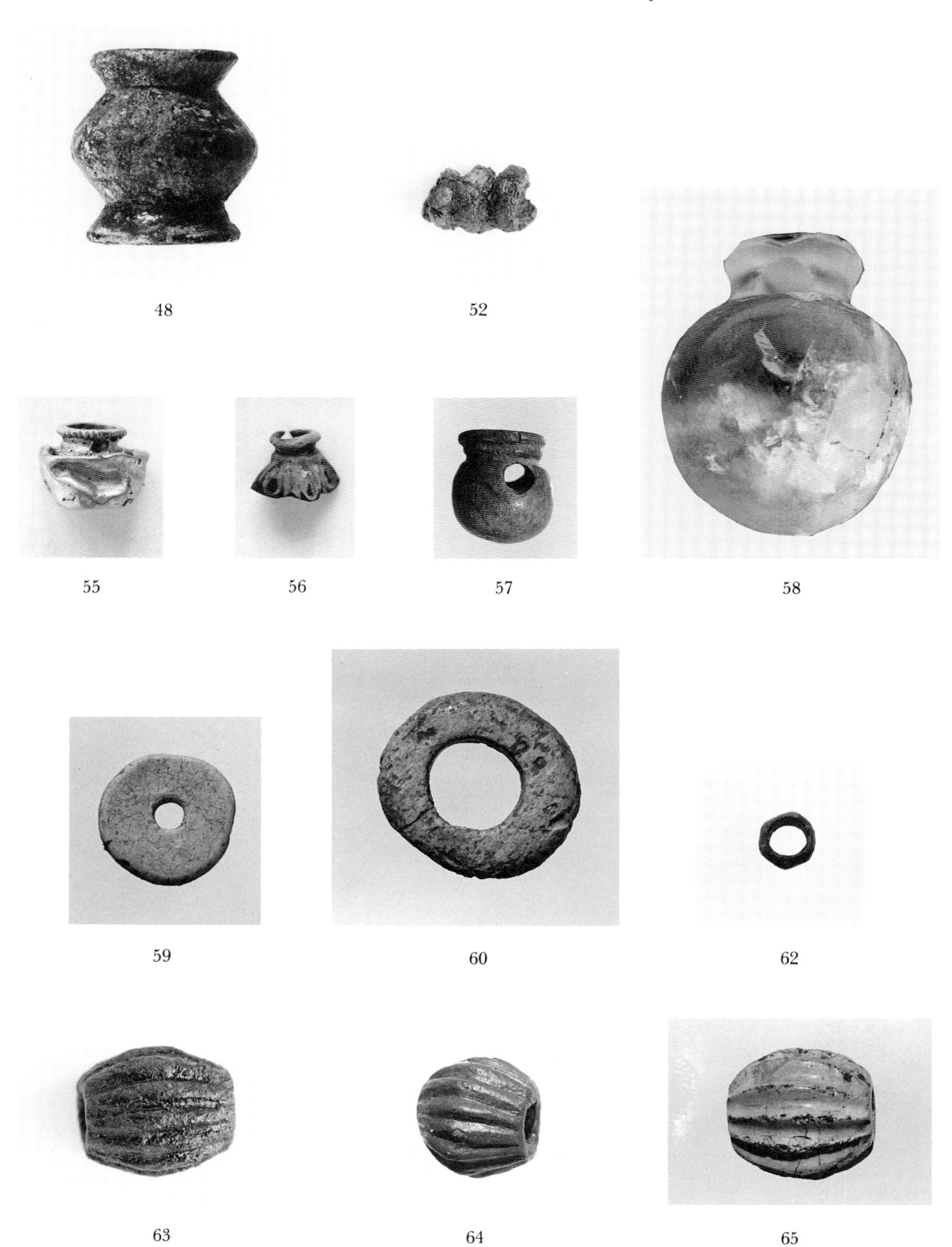

48   52

55   56   57   58

59   60   62

63   64   65

2:1

JEWELRY AND ORNAMENTS *WARDEN PLATE 15*

69

70  71

76  77

2:1

WARDEN PLATE 16   JEWELRY AND ORNAMENTS

78

80

81

82

84

85

2:1

JEWELRY AND ORNAMENTS   WARDEN PLATE 17

89   90   91

93   95   98   99

102   103

3:2

WARDEN PLATE 18 JEWELRY AND ORNAMENTS

106

107

108 109 110 111 112

113 114 115 116 117

118 119

3:2

JEWELRY AND ORNAMENTS WARDEN PLATE 19

120

121 123 124

125

128 130 131 132

1:1

WARDEN PLATE 20 JEWELRY AND ORNAMENTS

133

134 135 136 138

140 141

142

1:1

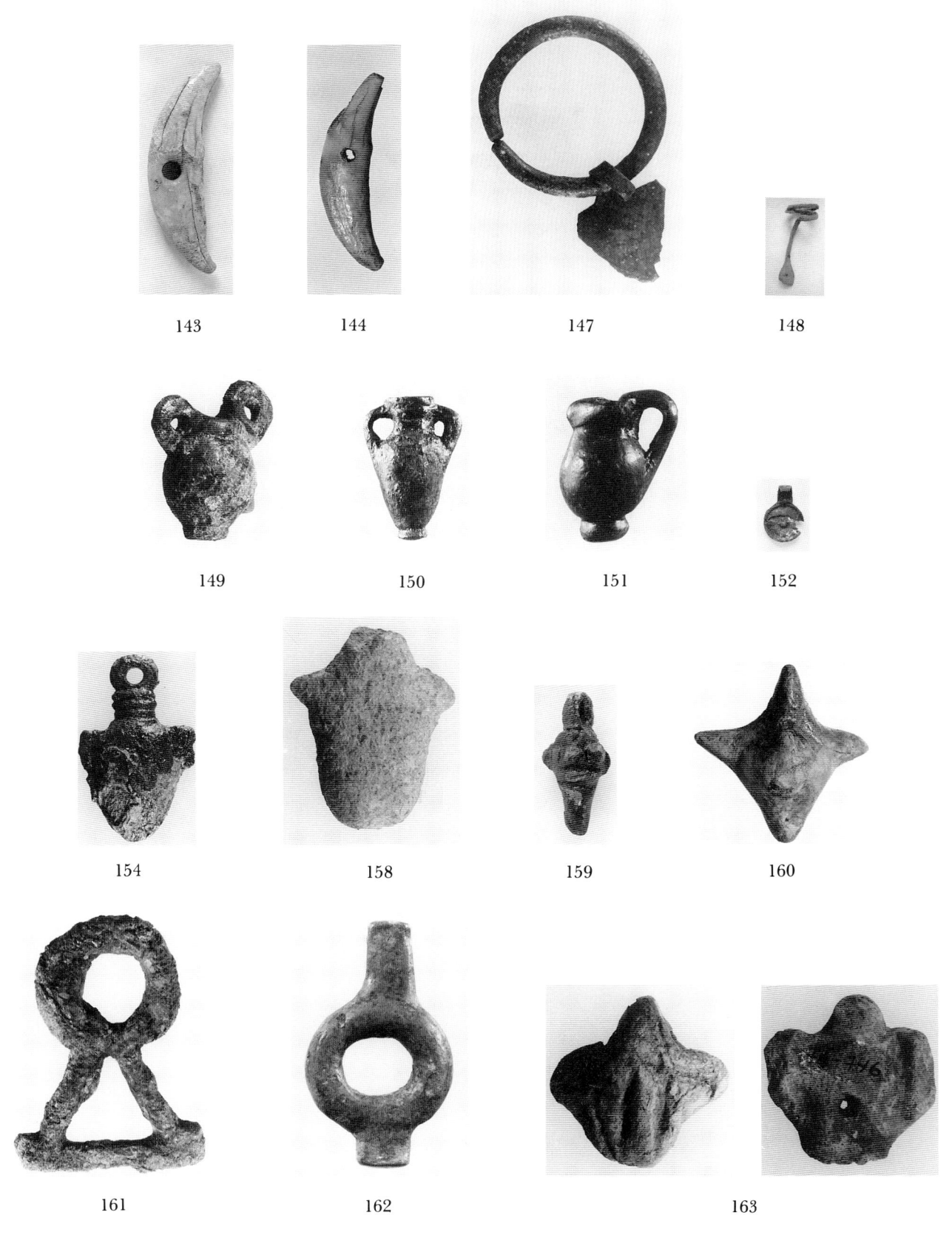

JEWELRY AND ORNAMENTS WARDEN PLATE 21

143 144 147 148

149 150 151 152

154 158 159 160

161 162 163

1:1

WARDEN PLATE 22   JEWELRY AND ORNAMENTS

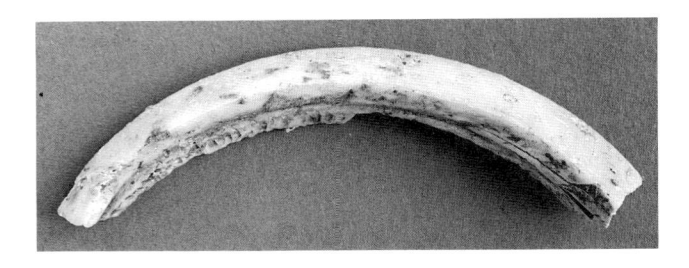

156

167

170   171   173   174

175   176

183   184   186

188   191

1:1

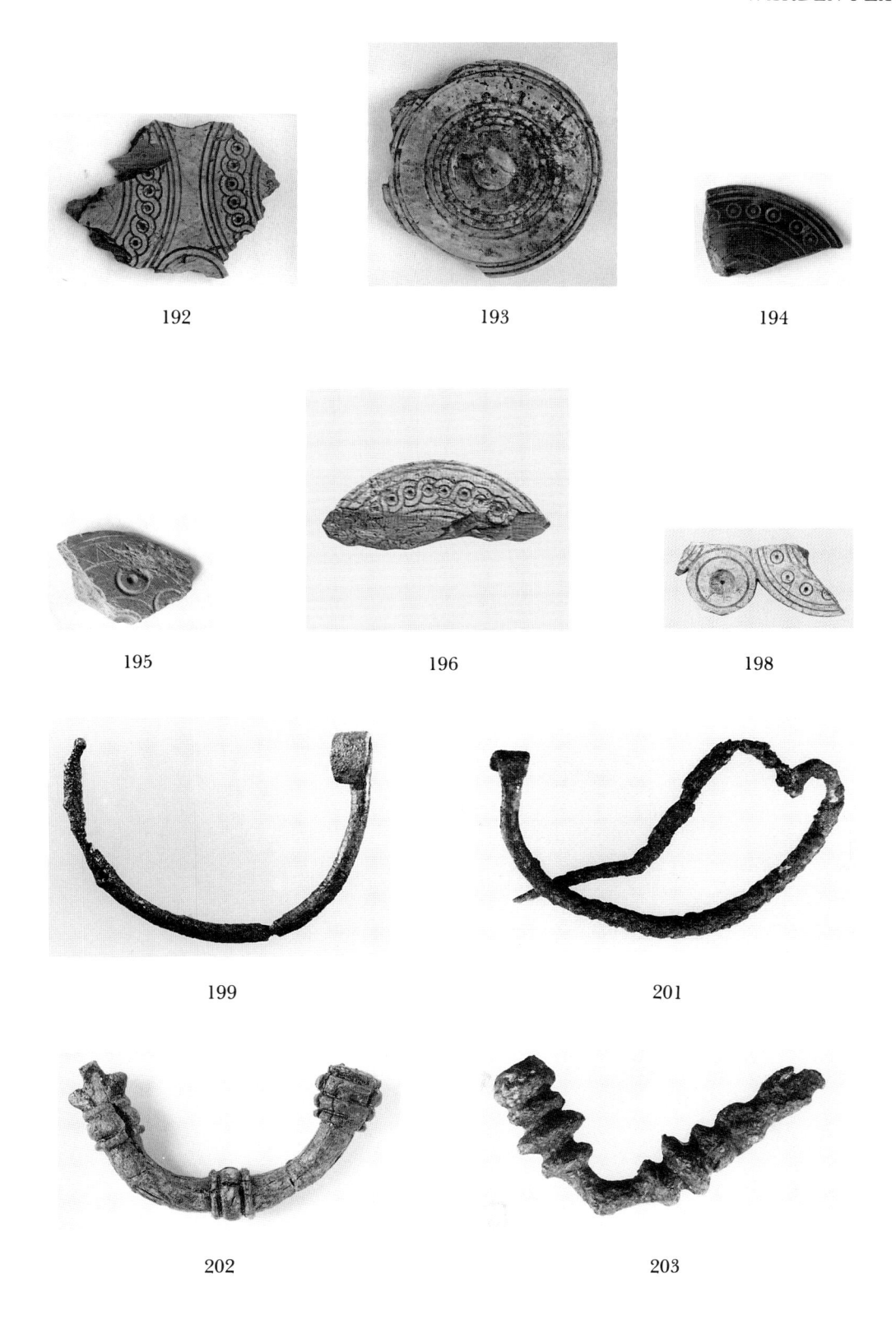

JEWELRY AND ORNAMENTS   WARDEN PLATE 23

192

193

194

195

196

198

199

201

202

203

1:1

WARDEN PLATE 24 JEWELRY AND ORNAMENTS

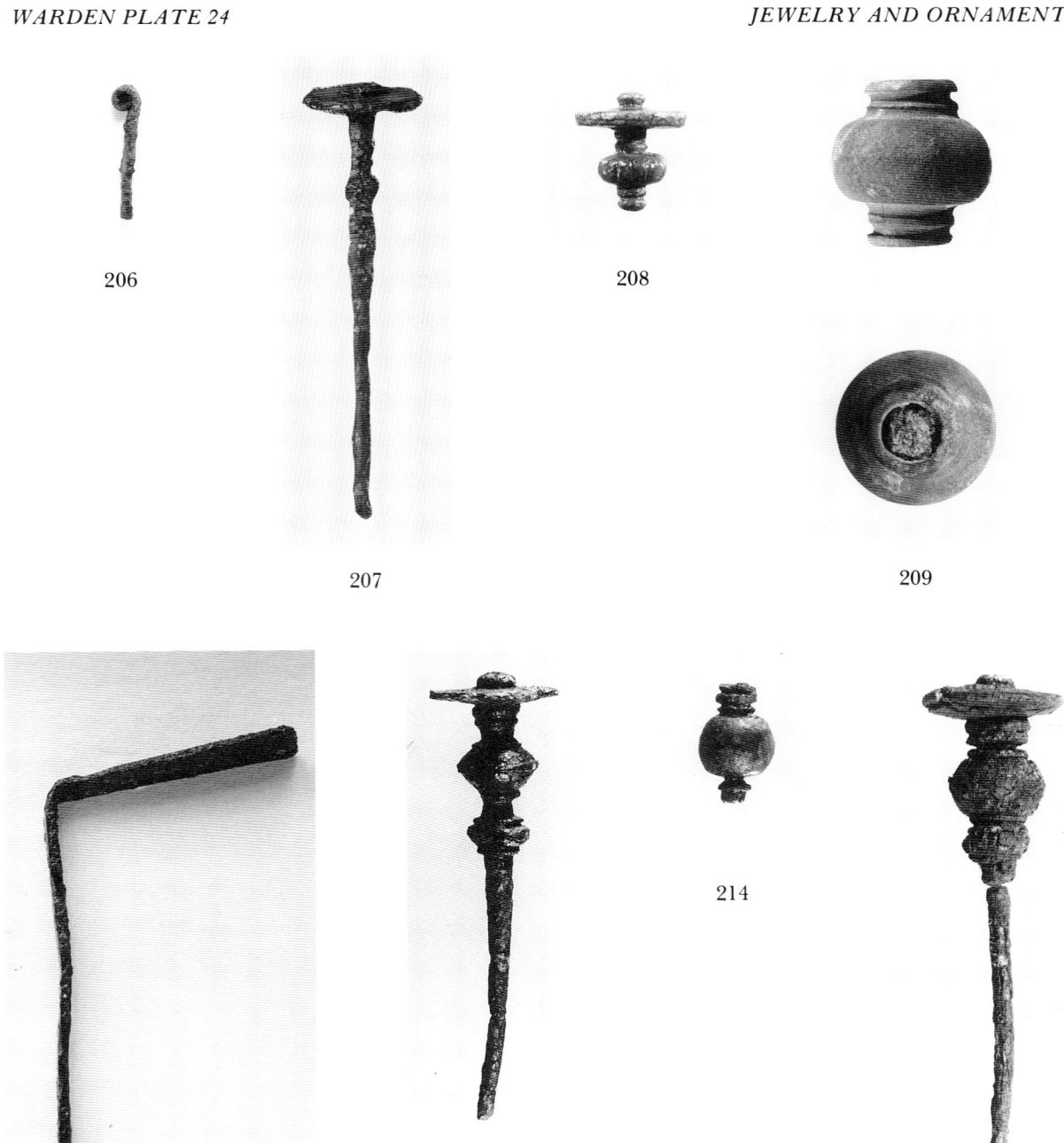

206

207

208

209

212

213

214

215

1:1

JEWELRY AND ORNAMENTS   *WARDEN PLATE 25*

216

219   220   221   223

224   225   226   227   229

230   232

231

1:1

WARDEN PLATE 26 JEWELRY AND ORNAMENTS

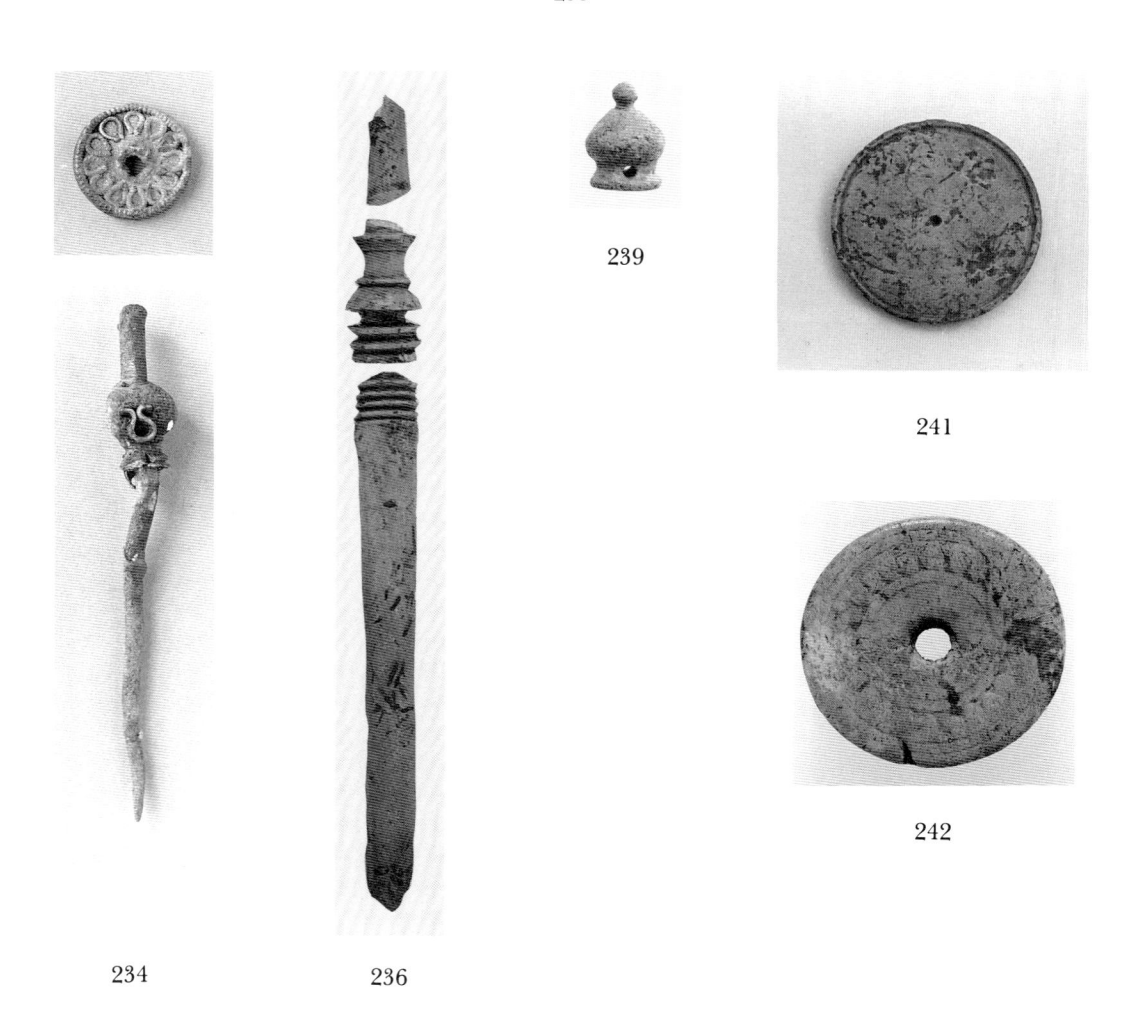

233

234   236   239   241

242

1:1

JEWELRY AND ORNAMENTS WARDEN PLATE 27

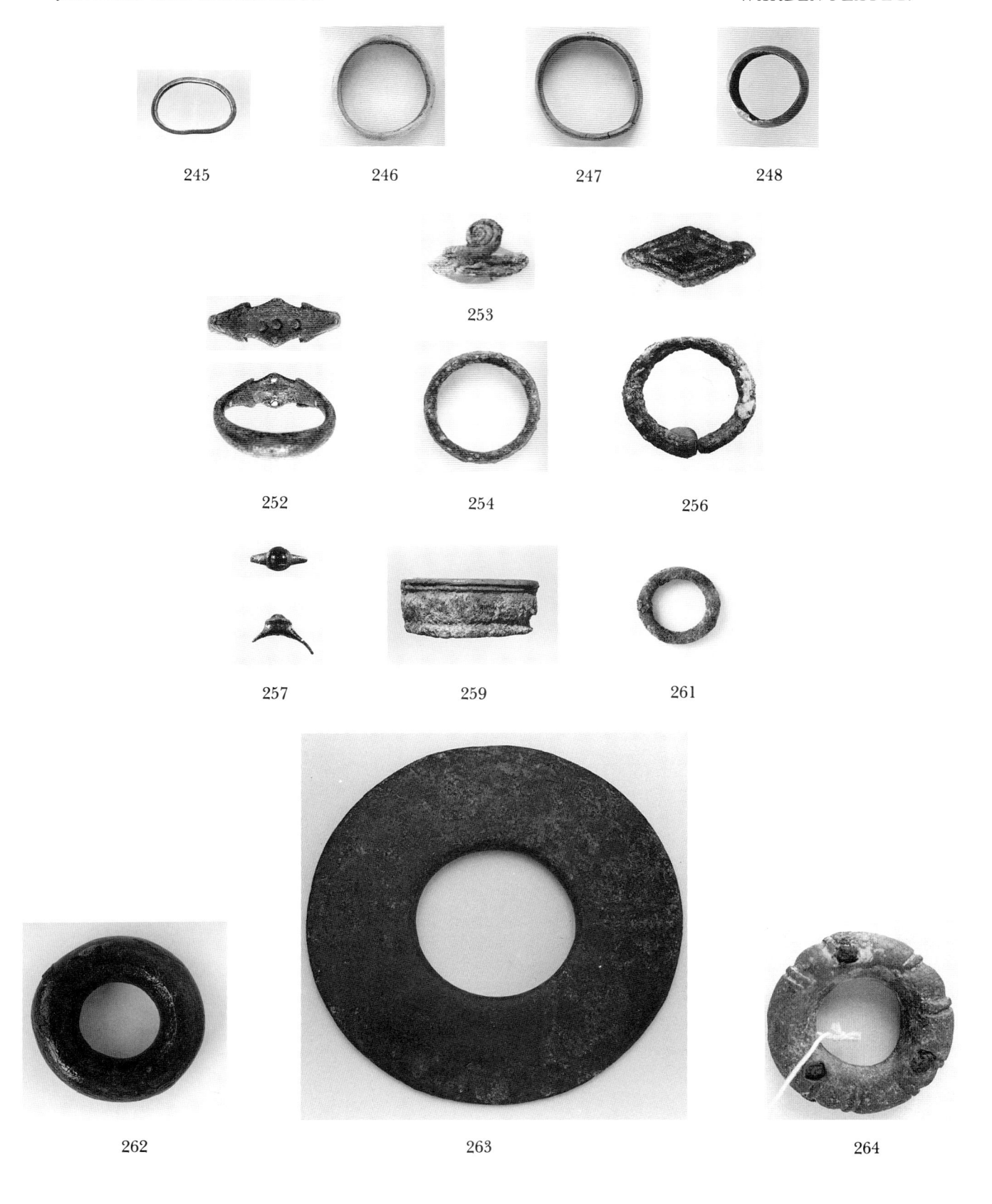

245 246 247 248

252 253 254 256

257 259 261

262 263 264

1:1

WARDEN PLATE 28 HARDWARE AND TOOLS

265

267

266

268

270

273

274

276

277

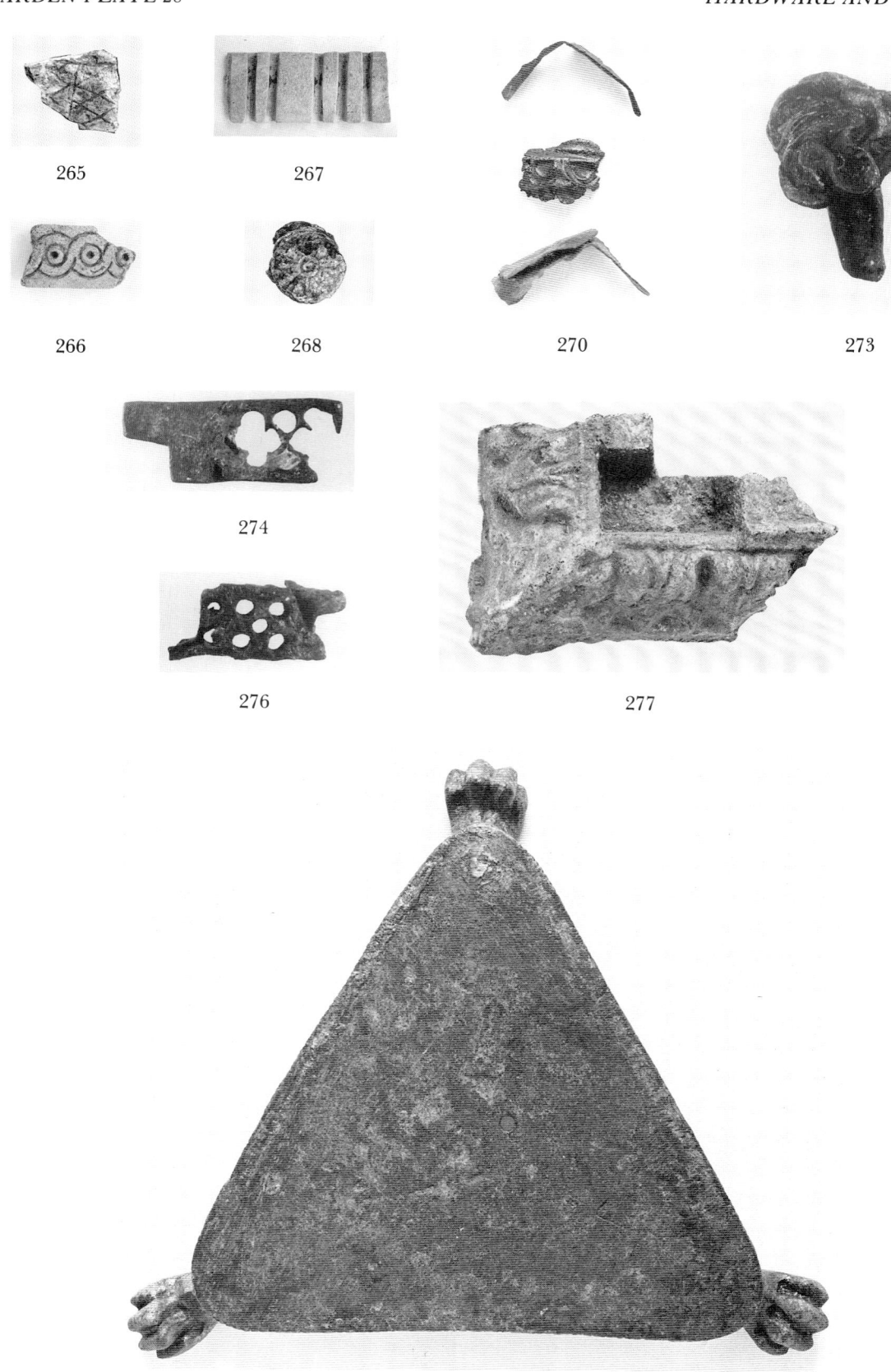

278

1:1

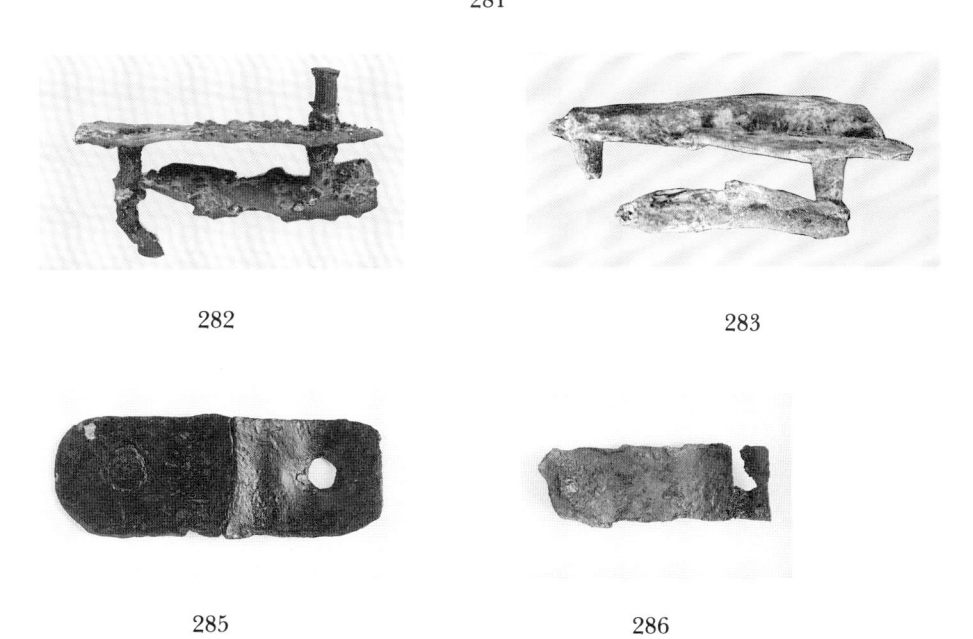

HARDWARE AND TOOLS WARDEN PLATE 29

279

280

281

282

283

285

286

1:1
280, 281-*1:2*

WARDEN PLATE 30 *HARDWARE AND TOOLS*

287

288

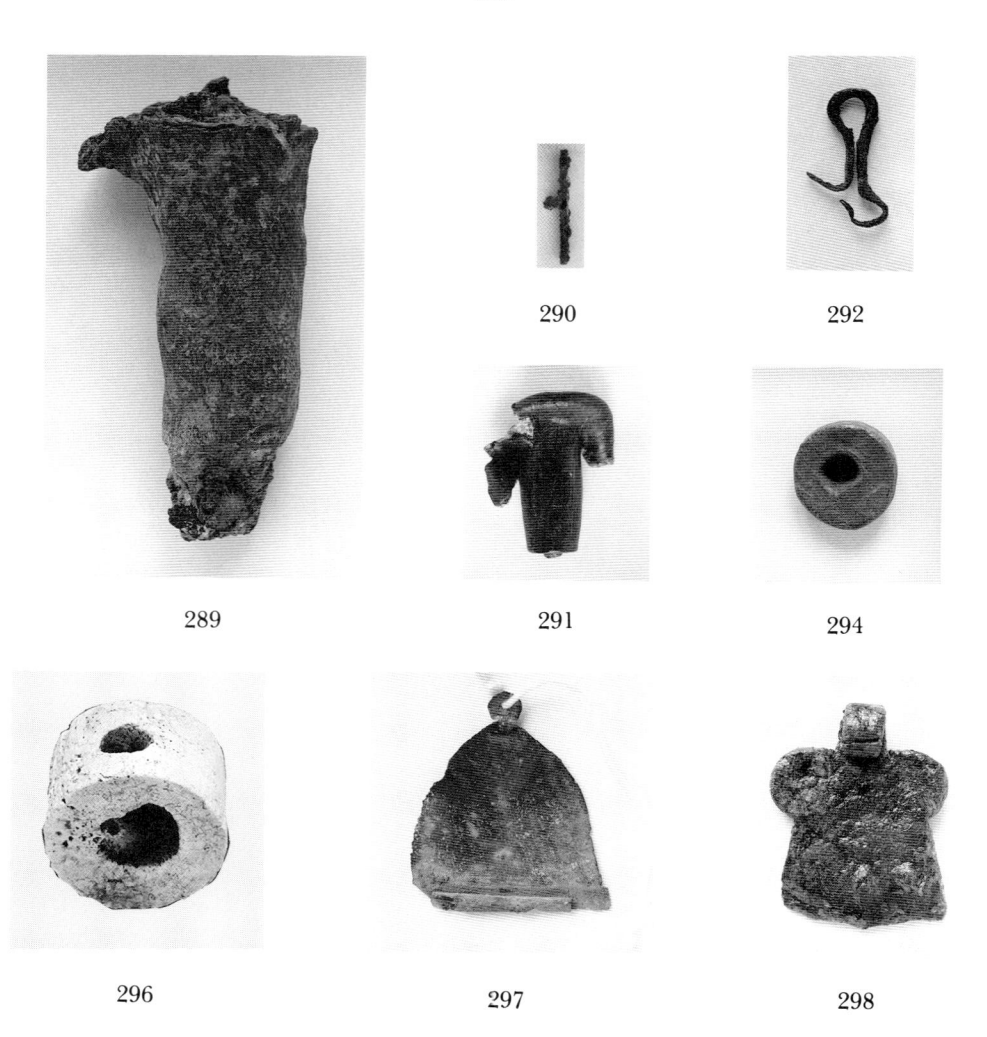

289 290 292

291 294

296 297 298

1:1
288-1:2

HARDWARE AND TOOLS   WARDEN PLATE 31

301

302

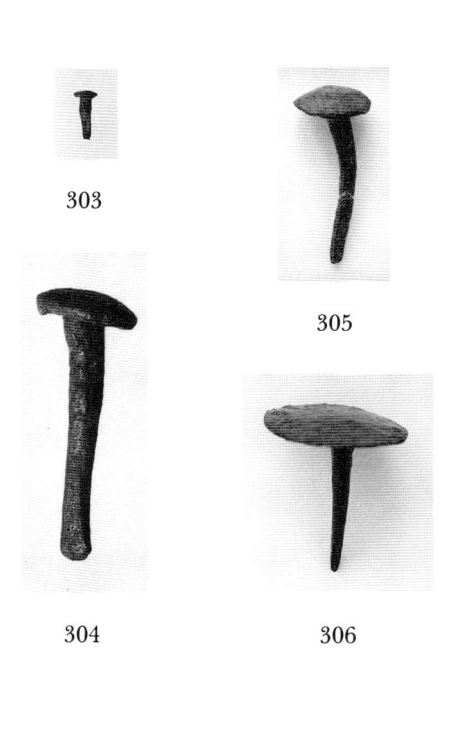

303

304

305

306

307

308

309

310

1:1

WARDEN PLATE 32　　　　　　　　　　　　　　　　HARDWARE AND TOOLS

311

312　　　313　　　314

315

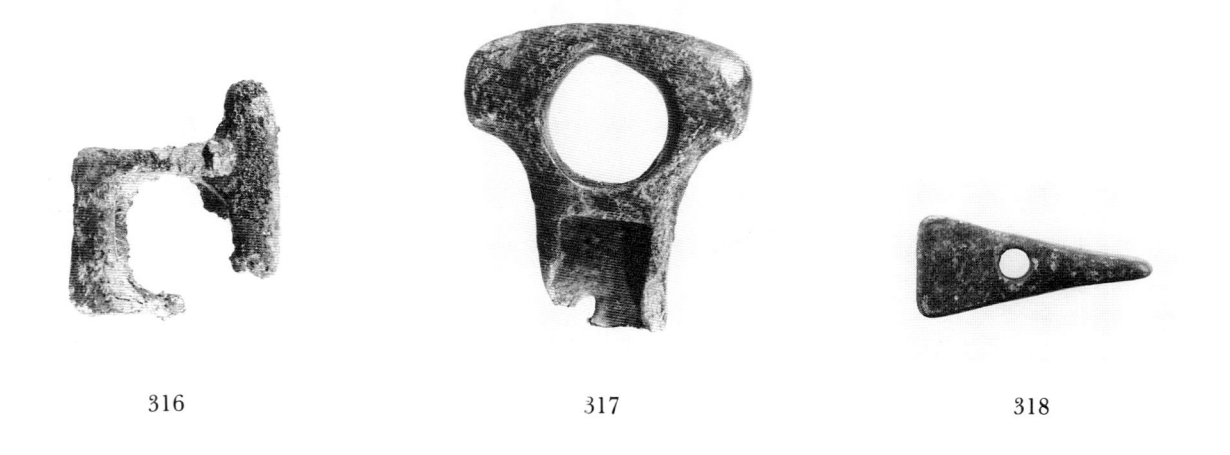

316　　　317　　　318

1:1

HARDWARE AND TOOLS WARDEN PLATE 33

319

320

324

325

1:1
320-1:2

WARDEN PLATE 34 *HARDWARE AND TOOLS*

328

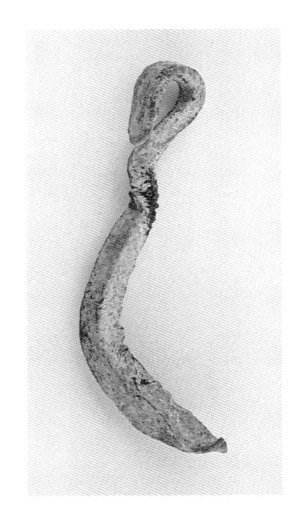

332 333

1:1

HARDWARE AND TOOLS *WARDEN PLATE 35*

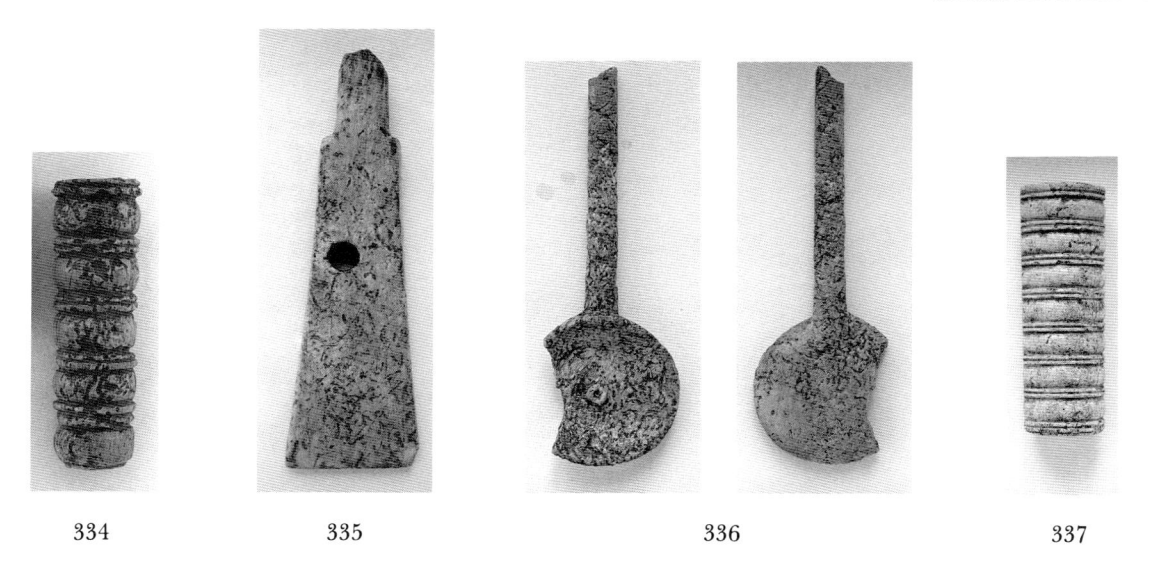

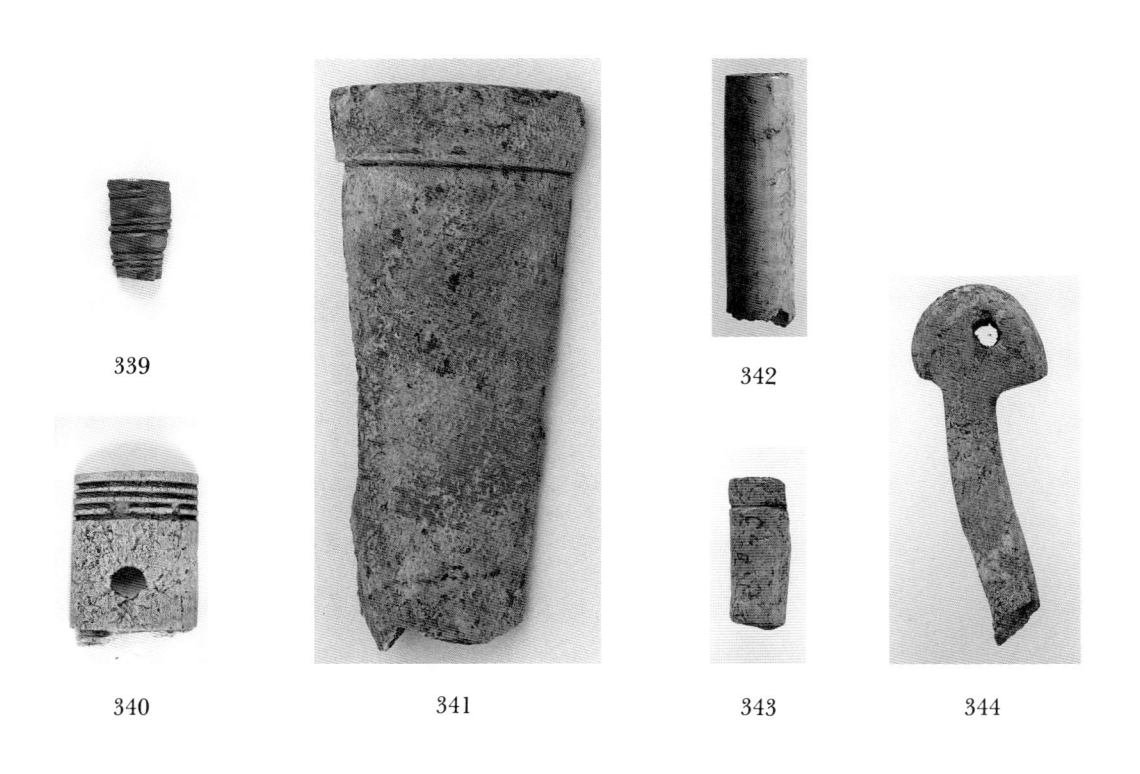

334

335

336

337

338

339

340

341

342

343

344

1:1

WARDEN PLATE 36　　　　　　　　　　　　　　　　　　　　　　　HARDWARE AND TOOLS

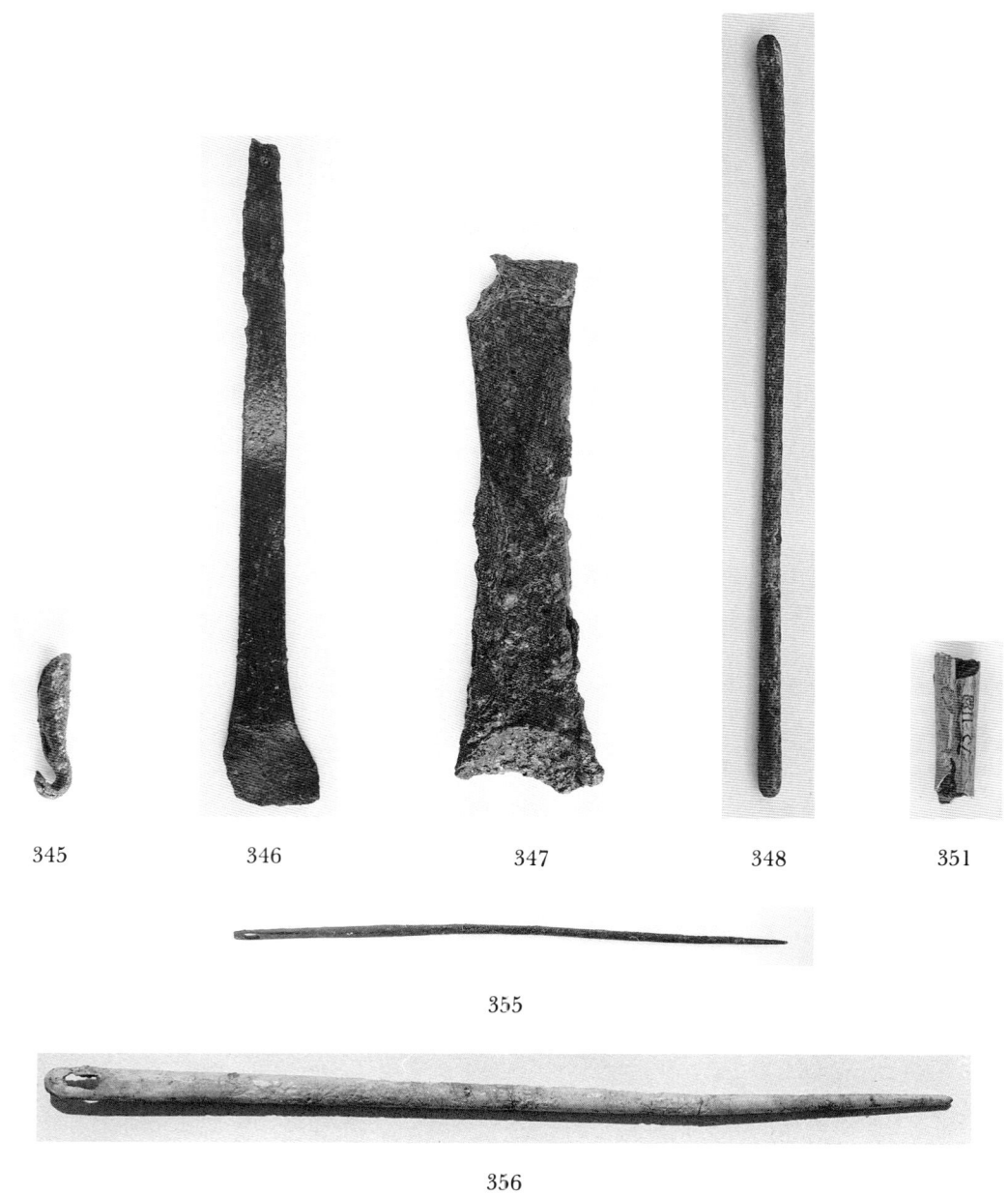

345　　346　　347　　348　　351

355

356

358

1:1
358-1:2

HARDWARE AND TOOLS   WARDEN PLATE 37

359

360

361   363   364

366

1:1

WARDEN PLATE 38　　　　　　　　　　　　　　　　　　　　　　　　　　WEAPONS

370

373

375

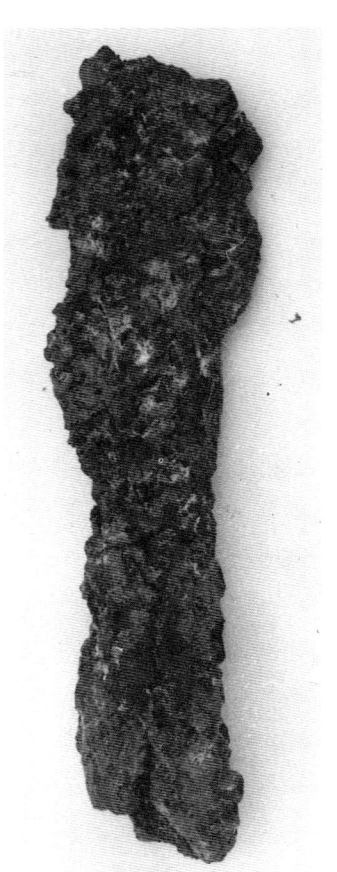

376

381

1:1

VESSELS WARDEN PLATE 39

383

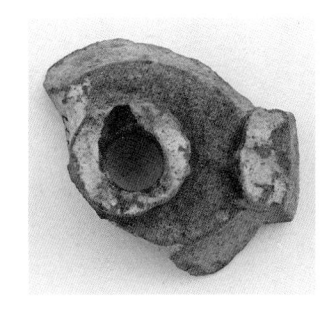

384

385

386

387

388

389

390

391

392

393

1:1

WARDEN PLATE 40　　　　　　　　　　　　　　　　　　　　　　　　　　　　　VESSELS

394

398

399

400

402

1:1
398-1:2

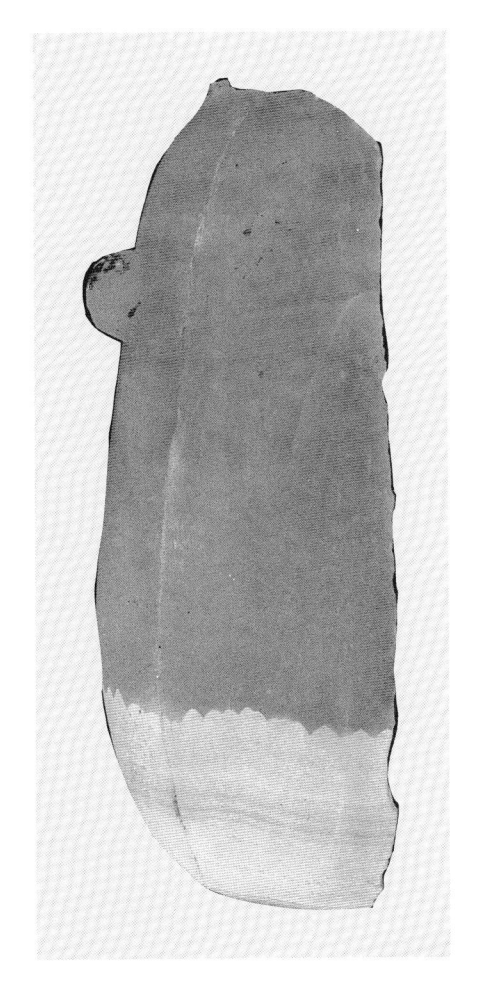

VESSELS *WARDEN PLATE 41*

405

406

408

409

412

1:1

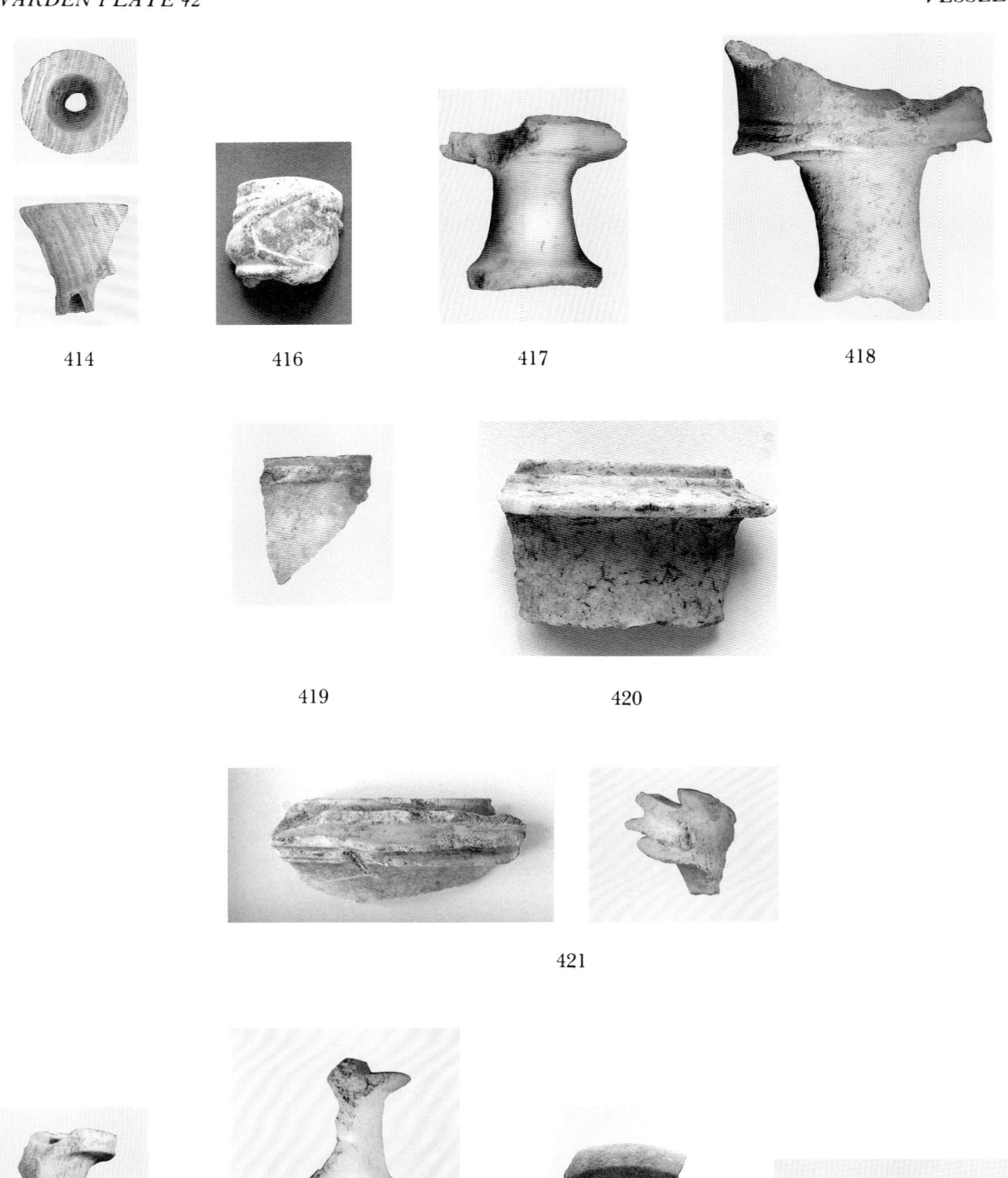

WARDEN PLATE 42   VESSELS

414   416   417   418

419   420

421

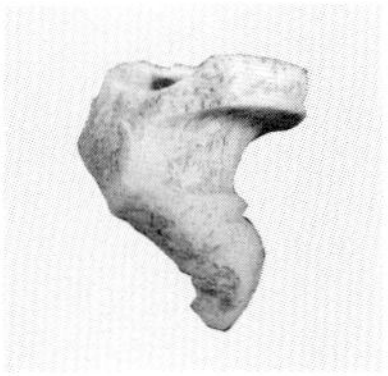

422   424    426 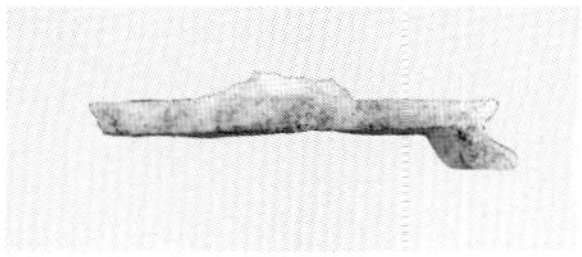   427

1:2

VESSELS *WARDEN PLATE 43*

429

430

431

432

433

434

435

436

1:2

WARDEN PLATE 44 VESSELS

439

441

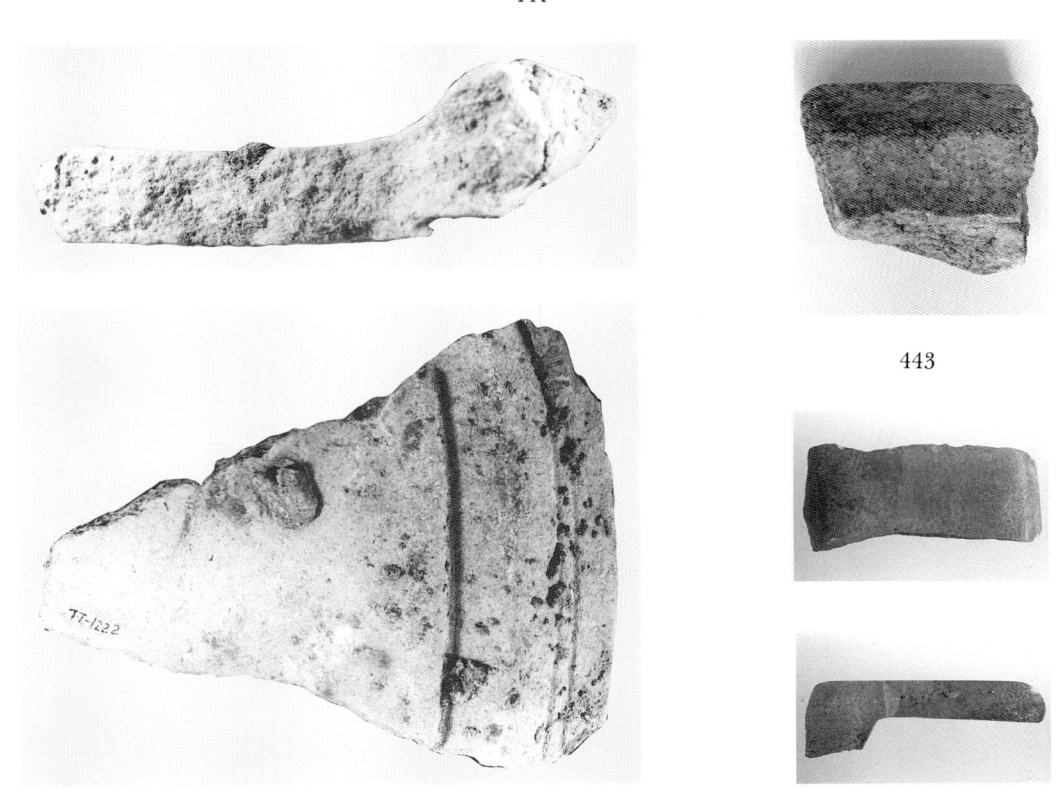

442

443

444

1:2

VESSELS WARDEN PLATE 45

445

446

447

450

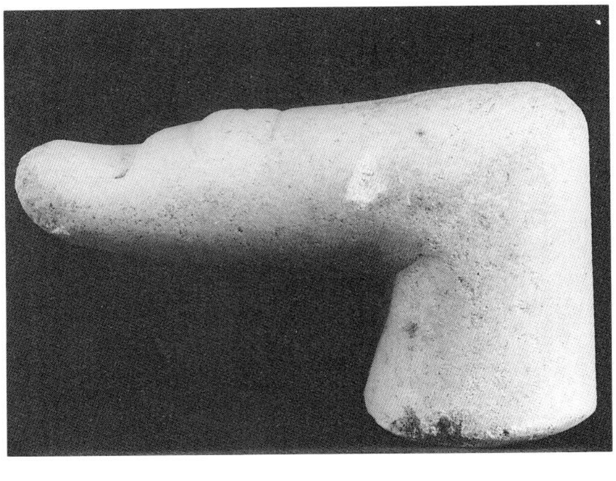

451

1:2
447-1:4

WARDEN PLATE 46   VESSELS

452

453

454

455

1:2

VESSELS *WARDEN PLATE 47*

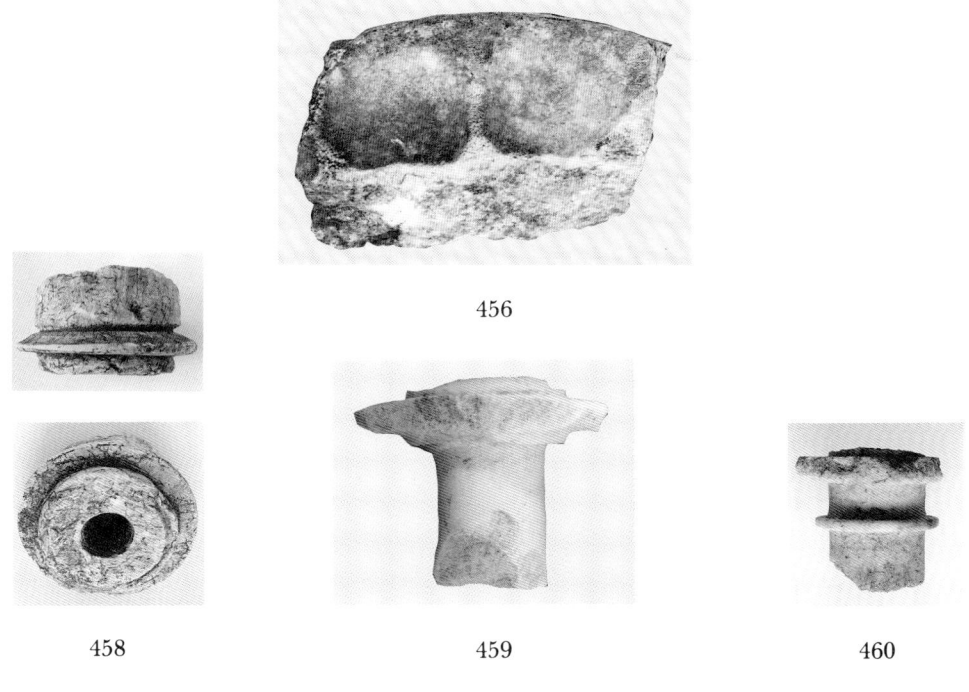

456

458   459   460

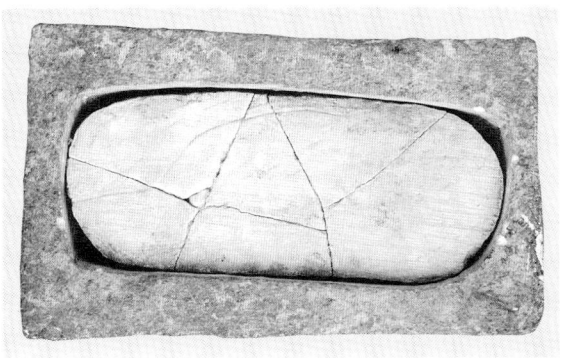

461

463

1:2

WARDEN PLATE 48

VESSELS

467

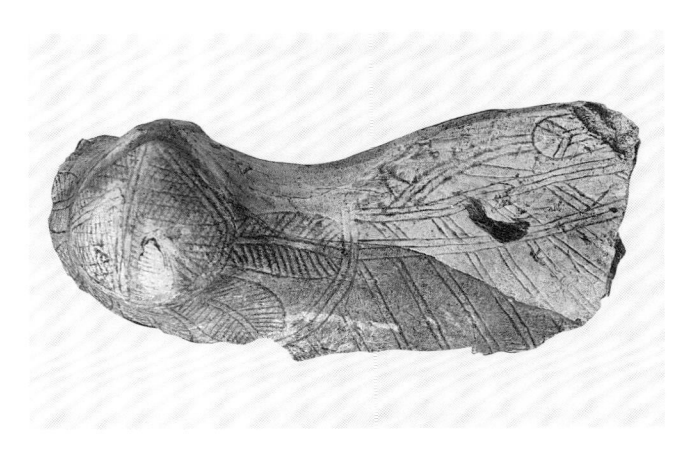

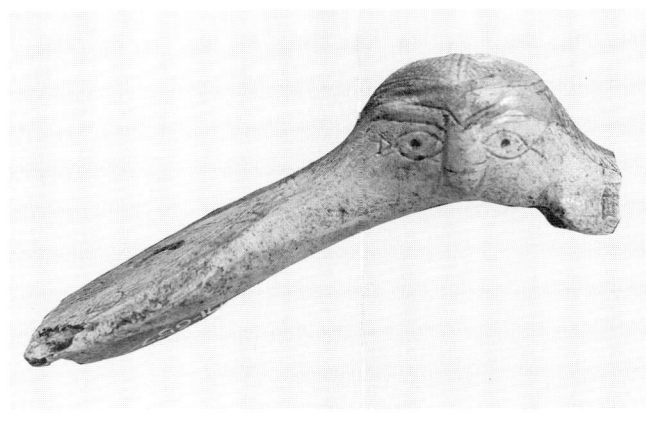

468

1:1

VESSELS WARDEN PLATE 49

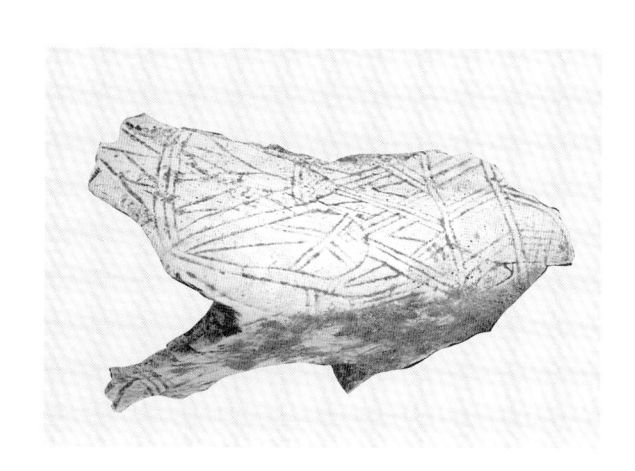

469

471

472

473

1:1

WARDEN PLATE 50 *MISCELLANEOUS FINDS*

475

476

477

478

479

480

481

482

483

1:1

MISCELLANEOUS FINDS *WARDEN PLATE 51*

485

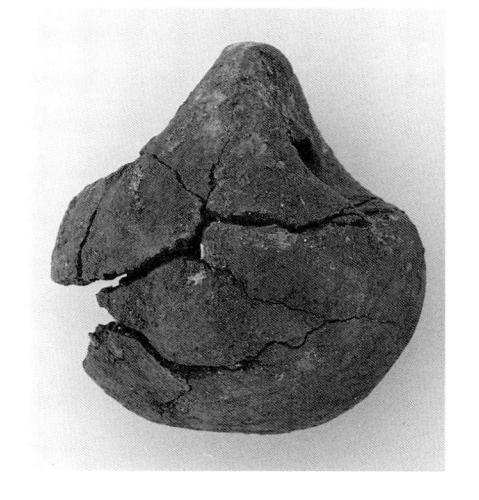

486

487

488

490

1:1

WARDEN PLATE 52　　　　　　　　　　　　　　　　　　　　MISCELLANEOUS FINDS

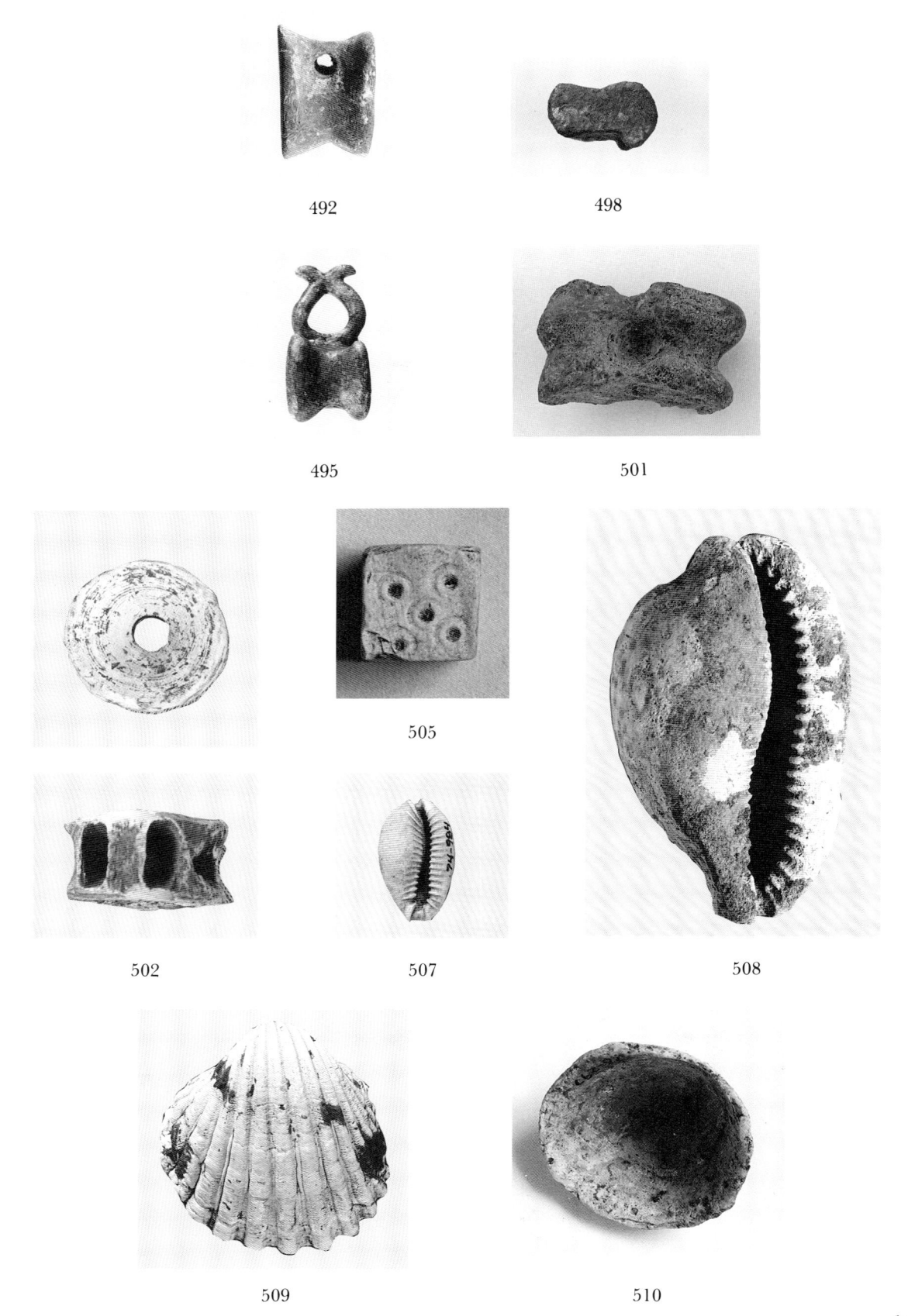

492

498

495

501

502

505

508

507

509

510

1:1

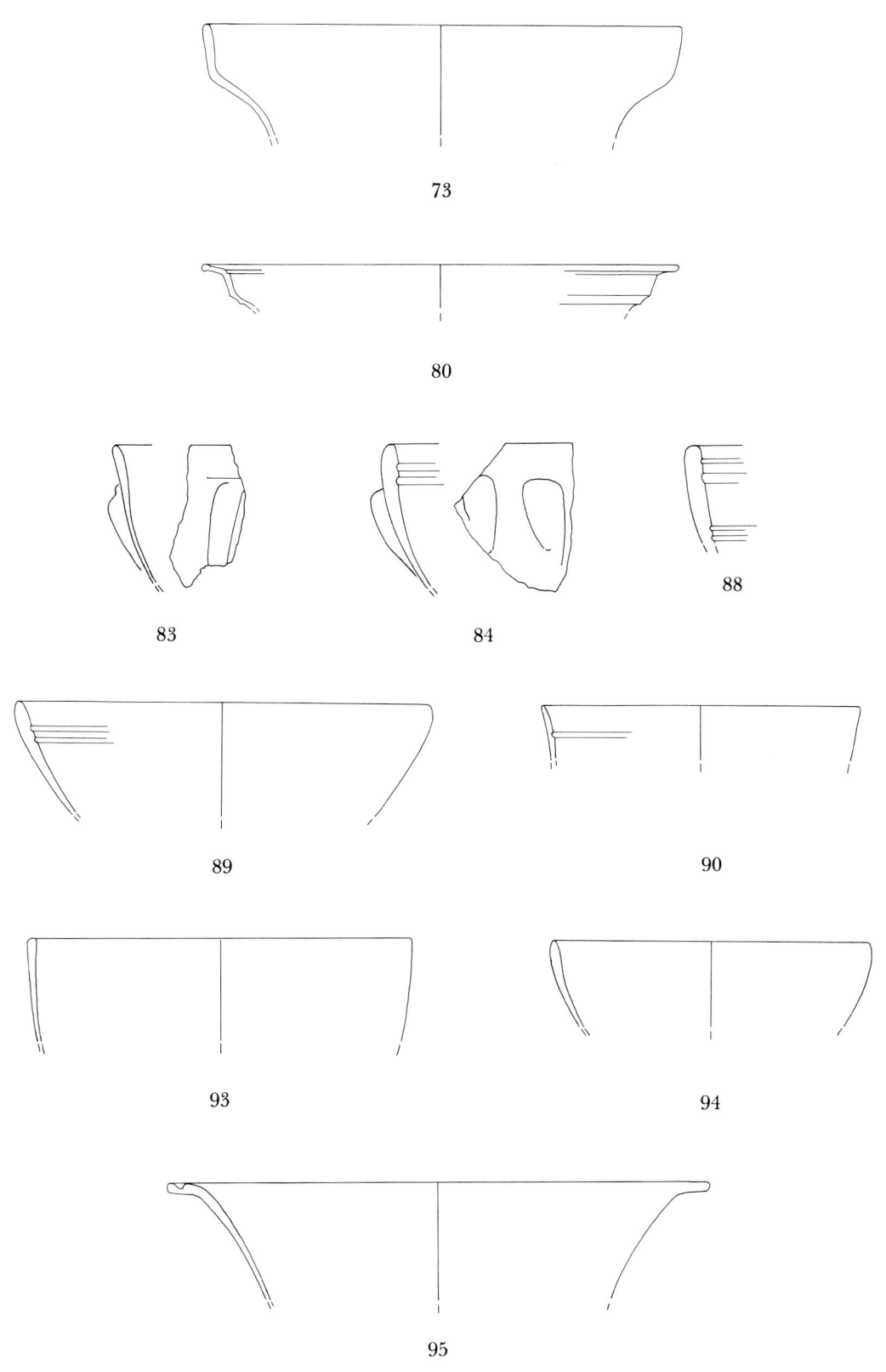

GLASS OLIVER FIGURE 1

73

80

83 84 88

89 90

93 94

95

1:2

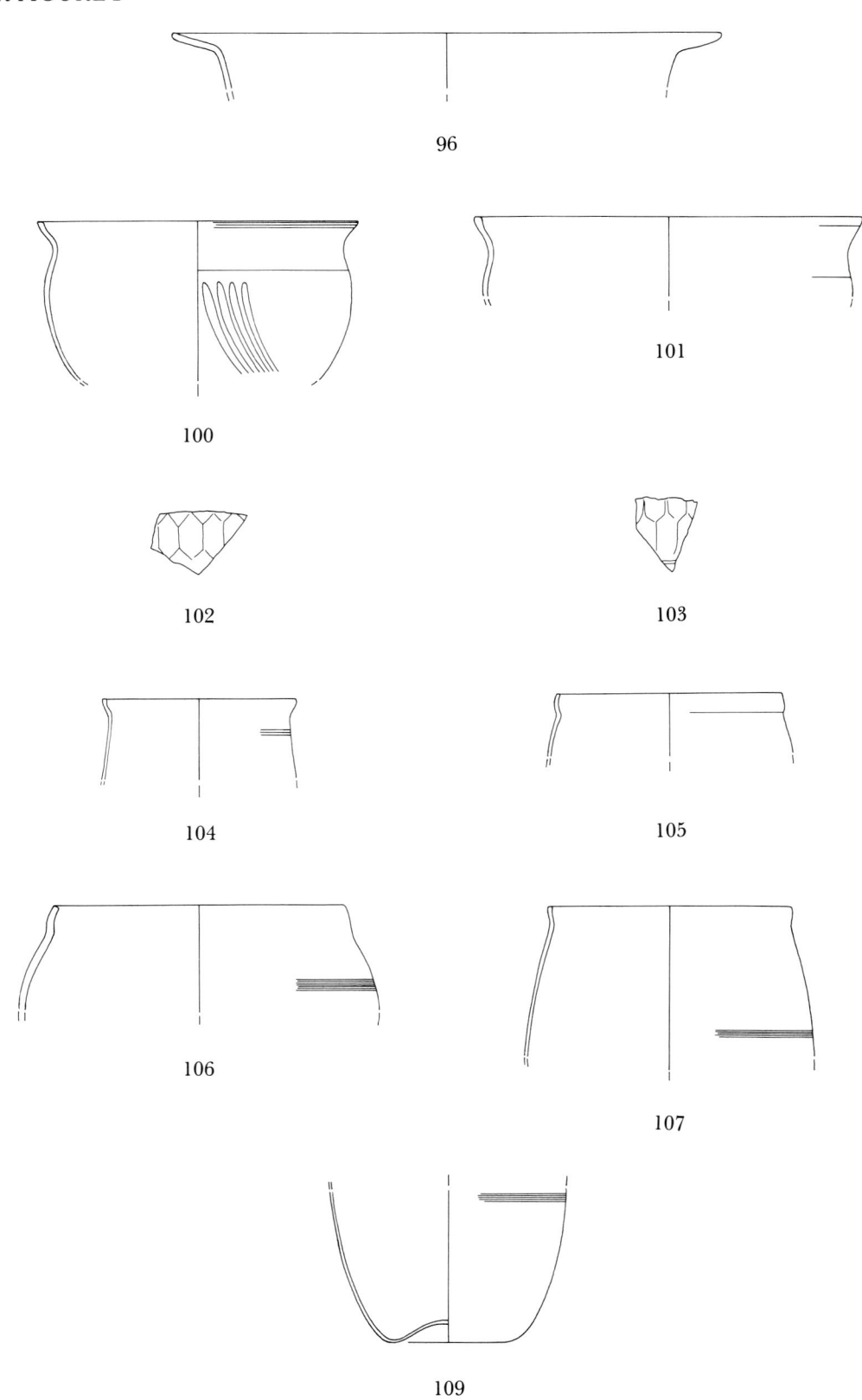

OLIVER FIGURE 2 *GLASS*

96

100

101

102

103

104

105

106

107

109

1:2

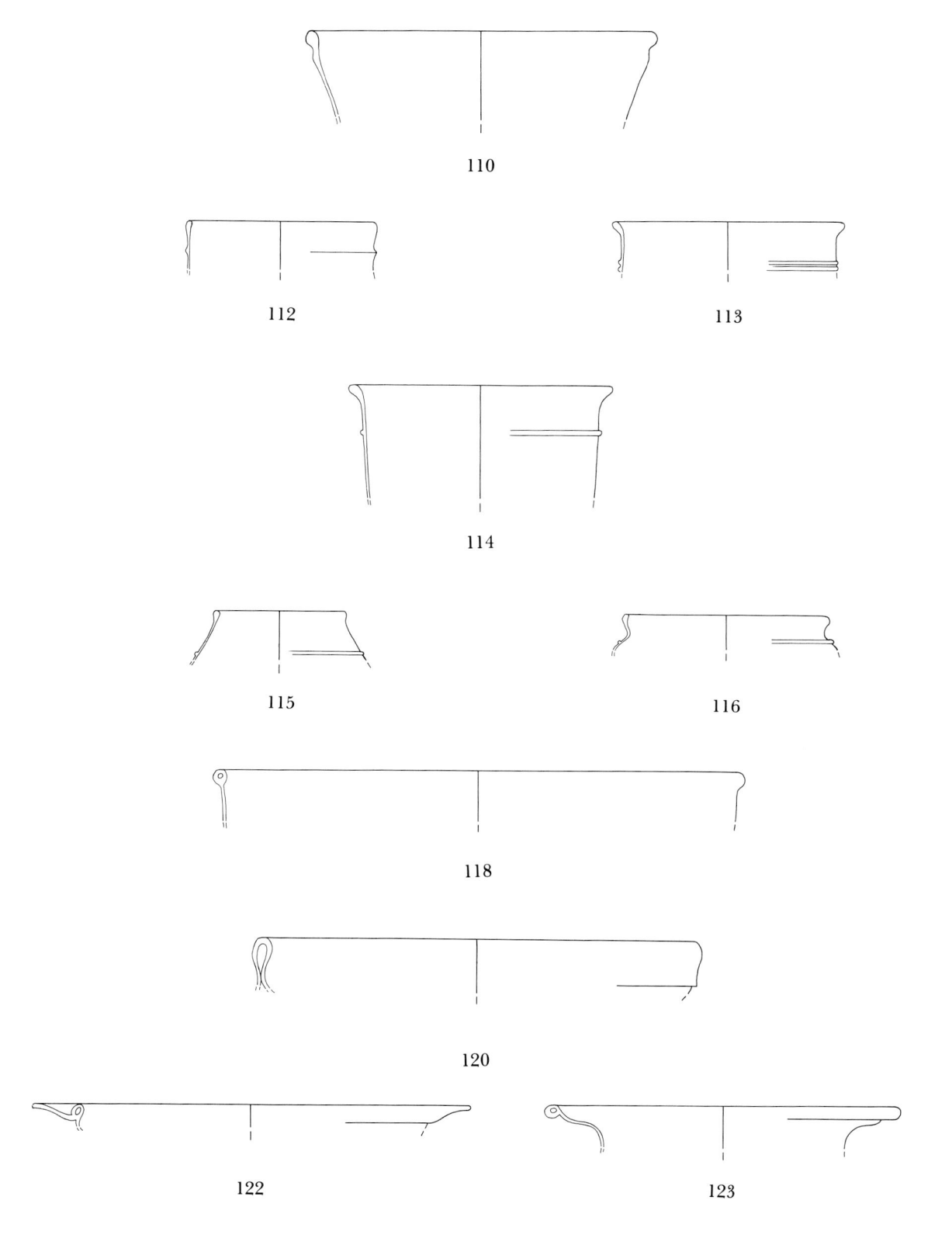

GLASS OLIVER FIGURE 3

110

112 113

114

115 116

118

120

122 123

1:2

OLIVER FIGURE 4 GLASS

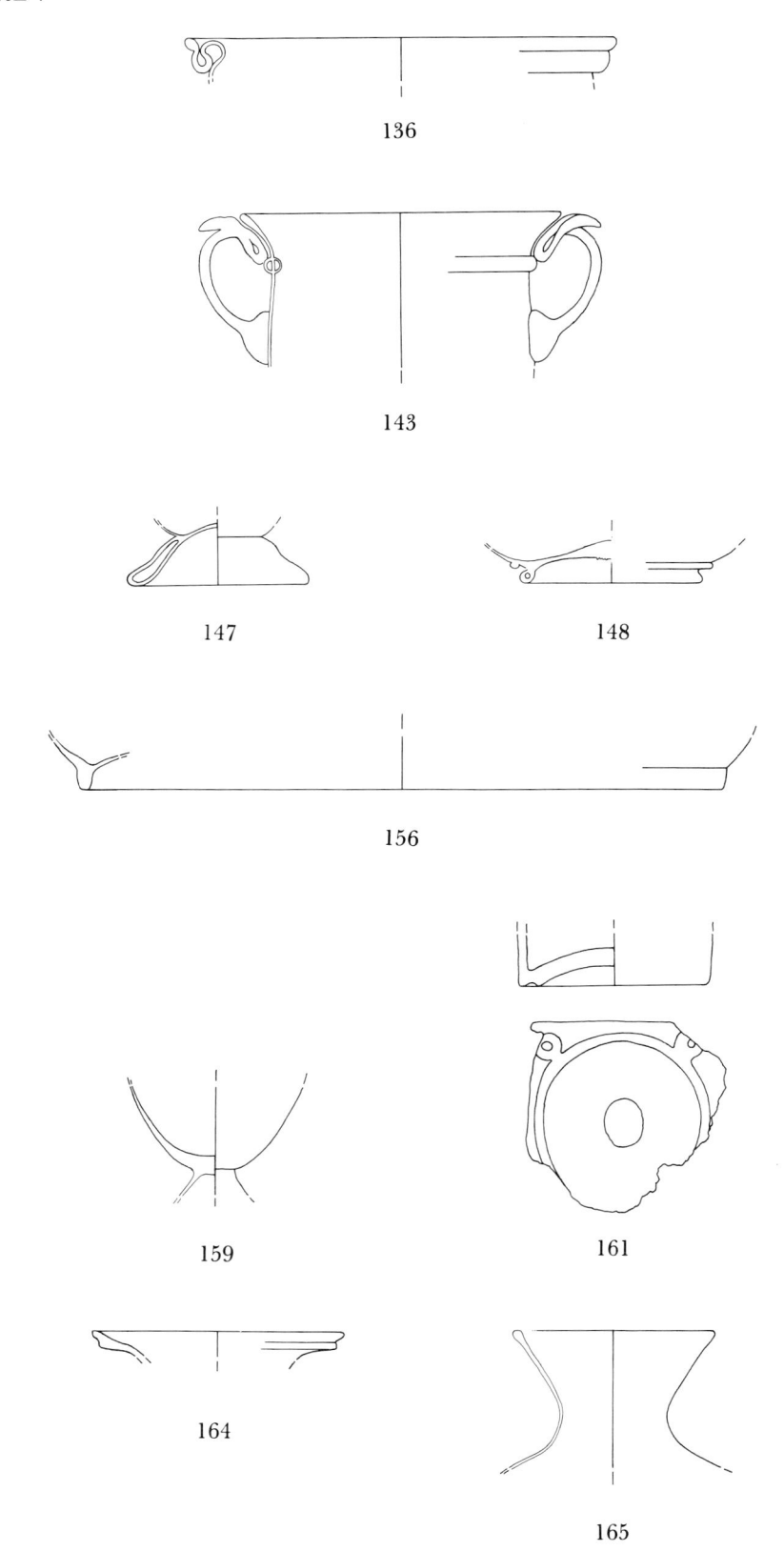

136

143

147 148

156

159 161

164 165

1:2

CORE-FORMED GLASS: ALABASTRA OLIVER PLATE 1

1

2

3

4

5

6

7

1:1

OLIVER PLATE 2 CORE-FORMED GLASS: AMPHORISKOI

8

9

10

11

12

13

14

15

16

1:1

CORE-FORMED GLASS: ARYBALLOI AND OINOCHOAI OLIVER PLATE 3

17

18

19

20

21

22

1:1

OLIVER PLATE 4　　　　　　　　　　　　　　　　CORE-FORMED GLASS: SHAPE UNCERTAIN

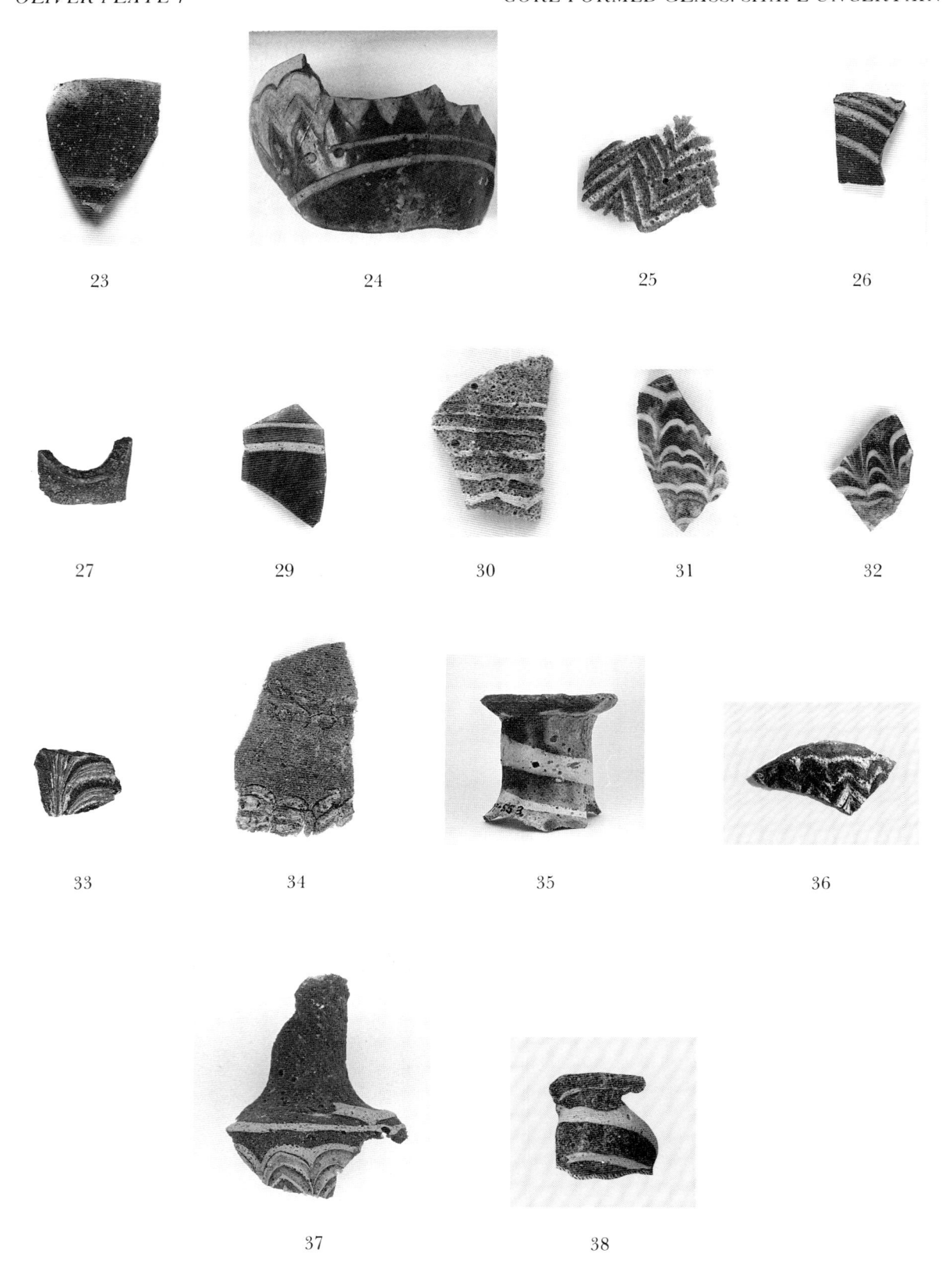

23　　　24　　　25　　　26

27　　　29　　　30　　　31　　　32

33　　　34　　　35　　　36

37　　　38

1:1

CORE-FORMED GLASS: PENDANT AND BEADS

OLIVER PLATE 5

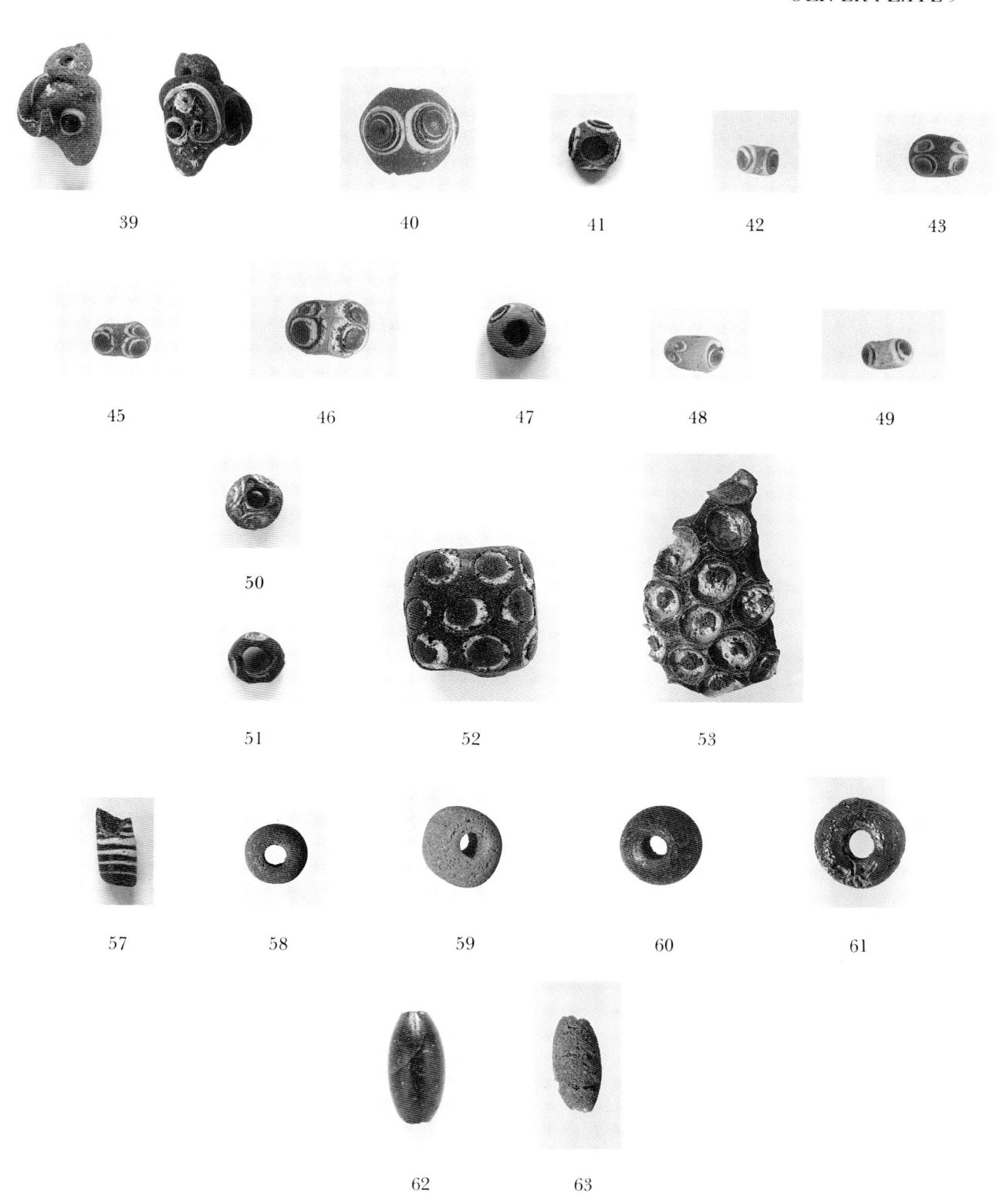

39   40   41   42   43

45   46   47   48   49

50
51   52   53

57   58   59   60   61

62   63

1:1

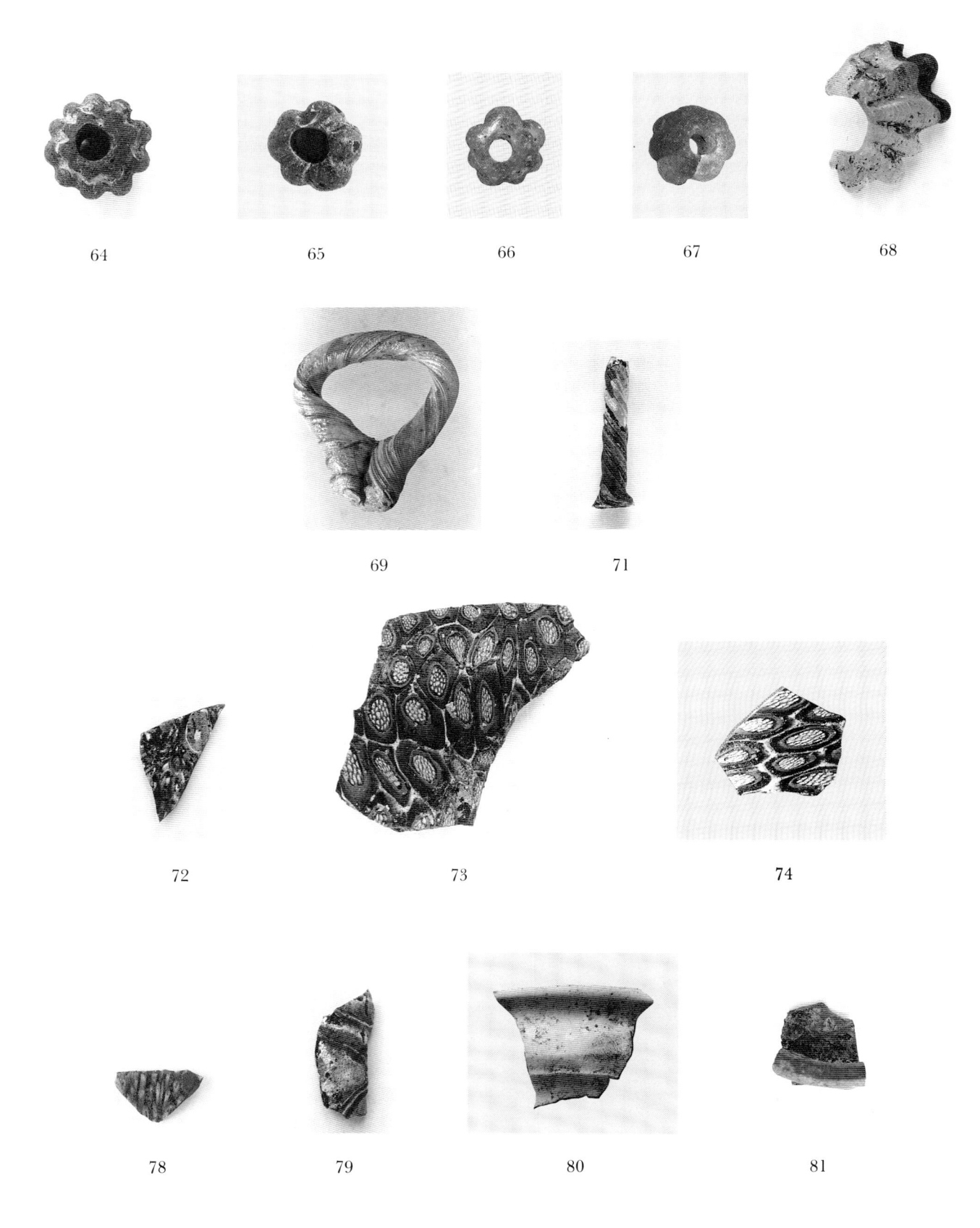

OLIVER PLATE 6   CORE-FORMED GLASS: BEADS AND RODS; CAST GLASS: OPAQUE

64 65 66 67 68

69 71

72 73 74

78 79 80 81

1:1

CAST GLASS: TRANSLUCENT AND MONOCHROME   OLIVER PLATE 7

82

83

84

85

87

88

89

90

1:1

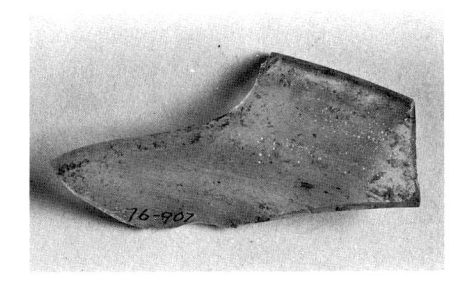

OLIVER PLATE 8 CAST GLASS AND BLOWN GLASS

93

94

95

96

98

99

1:1

BLOWN GLASS: OPEN SHAPES   OLIVER PLATE 9

100

101

102   103   104

105   106   107

1:1

OLIVER PLATE 10 BLOWN GLASS: OPEN SHAPES

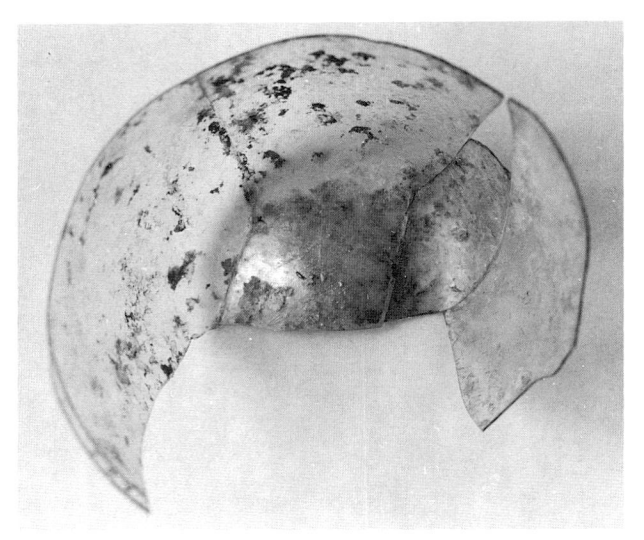

109

110

111

1:1

BLOWN GLASS: OPEN SHAPES   *OLIVER PLATE 11*

113

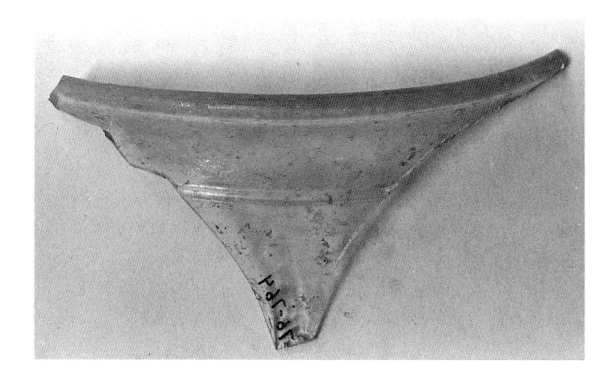

114

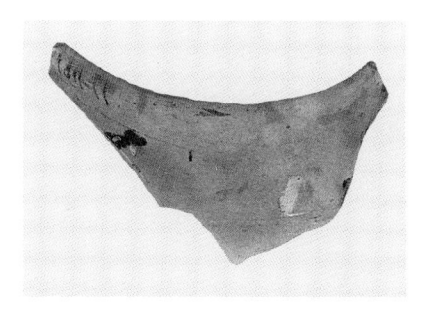

115

116    117

120    121    122

1:1

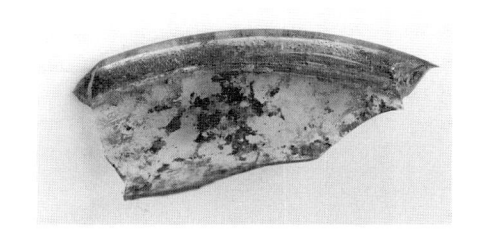

OLIVER PLATE 12 BLOWN GLASS: OPEN SHAPES

123

124

125  126

127  128

129 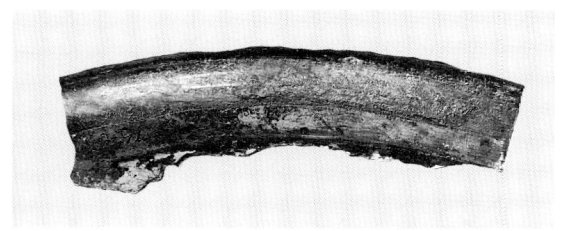 130

1:1

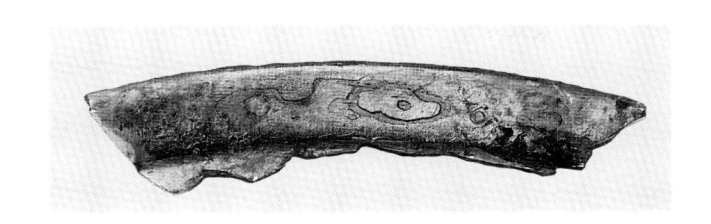

BLOWN GLASS: OPEN SHAPES   *OLIVER PLATE 13*

131

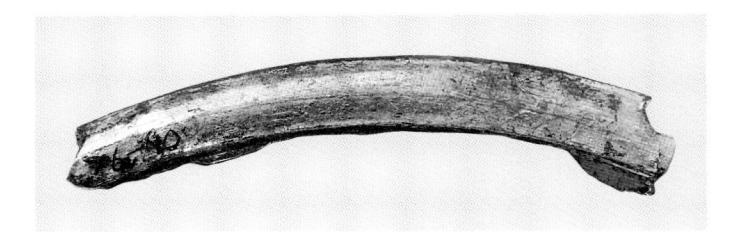

132

133 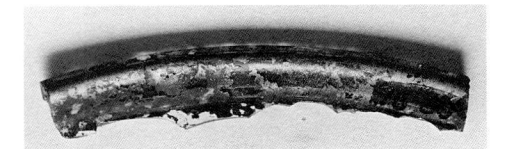   134

138 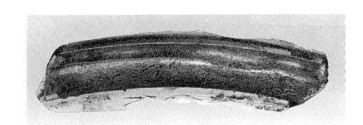   139 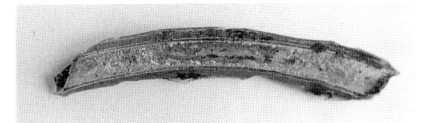   140

142    144

1:1

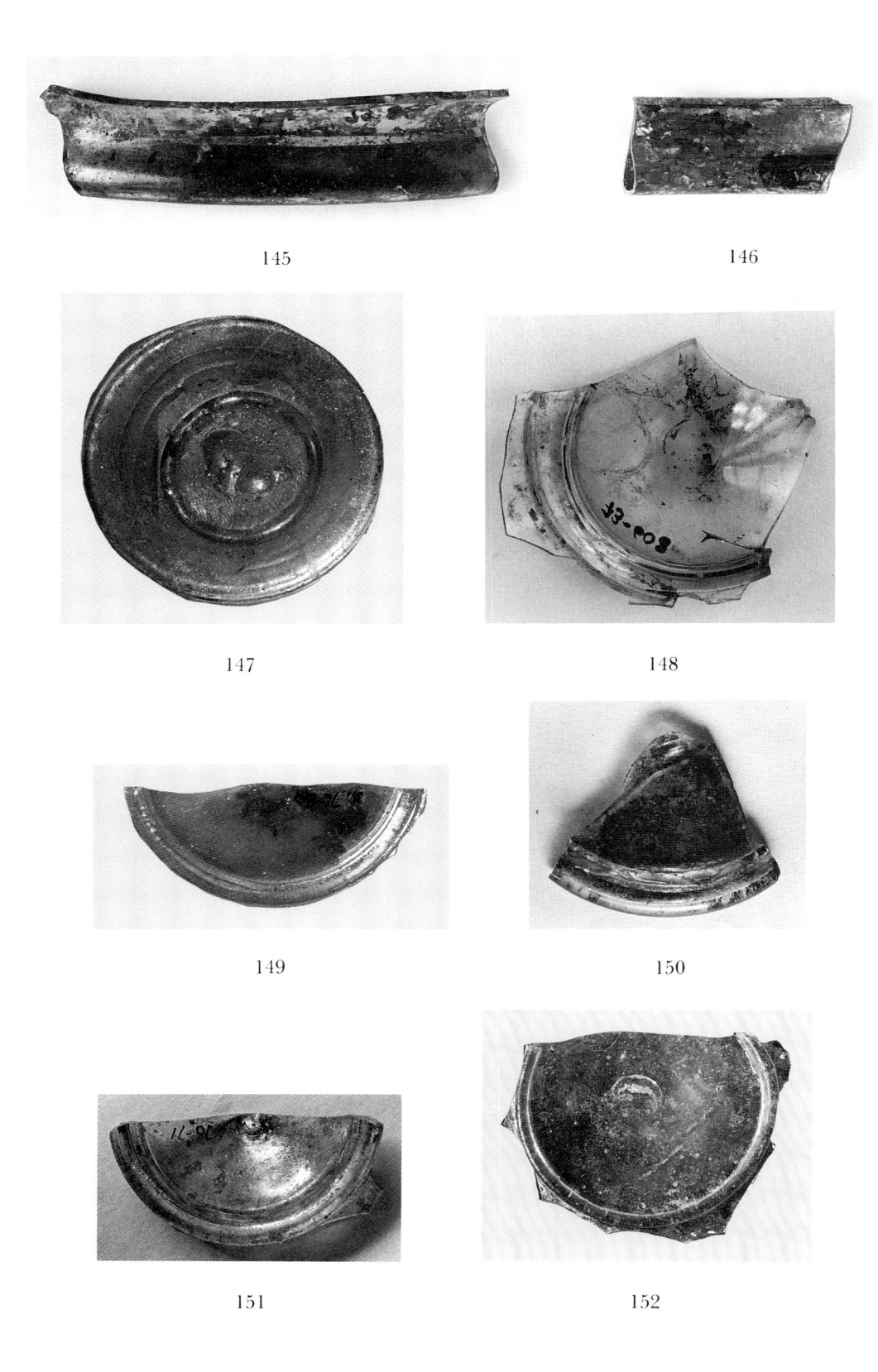

OLIVER PLATE 14
BLOWN GLASS: OPEN SHAPES

145

146

147

148

149

150

151

152

1:1

BLOWN GLASS: OPEN SHAPES *OLIVER PLATE 15*

153

154

155

156

157

158

159

1:1

OLIVER PLATE 16 BLOWN GLASS: OPEN SHAPES AND CLOSED SHAPES

160

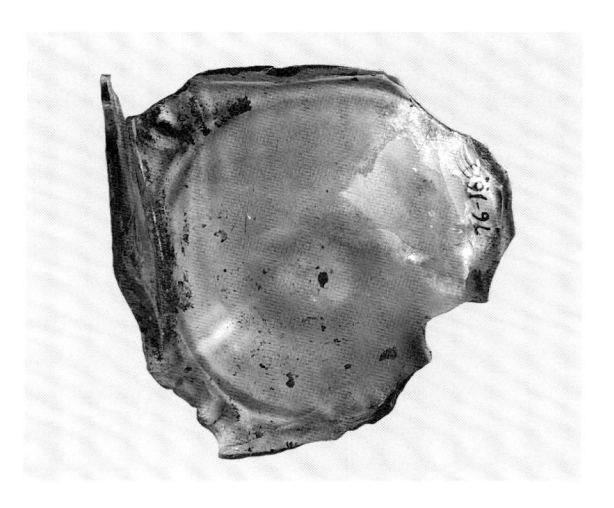

161

162 163

164

1:1

BLOWN GLASS: CLOSED SHAPES   *OLIVER PLATE 17*

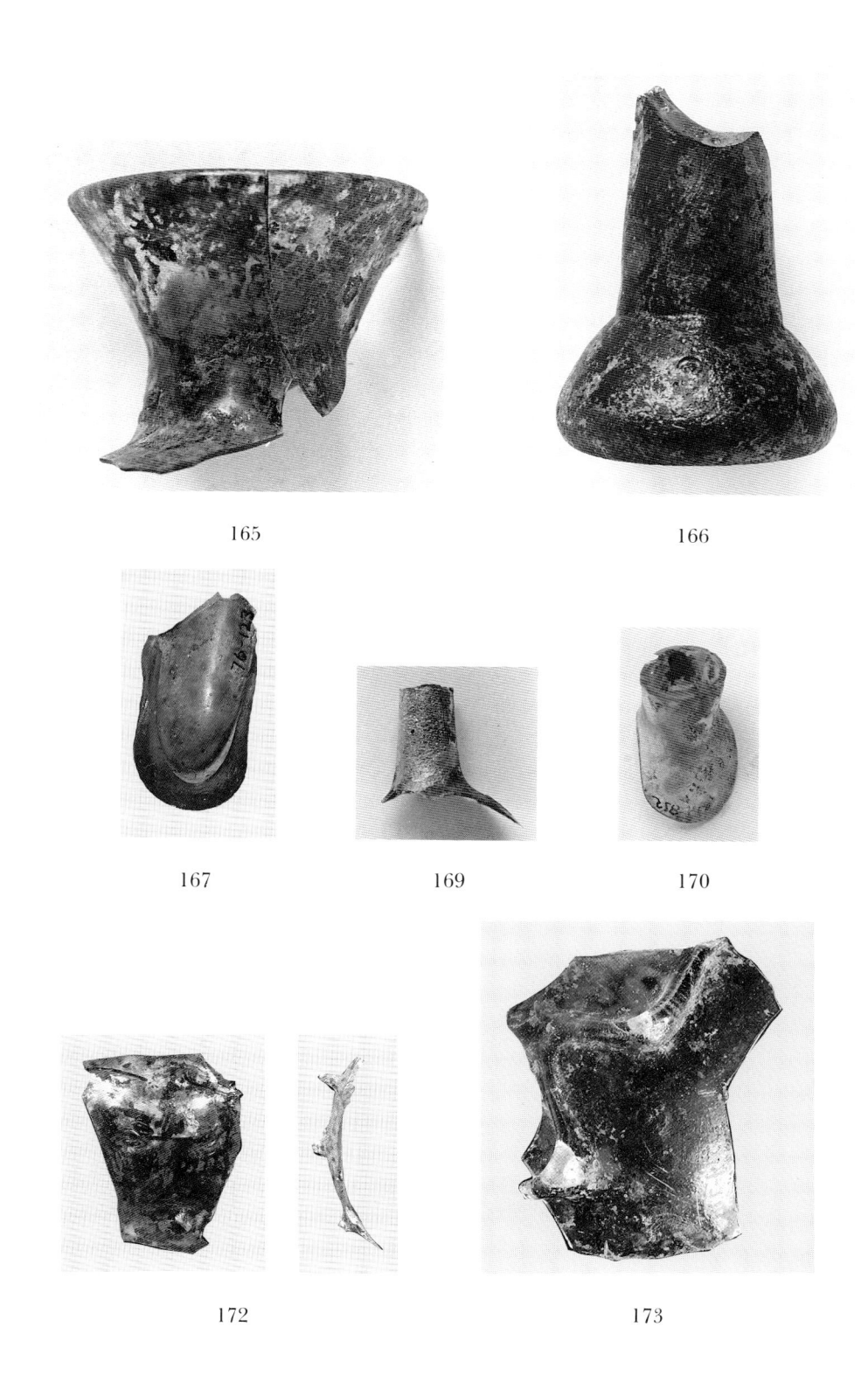

165

166

167

169

170

172

173

1:1

OLIVER PLATE 18, PRICE APPENDIX I   *GLASS HEAD*

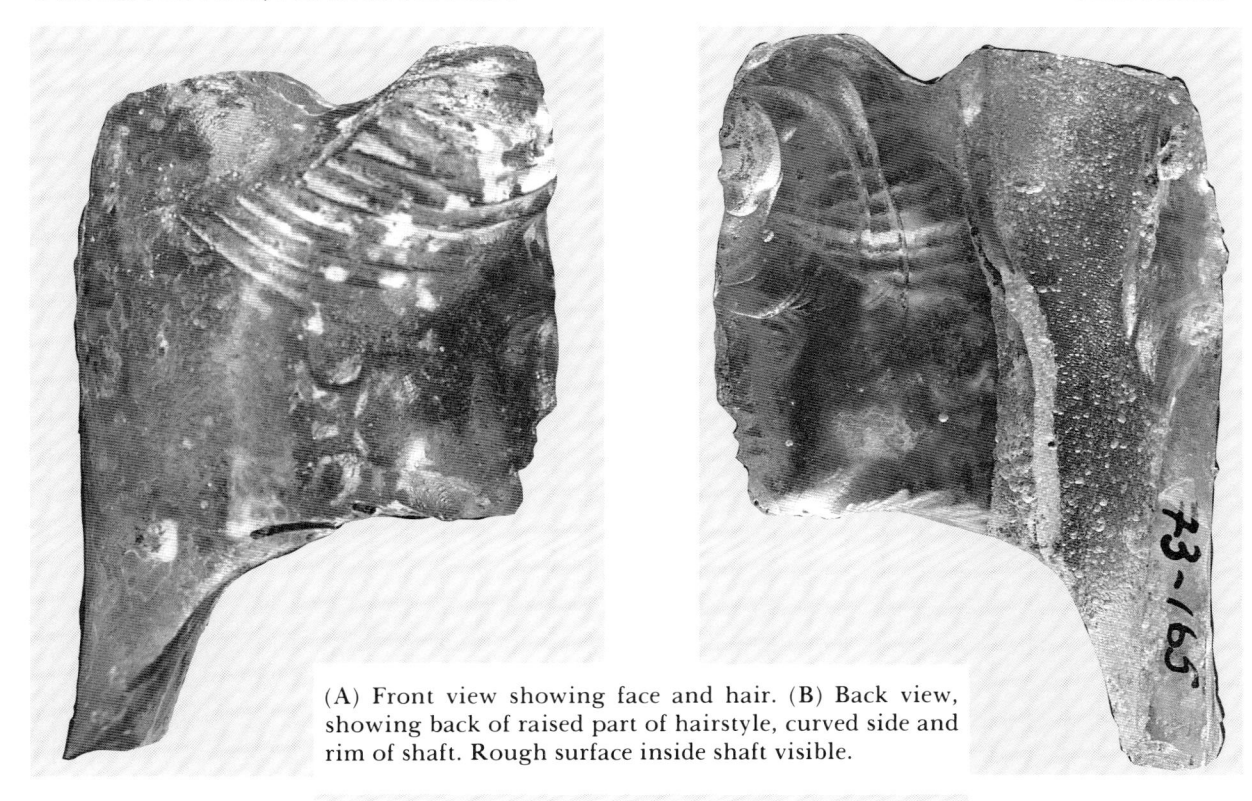

(A) Front view showing face and hair. (B) Back view, showing back of raised part of hairstyle, curved side and rim of shaft. Rough surface inside shaft visible.

A

B

(C) Side view, showing details of face and hair and rim of shaft behind head.

(D) Side view, showing section through fragment. The rough surface inside the tapering shaft is clearly visible, and some details of the face can also be seen through the thickness of the glass.

C   D

2:1

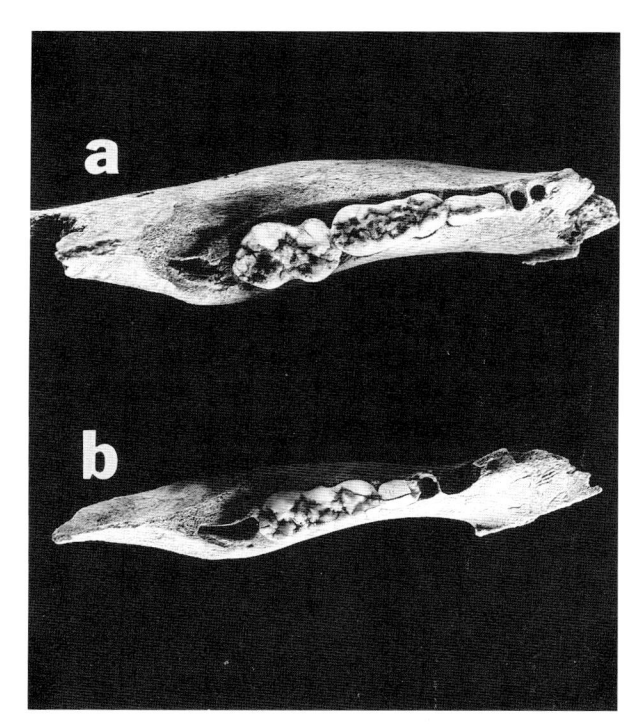

Two immature pig mandibles from Cyrene. The mandible (a) shows a fully erupted first permanent molar and an unerupted second molar. This pig was probably between six and twelve months of age when it was killed. The first permanent molar has not yet erupted on the mandible (b). This animal was slaughtered before six months of age. (Photograph courtesy of A.E. Mann, Physical Anthropology Section, The University Museum)

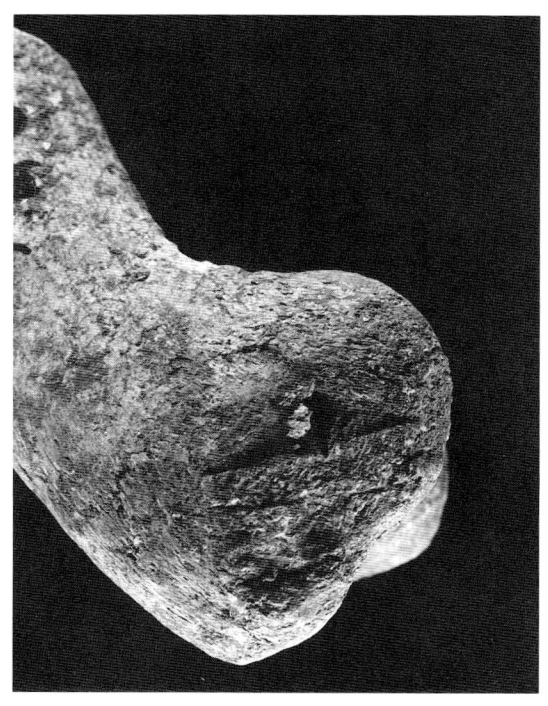

Distal humerus of a pig showing butchery marks on the medial surface. (Photograph courtesy of A.E. Mann, Physical Anthropology Section, The University Museum)

A

B

(A) Head broken from marble statuette of a piglet (Inv. 71-295) from Area E15, Trench 3, St. 1. (B) Terracotta figure of a pig (Inv. 78-406) from Area F14/G14, Trench 1, St. 2. Like many other Greek Demeter sanctuaries, the Cyrene site has been the repository of a significant concentration of either terracotta or stone votive models of the goddess of vegetation and the goddess' favorite animal of sacrifice, the pig. Susan Kane, who is responsible for the final report on animal figurines and statues, has catalogued 32 pig body parts.

POSITION and Plan of CYRENE.
By Cap.tn F.W. Beechey, R.N.

Lat.de 32°.49´.38˝N. Long.de 21°.49´.5˝E. Var.n 14°.30´W.

English Feet